Work and the Quality of Life

The MIT Press
Cambridge, Massachusetts, and London, England

Work and the Quality of Life
Resource Papers for *Work in America*

Edited by James O'Toole

Prepared under the auspices of the
W. E. Upjohn Institute for Employment Research

This book was set in Linotype Helvetica
by New England Typographic Service, Inc.,
printed on Finch Title 93,
and bound in G.S.B. 5/353/313 "Plum"
by The Colonial Press, Inc.
in the United States of America.

Library of Congress Cataloging in Publication Data

Main entry under title:

Work and the quality of life.
    Consists of 16 of the 39 papers prepared for a study, the results of which were issued in a report to the Secretary of Health, Education, and Welfare, published in 1973 under title: Work in America.
    "Prepared under the auspices of the W. E. Upjohn Institute for Employment Research."
    Includes bibliographical references.
    1. Manpower policy—United States—Addresses, essays, lectures. 2. Labor supply —United States—Addresses, essays, lectures. 3. Job satisfaction—Addresses, essays, lectures. I. O'Toole, James, ed. II. Upjohn Institute for Employment Research. III. Work in America.
HD5724.W64   331'0973   74-548
ISBN 0-262-15015-8

Contents

Foreword

Elliot L. Richardson

When I released the report *Work in America,* I likened it to another book, *The Limits of Growth.* Both of these startling studies draw our attention to controversial and sensitive issues concerning the quality of life. We may disagree with the conclusions of these books, but if they are anywhere near the truth, they are too important to be ignored, and too unsettling to be easily forgotten. Indeed, after having read *Work in America,* one begins to view the institution of work in a fresh light. It is impossible to slip again into the easy generalizations and glib assertions that abound in discussions of "The Work Ethic." The task force that produced *Work in America* made explicit what we only half recognized, that work is of central importance in the lives of Americans. "Consequently," they wrote, "if the opportunity to work is absent or if the nature of work is dissatisfying . . . severe repercussions are likely to be experienced" by the individual and society. They demonstrated that if the nation wishes to improve the quality of life, a good place to start is with the quality and quantity of work.

The findings of *Work in America* came as a shock to many readers. It was not easy for some to accept that the organization of work is adversely affecting the mental and physical health, family stability, and political behavior of many Americans. Moreover, evidence was adduced in *Work in America* to show that the "rationalized" design of jobs falls short of realizing the productivity potential of workers, organizations, and the nation. The approaches to meeting these problems that the task force advocated were long-term, indirect, and would impose the need for short-term sacrifice on the parts of management, unions, and school officials, among others. It is easy to see why the report was not universally praised.

But initial acceptance was not the goal of the task force. Any intelligent and careful exposition of the subject was bound to produce controversy. The report was specifically designed to stir responsible, rational, and widespread discussion and debate, and it accomplished that goal to a remarkable degree. As I wrote in the preface to *Work in America,* "This report is a beginning, not a conclusion." It was my intention at the time I first read the report to initiate appropriate follow-up activities at HEW. Unhappily, I was not able to carry through with my intention because I left HEW for the Department of Defense shortly after the release of the report. Washington has the reputation for being a burial ground for good reports. I am pleased that James O'Toole has bucked that trend and has not let the momentum of *Work in America* die. For example, at workshops held at the Aspen Institute, Dr. O'Toole is bringing together leaders from business, labor, government, and academia to build a meaningful approach to some of the problems outlined in *Work in America.* And this book, which is really volume two of *Work in America,* will provide more data for the ongoing national debate on the issue.

While I might not agree with everything that is included in these papers, I feel that they are important and stimulating documents that deserve widespread circulation and critical attention. These papers serve the purpose of providing more data on the issues raised in *Work in America* relating to health, education, and welfare. For example, we talk a great deal about prevention in health, but this usually means that we turn our attention to medical care, and run out of ideas very quickly. As the three papers included here on health show, in work there appear to be broad opportunities to prevent physical and mental illness, not only through occupational health and safety, but through the redesign of work to increase self-esteem and job satisfaction.

There is also a large number of important implications that follow from the conjunction of education and work. The design of jobs appears to be lagging markedly behind the enormous gains in educational attainments of the work force, and the elevation in credentials required of the worker has not been accompanied by an elevation in the content of work. With respect to welfare the papers included here help us to look at the employment reasons underlying the absence of fathers from homes. The key to welfare reform would appear to be jobs that contribute to the economic security and self-esteem needed for family stability.

Although after leaving the Department of HEW I no longer had direct cabinet responsibility for the problems of health, education, and welfare, I found myself dealing with these same issues in subsequent departmental assignments. For example, in trying to cope with the thorny questions of civil rights, crime control, and drug abuse at the Department of Justice, it was clear to me that the institution of work must be explored to see if there might be some preventive or rehabilitative measures to be found in that institution. Clearly, the issues of the quantity and quality of work affect us all. In *Work in America,* and again in this excellent volume, we are drawn to the realization that in the institution of work there is much that can be done to improve the quality of life. Accordingly, I commend this book to everyone for thoughtful and serious review.

Acknowledgments

This book is dedicated to William Herman, my friend, mentor, and coeditor of *Work in America*. I also wish to express my gratitude to the other members of the *Work in America* task force: Elizabeth Hansot, Neal Herrick, Elliot Liebow, Bruce Lusignan, Harold Richman, Harold Sheppard, Ben Stephansky, and James Wright. Overworked and undercompensated, each cheerily made a valuable and unique contribution to that report. In particular, I would like to thank Ben Stephansky and the Upjohn Institute for their unswerving support of the entire project over the last two years. Ben somehow managed to keep the proper perspective on the whole undertaking even in the face of incredibly trying bureaucratic roadblocks and oppostion from certain segments of HEW and the Department of Labor.

Recognition and thanks are also due to Joseph Slater and Rowan Wakefield of the Aspen Institute. They invested the institute's resources to keep the momentum of *Work in America* going and allowed me to bootleg the time needed to prepare this volume.

For this book, I also wish to extend my appreciation to Marilyn O'Toole, Martin Kaplan, and Ben Stephansky for their editorial contributions. And to the authors of the commissioned papers that we were unable to publish, my regrets that we did not have sufficient space to include their excellent pieces.

Finally, I wish to add my praise for a man who has been widely recognized for his contributions to American society. To those of us who participated in

the *Work in America* task force, Elliot Richardson's support for our relatively insignificant project is indicative of the integrity he has demonstrated so often on issues of greater political importance. Long before others in public life saw the relevance of the issue of the quality of working life, Elliot Richardson commissioned the *Work in America* study and, throughout the duration of the project, offered resources and encouragement. In a characteristic fashion, he released and endorsed the report publicly, even when there were pressures to suppress it or release it "out the back door."
J. O'T.

Contributors

Ivar Berg
George E. Warren Professor of Business
Columbia University

Louis E. Davis
Professor of Organizational Sciences
University of California, Los Angeles

Frank F. Furstenberg, Jr.
Associate Professor of Sociology
University of Pennsylvania

James S. House
Assistant Professor of Sociology
Duke University

Robert L. Kahn
Director
Institute for Social Research
University of Michigan

Stanislav V. Kasl
Associate Professor of Epidemiology and Psychology
School of Medicine
Yale University

Emanuel Kay
President
Emanuel Kay & Co., Inc.
Marblehead, Massachusetts

William H. Kroes
Psychologist
Behavioral and Motivational Factors Branch
National Institute for Occupational Safety and Health

David C. MacMichael
Senior Research Scientist
Center for the Study of Social Policy
Stanford Research Institute

Bruce L. Margolis
Psychologist
Behavioral and Motivational Factors Branch
National Institute for Occupational Safety and Health

James O'Toole
Assistant Professor of Management
Graduate School of Business
University of Southern California

Michael J. Piore
Associate Professor of Economics
Massachusetts Institute of Technology

Lee Rainwater
Professor of Sociology
Harvard University

Beatrice G. Reubens
Senior Research Associate
Conservation of Human Resources
Columbia University

Isabel V. Sawhill
Senior Research Associate
The Urban Institute

George Strauss
Professor of Business
University of California, Berkeley

Thomas C. Thomas
Senior Economist
Center for the Study of Social Policy
Stanford Research Institute

Eric L. Trist
Professor of Organizational Behavior and Ecology
University of Pennsylvania

Richard E. Walton
Edsel Bryant Ford Professor of Business Administration
Harvard University

Introduction

James O'Toole

In December 1972, an independent task force that I headed reported to the Secretary of Health, Education, and Welfare that "in the institution of work, we believe we have found a point where considerable leverage could be exerted to improve the quality of life."* Behind that assertion in the task force's report, *Work in America,* lie hundreds of studies that correlate work with key indicators of the quality of life. The sixteen papers published here review much of that evidence. These papers, commissioned for the *Work in America* study, aggregate, digest, and interpret an enormous body of research in order to pinpoint the relationships of work to health, to education, and to welfare.

In many ways *Work in America* was a summary of the commissioned papers, thirty-nine in all, and the dozens of other papers prepared by members of the task force and their student associates. The total volume of these documents amounts to several thousand pages. Consequently, there were many first-rate papers that could not be included in this book. A primary consideration has been to cover most of the major topics discussed in *Work in America;* each chapter of the report is represented here by two or three of the commissioned papers.

* *Work in America* (Cambridge: MIT Press, 1973), p. xv. *Work in America* was prepared under a contract with the W. E. Upjohn Institute for Employment Research and was submitted in December 1972 to Elliot L. Richardson, then Secretary of Health, Education, and Welfare.

These papers do not always agree with the findings presented in *Work in America*. This is one of the costs of selectivity: some of the arguments that convinced the task force are not included here, while some of the arguments that were rejected by the task force are included. And, as one might expect, the authors often disagree with one another on workplace issues. But all agree that work influences the quality of life both positively and negatively.

The "quality of life" is a convenient term. It covers a multitude of blessings. It is a measure of individual and national prosperity, happiness and commonwealth. As these papers show, there is a significant relationship between work and such important indicators of the quality of life as health, family stability, educational attainment, self-esteem, and productivity.

Lee Rainwater and Frank Furstenberg write here that people who are chronically unemployed have higher rates of family instability than the general population. James House and Stanislav Kasl offer evidence that these people also suffer from more symptoms of physical and mental illness. According to Michael Piore, the working poor—those with low-paying, unsteady jobs—also exhibit many of these symptoms. The authors indicate that steadily employed clerical and blue-collar workers with unfulfilling, low-skilled (but often high-paying) jobs in industry and government often have low self-esteem, support radical political causes, and have serious mental and physical health problems. Many of these workers suffer from the "hidden injuries of class": George Strauss shows that some of these workers are so psychologically crippled that they are unable to participate in re-creating leisure activities. Often, as Furstenberg reports, these workers manifest a tendency to limit their children's occupational mobility and educational success by restricting their adaptability to change and by crimping their self-confidence.

Emanuel Kay argues that workers in the professional classes also have problems stemming from working conditions. These conditions may lead to low self-esteem, alcoholism, marital problems, and obsolescence on the job. The papers by Bruce Margolis and William Kroes and by James House offer evidence that stressful work leads to heart attacks and other diseases. Those by Richard Walton and by Louis Davis and Eric Trist suggest that the design of jobs affects productivity for all classes of workers. Thomas Thomas, along with Furstenberg and Rainwater, implies that our failure to provide enough jobs is related to national costs such as welfare, crime, and delinquency. And Isabel Sawhill hits home with the assertion that the failure to recognize child-rearing as work and the failure to provide good labor force jobs for women are affecting both national productivity and "domestic relations."

But offering a litany of correlations between work and quality of life indicators often raises more questions than it answers. It is not at all clear what is cause and what is effect where social problems are concerned. Nor is it clear what course national and private policies should follow to alleviate these problems. (And some observers would argue that these problems cannot be solved by social policy or that the costs of treatment are unacceptably high in terms of side effects on national prosperity or personal freedom.)

Work in America was designed to open a broad discussion of these important national issues and to see which, if any, responses are called for. The purpose of this collection of papers is to provide the background for the views that were outlined in *Work in America* and to contribute more data to the debate about the future of work that is currently raging in unions, businesses, academia, and government.

I. Who Is Dissatisfied?

In the introductory chapter of *Work in America,* the task force outlined the functions of work: its centrality to the lives of most adults, its contribution to identity and self-esteem, and its utility in bringing order and meaning to life. It was asserted that when the opportunity to work is absent, or when the nature of work is dissatisfying, there are likely to be severe repercussions for individuals and the social system.

Evidence has been mounting that significant numbers of American workers are dissatisfied with the quality of their working lives. Dull, routine, and meaningless jobs are no longer acceptable to America's well-educated, well-paid work force. The lingering of Taylorism, the large scale of most work organizations, and the closing of the option of self-employment contribute to job dissatisfaction. But some observers assert that job dissatisfaction is not a serious problem. Some claim that poor people and manual workers have no right to expect satisfaction from work, others hold that there is no evidence that job dissatisfaction is increasing, and still others refuse to believe that a large number of people are dissatisfied.[1]

Ivar Berg recognizes the signs that workers are less satisfied with their jobs than they might be. He notes that workers who are unhappy with their jobs often appear to have lost their desire to work under any conditions—to have lost their willingness to work at all, not just merely to have an aversion to a certain task. Berg places much of the burden on management for the apparent unwillingness of workers to adhere to the "Protestant ethic." He writes that "corporate shenanigans, political deceptions, and a profession-al-executive class avowedly and conspicuously underworked, may simply not inspire the larger population to seek 'success' in the old way."

George Strauss offers a comprehensive review of the literature on job satisfaction in order to see whether there is a blue-collar revolt against work. Strauss explains why it is difficult to offer a simple, clear response to the question, "Is there a problem of job dissatisfaction?" There are several hun-dred studies of job satisfaction, and a discussion of them quickly becomes complex and methodological. (And it should not surprise anyone who has ever looked at a social science journal that these studies are inconclusive on many key points.) The greatest obstacle is that it is quite difficult, if not impossible, to establish norms in the critical domain of human experience. There is no index of "healthy" or "unhealthy" job satisfaction as reliable as the 98.6 on a thermometer.

But even without precise measuring devices some current trends are dis-cernable. Many of us are beginning to arrive at the point that futurists have been predicting for several years: we have decreasingly to "kill ourselves on the job" in order to put bread on the table. Many of us now have the luxury of dropping out of work for a while, and we have a choice among a wide array of jobs. Blue-collar workers are also sharing in this change: witness the auto workers who are trading off a day of salary for a day of free time.

Given these consequences of greater affluence and higher levels of edu-cation, the key question is: Do we *continue* to organize work in the fashion of the Industrial Revolution, when people were mostly ill-educated and on the border of poverty, or do we change work to reflect the needs of our new society?

The situation is not yet a crisis. It is an *opportunity* for change that we might seize to improve the quality of life in America. If we see the issue of improving working conditions in this light, we remove much of the talk about alienation and widespread job dissatisfaction that many find so objection-able. As a first step we could compile a list of basic assumptions about work that could serve as a guide to making it more satisfying:

• Some jobs are better than others, and no matter what is done all jobs can't be made uniformly satisfying.

• Almost all bad jobs can be improved, at least marginally.

• People differ widely in their psychological makeup and intelligence and hence have differing needs from their jobs.

• Intelligence and psychological makeup are better criteria for job placement than race, sex, class, or age.

• People with jobs that they don't like are less committed to their jobs than people who like their work.

• It is better for the individual, the workplace, and society for workers to be committed to their jobs than for them not to be committed.

Once agreement was reached about these assumptions, certain actions would be warranted. We would first try to improve the worst jobs in our economy through such means as offering higher pay, greater security, and effective participation in decision making and in profits; improving mobility; improving physical working conditions; and offering education options and higher status. Second, we would be particularly careful not to place intelligent workers in dull jobs because of irrelevant criteria: we would not give black workers janitorial jobs *because* they are black. Third, we would see to it that the interests and skills of workers better matched the requirements of their tasks.

What is clear from all available research is that each individual requires something slightly different to be satisfied with work. As young people put it, "Different strokes for different folks." The design of jobs, however, tends to be rather monolithic. This stems from the assumptions managers make about their workers' capabilities based upon the workers' race, sex, age, social class, or educational credentials. Using such criteria, employers assume, for example, that blue-collar workers are incapable of accomplishing tasks that require much intelligence. Accordingly, jobs for the poorly educated are usually designed to be repetitive, simple, and unchallenging. It is possible, however, to point to some facts about the labor force that belie employers' stereotypes and challenge the wisdom of simplified tasks for many blue-collar workers. We might look at the IQ range of workers to illustrate the point:[2]

Occupation	IQ Range	Mean IQ
Ph.D. (Professor)	100-169	130
Engineer	100-151	127
Clerk	68-155	118
Laborer	26-145	96

The data show that there are few dull Ph.D.'s, as expected, but we also find that there are many bright laborers. (In fact, three times more laborers than Ph.D.'s have IQs over 130; there are, of course, many more laborers.) The important point to be made here is that we design most laborers' jobs for the mean (or lower), which leaves many, many exceptionally bright laborers in jobs that are unchallenging and, *for them,* demeaning. Lynn Rigby, of Sandia Laboratories, has shown that these bright, dissatisfied workers are often the ones responsible for defects, failures, accidents, and errors in the workplace. From the *Work in America* perspective, it is clearly a waste of human resources to place bright people in bad jobs because we fail to recognize their potential. This indicates that at least some of the problems of job dissatisfaction might be lessened through better identification of worker talents and a better fit between person and job.

In short, as Strauss points out, because there is no single source of job satisfaction, there is no single way for employers to provide it. What we know is that different personalities, classes, and subcultures require different sources of satisfaction from work. Currently, the variety of job design is too limited to meet the wide array of changing human needs. What is required is more options in job design, more flexible working arrangements, and freer access to and information about jobs.

Some of the most convincing evidence of the need for new forms of job design came to the *Work in America* task force not only from the theoretical and survey findings of social scientists but from workers' own words about their expectations. Task force member James Wright took a small team of interviewers into the field and came back with a large and surprising body of taped discussions with truck drivers, auto workers, steel workers, clerks, and secretaries. Wright found that almost none of the workers had ever been asked questions about their personal happiness with their jobs—indeed, they were surprised that anyone cared. Rather taken aback, their responses were not the neat, well-organized, pat answers we give when someone asks a tough question that we've heard before. These respondents were full of bitterness about the conditions under which they toiled, and full of expletives that conveyed their frustration. They poured out the result of years of pent-up hostility toward their bosses, their unions, and their society. Significantly, the amount of drug and alcohol abuse Wright found among these workers was appalling.

Only fragments of these interviews found their way into *Work in America.*

But they provided a tenor and background that we on the task force could not forget when we sat down to write about the world of work. What was particularly memorable about the interviews was that time and time again the workers told of suggesting to their employers that there were better ways to organize their tasks—and of these suggestions invariably being met with indifference, disdain, or contempt. Finally, the workers gave up trying. They began to make the minimum possible commitment to their jobs that would still ensure a paycheck at the end of the week.

The messages of dissatisfaction that workers are sending to us are of the silent, sullen kind which the insensitive interpret as "not caring," "laziness," or "loss of the will to work." But we cannot reasonably expect greater worker articulation of discontent. Workers have seldom risen en masse in a social movement. American workers are a heterogeneous body—white, black, men, women, rich, poor, white-collar, blue-collar. The "worker" is a fiction. American workers are as different from each other as American citizens are —indeed, citizen is the only valid synonym for them as a body.

From our interviews we discovered that one reason that workers have not requested changed working conditions is that neither their employers nor their unions have led them to believe that change is possible. The attitudes of management and unions to these issues (whether these attitudes spring from indifference or from lack of knowledge) have led workers to conclude that the way we organize work is not subject to change. Like being born with a big, ugly nose, the condition of work is your lot, and you must learn to live with it. The only escape they see is a shorter work week, whether they get it through collective bargaining or through absenteeism.

As to why workers don't speak up at their local union meetings about the quality of their working lives, we might just as well ask why the millions of women who participated in coffee klatches in the 1950s and 1960s didn't discuss women's liberation. Similarly, why didn't Negroes in the 1940s and 1950s all demand their civil rights? Instead, they expended their energies in otherworldly escape in church or in the basic task of trying to eke out a living. Does the fact that at that time they weren't complaining mean that there was no segregation or that they liked being segregated? The issue just had not been focused, and they were unaware of what they could achieve through united action.

In almost all social movements, three things probably must occur before there is a widespread demand for change: (1) conditions have to be getting better, (2) the issue has to have crystallized, and (3) there must be knowledge of possible alternatives. Laborsaving devices were liberating women from housework, women were attending college in almost the same number as men, and women were entering the labor force in droves *before* women's liberation became a major issue. Negroes, many of whom were still serfs on southern farms until the 1950s, did not speak as a group until after the army had been integrated, after the Supreme Court's *Brown v. Board of Education* decision, and after the first civil rights legislation had been passed.

We are now starting to find parallels to the black movement and women's liberation among some workers. Conditions are generally improving in the workplace, and the auto workers at Lordstown have given job dissatisfaction a focus, so it is not surprising to find workers beginning to send signals that they are unhappy. As any candid personnel officer will admit, young workers are increasingly disrespectful toward the job and toward authority on the job, and management believes the rates of absenteeism and turnover are too high.

This worker discontent has not yet manifested itself in organized union activity because workers have not yet realized that their unions can represent them on noneconomic issues as well as on economic ones. Even more fundamental, perhaps, is that workers doubt their own potential as human beings. As research cited in several of the papers shows, workers who are in repetitive, unchallenging, and authoritarian work settings often fear the possibility of failure and answer no when asked if they want autonomy, an opportunity to make decisions, or an opportunity to learn and grow on the job. Significantly, after their jobs have been redesigned (or after they have been given a short training course to build their self-confidence), these workers refuse to go back to the old way of doing things.

As Strauss and Berg show, the extent of job dissatisfaction is too complex to be measured by simple tools like a Gallup poll. But the fact that social scientists cannot measure job dissatisfaction does not mean that it does not exist. Faced with the frustrating experience of trying to demonstrate to a nonbeliever that job dissatisfaction existed, *Work in America* task force member William Herman finally gave up and asked, "Why is it that we don't say, 'Thank God, it's Monday'?"

In summary, more important than the questions of the nature of job satisfaction or how widespread it might be, is the question of what benefits would accrue to the individual and to society from improvements in the quality of working life.

II. Problems of American Workers

In the second chapter of *Work in America* we argued that work problems impinge differently on different demographic groups. For example, for the generation of workers under thirty, work is one of the most perplexing institutions with which they must cope. They have never faced economic adversity, they are offered good and lengthy educations (which prolong their adolescence), they never see their parents at work, and they are told that they can achieve anything. With this kind of a preparation for adulthood, they enter the work force with high (some would say unreal) expectations. They take it for granted that their jobs will pay well; what they want are jobs that are beneficial to other people and challenging to themselves. Consequently, making a career choice is excruciating for them. All the options in the world appear open to them, but most of these young people are unable to find jobs that meet their expectations of wealth, happiness, and "relevance." They feel bored and cheated. The less fortunate of this generation are now giving foremen hell on assembly lines; those who had the best educations and the most options are now leading consumer and ecology activist groups against the system they feel let them down. Some members of this generation have adopted a disturbing quiescence—not engaging themselves in work, family, or politics. Some of this is reflected in a kind of mañana attitude in the workplace: notice how long it takes to get through the check-out line at the supermarket, how once efficient stores now seem to run out of goods that used always to be in stock, how increasing quantities of red tape are involved in getting the simplest service from government or private enterprise.

This generation (my generation) is not fully responsible for this "Latin Americanization" of our country's workplaces, but it has contributed more than its share. I would argue that the apparent unwillingness on the part of this generation to do certain jobs is not an unwillingness to work per se, but an unwillingness to discipline itself to tasks that are inflexibly organized or meaningless (in its view) or offer little in the way of pride of accomplishment. In communes, in businesses they've started for themselves, in storefront legal offices, and in the Peace Corps, young people are working very hard. The challenge we face, as I see it, is to make more jobs as valuable and as meaningful to young people as these enterpreneurial and public service tasks.

It is different with poor blacks and other disadvantaged people; their problems are not the by-product of parents' successes. They are unable to find enough work, or they find only work that fails to met the economic, social, and psychological functions necessary for a productive and responsible life. Michael Piore writes about the consequences of being trapped in the "secondary labor market." He also indicates that the work problems of blue-collar workers are indirectly related to the problems of the poor. In effect, the security of the organized worker rests parasitically on the insecurity of the unorganized secondary labor market worker. Piore's imaginative thesis is that union security agreements with industry, and the accompanying union accommodation to Taylorism, are at fault.

Unions have incorrectly interpreted the movement to improve the quality of working life as a jugular attack on them.[3] Traditionally, of course, the union has been the leading humanizing institution in the workplace. This is one of the reasons that people naturally look to unions for leadership in the effort to redesign jobs. That they have, to date, been noticeably willing to let management assume the lead does not mean that they cannot or should not exert themselves in this area. Piore argues, in fact, that the solution to many of the problems of the workplace is *more* widespread and *more* vigorous union activity.

Isabel Sawhill examines the economic problems involved in the sex-stereotyping of work roles. She makes it abundantly clear that women are discriminated against in their work both in the home and in the labor market. (Significantly, the fact that an increasing number of women are demanding jobs—and better jobs—is probably the best proof we have that the desire to work is not dead.)

In addition to carefully analyzing economic issues, Sawhill raises one of the most crucial questions to come out of the women's liberation movement: "Shouldn't men be more involved in the raising of children?" Although more child care centers may be a good thing, might it not be better for our children and our society if work conditions were more flexible so that men and women could share both work and home responsibilities? We know that children who are raised by both a loving mother and a loving father are usually mentally healthier than those who are raised by just one parent. We also know that those who are raised by one parent (which is probably the norm, given the hours the typical working father devotes to his children) are usually mentally healthier than those who are raised in institutions. Doesn't it make sense, then, if we are to have a revolution in family and work roles, to design policies that encourage joint parental rather than institutional responsibility for the raising of children? Can work be organized so that a husband and wife can split a job? Can we provide more half-time jobs for women *and* for men?

Emanuel Kay's paper is an examination of the workplace problems of another "neglected" group of workers—the relatively privileged middle managers. Kay argues that job dissatisfaction is not simply a blue-collar or clerical phenomenon. This is an important finding for public planning, for we know that middle-class Americans are reluctant to support programs that benefit only the poor. Since a program for improving the quality of working life would benefit all classes of workers, it has a greater likelihood of acceptance than a program focused solely on those in the worst jobs. Kay also points out that middle managers are in an organizational position to frustrate any attempts to make changes in the quality of working life for those below them. This is reason enough to try to improve their jobs, even if they are not needy in the traditional sense.

III. Work and Health

The papers included here by Stanislav Kasl, James House, and Bruce Margolis and William Kroes formed much of the basis for the chapter on health in *Work in America*. The task force concluded from these papers and other sources that various aspects of work account for many of the factors associated with heart disease—tension, high cholesterol, above normal blood pressure and blood sugar, etc. Work problems also correlate highly with symptoms of poor mental health (such as low self-esteem), although not necessarily with mental illness (such as schizophrenia).

Two aspects of the relationship of work and health are germane to public policy. First, workers and society appear to be bearing medical costs that have their genesis in the workplace, and many of them could be avoided if preventive measures were taken. Second, work can be transformed into a singularly powerful source of psychological and physical rewards that can be used to alleviate many of the problems of such groups as drug addicts, mental health patients, juvenile delinquents, and the handicapped. Significantly, a good job can also be "therapy" for those who are free from such problems—and who want to avoid them.

Margolis and Kroes present a broad overview of the factors that correlate with a variety of physical and mental health problems. They conclude that although we are largely ignorant of causal factors, the correlational, case history, and anecdotal evidence relating work conditions to both mental and physical health problems are too convincing to dismiss. House carefully documents the effects of occupational stress on phyiscal health. One of his most interesting conclusions is that workers who are motivated by extrinsic rewards (such as pay and security) are more likely to have heart disease than those motivated by intrinsic rewards (such as job challenge and self-actualization). He illustrates the methodological obstacles to greater knowledge in this field, but he argues that intervention is now warranted, even before more research is accumulated, for we presently know as much about the effects of work-related stress on the body as we know about the physical factors on which we are spending millions of dollars to reduce heart disease risk.

Kasl presents a thorough review of over 150 studies of work and mental health. He concludes that we do not know if work directly causes mental problems, but he demonstrates how the aspirations of some people, particularly those in low-status jobs, appear to be dwarfed by their work environment. He argues for a broader approach to the problem that would include questions of retirement, mid-career change, and the relationship between work roles and family roles. This is the perspective that the task force came to advocate.

IV. The Redesign of Jobs

The redesign of jobs was one of the central issues of *Work in America*. But work redesign is still only a part, albeit a crucial part, of an overall strategy to improve the quality of working life. In *conjunction* with increased opportunity for mid-career change, increased employment opportunities for the elderly, youth, minorities, and women, and decreased discriminatory obstacles to occupational mobility for these groups, job redesign *can* have an important and lasting effect on the social problems of America. Job redesign alone, however, is not a sufficient response to the problems of the workplace.

Robert Kahn argues in his paper that the following factors are causes of satisfaction or dissatisfaction at work: occupation, status, supervision, peer relationships, job content, wages, promotion, security, and physical working conditions. His proposal for the work module would relieve several problems associated with these factors and would also relieve another cause of job dissatisfaction—the inability to learn on the job. Kahn argues that there is no single formula to achieve satisfaction. Only experiments that try to change many of these factors simultaneously will succeed. (This is why so-called job enrichment, which usually changes only one or two features of a job, will fail in the long run to solve workplace problems.)

Richard Walton has a philosophical position similar to Kahn's. Walton feels that the roots of worker alienation go deep and that nothing less than comprehensive redesign of the workplace can sever them. The design of the General Foods pet-food factory in Topeka, Kansas, that he describes here touches on each of the key factors that Kahn identifies as important to the quality of working life.

In the Topeka plant, the workers are rewarded for learning new tasks. The goal is for every worker to be able to do every job in the factory. When I visited the plant I was amazed to find that even workers with little formal educational experience were able to repair the sophisticated electronic equipment and computer components in the plant's control room. I believe that there is a relationship between this learning aspect and the quality of life of the workers. The plant director, Ed Dulworth, told me that the number of workers at the plant who take advantage of the company's pledge to pay for formal programs of continuing education is three times the average for General Foods as a whole. Apparently, learning on the job has whetted the workers' appetites for more learning—or it has overcome the sense of not being able to succeed at school that afflicts so many blue-collar workers.

A second positive effect of the Topeka plant design on the quality of life is that the employees seem to participate in community and civic activities at rates high for blue-collar workers. One wonders if the habit of participation that has become natural for them on the job has spilled over into increased citizen participation.

Two serious objections have been raised concerning this plant.[4] First, several unofficial union spokesmen have claimed that the plant was designed to break union control over a part of General Food's activities. This is a serious charge. It is usually a mistake to question the motives of those who do good in this world—there are so few of them—but it would be a shame if job redesign becomes a tool for union busting. A response to this problem is to work with union and management in an organized plant to develop a unionized model that is as sensitive to the quality of working life as the nonunionized Topeka model. Indeed, Ben Stephansky and Harold Sheppard of the Upjohn Institute are working with UAW officials on just such a project. The second charge leveled against the Topeka plant is that it does not have a representative work force. When the plant was being staffed workers were carefully chosen from a multitude of candidates. This, of course, makes the work force untypical enough to raise some doubts about how much we can generalize about the plant. We need an experiment with a more conventionally selected group of workers if we are going to be able to generalize from it to industry as a whole.

Louis Davis and Eric Trist, a father of the movement to improve the quality of working life, present in their paper several case studies that formed the background for Walton's successful Topeka experiment. (Readers who enjoy disagreement among experts will find particular pleasure in contrasting George Strauss's concluding skeptical statement about the value of job redesign with the evidence presented by Davis and Trist.)

It is worth noting that the recent experiments in job redesign may owe much of their success to the well-documented "Hawthorne effect." In 1924, industrial engineers at the Hawthorne, Illinois, plant of the Western Electric Company found that productivity increased measurably when a group of workers was made the subject of an experiment. It has been shown countless times since then that there is invariably a spurt of productivity when management demonstrates interest in a group of workers. The increase in productivity is, unfortunately, short-lived, and workers soon slip back to their former pace. Contrariwise, recent experiments in job redesign appear to be eliciting long-term (and, perhaps, lasting) increases in productivity. As the key to job redesign is worker participation in decision making, it may be that the Hawthorne effect has been *institutionalized* in these new experiments. The fact of participation may be daily proof to the workers that management cares. Every time workers take part in a decision, the feeling that management trusts and respects them is reinforced, and the workers respond by making an effort to perform to their capacity. If the Hawthorne effect is being institutionalized and made lasting in these experiments then this would be an unusually important finding from the point of view of the science of behavior, because the Hawthorne effect is the only form of motivating humans that has ever been proved to work.

The publication of *Work in America* was followed by considerable attention in the media to job enrichment. Much of this interest was not a direct result of the report, but it all seemed to bubble up at the same time. Many articles pursued the same narrow themes about bored workers who needed "enriched" jobs. Response from industry and government to this publicity was immediate. Within the last year, several hundred companies have tried what they call job enrichment[5] (which in 99 percent of the cases simply means that a few workers are engaged in a little larger piece of a process than they were previously). In addition, national conferences on the "Changing work ethic" have been sponsored by industries and unions, countless job enrichment consultants have hung out their shingles, the Department of Labor reportedly allocated $2 million to study the quality of working life, the President's Productivity Commission has found some promising projects to fund, and the Congress has become concerned with alienation and productivity. As fast as superficial cover stories could appear in the popular press, job enrichment has been sold as a cure-all by some of the most distinguished snake oil salesmen of the modern era.

All this interest is better than no interest, but the debate has often sunk from the level of a serious discussion of public policy to the level of a fad. The problem with fads is that reaction inevitably sets in when the new medicine doesn't cure everything from gout to dandruff. Even if it is good for acne, it is discarded as quickly as it was introduced because it fails to meet our inflated expectations.

Fortunately, there has also been a serious level of response. There are people who recognize that the quality of working life is an important issue that will outlive the job enrichment idea. Responsible managers, union officials, and academic leaders acknowledge that while it is true that the redesign of jobs *can* have a positive impact on morale, productivity, social problems, and the quality of goods, it will *not* produce these marvels either automatically or invariably. To really improve the quality of working life requires hard work, careful planning and diagnosis, commitment, time, and a willingness to abandon old ideas and to accept some sound advice from those experienced in the field. If this effort leads to genuine participation by workers in decision making and profits, the desired outcomes will very likely follow.

But in many cases the return on the investment will be only marginal, particularly if it is measured in traditional, narrow economic terms.

But redesigning workplaces, even if the painstaking principles outlined in *Work in America* (and by Richard Walton here) are followed, will not create a new Jerusalem. Workers have many wants and needs, including more money (particularly for those on the bottom of the economic scale), better pensions, better security, and better health and safety on the job. Job enrichment alone will not meet these and countless other workplace needs. Clearly, some of the worst jobs in the economy cannot, because of their nature, be redesigned to make them satisfying for *intelligent* people. A person with an IQ of 130 is not going to find self-actualization in cleaning toilets, even if we give that person all the autonomy and participation in the world.

It is true that almost all jobs can be improved if the workers participate in decisions concerning their own production methods, recruitment, the internal distribution of tasks, internal leadership, what additional tasks to take on, and when they will work. But we must recognize that some miserable jobs can be made only barely tolerable by such redesign, especially for bright people (and young people, who have not yet had their expectations dwarfed by years of dehumanizing toil). Still, there are several things we can do about the worst jobs in the economy, in *addition* to redesigning them:

• *We can increase the pay of the people who do the tasks of civilization that the rest of us are unwilling to do.* We now pay the most to people who have the best jobs and the least to people who have the worst jobs. At a minimum, we can improve the quality of life by better compensating those who receive no intrinsic rewards from their work.

• *We can improve our matching of people to jobs.* It is probably the case that some dirty, dull, repetitive jobs *can* be made challenging and fulfilling to those unfortunates we call morons, cretins, imbeciles, or idiots. The problem now is that we don't offer these people any of the dignity that comes from contributing something to mankind or even from simply supporting themselves. Rather, we destroy them by locking them up in homes or institutions. Instead of using unattractive jobs in the only way that is positive (providing the mentally handicapped with a sense of usefulness) we give these jobs to those who have certain low market-value characteristics: blacks, Spanish-speaking people, women, ugly people, and so on. If we were to substitute intelligence and psychological need for race, religion, sex, national origin, and looks as criteria for job placement, we would do much to improve the quality of life.

• *We can automate the worst jobs.* This process began when an ox was substituted for a man in front of a plow. We can speed up the process and help it to occur where it is most needed—for humanistic as well as for economic reasons.

● *We can rotate the worst jobs so that no one is condemned to a life of drudgery on a single task.* Necessity is already beginning to bring this about. In Detroit, where absenteeism and turnover are high in the auto industry, unions and management have found that college students will gladly work a day or two a week on the assembly line. They do so because of the attraction of high pay, and because, unlike the regular workers who are playing hooky, students don't feel trapped in these jobs; they know they will not be there for the rest of their lives. They are not forced to adopt what for *them* would be the damaging identity of an assembly-line worker—they remain "students." In response to the call for public service jobs for youth, one might ask what greater public service a young person can contribute than to liberate a less fortunate soul from a dehumanizing task. After graduation from high school, young citizens could spend a year doing the dirty but necessary tasks of civilization.

● *Workers can be given a second chance in life.* Workers in the worst jobs can be given mid-career retraining to prepare them for a better job.

V. Education and Work

The *Work in America* proposal for facilitating mid-career change and recurrent education was necessary because job redesign is not a sufficient solution to the problems of the quality of working life: some people were just not meant to be stone cutters, no matter what is done to make stone cutting interesting. The fit between personality and the nature of the job is immensely important to satisfaction with work and life, and the only way to achieve satisfaction where the fit is poor is to permit a change of jobs. While changing jobs is relatively easy for young, mobile professionals, it is considerably more difficult for older, blue-collar and clerical workers. Task force member Bruce Lusignan's Worker Self-Renewal proposal, which economically facilitates a mid-career change for workers who are not affluent, is already a reality in Europe, where adult education is seen as an investment in the nation's future, much as youth education is viewed in this country.

Those of us who have had the benefits of education (and overeducation) and can thus afford to be cynical about the value of going to college should not lose sight of the fact that education is a singularly respected institution among lower- and middle-class workers. Many of these people feel that they missed the opportunity to learn when they were young, or that they were denied the opportunity because of economic, racial, sex, or class barriers. A recent confidential poll sponsored by industry indicates that what workers in industry want most—in addition to what they are already receiving from their employers—is the opportunity for continuing education.

Besides neglecting the needs of older workers, our educational system has shortcomings in relation to the world of work in such areas as the teaching of the work ethic, vocational education, and the credentials process. Concerning the work ethic, in *Work in America* we said that the schools were the anticipatory mirror of industry. As David MacMichael writes here, businessmen during the Industrial Revolution supported education "precisely as the means for teaching respect for authority, instilling conformity, inculcating the rewards of effort and obedience, and counteracting the blandishments of labor unions." The schools were designed to instill a working-class ethic of docility in preparation for a world of smoke, noise, and routine. Today, industrialists are less sure of what they want education to do, although most would still support the notion that "proper work attitudes" should be taught. Career educators are debating this point now, and there is a sharp division between those who would try to instill a work ethic and those who would leave this task to the family and to industry. *Work in America* advocated a middle ground: students should be able to have part-time jobs. In this way they would learn about the world of work and the attitudes they should develop without being indoctrinated in a *particular* work ethic. This is important, as MacMichael notes, because there is more than one work ethic (each is appropriate to a stage of economic development), and it is not clear which ethic one should instill in a rapidly changing economy. For reasons of personal freedom and economic flexibility, both MacMichael and *Work in America* advocate letting the young person choose his own ethical system with a little help from the schools on how to choose wisely.

Vocational education has failed to live up to its promise to make its graduates more employable than graduates of other high school curricula. Beatrice Reuben's paper examines how well vocational graduates fare in the work force as compared to other graduates. She looks at the following questions:

• Do graduates of vocational education use the skills of their training in the jobs they take?
• Do entry-level jobs require skills that can be learned in high school vocational education programs?
• How much upward mobility do graduates of vocational programs have?
• How do the graduates rate on job satisfaction criteria?
• Do the courses offered in vocational schools match the needs of the labor market?

- Do employers prefer to train graduates of basic education courses who have "learned how to learn" rather than vocational students who have learned specific skills?
- Are the unemployment records of vocational graduates appreciably better than those of any other demographic group?
- Does vocational education open up jobs for disadvantaged youth?

Her findings, derived from over a hundred studies, are that in general vocational graduates fare no better than other graduates on any of these criteria. This would seem to mean that support for vocational education (the most expensive of the high school curricula) would have to be based on criteria other than these, which are the ones that vocational educators advance.

One could offer an argument *for* vocational education based upon demand: (1) there are many students who prefer this form of education; (2) there are some who by nature are not equipped to handle academic subjects; and (3) there are others (such as juvenile delinquents and the mentally handicapped) for whom vocational education is the best way to find a place in society (and to be kept away from "normal" students). Questions are raised by these statements. (1) Would students prefer this form of education if they were not poor or disadvantaged in some other way? (2) Are many people actually born intellectually inferior? (3) Is it a good idea to segregate those with physical and social problems?

These are difficult questions—ones that strike to the core of many of our most basic democratic beliefs. The *Work in America* task force felt that the arguments in support of vocational education were outweighed by lingering doubts about the way it may track young people into a lower social class for life. We reasoned that specific skills might better be taught later in a young person's life, that high schools should be more flexible and democratic in their placement of students, that all young people should be given skills for family, community, and leisure, and that all should be taught how to learn about and cope with the world of work.

Vocational education has shared with education in general a tendency to stress the market value of credentials at the expense of other educational values. One consequence of this has been to require, needlessly, ever higher credentials for the same work. There appears to be no end to this trend. For example, a prestigious group of educators recently offered a proposal dealing with the fact that there will be 2.5 college graduates competing for every choice job in 1980. Their solution: raise the credentials requirements for jobs. While this might solve the problem for some educators, the effect of such a policy on the quality of life would be much more complicated:

• *Management scientists* tell us that overcredentialed people are the least productive workers on some tasks.

• *Political scientists* tell us that when we put overcredentialed people in boring jobs as a national policy (which has been done in Asia and Africa) a potentially revolutionary political climate ensues.

• *Economists* tell us that when people are overcredentialed for jobs the situation is, in some cases, inflationary.

• *Sociologists* tell us that when people are overcredentialed for jobs their job dissatisfaction is high, and absenteeism, turnover, sabotage, and mental and physical health problems are all likely to increase.

• *Philosophers* tell us that there are two reasons for not stressing solely the market value of educational credentials: (1) when one finds that one cannot cash in on one's education as promised, one begins to question the value of the entire institution of education, and (2) If one does not derive anything from education other than marketplace values, one will not have the skills needed to enjoy leisure and citizenship, which become increasingly important when jobs are not sufficiently challenging.

In summary, the position taken in *Work in America* is that we should direct our efforts to better understanding the important nexus of work and education, but in so doing we should be careful not to contort the function of education so that it serves only marketplace ends.

VI. Federal Work Strategies

If nothing else, the conclusions of *Work in America* regarding welfare illustrate the unrequited role of the intellectual in national policy making. Almost every researcher who has studied the problem of family disorganization in the ghetto has come to the same conclusion: the causal factor is probably the lower-class father's inability to get and to hold the kind of employment needed to provide the social, psychological, and economic security needed for a stable family life. The solution to the "welfare mess," then, is to provide good, steady jobs so that the men who are the fathers of welfare children can have the same marriage and remarriage opportunities as middle-class men and so that poor women can have the same kind of reduced economic risks in marrying and remarrying as middle-class women.

Although many of these studies have been prepared specifically for our national leaders, welfare proposals and programs still ignore the relationship between the underemployment and the unemployment rates of ghetto men on one hand, and the numbers of women and children on welfare rolls on the other. Even the latest welfare proposals unfortunately offer only puni- tive measures designed to force welfare mothers (not the fathers of welfare children) to work. This approach contradicts much of what we know about work and welfare: (1) we don't have to force people to work—almost all peo- ple will choose to work because of its economic, social, and psychological rewards; (2) welfare mothers are already working—they are taking care of their children; (3) to forcibly remove the mother from a home where the father is already absent is to invite further costs to society in delinquency, crime, drug abuse, and remedial education; and (4) the lower-class ethic calls for the man to support his wife and children—and any other arrange- ment is cause for disintegration of the family bond.

Because of these facts, *Work in America* called for increased employment opportunities for the *fathers* of children on welfare (men who probably are not on the welfare rolls themselves) as the long-range solution to the "wel- fare mess." In effect, we offered an indirect, macroeconomic solution in- stead of a direct transfer payment solution contingent upon mothers taking jobs in the secondary labor market. The three papers included here support this approach, which was developed by task force member Elliot Liebow.

Frank Furstenberg presents an overview of the extensive literature on the relationship between work experience and family life, and he finds a strong correlation between the kinds of work experience (particularly the father's) and the degree of family stability. He recommends a change in the structure of lower-level jobs to provide the basis for a strong family life.

Lee Rainwater argues that a program of guaranteed jobs plus one of guaranteed income can lead to the social, psychological, and economic well-being of families. Rainwater's guaranteed income plan will be rec- ognized as similar to the one offered by Senator George McGovern during his campaign for the Presidency. The plan is further evidence of the gap in understanding between politicians and intellectuals. Far from being an irre- sponsible and hastily conceived plan (as much of the electorate perceived it), it is a serious proposal that has adherents among both conservative and liberal economists. It is, in fact, the idea that Daniel Patrick Moynihan adopted from the work of Milton Friedman—and it was the basis of Presi- dent Nixon's first talk about welfare reform. Such are the permutations of public policy!

Thomas Thomas's proposal is even more precedent-shattering than Rainwater's. Thomas feels that workers in the secondary labor market (as described by Piore) have economic, social, and familial problems that they cannot escape as long as their employment opportunities are limited to this market. He feels that traditional approaches to welfare will not overcome the debilitating effects of the secondary market. He therefore proposes to build upon the resources of the poorer communities to provide employment that serves the economic and social functions of the *primary* labor market.

Conclusion

In one important respect, *Work in America* shares Thomas's unorthodox approach to social problems. The report departs diametrically from the prevailing mode of public policy analysis, which is dominated by the thinking of budgeteers, economists, managers, and administrators. *Work in America* is a planning document that takes a holistic and humanistic approach to public policy. It looks for indirect ways to solve social problems where frontal assaults have failed. For example, *Work in America* acknowledges that one of the most pressing problems in the nation today is the high rate of unemployment among certain groups (particularly among minorities in large cities). Direct job creation approaches to the problem have been rejected by decision makers because of the economic trade-off between employment and inflation. We feared that society will always choose low inflation over low unemployment, given a choice put in those narrow terms.

We therefore proposed a concept of social efficiency that would enlarge our accounting system of the costs to society of high unemployment. This accounting system would include, among other costs that are related to unemployment, the costs of welfare, crime, mental and physical health, and compensatory education.

We also proposed indirect methods to provide more employment—through job design, equity sharing, portable pensions, an end to discrimination in hiring, and worker renewal programs. All of these methods should improve the employment-inflation trade-off and thus permit a greater degree of job creation. These indirect methods would also help employed middle-class people and would, therefore, be more acceptable politically than direct programs that help only the poor.

Our national failure to find solutions to social problems may in the final analysis result as much from the difficulties inherent in social policy planning as it does from the political problems of competing interests. Planning is particularly complex because one issue cannot be isolated from other social and economic questions. Therefore, a holistic approach to planning is necessary if our policies and programs are not to be helter-skelter or conflicting or to lead us to a future we do not want.

Task force member William Herman suggested that we look to the physical sciences for one guide to social planning. It was discovered in the navy during World War II that one could not identify a passing ship at night by looking directly at it. After much experimentation, it was found that one *could* identify a ship if one fixed one's gaze considerably in front of (or behind) the vessel in question. Herman argued that perhaps this concept of peripheral vision can be profitably applied to social problems as well. For example, we find that medical care programs seldom have the desired effect on health status, that welfare programs seldom reduce the number of people on the dole, that school-based programs seldom increase the educational attainment of our youth, and that law enforcement programs seldom reduce the amount of crime. Solutions to such problems are often found to be indirect—through reducing poverty, increasing employment, strengthening the family, and so forth. Social planning, then, often requires a broad, peripheral perspective.

Work in America is an attempt at a holistic, indirect, interdisciplinary approach to complicated social problems using the institution of work as a focus and fulcrum. The subject of *Work in America* is not job satisfaction. Rather, the report is about how one might use the opportunity of changing the institution of work to improve the quality of life, to contribute to a more just society, and to strengthen our public and private institutions.

The reader will find the papers that follow far more meaningful if these larger issues are kept in mind.

Notes

1. Mitchell Fein, "The Myth of Job Enrichment," *Humanist,* September-October 1973; Harold Wool, "What's Wrong with Work in America," *Monthly Labor Review,* March 1973; Irving Kristol, "Is the American Worker 'Alienated'?" *Wall Street Journal,* January 18, 1973; William Winpisinger, "Job Satisfaction: A Union Response," *American Federationist,* February 1973; William Gomberg, "Job Satisfaction: Sorting Out the Nonsense," *American Federationist,* June 1973.

2. Lynn Rigby, *The Nature of Human Error* (Albuquerque: Sandia Laboratories, 1970).

3. Gomberg; Winpisinger.

4. Fein; Gomberg.

5. Roy Walters, *Job Enrichment Newsletter,* Glen Rock, New Jersey.

I Who Is Dissatisfied?

1 "They Won't Work":
The End of the Protestant Ethic
and All That

Ivar Berg

Dissimilar and divided as they have often appeared on other counts, it has been a long-standing commonplace about Americans that thrift, diligence in work, an instinct for craftsmanship, and a capacity for deferring gratification were traits they both exhibited and commended to the world. Such traits made us economically productive, and in being so we served our consciences no less than our pocketbooks; it is no wonder that the "Protestant ethic" in America has found adherents among Catholics and Jews and Muslims no less than among Presbyterians and Lutherans. The philosophical gap in this way of life—between personal worth and market value—we early and conveniently bridged by adorning economic necessity with all the medals of moral virtue. The net effect was to impart a high order of legitimacy to an economic system whose individual members could be credited or blamed for their own circumstances according to the degree of their prosperity.

Since the system is seen as the very vehicle of moral behavior, we have tinkered with it only occasionally—through homestead laws, antitrust statutes, selected regulatory measures, more benign collective bargaining laws, and, in recent times, provisions to broaden access to education. By these

Reprinted, with changes, from *The Columbia Forum,* vol. 2, no. 1 (winter 1973), by permission of the author and the publisher. Copyright 1973 by the Trustees of Columbia University in the City of New York.

adjustments we have sought to compensate for gross inequalities at the starting lines of the competitive race. That all but a very few citizens tried to enter the race was not remarkable. Poor Richard's aphorisms about the rewards of self-discipline, diligence, and the alert pursuit of opportunity are with us yet, in the inelegant but expressive slogan: "You can't get something for nothing." Few contest it.

But who has not recently heard the news, in one form or another, that after nearly two hundred years Americans are renouncing the Protestant ethic for new and spreading heresies? Decades ago a similar alarm was raised by persons who overestimated (long before Joe McCarthy and Whittaker Chambers) the allure of the European doctrines of "collectivism." In our own time, however, the news is passed among many more than that small contingent of witch-hunters of other times, and troubles those never seriously worried by the radical Left. Thoughtful parents, for example, who can abide their offspring's clothes and music and coiffure—even their questioning of marriage—are troubled by their insistence on "personal authenticity," by their attraction to communal values, and by their calling into question the worth of competition, of status seeking, and of material consumption. The impact of the so-called youth culture is threatening not because it has borrowed occasional terms of opprobrium from the orthodox Left—dependably, "people outgrow that"—but because questions are asked that have little to do with the state and ownership.

Additional evidence that stock in the Protestant ethic is low is readily inferred by some from the behavior of the working classes. We are told, for example, that workers are more independent, less attentive to their obligations, more prone to absenteeism, and generally less accepting of supervisory and managerial authority—and this despite the fact that unemployment rates have become uncommonly high. It is even more remarkable, perhaps, that absenteeism and other indicators of loose industrial discipline have allegedly risen among the hitherto well-behaved white-collar workers, whose own unemployment rates have also increased dramatically.

No one is accustomed to seeing such evidence of workers' deficiencies side by side with high unemployment statistics, and their rubbing together has produced heat. Thus one hears annoyance expressed over the fact that blacks are proportionately represented among the absentees from relatively high-paying auto factories. Surely when their own leaders deplore the blacks' unemployment rate, employed black workers should be happy with jobs and weekly paychecks; surely they ought not to tempt their employers by negligent attendance.

And when one looks at the unions, what should one make of, say, the rules requiring duplicative work in printing shops; the firemen who famously tend no fires on diesel locomotives; the work rules which prescribe the width of paint brushes, the size of crews, the number of plumbing vents to be installed in which houses by construction workers? Nor is there much sign of guilty feeling among workers over these (as Veblen dubbed them) "strategies of independence," an omission that amazes observers to whom the "withdrawal of efficiency" (as labor calls it) seems thoroughly shameful. All is insouciance and euphemism, apparently.

But beyond doubt the most inflammatory evidence offered for the end of the ethic is the testimony of the public welfare rolls, statistics rarely mentioned in editorials, summer cottages, seminars, or corporate boardrooms without the word "scandalous" appended. Indeed, so famous are the welfare figures now that they need no rehearsal here. It suffices to say that they are favored above all other demonstrations that "people don't want to work."

Another Diagnosis

The condition of the Protestant ethic may, however, be too glibly stated. "For instance" is notoriously not proof, and not all observers will infer the same conclusions from a given statistic or set of facts. Thus it is at least possible that the ethic is alive though not entirely well, and that a very different diagnosis can be made. That diagnosis suggests that work does occupy a central place in the lives of most Americans but that the legitimacy of "the system"—what and whom one works for—is much in doubt. Among the faithful who work in the old imperative way, this widening doubt can easily inspire resentment, for it could imply that they themselves are naive at the best, downright foolish at worst. This explains the censorious tone so often taken toward defectors, who might otherwise be seen only as deficient or self-damaging.

One could argue, first off, that the young are at least as interested in work as any generation has been at the school-leaving age. (Consider that even the so-called social dropouts who turn to communes enter into social compacts requiring individual contributions of labor the magnitude of which never fails to surprise the visiting journalists from the Sunday supplements.) But within the conventional labor markets and the jobs they offer, the skeptical young complain of, among other things, educational requirements that increasingly exceed what employers can actually use, a criticism which can be sustained in an extraordinarily large number and variety of work settings. The demonstrable consequence for those employed, of any age, is dissatisfaction with the work, frustration of talents, and turnover—whose statistics are more often cited as proof of a widespread indifference toward work than as signs of managerial irrationality. No one can accurately assess how much of business and industry's rates of mental illness and alcoholism begin with thwarted abilities. It should surprise no one, least of all modern employers spending vast sums on "morale" and "human relations" programs, that the dissatisfaction of underutilized workers can reflect itself in expensive personnel and production problems.

Nor is the "withdrawal of efficiency" news. Sociologists have been reporting for more than forty years, even before the pioneering studies of workers in Western Electric's Hawthorne works, that employees will "bank" work, will invent concealed timesaving improvements on their own machines, and, in general and wherever possible, seek their own ratio of monetary-to-nonmonetary satisfactions in their shops, offices, and factory lines. In other days, it was the rare top-level manager who would not, in unemotional moments, acknowledge that workers were no less rational for making the most of every comfort possible to them. That younger, bolder, and better-educated workers may have elaborated the preferences of older immigrant and depression-scarred workers should not puzzle us.

It may of course be true that workers' independence is on the rise. But it is not necessarily clear that workers' motivations have changed from those long ago adduced in social science studies of informal groups. Many of these studies, in their assessments of productivity, pointed specifically to the crucial work of managers. It may well be that we overlook that work in our assertions about employees.

Take the matter of featherbedding, about which publicists, managers, trade-association spokesmen, and others regularly remind us. The term is applied to work rules covering an enormous number of practices in innumerable work settings. The history of the most celebrated work rules, including those mentioned earlier, shows that they were formulated within the bargaining process, with employers obtaining something of great value in return for an "arrangement" managers never thought would be problematic. Railroad managers, for example, simply did not expect that diesel engines would revolutionize railroad technology, and traded a seat for firemen in these engines for a favorable wage settlement. The seat could of course be bought back in a reversal of the bargain: workers, no less than management, conform to that article of our creed which encourages us to husband our capital, whatever it might be.

The responsibility for nonwork can be similarly redistributed in other industries. Plumbing vents, for example, are typically required by building codes, whose terms most often reflect, not the sinful "make-work" instincts of construction workers acting unilaterally, but the effectiveness and ethics of municipal governments, contractors, and supporting union officials. Indeed, in much recent muttering about the devaluation of work, one might suppose that management had nothing to *do* with work.

Facts about Welfare Recipients
Even the shockingly large number of people receiving welfare payments—solely or in addition to wages—can be seen in more than one light. Those persons who suppose that the welfare increases in the nation's largest cities provide statistical indices of the ethic's demise must confront some inconvenient facts. For example, among heads of families who work full-time, about 7 percent earn an income at what has come to be called the poverty level. Among persons who are fully employed but without spouses or family, fully 30 percent are impoverished.[1] "In fact," wrote two sociologists recently, "about a third of all impoverished families (2.4 million in 1967) are headed by a fully employed person. Another million 'unrelated individuals' are in the same situation—fully employed but poor. Millions more live at the margins of poverty."[2] These millions may have something to tell us about the state of work in America. At the very least, they are Protestant ethic loyalists like none that we have imagined—or lately heard from.

If a sizable number of actual welfare recipients are fully employed, another sizable number are underemployed; and a very significant number of eligible underemployed, unemployed, and impoverished workers are not beneficiaries of welfare at all. A survey of low-income families in Detroit in 1965, for example, showed that 43 percent of eligible recipients in that city were not on the welfare rolls. In New York City in 1968, approximately 150,-000 families were eligible for wage subsidies, according to the city welfare department's estimates, but only about 15,000 families were claiming them.[3]

The total of the ineligible but poor, plus the eligible nonrecipients, plus the eligible but fully employed recipients, is large. One can juxtapose it with the number of able-bodied, unemployed recipients—after subtracting from the latter figure all the dependent children and aged persons it includes— and arrive at figures most unhelpful to the argument that welfare programs cosset a mob of lazy apostates who mock the Protestant ethic.

Meantime, the facts available on the attitudes toward work of typical welfare recipients—man, woman, or even dependent child—suggest that President Nixon's formulation last September of a "welfare ethic" is seriously flawed. A 1972 study by the staid Brookings Institution of the "work orientations" of the poor demonstrates that the poor as a body share with more prosperous Americans all those beliefs in employment, incentives, and rewards which the President claimed, in his celebrated Labor Day speech, help "build strong people" while "the welfare ethic breeds weak people." Welfare recipients, according to the Brookings study, viewed public assistance with favor—with *mild* favor—only *after* they had experienced serious occupational failures; these failures the researchers found attributable to labor market conditions, not to the inadequacies of those who had become public charges.[4] There is simply no evidence in this competent investigation (which took account of possible disparities between what respondents said and what they actually did about work) that we shelter from the chill winds of the marketplace large numbers of poor people who subscribe to what the President knows is out there: ". . . the new 'welfare ethic' that could cause the American character to weaken."

Some observers might even argue that our welfare policies tell a far sadder story about the values of the architects of these policies, and about the constituencies who encourage them, than about attitudes toward work in the larger population. Others might add, with Calvin Coolidge, that "the reason we have such high unemployment rates is that there aren't enough jobs." And carrying a suspicion of current policy a bit further, what should we make of the "workfare" concept? Does this considerable effort to get poor mothers of young children off the "aid-to-dependent-children" rolls serve the ethic? Or do our national income accounts, which assign no economic value at all to child-rearing, give testimony to an enduringly narrow and highly selective application of the ethic's prescriptions?

Corporate Morale

Our several logics, and our tendency to infer favored conclusions from selective facts, may suit our continuing need to equate necessity with morality. Can that be why no one suggests that the tenets of the faith have been toyed with by its own most ardent—and its most powerful—followers? Corporations, in whose corridors march the most articulate proponents of the ethic, face "the worst attitude climate in a decade,"[5] according to the Opinion Research Corporation, a subsidiary of the McGraw-Hill Company, whose own journal, *Business Week,* editorializes on the facts of a survey: "[Reversal of public disaffection with business] will take management that thinks in terms of long-run objectives rather than short-run profits. Much of the trouble that business has got into during the past five years has developed because executives were watching the security analyst and playing for a quick flash in the stock market instead of building for the future. Now the future they did not prepare for is here."[6] Deferred gratification? Saving for growth? The *Business Week* data on public attitudes toward business might well unsettle the *Business Week* editors. These data show that the "staunchest supporters" of business have an increasingly low opinion of extant businesses; the proportion of respondents reporting "low approval of companies" is 60 percent, up nearly 15 percentage points since 1965. In the same issue, *Business Week* provides a handy if incomplete summary of the reasons for this. It is a grim litany of rapacious conglomerates, "humiliating miscalculations" in aerospace, I.T.T. in the Justice Department, junk in the environment, and plain shoddy merchandise.

Try as they will to be objective about an important matter, however, *Business Week* cannot resist pronouncing a curse on the other house—a comfort to those executive subscribers who brood upon workers and the Protestant ethic. Thus, two tables purport to show that of late "people want more for less." These same tables are captioned: "They will not work harder to increase their standard of living, but they say they could produce more if they tried." Sure enough, the proportion of worker-respondents who "say they could produce more if they tried" can be seen to have risen appreciably since the late 1940s. From this, *Business Week* concludes that more and more workers want a higher standard of living but refuse to work harder for it. But a careful inspection of the tables and the several captions could as easily support the interpretation that larger numbers of respondents are content with their standard of living, thanks all the same, and in that respect see no purpose in working harder.

Indeed, in not yearning after new feats of consumption these workers seem well within the ethic, which never did put much stock in consuming but urged, instead, deferred gratification. Poor Richard could not have envisioned Miami Beach, and Horatio Alger knew not Neiman-Marcus. Conversely, of course, any society whose citizens consistently deferred their pleasures in the interests of security, liquidity, and growth would find little place for, say, credit-granting institutions and advertising agencies.

All in all, it seems a waste of good elbow grease for the executive classes to wring their hands unduly over the apostasy of workers from the ethic. Perhaps the least consolable have read the April 1972 Gallup poll, to which 57 percent of the "total public" admitted that ". . . they could produce more each day if they tried." But did those same executives notice that the figure for professional people and businessmen was *70 percent?* Only one group felt less productive still: 72 percent of young people between eighteen and twenty-nine years old.[7]

These last statistics suggest (though they do not prove; "for instance" is not proof) that the question of legitimacy higher up is an important one. Corporate shenanigans, political deceptions, and a professional-executive class avowedly and conspicuously underworked, may simply not inspire the larger population to seek "success" in the old way. One wonders if all of Madison Avenue's capacities for persuasion could blot out what millions see in their workaday lives: basic industries that turn tidy profits while great portions of their productive capacity stand idle through business-cycle swings; huge, unearned subsidies for inefficient aerospace firms; expense-account juggling, rapid corporate tax write-offs, and oil depletion allowances; railroads managed into bankruptcy; industrial wastes managed into rivers and lakes. It is naive to believe that the nonexecutive population is unaware of these things. Even *Playboy* has presented its leaders with a compendium of bare facts on the subject of malpractices. In a recent article Senator Philip A. Hart reviewed case after depressing case of mismanagement, managerial skullduggery, and breach of faith. Among the items: the nation's seventy largest corporations have run afoul of antitrust, false advertising, patent, copyright, and labor laws 980 times in a forty-five-year period; of the 980, "779 indicated that crimes had been committed."

Nor does it please earners to be told, most often by their elected leaders, that it is their wages and salaries which are to blame for an inflationary spiral that has very nearly consumed the economic gains of many years. Wage earners know that war is simultaneously expensive and unproductive, and many are also mindful of the spiraling costs of government. James W. Kuhn has pointed out that "Philadelphia pays its clerical employees a third more than the average paid in private industry, and in both Houston and Buffalo clerks' pay is a fifth larger; municipal data processors earn salaries about a fifth larger than those employed by private firms in Philadelphia, Newark, and Los Angeles; and maintenance workers in New York and Newark average 42 percent larger salaries than those in private industry."[8] Government is expensive in other ways: wage earners in New Jersey must read that their Secretary of State has ben indicted for exploiting his office to line his pockets on the very eve of his predecessor's incarceration for the same behavior; this, only months after Newark's former mayor and some other public servants had been jailed for similar violations of the public trust.

Yet we are continually warned that the wage earners subvert the work ethic. The journalist recently published in *Reader's Digest* who spent "much of 1971 . . . interviewing 500 representatives of construction companies" so as to inveigh against work rules unaccountably missed the wholesale corruption, involving builders and New York City inspectors, documented in the *New York Times* in the same month that *Reader's Digest* exposed the workers.[9]

Conclusion
To put it judiciously, evidence that workers are misbehaving as never before is less than abundant. All the recently fashionable conferences on "work alienation" and "the changing work ethic" would have us believe that there is a new crisis and that productivity has suddenly given way to job turnover, industrial conflict, and worse. Yet the "quit rate" per 100 workers in manufacturing went *down* from 2.7 in 1969 to 1.8 in 1971, the last full year for which data are available. (Data on other employees are not recorded by the Bureau of Labor Statistics; exceedingly few managers have trend data on white-collar workers or consider them if they have them.) And President Nixon reminded us, in his Labor Day speech, that "today, we have achieved an era of relative calm on the labor-management front, with work stoppages at a six-year low."

Now it would be quite wrong to suppose that there are not some complex difficulties connected with work in contemporary American society. There are organizations in which absenteeism, turnover, conflict, and other offenses against productivity are of some moment and the causes of these and other problems deserve systematic study. But it is well to view with skepticism all simplified explanations that focus only and owlishly on the worker's philosophy and to examine a number of the currently popular prescriptive solutions with care.

Consider, for example, that E. Daniel Grady, division traffic manager for Michigan Bell Telephone Company, reduced the absenteeism of Detroit operators from 7.5 percent to 4.5 percent in one quarter by keeping attendance records on a weekly rather than a monthly basis. Mr. Grady, after digging into the matter, discovered that telephone operators felt that a month's record had already been marred if they were absent early in that month; in for a penny, they went in for a pound. By recording in a shorter unit, he removed that easy rationale for multiple absences. And Edward J. Feeny, a vice-president of Emery Air Freight Corporation, was able to increase his employees' care and skill at packing cargo containers to capacity by the staggeringly simple expedient of *telling* the workers the difference in profits between filling to 45 percent and filling to the 90 percent they quickly achieved. The result: a $520,000 annual cost reduction. These illustrations could be multiplied to a degree that is dumbfounding; they may be found in any second-rate textbook on "human relations."

The plain truth is that the overriding majority of Americans are not lazy malcontents who soldier on the job at every opportunity. Even auto workers, universally famous for having the best reasons to be unhappy with their work, *act* upon their disenchantments with surprising inconsistency. Only about half of the production workers employed by the Big Three retire before reaching sixty-five, according to Melvin Glasser, director of the UAW's Social Security Department. This, despite a "thirty and out" retirement plan for workers fifty-eight or older with thirty years service. Many keep working for financial reasons—to maintain preretirement pay and to benefit, ultimately, from any expansion in retirement benefits. The indication, says Mr. Glasser, is that the retirement age will be lowered, but he does not believe it will be lowered much.

We have dissatisfied workers in America, but work dissatisfaction is not laziness or historicocultural sabotage. One might expect management, at so late a date, to know that. But that is another matter—for, as some of the observations in these paragraphs suggest, there are grounds for doubt about *managers'* willingness, in any sector of the economy, to get on with it. Dissatisfied workers may well become less productive in the face of evidence that managers don't know what they are doing themselves; evidence that employers are so protected from market pressures that they can afford to be inefficient; evidence that they will blame employees for their own miscalculations; or evidence that managers will seek to deceive the workers.

It is interesting to note in this regard that the single most frequent complaint listed by employees in a University of Michigan study was over the difficulty of getting their jobs done and done properly amid faulty materials, badly scheduled deliveries, and other manifestations of mismanagement. The second largest category of job dissatisfactions involved health and safety hazards, the overriding majority of which are wholly under management's control.[10]

Readers unfamiliar with life in the basic industries might contemplate the experience of workers with avoidable occupational accidents and illnesses. In 1968, a total of 14,300 people died in industrial accidents—about the equivalent of American fatalities in Vietnam that year. "In the same year," report Patricia Cayo Sexton and Brendan Sexton, "90,000 workers suffered *permanent impairment* from industrial accidents, and a total of 2,100,000 suffered total but temporary disability. . . . In 1969 [exposures to industrial pollutants in the workplace] caused one million new cases of occupational disease. Among the casualties were 3,600 dead and over 800,000 cases of burns, lung and eye damage, dermatitis, and brain damage."[11] It is simply fatuous to believe that managers whose employees have an intimate, daily association with unnecessary risks to life and limb should be thought competent, never mind "legitimate," by those same employees. The "staunchest supporters" of industry questioned by *Business Week* may consult the front page of the *Wall Street Journal* for August 5, 1969, where an executive pronounced, "When you come right down to it, a lot of our safety decisions are really cost decisions. We give our workers safety glasses because they cost just $3.50. Safety shoes, which they also need, cost $14. . . ."

It is equally fatuous to believe that the current rash of experiments in "work enlargement" or "work enrichment" will fool workers anywhere when these programs are only ostensibly designed to enhance satisfaction in work. Well-intentioned social scientists who lecture managers on the currently favored techniques for elevating the "self-actualization" of workers may be in deeper than they know. Edwin Mills, director of the "Quality of Work Program" of the much touted National Commission on Productivity, told a Chicago business audience, just before the turn of the year, that 80 percent of 150 firms currently conducting experiments designed to "enlarge" and "enrich" work were nonunion. Their managers reported in a private poll, according to Mr. Mills, that these experiments were part of such firms' overall antiunion policy. It is doubtful, on historical grounds, that the dissatisfactions and needs which move workers to collective bargaining will be dissipated by "self-actualization." And deceptions will not help; employees will not be blinded to management incompetence by such strategies.

The fact is that management has lately become far more visible to the American employee, and the close-up is not flattering. The sociologist Fred Goldner has argued compellingly that the growing ranks of managers have themselves become a work force of extraordinary magnitude. Managers' habits, their technical competence, and their dedication to work are on display as never before, and are as open to interpretation as their workers'. Particularly in a "service economy," in which so many of us "work with our heads," it is not difficult to justify visits to the barber shop or the hairdresser as being, so to speak, continuing work toward the same end. After all, "the mind doesn't punch in and out," and "we're really working all the time." To the extent that we believe and act on that premise we will be observed doing so. That is, we will ourselves be judged by the rest of our countrymen who have brought their ascetic heritage into a convenient—a necessary—synthesis with the impulse toward comfort.

It was Max Weber, the German sociologist and economic historian, who explored most fully the role of the Protestant ethic in the genesis of capitalism. And it was Weber who examined at length, in his studies of authority, the concept of legitimacy. He concluded that in large, complex organizations, technical competence was a central inducement to the acceptance of authority by subordinates. Weber might see in those facts of contemporary American life I have touched on signs of damage, not to the ethic that stimulates workers under legitimate conditions, but to management's claim to the loyalty and industrious output of its millions of charges.

Notes

1. Patricia Cayo Sexton and Brendon Sexton, *Blue Collars and Hard Hats: The Working Class and the Future of American Politics* (New York: Random House, 1971), p. 68.

2. Ibid., p. 69.

3. Frances Piven and Richard A. Cloward, *Regulating the Poor: The Functions of Public Welfare* (New York: Pantheon Books, 1971), p. 74.

4. Leonard Goodwin, *A Study of Work Orientation of Welfare Recipients Participating in the Work Incentive Program* (Washington, D.C.: Brookings Institution, 1971).

5. "America's Growing Antibusiness Mood," *Business Week,* June 17, 1972, p. 100.

6. "Why the Public Has Lost Faith in Business," *Business Week,* June 17, 1972, p. 116.

7. "America's Growing Antibusiness Mood," pp. 100–101.

8. James Kuhn, "The Middle of Inflation: A New Answer," *The Public Interest,* no. 27 (spring 1972), p. 66.

9. Sexton and Sexton, pp. 103–104.

10. Neal Q. Herrick and Robert P. Quinn, "The Working Conditions Survey as a Source of Social Indicators," *Monthly Labor Review* 94, no. 4 (April 1971): 15–24.

11. Sexton and Sexton, p. 103.

2 Is There a Blue-Collar Revolt against Work?

George Strauss

In recent years we have seen an upsurge of interest in the blue-collar worker. Some observers have emphasized an "ethnic" revolt of the worker against his political and social conditions. They offer as evidence of this revolt the support for George Wallace in the 1968 and 1972 elections, the "hard-hat" demonstrations of 1970, and the widespread opposition to school busing. Others—mainly journalists and politicians—have maintained that there is a revolt against *work*, "a new 'anti-work ethic' . . . a new, deep-seated rejection by the young of the traditional American faith in hard work."[1] Although these two phenomena are probably interrelated, the emphasis here will be on an examination of the evidence concerning the blue-collar revolt against work.

This paper presents a brief overview of our present state of knowledge as to blue-collar attitudes toward work and stresses areas of controversy and uncertainty. Despite a good deal of research, our understanding is still very limited.[2]

Social critics and representatives of the Establishment alike have warned that discontent is increasing rapidly and that workplace reforms are urgently required:

More and more workers—and every day this is more apparent—are being disenchanted with the boring, repetitive tasks set by the merciless assembly line or by bureaucracy. They feel they have been herded into economic and social cul-de-sacs.[3]

The explosive potential of this discontent has the capacity to destroy the fragile facade of American democracy. . . . Positive action [is required] if anything is to be salvaged of the original American dream which dies a little every day in the dismal workplaces darkening the landscape from sea to shining sea.[4]

Concern with workplace problems has spread even to the President, who has deplored the apparent decline of the work ethic on numerous occasions: "Scrubbing floors and emptying bedpans have just as much dignity as there is in any work done in this country—including my own. . . . We must always remember that the most important part of the quality of life is the quality of work. And the new need for job satisfaction is the key to the quality of work."[5]

Not everyone agrees about the extent of the problem. Nor is it clear—even on the assembly line—that workers are as much concerned about the alleged dehumanizing *intrinsic* aspects of work as they are about more traditional concerns such as pay, fringe benefits, and job security.

" 'Blue-Collar Blues' Overrated: Sociologists Misread Attitudes of Young Workers on Jobs," reads a headline in the *AFL-CIO News*, which cites Machinists Vice-President William A. Winpisinger as refuting "the invalid conclusion that today's generation of young workers is rejecting the world of work . . . the real significance of studies showing that one worker in five finds fault with aspects of his job is that 80 percent are satisfied."[6] Much the same view is expressed in another AFL-CIO publication:

Substituting the sociologist's questionnaire for the stopwatch is likely to be no gain for the workers. . . . Much is being made these days in radical chic academic and intellectual circles of the recent strike at Lordstown, Ohio, Chevrolet Vega plant, where a predominantly young workforce struck over the speed-up safety and other work conditions. The role of the United Auto Workers in formulating negotiable issues out of vague discontents and specific grievances was totally ignored by intellectuals and mass media alike. From the newspaper and magazine accounts one would think that these young workers were on strike not only against General Motors but chiefly against the older workers and their union. Legend now has it that the strike was part of the youth rebellion! In fact it was another strike in the long struggle of auto workers to improve their lot. A similar strike over like issues in Norwood, Ohio, received zero attention. . . . The Norwood workers, you see, are older.[7]

Which position is correct? Are we facing a radically new phenomenon, a widespread revolt against work (particularly by the young) or merely a continuation of the age-old struggle of workers to improve their economic posi-

tions? Are higher pay, better job security, and a stronger grievance procedure the answers to worker dissatisfaction—or are more radical measures
required? To what extent does boring, unchallenging work lead to work dissatisfaction? How central is work to life? How do people adjust to boring
work? Is dissatisfaction with work likely to increase in the future? Is it a revolt against *all* work or only against unchallenging work? Despite a great
deal or research, our understanding of these issues is still limited. In what
follows I will try to bring some order to what we know about these controversial questions.

Indices of Morale

To start, let me make it clear that the evidence we have to date, though incomplete and contradictory, does not support the hypothesis of a substantial
recent increase in blue-collar dissatisfaction with work. Most of the discussion has been based on specific incidents that have hit the headlines, and
there has been too little effort to look at the issues in perspective. The Lordstown strike, for example, made good copy, but strikes over production standards are common in the automobile industry, particularly when new processes are being introduced. Much of the other anecdotal evidence of increased dissatisfaction also comes from automobile plants—an atypical example of work life; in few other activities is the worker's autonomy so severe-
ly restricted as it is on the automobile assembly line.

How about statistical indices? Quit rates in manufacturing went up from
1.1 in the recession year of 1958 to 2.7 in 1969 (but dropped to 1.8 in 1971,
went up again in 1972, and generally seem to have behaved inversely to unemployment). Absentee rates in automobile plants went up from 2–3 percent
in 1965 to 5–6 percent in 1970—and then dropped in 1971.[8] Productivity declined in the late 1960s but recently has climbed quite sharply (though factors other than worker attitudes are, undoubtedly, primarily responsible).

How about opinion polls? A major 1969 survey suggests that, insofar as
comparisons can be made, workers' dissatisfaction with their jobs is not
much changed from the 1950s.[9] Further, this study suggests that dissatisfaction with work of blue-collar workers is not much different from that of anyone else.[10]

Since 1949, the Gallup poll has been asking "On the whole, would you say
you are satisfied or dissatisfied with the work you do?" Doubts have been
expressed about the meaningfulness of this question. (And there appear to

Table 2.1. Gallup Poll on Satisfaction with Work

	Satisfied		Dissatisfied		No Opinion	
1949	69%	(55%)	19%	(33%)	12%	(12%)
1963	90	(54)	7	(33)	3	(13)
1965	87	(48)	9	(38)	4	(14)
1966	87	(69)	8	(18)	5	(13)
1969	88	(76)	6	(18)	6	(6)
1971	85	(68)	9	(21)	8	(11)
1973	80	(53)	10	(22)	10	(25)

Source: "Job Satisfaction and Productivity," Gallup Opinion Index, no. 94 (April 1973).
Note: Responses of whites are followed by those of nonwhites.

have been some changes in the way answers have been tabulated over the years.) For what they are worth, the responses are presented in table 2.1. Somewhat similar evidence comes from the 1968 Manpower Report of the President (which uses yearly averages of published reports as an index). The percentage of those reporting dissatisfaction with work dropped from 21 percent in 1946–47 to 12–13 percent in 1964–65.

Although this evidence does not indicate increased dissatisfaction or imminent revolt, neither does it prove that workers are truly satisfied. Quite to the contrary. Though most workers accept (or become resigned to) their lot, the adjustment process is not always easy. To me it is far more useful to examine this adjustment process–the question of how workers come to terms with their jobs–than to become excessively concerned with short-run indices of morale. But before examining dissatisfaction with work from this perspective, there is value in discussing several related forms of dissatisfaction.

Causes of General Discontent

A number of studies have suggested that at least some relationship exists between dissatisfaction with work and dissatisfaction with politics, with society, and even with life itself—a syndrome of malaise that has been often called "the blue-collar blues" or alienation.[11] In a society with a short fuse all causes of discontent tend to exacerbate each other. The forms of discontent are far from being identical or even highly correlated, however. (Building tradesmen were among the leaders of the hard-hat revolt of 1970, but they are hardly high in job dissatisfaction.)

At least four causes of blue-collar dissatisfaction have been suggested. I shall mention the first three briefly, chiefly to indicate their relationship to the fourth, dissatisfaction with work.

Economic Squeeze

As Jerome M. Rosow puts it, the average blue-collar worker "reaches his peak earning power and chances for promotion early in life. Unlike the white-collar worker, he earns wages that remain steady even though expenses mount as his children become ready for college or he has to support aging parents."[12] This feeling of squeeze presumably has been accentuated during the recent periods of combined inflation and unemployment in which real income for many blue-collar workers has fallen or remained constant.

This hypothesis can be disputed on a number of economic grounds. One thing seems clear: for the hypothesis to be true, dissatisfaction should climb as the blue-collar worker gets older, but, if anything, the evidence from attitude surveys suggest the reverse.[13] Further, the economic squeeze hardly explains the presumed rise in absenteeism and turnover.

Social Squeeze

The second hypothesis is that blue-collar workers (and particularly ethnics) feel threatened by the invasion of blacks who are moving into their community and being bussed into their schools. Second and third generation ethnics —who have escaped the mid-city slums (where their parents and grandparents had lived)—now feel that their newfound status in the working-class suburbs is jeopardized.

Further, ethnics who have gone to school or gradually worked up the seniority ladder in order to obtain white-collar or supervisory jobs find themselves jumped over by blacks who they feel have failed to earn their rights in the conventional fashion. To compound this resentment, middle-class young intellectuals seem to deprecate the very concepts of success that the blue-collar ethnic has suffered so long to achieve. The educational route to success through winning credentials is thus threatened from both above and below—and patience and hard work no longer seem to pay off.[14] Similarly, manual work appears to be degraded by both schools and society generally. (And note that on television Archie Bunker is the "dumb" blue-collar worker.) Finally, the value of skill differentials in terms of money or prestige have been considerably reduced. Even the skilled craftsman, once a man of high social status, is now a nobody. (But note the resurgence of interest in craftwork and other manual activities among middle-class youth.)

Dissatisfaction of this sort undoubtedly occurs, and it very likely has an impact on the workplace. The social squeeze may make the job squeeze less tolerable. According to Ely Chinoy, many blue-collar workers look upon their jobs as something temporary, to be endured until something better comes along.[15] Or they may look upon work instrumentally, as a means toward an end (such as a home of their own). In either case, if the temporary job turns permanent or the end turns sour, willingness to endure may drop precipitately.

Youth Rebellion

To what extent is blue-collar dissatisfaction largely a youth phenomenon, an extension of the revolt that previously took place on campus? Certainly there is evidence that younger workers are less satisfied with work than older ones. Some elements of the "youth culture" have spread to the factory. Long hair, hip clothes, and the use of drugs seem to be becoming more popular among young workers; possibly they are reacting against the disciplined acceptance of authority and the status quo. But one may question the extent to which young blue-collar workers also reject conventional standards of material success. If anything, young blue-collar workers have been more hostile to student power and black demands than their blue-collar elders.[16]

Even though it may be difficult to explain blue-collar dissatisfaction in the same terms as dissatisfaction among middle-class youth, there is a strong possibility that young workers are less willing to tolerate the forms of boring work that their fathers were willing to accept. The typical blue-collar worker today is younger and much better educated than in the past, and having grown up in an atmosphere of prosperity he may be less concerned with job security.

Dissatisfaction with Work

Over the years, out of the contributions of individuals such as Chris Argyris, Norman Maier, and Douglas McGregor has come a fairly consistent hypothesis which suggests an almost inevitable conflict between organizational and individual needs, especially in mass production industry.[17] This view, which might be called the personality versus organization hypothesis, runs as follows:[18]

• Workers seek social belonging, independence, and personal growth. In other words, they seek to ascend the Maslow needs-hierarchy ladder from physical, through safety, social, and egoistic, to self-actualization needs. (By "hierarchy" it is meant that a higher, less basic need does not provide motivation unless lower, more basic needs are satisfied. Moreover, once a basic need is satisfied, it no longer motivates.) A critical point is that such satisfactions are desired *on the job.*

• Organizations fail to recognize these needs and instead follow what Mc-Gregor calls "Theory X" assumptions, that is, that workers dislike work and wish to avoid responsibility. In so doing, organizations force workers to behave in an immature and dependent fashion.

• As a consequence, workers become alienated from their jobs. Either they fight back (through union activity, sabotage, or output restriction) or they withdraw and produce no more than a minimum amount of work. Whichever response workers make, management is forced to supervise them more closely, which in turn makes workers still more frustrated and still more likely to withdraw or fight back.

• The only way to eliminate this vicious cycle is for management to adopt "Theory Y" assumptions about human nature, that is, that people can enjoy work and can exercise self-control and that they are imaginative and creative. Management should therefore develop policies that promote intrinsic job satisfaction and individual development. It should especially promote job enrichment, general supervision, and strong cohesive work groups. Higher pay, better job security, and stronger grievance procedures are important but are not enough.

It is not my purpose to test the validity of this hypothesis here. It does suggest some important questions, however, particularly relating to the role of work in life, and it provides a convenient introduction to the discussion that follows.

Workers' Needs

There is considerable evidence that at least for some workers dissatisfaction appears directly related to short job cycles, low autonomy and control over work pace, and lack of challenge.[19] Such factors also relate to absenteeism,[20] to turnover,[21] and to strikes.[22] At least two studies suggest that poor mental health is correlated with low-skilled jobs.[23] A different kind of evidence is provided by studies that compare mass production, assembly-line workers with craftsmen (such as printers) and workers in automated process technology (such as oil refineries).[24] These studies agree that by all indices job satisfaction is significantly higher for craftsmen than for assembly-line workers, with the position of automated workers less clear, but certainly above that of assembly-line workers.

On the other hand, the need for challenging work needs to be put in perspective. A recent thorough study suggests that factors relating to supervision, management policies, and the work environment—having a "nurturant supervisor," receiving adequate help, having few "labor standards problems" (such as safety hazards, poor hours, and poor transportation)—all seem to relate at least as closely to job satisfaction as having a challenging job with "enriching" demands. In other words, improving managerial practices may improve job satisfaction as much as changing the nature of the job.[25]

Though challenging work is not the sole determinant of job satisfaction, it clearly plays a part for *some* workers. Granted this, the critical question is *how* important is work challenge for the healthy human being?

Supporters of the personality vs. organization hypothesis often phrase their arguments in terms of the Maslow hierarchy. According to Maslow, as individuals mature they seek opportunities for self-actualization—that is, they seek the freedom to be creative, to develop their skills to the maximum, to exercise autonomy, and the like. The oversimplified Maslow scheme can be criticized on a number of grounds. For example, it is stated in a nonoperational manner which makes it very difficult to prove or disprove (especially since most forms of human behavior satisfy more than one need). Further, there may be substantial differences among people in the relative weight they give to the "basic" needs (physical, safety, and social) as against the "higher" needs (such as esteem and self-actualization). Compare Archie Bunker's glorification of basic needs to the poet or the scientist who seems to shun such needs and devotes himself to self-actualization in his garret or lab. Maslow himself never claimed that all people would wish to climb his ladder, and he never claimed that people would climb it in the same way. In fact, as his later writings make clear, his "mature," "normal" individual is a rather special breed.

The Maslow scheme is not essential to the broader hypothesis, however. All the broader hypothesis requires is that a substantial portion of human beings (and, for our purposes here, blue-collar workers) have a strong need for self-actualization. There can be little doubt that all people have such needs to some extent. The main questions relate to how important they are relative to other needs and how people react when they are denied.

The work of McClelland and his disciples suggests that people vary substantially in the relative importance they attach to various needs.[26] Further, they find that there is no necessary ladder, that people don't inevitably emphasize self-actualization after lesser needs are reasonably well satisfied. McClelland posits three needs besides physical ones: *need achievement, need affiliation,* and *need power.* Persons who are high in need achievement react well to challenge; those who are low in it are concerned primarily with playing it safe and avoiding failure. Presumably this latter group (particularly those high on need affiliation) prefers direction to autonomy. McClelland's research also suggests that these needs are rather easily malleable; a relatively short training course can substantially increase need achievement (and also managerial success). If so, perhaps training can also induce high affiliation; workers can be trained to prefer unchallenging work. Shades of Huxley's *Brave New World* in the corporate state!

Aside from this probably extreme interpretation of the implications of McClelland's work, it does seem reasonably clear that because of personality differences people do vary substantially in their needs for challenge and autonomy.[27] These personality differences, in turn, may well be due to variations in culture and family child-rearing practices (and possibly even genetic factors). A question to be considered later is whether child-rearing practices may be changing sufficiently to cause substantial differences in attitudes toward work. But for the moment let us consider a narrower issue: To what extent do cultural differences, especially rural-urban differences, affect workers' attitudes toward challenging jobs?

Cultural differences. A major corollary to the personality versus organization hypothesis is that there is a positive relationship between job challenge and job satisfaction and that job enlargement is an almost surefire way to raise morale. The findings of Arthur Turner and Paul Lawrence seriously challenge this assumption.[28] In a study conducted in eleven firms, these researchers sought to measure the relationship between job satisfaction and complexity of work. They found that small-town workers reacted positively to more complex tasks, as expected, but that urban workers reacted less positively to them. The latter finding, which was unanticipated, is further supported by Hulin and Blood, who reported on research involving 1,900 workers in twenty-one plants in a wide variety of communities.[29] Where urban and slum characteristics were high, they found that correlations between blue-collar satisfaction and job skills were low or negative. The reverse was true in more rural areas. (The nature and location of the community seemed to make no difference for white-collar workers.) In another study it was found that rural workers react to job discretion with greater pride in their job accomplishments.[30] For urban workers, greater discretion is related only to a sense of involvement and to making time seem to "drag" less often.

This research may be subject to methodological criticism. But assuming it is valid, there are a number of possible alternate (and partly contradictory) explanations for these unexpected findings:

(1) It may be that rural and small-town workers have internalized the old-fashioned Protestant, middle-class ethic which glorifies work for its own sake and insists on individual achievement. The city worker belongs to a different culture (or is at least alienated from the traditional culture). Why should the urban blue-collar culture be different?

• Small towns are small, and it is therefore difficult for blue-collar and white-collar values to develop in different directions. The big city permits greater diversity.

• Turner and Lawrence point out that their sample of rural workers was largely Protestant and their urban workers largely French Catholic, thus suggesting that the two sects have different values toward work.

• Urban workers (many of whom are black or ethnics) may reject the Protestant ethic because their experience (rather than religion) has *not* taught them that hard work pays off. Indeed, rural parents may stress need achievement to their children while the urban child learns need affiliation or need power. (As far as ethnics are concerned, this explanation would seem to fly in the face of the "social squeeze" hypothesis, which argues that ethnic blue-collar discontent arises because blacks threaten their *achievements.* It should be noted that the Hulin and Blood sample excluded blacks.)

• The explanation may relate to the Maslow hierarchy. Hackman and Lawler report that urban workers are relatively more concerned with satisfying physical and social (as opposed to egoistic) needs than their country cousins.[31] The explanation for this is unclear; possibly it relates to the higher cost of living and the greater difficulty in developing meaningful social relations in the city.

(2) A second explanation is fairly simple. No one wants unlimited challenge in his life. The research scientist, for example, may relish the novelty and uncertainty of laboratory work, but he insists that his secretary always be on call, his lab technician give predictable responses, and his car start with complete regularity. For urban workers, already surrounded with uncertainty, the degree of challenge desired on the job may be far less than that of his rural counterpart.

(3) It could be that urban workers are less well endowed than rural workers with manual skills or even intelligence. As a consequence, even relatively simple tasks may seem taxing. (We know that feebleminded persons often have a relative advantage on simple jobs.)

(4) Another explanation may be offered in terms of "equity theory." Challenging jobs usually require more work (certainly more responsibility), but

they also command higher status and pay.[32] In rural areas, taking on more challenging work may lead to greater *relative* social and economic payoff than it does in the big city, where some higher-paid blue-collar workers may still be quite low on the overall social and economic totem pole. The city worker may decide that the reward for taking on more responsibility is not worth the effort.

(5) Work and the job may be more central to workers' lives in rural areas than they are in big cities, where there is a wide variety of other areas upon which life interest may be focused.[33]

This last suggestion raises a much broader question to which we now turn: How central is the job in determining satisfaction with life? *Importance of the job.* Must workers satisfy their higher needs on the job, or can they satisfy them after work, with their family, through hobbies and recreation, or in social and community activities (such as unions)? Arguably, the center of many people's lives is not the job (which is merely a way of earning a living), but the home or the community. As Robert Dubin writes: "Work, for probably a majority of workers, and even extending into the ranks of management, may represent an institutional setting that is not the central life interest of the participants. The consequence of this is that while participating in work a general attitude of apathy and indifference prevails. . . . Thus the industrial worker does not feel imposed upon by the tyranny of organizations, company or union."[34]

How important is work in human life? In classical Greece, work was devalued, it was at best *instrumental,* a means to an end. In many societies, "gentlemen" don't work. In Communist China, on the other hand, strenuous efforts are being made so that all work will be *expressive,* a valued end in itself. In our society, work is more clearly the central life interest of artists and professionals than it is of casual laborers. The college professor's career is both his work and his leisure. He thinks about his work even when off the job. His self-image is tied up in work. Even his friends are likely to be college professors—and they talk shop. To a lesser extent, skilled craftsmen behave in the same way. As Harold Wilensky suggests: "Where the technical and social organization of work offer much freedom—e.g., discretion in methods, pace or schedule, and opportunity for frequent interaction with fellow workers . . . then work attachments will be strong, work integrated with the rest of life, and ties to the community and society solid. Conversely, if the task offers little workplace freedom . . . then work attachments will be

weak, work sharply split from leisure and ties to community and society uncertain."[35]

How do workers respond to jobs that provide little opportunity for being
expressive? A few seem to adjust easily enough to viewing their jobs as
purely instrumental. In my own interviewing experience in factories, I have
often run across women who say something like, "I like this job because it
gets me away from all the kids and pressures at home." Similarly, I have run
into artists who have deliberately taken on high-paying but boring jobs in
order to earn enough to support their real interests. (A related phenomenon
is the college-educated hippie postman who has "dropped out" of seeking
creative work, perhaps interested in earning just enough to support his
habit.) John Goldthorpe concludes that English auto workers consciously
take on assembly-line jobs because they view them as an instrument for the
attainment of economic ends.[36]

Nevertheless, these may be exceptional cases. As Wilensky and others
have implied, the nature of one's work in our society does much to provide
meaning to life for most people, particularly for males. What does this mean
for those for whom the job provides little meaning? Can they make a trade-
off between off-the-job and on-the-job satisfactions? Can the worker who
desires higher-order satisfactions on the job make up for this loss off the
job? And what is the cost in doing so? These are difficult questions to research, but several approaches to the problem have been suggested.

Satisfaction with life generally seems to be correlated with satisfaction on
the job—that is, those who are unhappy with their jobs are also unhappy
with life generally. This may only mean that some people are perpetual malcontents. Or it may mean that people with unsatisfactory lives *report* dissatisfaction with their jobs. For example, unmarried workers (who possibly
have less happy lives than those who are married—a heroic assumption)
report less work satisfaction than married workers do.[37]

But workers on *objectively* less challenging jobs report less satisfying
lives. Further, there are the previously cited mental health studies that suggest that unskilled factory workers suffer from poorer mental health than
those in more skilled work. Assuming these studies are valid, the question
remains whether poorer mental health and less satisfaction with life are
caused by low job challenge or by other factors. The unskilled or semiskilled blue-collar worker suffers not just from boring work but from low
social status, low pay (at least compared to those on higher-skilled jobs),

and relatively irregular work. The last two factors lead to his having a less desirable standard of living, living in a less desirable part of town, and being less able to afford adequate medical and psychiatric care. Thus it is far from clear whether poorer mental health is caused primarily by the intrinsic nature of unskilled work or by the fact that such work pays poorly and has low status both on and off the job. Insofar as mental disturbances and dissatisfaction with life are caused by economic and social pressures at home, higher wages may be a better solution than improved human relations or job enrichment.[38]

Another approach involves looking at *recreation and the use of leisure time.* Do those on unchallenging jobs make up for them with challenging recreation and the creative use of leisure time? Value judgments are involved here, of course. What the professor-researcher might find creative and self-actualizing (for example, bird watching, mountain climbing, or listening to Bach) the blue-collar worker might find completely boring.

According to one study, people with active jobs that permit substantial discretion tend to engage in active forms of recreation, such as participating in voluntary organizations, active sports, house building, and various hobbies.[39] Those whose jobs permit social contact but little discretion engage in social forms of recreation, such as visiting and receiving visitors, going on outings, drinking beer, and talking. Finally, workers with limited discretion and social contact at work tend to participate in "passive" activities, such as fishing, going to church, shopping, going for a drive, watching TV, and listening to the radio. According to this study, at least, workers do not counteract the effects of dull life through active recreation.

Perhaps this should not be surprising. Participant accounts of life in mass production factories stress that the work pace normally leaves one so exhausted at the end of the day that one has energy left only to drink a few beers or watch television.[40] But there is another, less kind explanation: it isn't dull work that causes dull recreation, but dull people who pick dull recreation and through natural selection drift into dull work. In any case, for most workers the quality of life at home seems closely related to the quality of life on the job. The limited evidence to date does not support a trade-off hypothesis.

Further evidence of the importance of work is provided by a 1955 survey by Nancy Morse and Robert Weiss in which a sample of white male workers were asked, "If by chance you inherited enough money to live comfortably without working, do you think you would work anyway?"[41] The vast majority (80 percent) of all respondents responded positively (see table 2.2), although the percentages were slightly higher for middle-class (86 percent) than for working-class workers (76 percent). Why would they work? Here a surprising phenomenon is revealed. As expected, the main reason middle-class workers would continue working was for "interest or accomplishment," but for blue-collar workers the main reason for continuing to work was "to keep occupied." This latter group would rather work than not work, even though working involves just filling in time.[42] This may be a depressing commentary on the meaninglessness of life off the job, but at least it suggests the centrality of work to the average American white male. It also suggests that workers do adjust to boring work, though perhaps at a cost.

Adjustment to Unchallenging Work

There are two sets of data in table 2.2 that I have not yet discussed. The first is that most blue-collar workers would prefer another job, and the second is that the vast majority report they are satisfied or even very satisfied with work. The second finding is consistent with the Gallup poll results shown in table 2.1 and with almost all other research in this area.[43] In the typical study, only 10–20 percent of those who reply report that they are dissatisfied with their jobs. Even among auto assembly-line workers, 66 percent report that their jobs are "interesting." [44]

Table 2.2. Selected Attitudes toward Work

	Middle Class	Working Class
Would continue working, even if inherited enough not to	86%	76%
Reasons for doing so		
Interest or accomplishment	44	10
To keep occupied	37	71
Would continue working at same job	61	34
Attitude toward job		
Very satisfied	42	27
Satisfied	37	57
Dissatisfied	21	16

Source: Nancy Morse and Robert Weiss, "The Function and Meaning of Work," *American Sociological Review* 20, no. 2 (April 1955).

To put the question rather naively, does this mean that such a high percentage of blue-collar workers are *really* satisfied with their jobs? I think not; the figure relating to *very* satisfied may be more meaningful. (It is a far less stable figure and varies greatly from job to job.) If a substantial proportion of blue-collar workers report that (1) they are satisfied with their job but wish to change it and (2) they would continue working even if they didn't have to, but only to fill time, then this can only mean that these workers accept the necessity of work but expect little fulfillment from their specific job.

Apathy

The simple personality versus organization hypothesis proposed by Argyris suggests that organizational restraints cause workers to become frustrated and to react to this frustration either by fighting back (through union activity, sabotage, or output restriction) or by regressing and producing no more than a minimum amount of work. By 1964 Argyris considerably softened his harshly pessimistic original view. He recognized that many workers seem to adjust to an unchallenging work environment. Though such individuals may be psychologically "immature," their expectations of what the job offers them are low, and they suffer few overt pangs of aggression. (Or, to put it another way, since their expectations are low, it requires relatively little objective satisfaction for them to report themselves "satisfied.") They do routine jobs in an adequate fashion, though their performance is not innovative and they are resistant to change. These workers may not be overtly dissatisfied but still are not motivated.

Implicit support for Argyris's view has come from the research of Frederick Herzberg and his colleagues.[45] On the basis of imaginative research, Herzberg concludes that job satisfaction and job dissatisfaction are not opposite points on a continuum but are, in fact, two separate dimensions. "Extrinsic" factors, such as company policy, incompetent supervision, and unsatisfactory working conditions, may lead to dissatisfaction. This dissatisfaction may be reduced by "hygienic" measures, such as fringe benefits, "human relations" training for foremen, and better company policies, but these measures will not make workers satisfied, only apathetic. For true satisfaction to be obtained, "intrinsic" factors must be provided, such as achievement, accomplishment, responsibility, and challenging work. Note that satisfaction is obtained primarily from the *content* of the work itself, dissatisfaction from its *context,* or *environment.* Only satisfaction relates to productivity. The presence of dissatisfaction may lead to low morale or absenteeism, but its elimination will not raise motivation or productivity. Herzberg concludes that it is a mistake to emphasize traditional "hygienic," "extrinsic" measures which serve only to make the work environment more tolerable. Instead, management should seek to enrich (not just enlarge) jobs to make them seem interesting and important.

Herzberg's work has led to substantial controversy and considerable research. On the whole, those who have used his methodology have obtained his results; those who have used different methodologies have obtained different results. But whatever the limitations of the research, there seems to be a convergence on the view that there can be a middle ground between the overly pessimistic view that workers actively fight routine jobs and the overly optimistic one that these jobs make workers truly happy. This middle ground is illustrated by an interview I once held with a blue-collar worker on a routine job. This worker told me, in a rather offhand way, "I got a pretty good job." "What makes it such a good job?" I responded. He answered, "Don't get me wrong. I didn't say it is a *good* job. It's an OK job—about as good a job as a guy like me might expect. The foreman leaves me alone and it pays well. But I would never call it a *good* job. It doesn't amount to much, but it's not bad."

This middle ground might be called apathy. The worker's expectations are low, but he accepts the situation. In a sense, he has made a bargain with his employer and does not feel badly cheated.[46] Attitudes such as this are not likely to lead to revolt. (On the other hand, changing expectations may change the picture considerably, as I will discuss below.) As Blauner puts it, "The majority of blue-collar workers are committed to their roles as producers, and are loyal (although within limits) to their employers."[47]

Substitutes for Intrinsic Job Satisfaction

Too little is known about the process by which workers adjust to boring work, but it is reasonably clear that adjustment is easier for some people than others and easier in some technologies than in others. At least three factors facilitate the adjustment process.

Social life. For many workers the social life on the job can provide satisfactions that substitute for those lacking in the job itself. In a context of humdrum routine, human sociability is able to extract surprisingly rich rewards from seemingly trivial events. Horseplay, lunchtime card games, gossip around the watercooler, football pools, and the like provide satisfaction, particularly for those with strong need affiliation. As the job becomes less rewarding, the social group may become more so.[48]

But this is not always the case. Cohesive work groups do not arise automatically whenever the work is boring. Jobs differ substantially in the opportunities they provide for social interaction. Once again, the automobile assembly line—which permits the typical worker to communicate only with the men directly ahead and behind him in the flow of work—provides relatively less opportunity for interaction than most other types of work. Similar problems have been created on continuous-strip steel mills where the work stations have been placed so far apart that workers are unable to communicate with each other.

Success in bargaining with management, either formally through the union or through wildcat strikes and other informal methods, can help create group cohesion, just as failure can fracture unity. But success of this sort is also partially a function of technology. Leonard Sayles has distinguished among Strategic, Conservative, Erratic, and Apathetic work groups.[49] Only the first two are successful in terms of bargaining. Members of Erratic groups may work together more closely than members of Strategic groups, but, for a variety of reasons, differences within these groups prevent them from developing effective teamwork.

High turnover, as well as heterogeneity of employees in terms of age, ethnic and educational background, or job duties, all inhibit the development of cohesive work groups. Social cohesion is also affected by the opportunity for association off the job: "The evidence of the work literature supports the notion that levels of work satisfaction are higher in those industries and in those kinds of jobs in which workers make up an 'occupational community.' One such industry is mining. Not only is the actual work carried out by solitary work groups, but in addition miners live in a community made up of fellow workers. This kind of 'inbreeding' produces a devotion to the occupation which is not characteristic of many other working class jobs." [50]

Those who live in isolated, small communities, who work odd shifts, or whose jobs frequently take them from home (such as sailors, railroadmen, or traveling construction craftsmen) are more likely to develop occupational communities of this sort.

The union also helps provide solidarity, at least for a small group of activists, but participation in union activity is not likely to be high in groups that are not already socially cohesive. Indeed, substantial evidence suggests that workers who are dissatisfied with their jobs also tend to be dissatisfied with their unions.[51]

To summarize, a rich social life on the job can substitute for boring work to some extent. Unfortunately, however, those occupational work groups that have the greatest need for the kind of social support that a cohesive group might provide frequently are the very ones that find it most difficult to develop such cohesion in the first place.

Dreams of advancement. Ely Chinoy's 1955 study, *Automobile Workers and the American Dream,* explains in vivid terms one aspect of how blue-collar workers adjusted at that time to the frustration of the assembly line. (The past tense is intentional because it is possible that this form of adjustment is no longer feasible.) Despite the seemingly dead-end nature of their jobs, a high percentage of Chinoy's respondents looked upon their job as only temporary and fantasied the day when they would be able to quit the factory and establish their small business or engage in some other independent occupation. When the pasage of time proved these dreams false, they projected their frustrated ambitions onto their children and planned how they could go to college and thus escape the assembly line. In either case, as Blauner puts it, "their daydreams serve as a safety valve for day-to-day frustrations."[52]

Economic security. Older blue-collar workers may have been able to adjust to the conditions of their work because these conditions have been constantly improving, and changes in the workplace have met their expectations. Compared with the 1930s, strong unions and the relative prosperity of the 1950s and 1960s brought the worker, particularly the man with high seniority, a considerable degree of job security, protection against tyrannical foremen and arbitrary rules, and an ever growing stream of fringe benefits. These developments led Daniel Bell to conclude: "Workers, whose grievances were once the driving energy for social change, are more satisfied with the society than the intellectuals. The workers have not achieved utopia but their expectations were less than those of the intellectuals and their gains correspondingly larger."[53]

A Game with the Environment

Recent research suggests that the process of adjusting to work may be even more complex than we had previously thought. In discussing work attitudes (of French white-collar workers), Michel Crozier suggests that "feelings are not the product of circumstances . . . feelings are escape routes . . . [ploys in a] game with the environment." [54] There is no reason to believe that attitude questions are answered 100 percent honestly or that conscious attitudes, or even unconscious ones, accurately reflect a person's objective situation. When workers report that they are "satisfied" with totally boring jobs, it may mean only that their self-respect forces them to answer in this way. Work may be so central to life that to report that one's job is unsatisfactory is almost to admit failure in life itself. This may be more than an attempt to deceive the interviewer; one's need for mental balance (to reduce cognitive dissonance) may require one to believe that he is really satisfied.

If attitudes toward the job represent a game with the environment, then different strategies are possible for playing the game. Although Crozier's study dealt with white-collar workers in a French insurance company, he suggests strategies that may be employed by American workers as well. In his study, lower-ranking employees reported greater satisfaction with their "position" in the insurance company than those in higher-ranking jobs, but they also reported less interest in their work. Why? For those of lower ranks (many of whom came from working-class backgrounds), merely working for an insurance company added to their status, even though their own particular work was menial. Those at higher levels had the security to cast aspersions on their employers and to suggest that they could do better elsewhere. Those at lower levels felt that they could "better safeguard [their] independence by submitting to orders than by seeking to participate in the elaboration of decisions." [55] They preserved their independence not by solidarity but by apathy and demanding close supervision. They felt that the permissive supervisor who engaged in general supervision showed "lack of candor"; they preferred "the forceful manager who makes clear and categorical decisions. . . . Subservience [is] a marvelous tool by which to control and manipulate management." [56]

For these low-ranking French white-collar workers, the strategy was to lie low, to avoid involving themselves in the job, and so to protect their egos. There is certainly a similarity between these workers and their U.S. counterparts who report that they are "satisfied" with their jobs but work only to "keep busy."

Argyris reports that many lower-skilled workers express needs to "be left alone," to "be passive," and to "experience routine and sameness." [57] He suggests that these attitudes are caused by the organization's stifling of individual maturity. Arthur Kornhauser reports interview responses like "There's such a thing as beating your brains against the wall," "Some things you just can't change; might as well accept them and adjust yourself to them." [58] He sees in such "passivity, fatalism, and resignation" evidence of poor mental health. Even assuming that the job caused the attitude (rather than that the attitude caused the employee to accept the job), the worker who expresses such attitudes may not have poor mental health but may be realistic, a shrewd player in the game with the environment, and very helathy indeed.[59]

Apathy is one ploy, resistance is another. Blauner suggests that the automobile worker, though still on the whole "satisfied" with his work, reports greater dissatisfaction than any other worker in a major occupation. For the auto worker, "Dissatisfaction is a reflection of his independence and dignity. . . . This independence and dignity is expressed in other ways besides generalized dissatisfaction. The auto worker quits his job more frequently than other workers. He is characteristically a griper, a man who talks back to his foreman, in contrast to the more submissive textile employee." [60] He also submits more grievances and is more likely to revolt against his union or to sabotage the production process. For at least some auto workers, "dissatisfaction is dignity."

The point here is that we should not take expressions of satisfaction or dissatisfaction too literally. A worker may switch quickly from one strategy to the other, with little objective change in the work conditions. And apathy may quickly change to revolt, just as it did for blacks in America, when conditions suggest that this particular strategy will provide a greater payoff in the game against the environment.

Summary
What sense can we make of this confusing and contradictory data? It seems clear that not everyone feels oppressed by his work organization. We know that dissatisfaction with work often seems to be a function of technology. We also are reasonably certain that the most dissatisfaction is reported on jobs with short job cycles and relatively little challenge and in industries in which such characteristics are common, especially the automotive industry (and also in wholesale and retail trade).

But degree of job challenge alone does not determine attitudes toward work. Dissatisfaction is also high in jobs that are paid poorly, are low in status, and prevent the development of group life. Supervision too is important. And some theorists would suggest that good supervision may perhaps be more crucial than challenging work.

Personality and culture enter the picture in a puzzling fashion. There are two alternative hypotheses as to why some workers seem to adjust easily to boring work:

(1) Unchallenging bureaucratic jobs inhibit the normal development of the human personality and thus lead to poor mental health, apathy, and even to the delusion that one prefers highly structured work. Workers suffering from such conditions attempt to redirect their limited energies to activities of the job, to social life on the job, or to sheer fantasy (but never with great success and always with considerable emotional cost).

(2) For genetic or cultural reasons, some people have low levels of aspiration and/or ability to handle challenging work, have low need achievement, and/or wish to center their lives off the job. Their primary demands from the job are economic and instrumental. To the extent they can, they pick jobs that pay well or make few mental or physical demands.

Incompatible as these two explanations of the evidence may seem, both may be partly true. Whole cultures may adjust to job opportunities that call for little challenge (as blacks did until recently) and so change their "personality." Although such adjustment may be unhealthy, it can be stable and not lead to revolt unless the underlying conditions change.

To put it another way, there are a variety of forms of adjustment to "objectively" unchallenging work (that is, work which most observers— and especially college professors—report as unchallenging). Some workers are able to develop rich social lives on the job or are active in their unions. Others obtain a large part of the challenge they seek off the job, through recreation or family activities (though the evidence suggests that for many this recreation may be rather passive). A worker may "adjust" by dreaming of better work, either for himself or his children. Alternatively, he may "enlarge" his job through sabotage or output restriction,[61] or he may lower his aspirations and delude himself into thinking that he is truly happy—and thus become resigned and apathetic (and even classified as being in poor mental health). Finally, he may become a chronic griper and even express his feelings through strikes, absenteeism, or quitting his job, that is, through "revolt."

Some of these forms of "adjustment" are more costly to society and the individual than are others. "Revolt" is one possibility, but not the only one. And the extent of revolt seems unlikely to increase substantially unless underlying conditions change to make it more attractive than other forms of reaction.

Trends for the Future
Much of the discussion relating to blue-collar dissatisfaction seems to assume that it has intensified in recent years. Although we have little evidence that dissatisfaction with *work* has increased, there are a number of hypotheses available to explain an increase *if* it becomes apparent.

One hypothesis is that the characteristics of work itself have objectively altered. But other than gross census data concerning occupational distribution, we have little evidence of changes in jobs. Perhaps there has been some movement away from assembly-line work toward process automation. If so, as I said earlier, this might actually increase satisfaction. More likely, the change has been too gradual to lead to any sharp increase in dissatisfaction.

On the other hand, there have been some changes in the job environment. Managers, as well as workers, are better educated. Unionism and the human relations movement have had an impact. Although we have little firm evidence, we have every reason to believe that workers today are better treated by their bosses, company policies more humane, safety hazards reduced, and job security improved. Herzberg's "hygienes" are more prevalent, making the job more tolerable.

Changes in the Work Force
Although jobs do not appear to have changed, workers have, and the changes are quite significant.

Younger. Blue-collar employment in manufacturing declined by 14 percent from 1953 to 1961. This led to the hiring of fewer young men, and the average age of blue-collar workers rose substantially. Since 1961, employment has expanded rapidly, and the bulk of the employees hired during the 1920s have retired, with early retirement provisions accelerating the trend. The result has been a substantial reduction in the average age of workers in many industries, especially the automotive. During the 1960s the average age at Ford dropped four years, and in 1970 roughly one-third of the hourly employees in the automobile industry were under thirty. The average age at Lordstown was twenty-five.[62]

Young men are, in general, less satisfied than their elders with work;[63] and young blue-collar workers are influenced by at least *some* of the trends that led to revolt on campus. Like their peers in college, they have been brought up in a much more permissive environment.

This trend toward an increasingly youthful labor force will not continue, however. The bonanza crop of postwar babies (born in 1946–51), who entered either the workplace or college during the hectic years of 1964–69, are now in their mid-twenties, the older ones no doubt burdened with children and mortgages. The number of young workers entering industry will actually decline.

Better educated. In 1948 the average education of craftsmen, operatives, and laborers was nine years; in 1971 it was twelve. Nine percent had three years of college. During this period the educational attainment of the blue-collar work force soared beyond job requirements. Automobile manufacturing, especially, has "old, ultra-simplified methods originally designed not only to avoid waste motions but to accommodate unskilled immigrant labor and farm youths." [64] Understandably, there is evidence that where job level is held constant, education is inversely related to satisfaction.

We see cognitive dissonance here. The extra investment involved in increased education has given rise to increased expectations, which have not been met. For these workers, education has not been a route to success. And a substantial proportion of workers feel that their skills are underutilized on the job, and this is especially so among those who report attending "some college." (Among whites, those thirty years or younger with "some college" report the greatest job dissatisfaction of any group.)[65] Better-educated blue-collar workers may demand higher wages just to counteract their boredom. Indeed, they may compare their wages with those of their age group who have "made it" in white-collar work.

Education may have two other effects. It may increase the worker's opportunities to find meaningful recreation off the job, which suggests that he will more easily make a trade-off between boring work and interesting leisure. On the other hand, it may also reduce his sense of alienation and increase his sense of control over the environment.[66] To the extent the second effect is true, he will be less willing to accept apathy as his strategy in the game against the environment and may be more inclined to engage in active revolt.

Changes in Values

During the 1940s and 1950s workers called *steady work* the most important thing they wanted from their jobs. A comprehensive 1957 study that summarized the extensive literature to date listed job factors influencing satisfaction in roughly this order: job security, opportunities for advancement, company and management, wages, and intrinsic work—with intrinsic work coming fifth.[67] By sharp contrast, in a 1969 survey *interesting work* came first and job security was rated seventh, and six of the eight most desired aspects of work related to job content.[68]

These data may be but a statistical artifact, but if confirmed by other evidence they would suggest a substantial shift in the value ordering of American workers, one which is consistent with the Maslow hierarchy. After all, this is the first generation not to grow up in the shadow of the Great Depression; the specter of job insecurity may have been dispelled. With low-level needs largely fulfilled, workers may now be in a position to demand satisfaction for their egoistic and self-actualization needs.[69] If so, such workers are less likely to settle for apathy or even for a job that offers high income and the possibility of a rich social life but not intrinsic satisfaction from the work itself. For such workers, money alone may no longer motivate—or, as economists put it, it may have declining marginal utility.

Two studies seem consistent with this view. The first, by Charles Hulin, suggests that when work content is held constant, job satisfaction is negatively correlated with community income.[70] In other words, as the community and the workers in it grow more prosperous, but the worker's job remains unchanged, his satisfaction drops. The second supporting study, by J. Richard Hackman and Edward E. Lawler, tends to confirm the commonsense expectation that the relationship between job challenge and job satisfaction is highest when workers are motivated to satisfy higher-order needs.[71]

Ely Chinoy suggested that one escape route for the automobile worker was to dream of setting up his own business. (Other studies suggest that ambitious workers in some industries once felt they had a real chance to move into management.) One may wonder whether these escape routes still are psychologically meaningful, even for workers with some college education.

We come to a final difficult question. Assuming there is a revolt at all, is it against all work or only boring work?

A case can be made that it is a revolt against all work. The Hulin and Blood studies suggest that a significant portion of our population rejects the Protestant ethic and feels no increase in satisfaction when given challenging work. In addition, certain segments of our youth culture have dropped out of the "rat race." (Consider the college-educated hippie postman.) To some extent there seems to be a drop in competitive motivation and the Protestant ethic among college students.[72]

By and large, this case is weak. As suggested earlier, Hulin and Blood's workers from the city slums may have given up and settled realistically for steady but boring jobs. Their better-educated children, having grown up in relatively greater economic security, feel greater control over their destiny and reject their parents' low-risk solutions. If those at the very bottom of the pile—blacks, Indians, and Chicanos—can revolt, why not these workers who are slightly higher up? Anyway, the youth culture may not represent a revolt against all work, but only against meaningless work. "Meaningful" work may mean more than challenging work. Work may also have to serve some broader social or aesthetic end. Witness the rise of handicraft industries.

Earlier I argued that too many sociologists apply professors' standard values in judging the plight of blue-collar workers. But as the worker becomes better educated and more affluent, he too *may* become more like the professor. Possibly. But as long as access to education in our society remains relatively open, the vast majority of those who really want white-collar, professional, or managerial jobs will go on to obtain the degree of education required to obtain them. (Mine may be an elitist view). When almost everyone has a high school education, the social and psychological meaning of that degree may drop, as will the expectation that it should guarantee meaningful work.

Conclusion

Recent political developments do suggest some sort of socioeconomic revolt among blue-collar workers or, perhaps, among lower-middle-class groups generally. But given the 1972 Nixon landslide, it is a strange revolt— a revolt against change rather than for it. However, the evidence to date is less clear about a sudden increase in dissatisfaction with work. The two phenomena may be related, but they are not identical.

A boring job is a boring job, but some adjust to it more easily than others. All of a sudden, businessmen, economists, and politicians have begun to talk about job enrichment as the remedy for a host of maladies—even as a means of improving our balance of payments. It is not clear that all workers want job enrichment or that job enrichment alone, without increased wages, increased promotional opportunities, and a higher social status for blue-collar work would resolve the blue-collar dissatisfaction that does exist. Job enrichment may also require redesigning production processes and may reduce technological efficiency. Further, it may necessitate a revamping (inevitably upwards) of our pay scales, retraining of management, and possibly a reduction in the rigidity of our seniority rules. After these costs are deducted, the net advantage of job enrichment, either to our economy or to our remaining society, may be low.

Notes

1. *Economist,* April 30, 1972, p. 71.

2. This renewed interest among social scientists in attitudes and blue-collar workers is a throwback to the 1940s. During the 1950s and 1960s our interests tended to climb the status ladder from blue-collar workers to supervisors and then to managers and professionals, while as variables our concerns were more and more centered on motivation, productivity, and organizational climate.

3. Harold L. Sheppard and Neal Q. Herrick, *Where Have the Robots Gone?* (New York: Free Press, 1972), p. xi.

4. Harvey Swados, "Foreword," in ibid., p. x.

5. Labor Day Address, 1971.

6. *AFL-CIO News,* January 27, 1973, p. 5.

7. Thomas R. Brooks, "Job Satisfaction: An Elusive Goal," *AFL-CIO American Federationist* 79, no. 10 (October 1972): 1–8.

8. *New York Times,* April 12, 1972, p. 8.

9. Survey Research Center, University of Michigan, *Survey of Working Conditions* (Washington, D.C.: U.S. Department of Labor, Employment Standards Administration, 1971).

10. Stanley E. Seashore and J. Thad Barnowe, "Demographic and Job Factors Associated with the 'Blue Collar Blues,' " mimeographed (1972).

11. Sheppard and Herrick; Seashore and Barnowe; Sar A. Levitan, *Blue Collar Workers: A Symposium on Middle America* (New York: McGraw-Hill, 1971).

12. Jerome M. Rosow, Assistant Secretary of Labor for Policy, Evaluation, and Research, memorandum for the Secretary of Labor, April 16, 1970, p. 3.

13. Satisfaction with pay and benefits is higher among blue-collar workers under fifty with children than it is among those thirty or under without children. (See Seashore and Barnowe; Sheppard and Herrick, pp. 5–6.)

14. Edward Ransford, "Blue Collar Anger: Reactions to Student and Black Protest," *American Sociological Review* 37, no. 3 (June 1972): 333–346.

15. Ely Chinoy, *Automobile Workers and the American Dream* (Garden City, N.Y.: Doubleday, 1955).

16. Ransford.

17. Chris Argyris, *Personality and Organization* (New York: Harper & Row, 1957); Norman R. F. Maier, *Psychology in Industry* (Boston: Houghton Mifflin, 1955); Douglas McGregor, *The Human Side of Enterprise* (New York: McGraw-Hill, 1960).

18. George Strauss, "Some Notes on Power Equalization," in *The Social Science Organizations,* ed. Harold J. Leavitt (Englewood Cliffs, N.J.: Prentice-Hall, 1963).

19. Charles R. Walker and Robert Guest, *The Man on the Assembly Line* (Cambridge: Harvard University Press, 1952); Robert Blauner, *Alienation and Freedom* (Chicago: University of Chicago Press, 1964); Seashore and Barnowe.

20. Walker and Guest; A. N. Turner and Paul R. Lawrence, *Industrial Jobs and the Worker* (Boston: Harvard Graduate School of Business Administration, 1965). But see also Maurice Kilbridge, "Do Workers Prefer Larger Jobs?" *Personnel* 37, no. 5 (September 1960): 45.

21. Charles S. Telly, Wendell French, and William G. Scott, "The Relationship of Inequity to Turnover among Hourly Workers," *Administrative Science Quarterly* 16, no. 2 (June 1971): 164–172.

22. Leonard R. Sayles, "Wildcat Strikes," *Harvard Business Review* 32, no. 6 (October 1964): 84–92.

23. Arthur Kornhauser, "Mental Health of Factory Workers," *Human Organization* 21 (spring 1962): 43–46; Gerald Guerin, Joseph Vernoff, and Sheila Feld, *Americans View Their Mental Health* (New York: Basic Books, 1960). The works cited in notes 18–23 are critically examined by Charles L. Hulin and Milton R. Blood, who suggest that few of the studies have been properly conducted and that overall the evidence lacks credibility ("Job Enlargement, Individual Differences, and Worker Responses," *Psychological Bulletin* 69 (1968), no. 1: 41–55).

24. Blauner; Jon Shepard, "Functional Specialization and Work Attitudes," *Industrial Relations* 8, no. 2 (May 1965): 185–194.

25. Survey Research Center, p. 432.

26. David McClelland, *The Achieving Society* (Princeton: Van Nostrand, 1961).

27. One study by Victor Vroom, for example, suggests that workers who have a high need for independence and weak authoritarian attitudes are likely to respond to consultation with their supervisors by being more satisfied with their work; those with low needs for independence and strong authoritarian values are less likely to respond in this manner (*Some Personality Determinants of the Effects of Participation* [Englewood Cliffs, N.J.: Prentice-Hall, 1960]).

28. Turner and Lawrence.

29. Hulin and Blood.

30. Gerald I. Susman, "Job Enlargement: Effects of Culture on Worker Responses," *Industrial Relations* 12, no. 1 (February 1973): 1–15.

31. J. Richard Hackman and Edward E. Lawler III, "Employee Reactions to Job Characteristics," *Journal of Applied Psychology* 55, no. 3 (June 1971): 259–286.

32. According to the 1969 Survey Research Center study, jobs which are high on "enriching job demand" are also high on "job related tensions."

33. It should be noted that the research of Jon M. Shepard seems to contradict all these explanations. His findings suggest that job satisfaction is positively correlated with job challenge even for alienated workers ("Functional Specialization, Alienation, and Job Satisfaction," *Industrial and Labor Relations Review* 23 [January 1970]: 207–219).

34. Robert Dubin, "Industrial Research and the Discipline of Sociology," in *Proceedings of the 11th Annual Meeting* (Madison, Wis.: Industrial Relations Research Association, 1959), p. 161.

35. Harold Wilensky, "The Uneven Distribution of Leisure," *Social Problems* 9, no. 1 (summer 1961): 32–56.

36. John H. Goldthorpe, "Attitudes and Behavior of Car Assemblers: A Deviant Case and Theoretical Critique," *British Journal of Sociology* 69 (January 1966): 41–55.

37. Survey Research Center.

38. A hasty glance at the research makes it abundantly clear that unskilled workers are not the only ones to suffer from poor mental health. Depending on the study one looks at and the mental health index used, one can conclude that executives, clerical personnel, salespeople, and lower-level supervisors all suffer from one form of below-average mental health or another. The evidence makes one sympathize with the old Quaker, "All the world is queer except me and thee; and sometimes I think thee is queer." The 1969 Survey Research Center study, for example, concludes that those in higher-status occupations suffer more from job-related tensions, those in lower-status occupations more from somatic complaints.

39. Martin Meissner, "The Long Arm of the Job: A Study of Work and Leisure," *Industrial Relations* 10 (October 1971). See also Kornhauser.

40. Studs Terkel, "A Steelworker Speaks," *Dissent* 19, no. 1 (winter 1972): 9–20.

41. Nancy Morse and Robert Weiss, "The Function and Meaning of Work," *American Sociological Review* 20, no. 2 (April 1955): 191–198.

42. In the 1969 Survey Research Center study, 67.4 percent of the respondents responded positively to the question, "If you were to get enough money to live as comfortably as you'd like for the rest of your life, would you continue to work?" Yet doubt can be cast on both these studies, as far as automobile workers are concerned, by the large proportion of such workers who elected to take early retirement when this option became available in 1970.

43. Results of the 1969 Survey Research Center study: 46.4 percent very satisfied, 39.0 percent somewhat satisfied, 11.3 percent not too dissatisfied, 3.2 percent not at all satisfied. The only report I know in which less than a majority expressed satisfaction was the 1965 Gallup poll in which only 48 percent of the black respondents expressed satisfaction (compared to 87 percent of the whites). Arguably this exceptional finding represents an attitude toward life or toward politics rather than toward the job.

44. Blauner, p. 204.

45. Frederick Herzberg, *Work and the Nature of Man* (New York: World Publishing, 1966).

46. This does not mean that workers never feel cheated. Tyrannical actions of individual foremen, efforts to speed up the production line, and the like can often lead to feelings that the basic bargain has been broken. My point is merely that available evidence suggests that a broad spectrum of workers are at least resigned to their lot.

47. Blauner, p. 181.

48. See particularly Donald F. Roy, "Banana Time: Job Satisfaction and Informal Interaction," *Human Organization* 18, no. 4 (winter 1959–60): 158–166.

49. Leonard Sayles, *Behavior of Industrial Work Groups* (New York: Wiley, 1958).

50. Blauner, p. 351.

51. Leonard Sayles and George Strauss, *The Local Union,* rev. ed. (New York: Harcourt Brace, 1967).

52. Blauner, p. 120.

53. Daniel Bell, *The End of Ideology* (New York: Collier Books, 1961), p. 399.

54. Michel Crozier, *The World of the Office Worker* (Chicago: University of Chicago Press, 1971), pp. x–xi.

55. Ibid., p. 132.

56. Ibid., p. 130.

57. Chris Argyris, "The Individual and the Organization: An Empirical Test," *Administrative Science Quarterly* 4 (1959), no. 2: 162.

58. Kornhauser.

59. In *Work and the Nature of Man* Herzberg looks upon mental health and mental illness as two separate dimensions (making the same distinction as that between job satisfaction and dissatisfaction). Presumably Kornhauser's workers are neither healthy nor ill. A broader question is how to characterize the deviant worker who makes work central to his self-image in a situation where most of his peers seek satisfaction elsewhere. In a crazy world, what is sanity?

60. Blauner, p. 122.

61. William F. Whyte et al., *Money and Motivation* (New York: Harper & Row, 1955).

62. Judson Gooding, "Blue Collar Blues on the Assembly Line," *Fortune,* July 1970, p. 69.

63. Survey Research Center, p. 70.

64. Gooding, p. 70.

65. Survey Research Center, p. 40.

66. Arnold Tannenbaum (work in progress, 1972).

67. Frederick Herzberg et al., *Job Attitudes: A Review of Research and Opinion* (Pittsburgh: Psychological Service of Pittsburgh, 1957).

68. Neal Q. Herrick, "Who's Unhappy with Work and Why?" *Manpower* 4, no. 1 (January 1972): 5.

69. Arguably blue-collar workers now receive middle-class wages and now want middle-class type jobs. Such a view would seem to be inconsistent with Rosow's economic squeeze.

70. Charles Hulin, "Effects of Community Characteristics on Measuring Job Satisfaction," *Journal of Applied Psychology* 50, no. 2 (1966): 185–192.

71. Hackman and Lawler.

72. John B. Miner, "Changes in Student Attitudes toward Bureaucratic Role Perceptions during the 1960's," *Administrative Science Quarterly* 16, no. 3 (September 1971): 351–364.

II Problems of American Workers

3 Upward Mobility, Job Monotony, and Labor Market Structure

Michael J. Piore

This essay represents an attempt to understand worker complaints about American society in terms of a single set of hypotheses about the structure of American labor markets. The term *hypothesis* is used advisedly. The theory of discontent developed here is logically consistent: it is consistent with the facts of American labor history in the twentieth century, and more or less consistent with the conventional wisdom about the causes of worker complaints, but neither the facts as stated, which constitute input into the theory, nor the implications drawn from these facts, which are the theory's output, have been the subject of rigorous empirical examination.

The complaints that the theory attempts to explain come, on the one hand, from low-income minority-group workers and, on the other hand, from higher-income blue-collar workers and middle-income white-collar workers. These groups correspond more or less to what sociologists term the lower class and the working class, although the inclusion of white-collar workers stretches the conventional usage of the latter term. The discontent of these groups seems to be real enough. Among the lower class, it has made itself felt in urban riots and lesser forms of unorganized unrest and in an increased political awareness and support for organized campaigns and protests. Symptomatic of the discontent among the working class has been political support for protest candidates such as George Wallace and the increasingly high votes of rejection of union contracts. For reasons that will become apparent, I would also include here the pressures that led to concerns about technological change and automation which predominated in the late 1950s and early 1960s.

Diagnosis of the Problem

While the discontent of these two groups of workers is apparent, the genesis of their discontent is less clear. It was felt for some time that the basic reason for the discontent of the lower class was unemployment. While the rates of unemployment for the statistical categories that are dominated by lower-class workers (Negroes, the Spanish-speaking, those from slum neighborhoods) are indeed high, the research that a number of us conducted among these groups in the boom period of the middle sixties suggested that this discontent centered upon the quality of available jobs.[1] Moreover, high rates of unemployment were derivative of either the characteristics of the jobs themselves (they had unusually high rates of layoff and discharge) or of the workers' attitudes toward these jobs. This is probably not true in the recession labor markets that currently prevail—even poor jobs are now scarce. But presuming the economy is brought back to what has been considered full employment in the past, the research suggests that the discontent of lower-class workers will continue to be based on the quality of their employment opportunities. It is perhaps worth pointing out, parenthetically, that the technology for achieving full employment has been available for some time. What is lacking is the will on the part of policy makers to vigorously pursue the goal of full employment.

I have argued in detail elsewhere that the problem I describe above is best defined in terms of a dual labor market, with a primary and a secondary sector.[2] Jobs in the secondary sector are distinguished by the fact that, relative to primary jobs, they tend to offer low wages, poor work conditions, and little chance of advancement; to be managed by harsh—often capricious—supervision that is unrestrained by a cohesive set of work rules or a formal grievance procedure; and to exhibit great instability and offer little employment security. The crux of the problem of lower-class workers is that they are confined to this secondary sector.

In assessing the problems of the lower class, it should also be noted that its discontent has been concentrated in urban areas among second generation immigrants from rural areas (of the United States and abroad), although in terms of the characteristics defining secondary jobs, those who were born and raised in the rural South or abroad probably have the worst jobs. The really poor seem to be more accepting of their lot.

Putting these two facets of lower-class discontent together suggests that the complaint might best be diagnosed as a lack of upward social mobility. The process of immigration gives a sense of mobility to those who move; and the possibility of moving gives a sense of opportunity to those who remain behind. Discouragement and discontent are felt only by the children of those who originally moved, who now find themselves trapped in the jobs that, if they are not precisely those of their parents, have degrading aspects similar to those of their parents' jobs and fall miserably short of the jobs to which they aspire and to which their parents aspired for them.

Working-class people's discontent does not seem to be so clearly associated with social mobility in this sense. It would be too strong a statement to say that they do not have higher aspirations for their children; they would be pleased and proud for their progeny to achieve great wealth or professional status. But they are relatively content with their own economic positions, and they would be satisfied to see their children follow them into similar jobs and life-styles. This feeling seems, moreover, to be shared by the children themselves.

The discontent of the working class seems rather to center on the precariousness of what has been achieved—to be an expression not of frustration at an inability to advance but of the fear of falling behind their present positions. Thus, in the early 1960s, the working class was preoccupied by the threat of technological change; in the late 1960s it was preoccupied by the threat to its life-style and employment security that it felt was posed by black and other lower-class groups pressuring them from below.

This sense of insecurity is particularly apparent in contrast to the attitudes of middle-class or professional workers, who are also relatively satisfied with what they have achieved and who expect their children to follow them into comparable careers. What is something of a problem for these people is that their children may not *want* to pursue professional careers, but the idea that their children might not be *able* to do so, or that their own professional status and associated economic and social styles of life might be threatened—which seems to be in the forefront of working-class thinking— is completely foreign to the thinking of professionals, at least among those of my acquaintaince.

The other source of discontent among working-class people is the quality of their jobs. This problem includes issues of industrial health and safety and, recently, the monotonous nature of many blue-collar jobs. It is always difficult to know exactly how to assess this problem; one never knows whether the middle-class professionals who diagnose it are reading their own preferences into the attitudes of other workers. It seems to me that most discussions of this phenomenon do underestimate the capacity of human beings to mold themselves to, accept, and ultimately come to like even the most monotonous work—at least in the negative sense that they are very uncomfortable in a challenging work environment. Nonetheless, the revolt of the rank-and-file (especially younger members), which was the most spectacular at Lordstown, Ohio, does suggest that monotony is a problem. If one cannot interpret the current revolt as indicative of older workers becoming psychologically unstuck, or even of younger workers not eventually conforming, at least one can argue that at the point in the life cycle when the adjustment to monotony must be made there is increasing resistance to it.

The Underlying Causes

The continuing job anxiety of working-class people and their concerns about monotony and health and the complaints of lower-class people about the quality of their jobs and their limited employment opportunities may be viewed as joint products of a single phenomenon: the structural adjustments in the organization of work that are attributable to the pursuit of employment security by industrial unions. In this sense, they can be traced to the labor legislation of the 1930s that permitted these unions to organize and placed them in a position to negotiate employment security arrangements.

Two aspects of these arrangements are critical. First, they are negotiated on a decentralized basis between individual employers and representatives of their own employees. There is thus considerable variation in the amount of security that has been achieved. More importantly, a large sector of the economy has never been under the real threat of organization, and hence there is no employment security for workers in some industries at all. Second, in very few cases is the employment security that has been achieved absolute, and a good deal of attention has focused upon a set of rules for distributing scarce jobs and income among the labor force.

The decentralized nature of employment security arrangements and the incompleteness of unionization to which it is related act to aggravate the dichotomy between the sectors of the dual labor market. To the extent that unions have succeeded in stabilizing employment in the primary sector, what they have essentially done is to shift the cost of variations in and uncertainty about the demand for output, which seems to adhere in industrial economies, from their constituents to the employer. The employer has, in turn, looked for ways in which he can shift these costs to other parts of the economy, and the existence of an unorganized sector—with no deterrents to varying employment levels to fit demand—has provided a means of doing so. Thus primary employers avoid putting new workers on their own payroll during periods of unsustainable increases in demand and instead seek to transfer these peaks to employers in the secondary labor market. It should be emphasized that this is not simply a question of variation in demand over the business cycle—although this is certainly the case in part —but it also relates to the fluctuations in demand in the course of a year, from season to season, or at random, because of a hundred factors which may be peculiar to an industry or an enterprise. Thus, employers who are under pressure from unions to stabilize jobs look periodically to transfer demand, even in a full employment economy. There are a variety of institutional arrangements through which this transfer is accomplished. The most prominent methods are probably subcontracting and temporary help services. There are also ways in which employers can maintain a secondary sector within their own establishment, although this often requires the acquiescence of the trade union. For example, there may be certain departments composed of low seniority workers in which employment fluctuations are concentrated. Such departments are particularly easy to spot in southern plants, where they are reserved for black workers, although it often turns out that once one knows where to look an analogue can be found in the North. During peak demand in paper and steel mills, yard workers get temporary assignments to production departments. Another common way of handling peak demand "in house" is to cycle people through the union probationary period, discharging workers and hiring replacements just before the probation is completed and before they become subject to the protection of the union contract.

Many of the other characteristics distinguishing secondary and primary jobs can be seen as derivative of this process of employment stabilization in the primary sector. The lack of clear, formal work rules and disciplinary standards and the capricious and highly personal manner in which foremen are allowed to discipline workers was characteristic of most American industry before union organization in the thirties—and appears directly attributable to the weakness of trade unions in the secondary sector today. The lack of training and chance of advancement can be traced to the temporary nature of employment opportunities which provides no incentive to the employer to invest in his work force (or, for that matter, for the worker to invest in himself).[3] In fact, the employer's strategy of transferring peak demand to the secondary sector is generally to preserve the skilled aspects of the job in house and to have unskilled tasks done outside. When demand slacks off, the unskilled tasks are brought back to the primary establishment and assigned to skilled employees in order to provide enough work to meet employment obligations. Even the harsh working conditions that characterize the secondary sector are sometimes the by-product of the temporary nature of the work and the short time horizon of the employer, which deter investment in physical plant.

The aspects of primary work that seem to underlie the complaints of the working class—job monotony and industrial safety—may be seen as a by-product of employment stabilization. The variety and complexity of work required to hold the interest of an employee in a job is a lot greater when the job is permanent than when it is temporary; the same work seems a good deal more monotonous for permanent workers in the primary sector today than it appeared in earlier periods when job tenure was shorter and less secure. Similarly, a number of the industrial health problems that have become matters of concern in recent years are the result of prolonged, continuous exposure to materials, air, or noise, which are unlikely to affect in any important way a person who holds the job temporarily, or even over a prolonged (but intermittent) total period.

But probably the more important factor in monotony and health, and cer-tainly the basic explanation for the continuing anxiety about security among the working class, is the particular manner in which the issue of employ-ment security has been resolved in American industry. Although the unions have consistently sought guarantees of security, they have only recently— and even now only in very limited sectors of the economy—begun to achieve anything approaching such guarantees. In the automobile industry, with its supplementary unemployment insurance, there is a large-scale example of such a guarantee, but it is a guarantee of income, not of employ-ment. There are other examples of a less quantitative significance: IBM,

Procter and Gamble, and the sugar refining industry. Elsewhere, unions have been forced to settle not for guarantees but for arrangements for distributing scarce employment and income among the labor force. These arrangements make it more costly for the employer to lay off and rehire and in this way act to deter layoffs, thus indirectly tending to stabilize employment.

It is these indirect effects that constitute the basis for the hypothesis that the management of fluctuations in labor demand in the unionized sector fosters the development of secondary employment. But for the work force, the union, and the firm they act to shift attenion from the management of employment fluctuations per se to the procedures for distributing the impact of these fluctuations among the firm's own employees.

The procedures that have been developed rely heavily upon a system of job assignment by seniority. The details vary substantially among plants, but the basic idea is that a worker's seniority is defined by his date of hire, and the employer is obligated to permit senior workers whose jobs are temporarily or permanently eliminated to "bump" (displace) junior employees from their jobs. Workers so displaced have the right to bump their juniors so that in theory (it does not quite work out this way in practice) it is the most junior employee who goes out the door. Seniority is also used to allocate promotion opportunities, although in the case of promotion, ability is frequently used as a criterion in combination with seniority. In most American industries, the wage is linked to the job, and thus the seniority rules for job allocation determine pay as well.

Through the seniority system, therefore, both the worker's employment security and his pay have come to be uniquely connected to a specific job assignment. And thus not only has movement between enterprises been reduced, but movement among jobs or work assignments within an enterprise has also been narrowly restricted. Any attempt to remove these restrictions is deterred by the fact that job definition is so closely connected to pay and security. In a sense, reliance upon seniority has generated a conflict between job security and work variety.

This conflict has been further aggravated by the trend in industrial engineering to design jobs so that the range of tasks connected with each work assignment is narrowed and routinized. There is no clear scientific basis for this trend. The number of experiments that suggest that productivity is enhanced by job enrichment are sufficient to warrant at least a careful examination of the issue, but industrial engineering practice has been virtually unaffected by this possibility, and in fact the profession has been largely uninterested in the issue. This suggests that the idea of job simplification has some profound hold upon the imagination, and it would be intellectually satisfying if I could locate that hold in relation to job security. But the idea has a history that stretches back in engineering to Taylor's scientific management and in economics to Adam Smith in the late eighteenth century, and there is little that connects it directly to the stabilization of employment in the recent past.

What does seem to be related to job security, however, is the attitude of trade unions toward industrial engineering. On the whole, in the postwar period that attitude has been one of cooperation. The basic tools of industrial engineering—time-and-motion study, job evaluation, and the like— have in most establishments become the language of industrial relations. In a number of situations unions have actively cooperated with management in industrial engineering. The negotiation of the Cooperative Wage Survey (CWS) Plan in steel is the most well known. In the garment industry, unions have actually originated campaigns attempting to induce employers to accept and apply industrial engineering principles. Where unions have not played an active role, they have generally acquiesced in management-initiated applications of industrial engineering precepts and have trained their own people to review management decisions in this context.

The degree of cooperation between labor and management in this area lies in the face of the stereotypical conflict between the time-motion man and the industrial worker. It is all the more remarkable in view of the early history of the scientific management movement and the fervent antiunion bias of Frederick Taylor. It belies an inherent antagonism between the engineer's view of man as an extension of the machine and the essentially political and humanistic view of the worker that is characteristically held by union leaders. It also belies the assumption that job simplification is believed by both the engineers and the unions to foster automation and technological change, a belief that would constitute a real, as well as a philosophical, basis for conflict.

For an explanation of the acceptance of industrial engineering that unions have evinced, one must look to the role of seniority and the reasons for union reliance upon it. Seniority is not the only basis upon which jobs and income could be distributed. Alternatives include ability, qualifications, need, and work sharing. These are used in some parts of the economy but are nowhere near as prevalent as seniority. Why this is so is not altogether clear, but of considerable and possibly overriding importance is the unambiguous character of seniority. The distribution of jobs and income present union leaders with the task of choosing among the members of their organization in a situation in which the gains of one group inevitably result in losses of the most serious kind to another group. Such a choice is a threat to the political position of the union leaders and has the potential as an issue for completely destroying the organization. The importance of this last point cannot be overestimated; it presents the nightmare of an anxious work force fighting with each other for limited jobs. Historically, this has been the major deterrent to the stability of American trade union organizations. The seniority system resolves this issue once and for all; it is an objective criterion, is easily defined, leaves no room for interpretation, and hence bars manipulation by union leaders, employers, or any group of workers.

But the ability to use seniority as an unambiguous tool for the distribution of pay and security depends upon unambiguous job assignments. And this creates an interest among union leaders in the kind of rationalization of the job structure that industrial engineering has introduced—an interest which, it may be noted, is as strong as the unions' interest in the principle of seniority itself. The use of seniority also presupposes that the requirements for performance of the job are small enough that virtually any worker can move into it. This creates a union interest even in the kind of job simplification that increases the threat of technological change.

In sum, what is being argued is that the fact that security was limited and that unions were forced to worry about its distribution worked to further enhance monotony in primary sector employment. The distributional rules that developed linked security to specific job assignments and encouraged the unions to acquiesce in the further narrowing of these assignments through industrial engineering and job simplification. Paradoxically, in acquiescing to the engineers, unions may have heightened the very insecurity with which they were attempting to deal, for the definition of a job in terms of a limited number of narrow, carefully defined tasks certainly enhances the possibility of its being mechanized out of existence. In any case, the fact that unions were unable to provide employment guarantees left the working class with continuing job anxiety and renders them extremely sensitive to pressure from below them in the social structure.

Solutions

If the root of the problems with which we are concerned lies in the job security arrangements negotiated by the industrial unions, it would seem that the cure is to be found in changes in those arrangements. One direction of change is a weakening of unions' power, which would permit the degeneration of existing security arrangements. Such a solution would reduce the barriers between the primary and secondary markets and would enhance the variety of the work experience, presumably reducing monotony and possibly enhancing industrial health. It would do so, however, at a substantial cost in terms of the security of workers now in the organized sector and would sacrifice the procedures to insure equity and due process that unions have painfully built up in the workplace over the last thirty years.

The alternative is to look for more job security rather than less. In particular, if current difficulties among blue-collar workers are caused by efforts to ration scarce jobs among a firm's work force, this could be remedied by imposing a complete guarantee. In other words, there could be insurance that there will always be employment for workers who have already been hired. The Japanese economy provides a model of such guaranteed employment in much of its manufacturing industry, and there is reportedly considerably greater freedom in job assignment there than in similar American enterprises. Also, in Japan the employment guarantee has produced a pay system in which wage is based upon seniority and is largely divorced from the particular job. The limited experience with employment guarantees in the United States also points to greater freedom in job assignments. Indeed, in union-organized industries, such guarantees have generally arisen as an effort on the part of management to obtain precisely that freedom to vary work assignments.

Freedom of job assignment is not, of course, the same thing as job enrichment, but it permits far greater experimentation with this and other means of reducing the monotony of work experience. If the earlier arguments are correct, moreover, the employment guarantee would free union leaders to press for changes in this direction. The development of such pressure might quite possibly have to wait for a new generation of union leaders, however. An acceptance of industrial engineering and its bias toward rigid and confining job assignments has been built into the ideology of American business unionism, and leaders who reject it are generally viewed by the movement's elder statesmen as immature, radical, or demagogic. And it will certainly take a new generation of industrial engineers to respond to such pressure.

It is possible that collective bargaining is already evolving in the direction of employment guarantees. The logic of the supplementary unemployment insurance in the automobile industry and similar arrangements negotiated in allied industries is to make labor costs independent of layoffs. If this is indeed the natural direction of evolution, then any one of a half dozen proposals designed to increase union bargaining power—including repeal of the Taft-Hartley Act's section 14B, the mandatory provision of unemployment benefits to strikers, and increased limitations on employer election propaganda—should hasten the introduction of guarantees. Similarly, policies designed to reduce the cost of employment fluctuations to the employer and make him more willing to provide guarantees should have a positive effect. Of such policies, a renewed commitment to full employment is probably the most important. One can also imagine a variety of governmental insurance systems or reinsurance systems that would protect the employer against extreme situations in which an employment guarantee would prove an intolerable burden. The case for such systems is probably strongest for those situations in which government policy is the controlling factor in job security, such as defense-related employment or industries threatened by foreign competition.

It seems unrealistic, however, to expect *extensive* employment guarantees to develop through private collective bargaining. Existing labor legislation produces great variations in union power across the economy. We have been very reluctant to tailor these laws to the realities of individual industries. And so long as a single code is applied more or less uniformly, it is very difficult to give unions the power to obtain guarantees in sectors where they are weak without creating intolerable concentrations of power in sectors where unions are already strong.

The alternative to efforts to foster guarantees through collective bargaining is simply to impose such guarantees by law. This might be done either by direct prohibition of terminating employment or by a system of fines (or enforced severance pay). To a certain extent, fines are already inherent in the "experiencing rating" provisions of the unemployment insurance system; and the kind of continuity of policy so highly prized in American politics could be preserved by strengthening them. Fines are to be preferred to prohibition in principle since they can be tailored to different situations without risking perverse incentives. For example, the penalty for discharge should probably be related to age and seniority, but prohibition would create an incentive to fire the employee before he reaches the critical age or seniority date. With fines, this can be avoided by making the fine a continuously increasing function of seniority. (If it is linked to age it will discourage the hiring of older workers.) I am under the impression that something of this sort has emerged in France as an attempt to monetize legal prohibitions of discharge.

The cost of all of these efforts to further stabilize employment in the primary sector will be increased pressure to transfer variations in demand to the secondary sector. These proposals must be reviewed in this light. To do this adequately requires a much more elaborate view of the dual labor market distinction than I have thus far developed, or have time to develop in the space which remains. It is perhaps possible to sketch briefly some critical elements. These involve two basic points. First, the lower-class workers seeking upward mobility with whom this essay is concerned are not the only people in the secondary market. This sector also includes youth whose intermittent work patterns are connected with their preoccupation with school and leisure time activities and who have a great deal of flexibility in their income needs and in the timing of their work activites. A number of working women whose first commitment is to family responsibilities are also found in the secondary market, as are first-generation immigrants working to accumulate a fixed sum of money and planning to return to their native homes. For these people, the kind of short-duration jobs generated by the efforts of primary employers to evade permanent commitments during temporary peaks in demand are not a major problem, particularly if the economy is at full employment so that new jobs appear as older ones run their course. So long as one can separate and free the disadvantaged workers for whom confinement to secondary jobs is not part of a socially acceptable life pattern, the existence of a secondary sector per se need not constitute a social problem.

Employment in the secondary sector is not composed solely of the temporary employment transferred from the primary market during peak periods of demand. A number of secondary jobs are of inherently short duration: seasonal jobs in some forms of construction; seasonal agricultural work; resort, hotel, and kitchen jobs; and so on. Other secondary jobs are relatively permanent but for one reason or another are adjusted to a transient labor force (menial jobs in hospitals, for example). It is possible to stabilize many of these employment opportunities. A number of the inherently short-duration jobs can be built into some continuous employment experience through the development of hiring hall arrangements of the kind that unions in the construction and maritime industries use to give continuity in employment to their members. Existing labor legislation tends to penalize such arrangements (construction and maritime unions are protected more by their own skill monopolies than by the law), but it would be possible to compensate for this either by substituting governmental arrangements, as on the New York waterfront, or by changing labor law. Much could be done to change the jobs that are already stable—and some that are not—by amending existing legislation to encourage union organization among employees in agriculture and in the public and nonprofit sectors.

What these considerations suggest, in short, is that both the composition of workers in the secondary sector and the composition of jobs are susceptible to rearrangement through public policy. It may be possible to reduce through policy the number of jobs now in the secondary sector. The level can be reduced not simply so that disadvantaged workers are no longer required to fill them but so that the remaining force of workers—those for whom a short-term job carries no social stigma—is large enough to handle the increased spillover of temporary work that more stringent employment guarantees in the primary sector would create.

Mention should be made of the behavioral problems of disadvantaged workers now in the secondary sector. The preceding discussion has proceeded as if the secondary sector were a phenomenon related exclusively to the character of jobs. This is clearly an oversimplification, however. Experience with manpower programs over the last decade suggests that many workers have considerable trouble adjusting to the requirements of primary jobs when such jobs become available to them. At least one of their problems is the monotony of work in the primary sector, and this particular barrier should be reduced by the reforms proposed above. But many of these difficulties appear to reflect a life-style off the job, in their homes and neighborhoods. In this sense, the home environment and the work environment are adjusted to each other. It is impossible to know which, if either, is cause or effect, but it is undoubtedly true that the fact that one is embedded in the other makes it difficult to change either. None-theless, it is also true that we know quite a bit about how to change the work environment both through attaching financial rewards and penalties to certain employment characteristics and through making institutional changes. I personally am impressed by the ingenuity of enterprises in inducing workers to respond to their needs when management feels a compelling reason to do so. I tend to discount all of the discouraging experience of the manpower and poverty programs because they were not accompanied by any strong pressures upon employers. Where such pres-sures in the form of riots or civil rights suits did exist, the results were more encouraging. Still, it is ultimately a matter of faith that workers will respond, and respond in a relatively short space of time, to changes in the work environment; a matter of faith and also, I should say, a matter of judgment as to where, in the face of uncertainty, the greatest social costs of certain policies lie. In the United States, the social cost of changing the economic and institutional environment faced by a private employer is never adjudged small, but it must be smaller than the cost of attempting to tamper directly with the home and family or of ignoring the poor and underprivileged to whom the American ideal has promised so much.

In closing, it would seem important to point out at this time, when it is becoming fashionable once more to argue that the significant characteristics of man are determined by heredity or by events in early childhood, that the difference between the working class and the lower class, and between secondary and primary work, are consistent with quite a different set of facts. However frozen certain behavioral traits may be by early experience, much of the behavior associated with work undergoes fundamental changes quite late in life. In virtually all social classes, work histories in adolescence involve a very weak labor market commitment and an erratic pattern of work and attendance which appears to be embedded in leisure time activities. Middle-class and working-class youth then settle down in their twenties to a pattern of regular and very routine work. This settling down appears to be associated with marriage and family formation and to be something that happens not to an individual alone but to most of his close friends as well. Among lower-class youth, this transition frequently fails to occur, and the failure of the transition to a stable job is accompanied by a higher rate of failure in family formation. It seems plausible, therefore, that what is involved is a series of reinforcing events. It may not be enough, in other words, to find a stable job in order to make a transition to a stable work pattern. It may be necessary to find such a job at the time one is getting married. It may also be necessary for this to occur at the time one's friends find jobs in order to enforce the new life-style that the primary job market requires. For the lower classes, there are just not enough stable jobs to make the probability high that all these events will happen simultaneously. If this is what is going on, then an increase in the number of stable jobs may alone be sufficient to free disadvantaged workers from the syndrome in which they are trapped.

Notes

1. Much of this research is summarized in David Gordon, *Theories of Poverty and Unemployment* (Lexington, Mass.: D. C. Heath, 1972).

2. Michael J. Piore, "On-the-Job Training in the Dual Labor Market," in *Public-Private Manpower Policies,* ed. Arnold Weber et al. (Madison, Wis.: Industrial Relations Research Association, 1969), pp. 101–132; idem, "Jobs and Training," in *The State and the Poor,* ed. Samuel H. Beer and Richard E. Barringer (Cambridge, Mass.: Winthrop, 1970), pp. 53–83.

3. On-the-job training generally represents an investment either by the employer in his work force or by the worker in himself. When employment is temporary, the employer certainly has no incentive to make such an investment. If the worker had an incentive, the employer might find it worthwhile to structure his work environment so that workers could train themselves; but in secondary work, not only is employer attachment temporary, but occupational and industrial attachment is as well.

4 Perspectives on Women and Work in America

Isabel V. Sawhill

In looking at the special problems of women in the world of work, one finds an environment that is very much in flux. Although one can discuss at least some of the causes and consequences of the observed changes, a critical evaluation of the picture that emerges must rest on some normative assumptions. Thus, it is not as difficult where women and work are concerned to say what *is* as it is to say what *should* be. The fact is that the welfare of women may not always be synonymous with the welfare of men (or of children). Furthermore, since women are a diverse group, improving the lot of some could impair that of others. There are some women who have made a large investment in the present scheme of things and their status is undermined if the rules of the game are changed too rapidly. There are others who are pressing for a radical revision in the sexual division of labor and a restructuring of the institutions of marriage and child care. Although these conflicts of interest should not be exaggerated, they do pose obvious problems for public policy. In general, there may be no unambiguous way to identify a change for the better, given the lack of consensus in this area.

There are, however, a number of more modest goals that policy makers may wish to adopt, including greater equality of opportunity (equity) and better utilization of human resources (efficiency). The very act of studying women as a separate group is evidence that being female implies that status in our society is still largely determined by sex as well as other circumstances of birth—a fact that should be an affront to our democratic ideals. Thus, true equality of opportunity requires new options for women. In addition, women can furnish the talent and energies needed to build a healthier society if they are given the opportunity to participate more fully in the world outside the home. These ideas about equity and efficiency are not new; they are rather widely accepted and have been around long enough to be respectable. There is, of course, the possibility that they may miss the point. Work, especially "meaningful work," may increasingly be an end in itself, a means of personal fulfillment, or a source of personal worth. Lester Thurow has aptly described this phenomenon:

Unfortunately, the conventional wisdom ignores the non-economic benefits of work—benefits that seem to be superior goods. I make interesting friends there; I do interesting things; it defines my status; it makes me eligible for the non-monetary rewards of the community. The wants satisfied in the production process may be more important than the wants satisfied by it. An hour of work may well be more enjoyable than an hour of leisure. If the conventional myth about the superiority of leisure was held only by economists making forecasts, it would not be a serious problem, but unfortunately it also seems to be held by public policy makers.[1]

With these issues in mind, we can turn to a closer examination of work in the lives of women. Almost all women work unless they are students, disabled, or elderly. Some work in the market for pay, others work in the home, and many do a little of both. In what follows, we will look first at their market work and then at their home work. This will be followed by a discussion of the earnings and job opportunities of women in the labor force. Finally, some attention will be given to the possible social consequences of changes in the earnings and employment of women outside the home.

Market Work

Trends in Participation
American women have always worked—it is only the nature of their productive contribution that has changed. During the colonial period, most of their work was carried on at home. Women did the spinning, weaving, sewing, and related work not only for their own families but also as part of the domestic system of industry which prevailed until the beginning of the nineteenth century. In addition, many were employed as servants. In the

late eighteenth and early nineteenth centuries women began moving from home to factory to become operatives in the new textile mills, and they were increasingly utilized as teachers. By the end of the nineteenth century, they were finding employment as office workers and salesclerks. During the twentieth century, census statistics document a tremendous expansion in the employment of women, especially in the growing number of white-collar occupations. The result has been a dramatic increase in the proportion of the labor force that is female. Whereas in the early nineteenth century probably no more than one out of every twenty workers was female, by 1890, one out of every six was female, and by 1960 one out of every three.[2]

The increases in female labor force participation have been particularly large since 1940. In fact, it has been argued that some of the pre-1940 increases may be a statistical artifact created by improvement in census procedures with respect to the enumeration of working females. Any explanation of these trends must therefore deal with the *acceleration* in participation rates in the postwar period and the changing composition of the female labor force that has made this tremendous expansion possible.[3]

At the turn of the century, the typical female worker was young and single. As late as 1940, only 30 percent of working women were married and living with their husbands, whereas today about 60 percent fall in this category. In short, most of the growth of the female labor force in the postwar period is due to the increased employment of mature married women, many of whom enter or reenter the labor force once their children are grown or in school. More recently, there has also been a rapid increase in the participation rates of younger married women, including those with children under six or in school.

The result is that statistics on the composition of the current female labor force show that many different categories of women are working, and working for different reasons. Furthermore, these women are quite similar to those who stay home with respect to marital status, age, education, and other characteristics. If one were to try to identify the "typical" female worker she would be middle-aged, married to a man earning $5,000 to $7,000 per year, high school educated, and employed as a secretary. She might well have several school-age children and be working for financial reasons or to provide her family with a new car or home improvements that it could not otherwise afford. Her earnings would increase family income by about 25 percent and might permit her lower-middle-income family to achieve middle-class status.[4]

Causes of Increased Participation

While the long-run historical data show increasing labor force rates for women, they show decreasing rates for males (chiefly younger and older males) and, on balance, little variation in the total proportion of the population at work. In attempting to explain these trends, social scientists have turned to an analysis of demographic, economic, and cultural variables.[5]

Demographic variables. Changes in the composition of the population (by sex, age, race, nativity, marital status, residence, and family size) can have an effect on labor force participation. For example, changes in the ratio of females to males in the working-age population would tend to increase the ratio of females to males in the labor force even without any change in participation rates. Similarly, urbanization and smaller families could be expected to increase the proportion of women in paid employment. The empirical evidence suggests that none of these factors has been of great importance in explaining changes in the sex composition of the labor force, however. In other words, changes in participation rates within demographic categories have been much more significant in explaining the observed trends than changes in demographic composition.

Economic variables. Economists postulate that as income rises people respond either by working more or by working less. They may work more because higher wages make each hour of leisure more expensive, or they may work less because a higher income permits them to "afford" more hours of leisure. Most empirical evidence has indicated that the latter effect is the stronger one: as incomes have risen over time, the workweek and the workday have been shortened, retirement has been earlier, and schooling has been prolonged. In addition, cross-sectional studies reveal an inverse relationship between the work rates of married women and husbands' incomes. The major piece of evidence to the contrary is the increased labor force participation of women over time in the face of continually improving standards of living.

A major step in resolving this paradox was taken by Jacob Mincer in his analysis of the determinants of the labor force participation of married women. Mincer's contribution was to suggest that women who seek employment are not necessarily foregoing leisure as much as they are substituting work in the market for work in the home. His empirical study showed that women's market work is negatively correlated with husband's income but that it is even more strongly related (positively) to their own earnings. As the earnings opportunities of married women have improved, these women have responded by entering the labor force in large numbers. It is simply too "expensive" for them to stay home. This movement from home to market has undoubtedly been facilitated by the declining importance of work in the home as a result of smaller families and the greater availability of laborsaving devices and commercial substitutes for home-produced goods and services (baby-sitters, nursery schools, restaurant meals, commercial laundries, prepared foods, electrical appliances, and so forth). But these factors have probably not been the underlying determinants of the observed change. First, they may be a consequence as well as a cause of women's working. Second, they are not consistent with the timing of the change: the acceleration of female labor force participation rates in the postwar period coincided with higher fertility rates and increasing shortages of domestic servants, while most of the improvements in technology within the home took place long before the observed upsurge in female employment.

In a recent study of the growth of the female labor force, concentrating on the 1940–60 period, Valerie Oppenheimer presents many of the above arguments and others to support her conclusion that "the most likely explanation of the postwar rise in the female work rate is that an increasing number of women have been drawn into the labor force in response to an expansion in job opportunities. In other words, it appears that demand has been the dominant factor in the situation, and supply has adjusted itself to demand."[6] Underlying this thesis is the idea that there is a specific demand for *female* labor as a result of the sex typing of certain occupations and industries that expanded rapidly in recent years. Simultaneous with this increase in demand, there was a decline in the availability of young, unmarried women, as girls stayed in school longer and married earlier, forcing employers to turn to alternative sources of labor—older, married women. The rapid increase since 1960 in the employment rates of mothers with young children suggests that the strong demand for *female* labor may be partly responsible for pulling this group into the market as well.[7]

These conclusions are further strengthened by studies that show that (1) the labor force participation of women is highest in the areas where employment opportunities for women are greatest (such as Washington, D.C.); and

(2) the labor force participation of women is highly responsive to wartime demand and the ebb and flow of the business cycle.[8]

Finally, it is well known that better-educated women are much more likely to seek employment than the less well educated. In 1968, participation rates were 17 percent for those with less than five years of schooling, 31 percent for those with eight years, 48 percent for those graduating from high school, 54 percent for college graduates, and 71 percent for those with any education beyond college.[9] If one keeps in mind that participation is inversely related to husband's income and that well-educated women tend to marry high-income men, these statistics again suggest that women's employment is highly sensitive to their own earnings potential. A large group of women who are able to find well-paid and interesting work are not staying home even when they can afford to. This could be partly because the jobs open to well-educated women provide not only better pay but also better working conditions and higher status than that of a housewife, whereas jobs open to less well-educated women have the opposite characteristics. In other words, women prefer semiskilled work at home to unskilled work in the market, but they prefer skilled work in the market to either of these alternatives.

The implication is that if women are provided with more challenging and higher-paid job opportunities, many more will opt to leave the home. In the process of doing so, they will not be foregoing leisure as much as they will be changing jobs—that is, substituting work in the market for work in the home or possibly leisure consumed on the job for leisure consumed at home.

Cultural variables. Although economic variables appear to be strategic in understanding the greater employment of women outside the home, they undoubtedly interact with a variety of social or cultural variables in a rather complex fashion. Certainly the attitudes of women themselves (as well as those of their husbands, relatives, and friends) and the willingness of employers to hire women should not be neglected. Although it is difficult to interpret what little hard evidence there is on this question, one is left with the impression that attitudes adjust to changes in the facts rather than that they are the underlying cause of such changes. Nevertheless, once change is initiated, the gradual shift in attitudes that follows helps to create secondary waves of activity which sustain or build on the initial momentum.

Most of the public opinion polls of the thirties and forties showed that the great majority of men and women disapproved of married women working (except to support the war effort). More surprising perhaps is the fact that as late as 1960, a poll conducted by the University of Michigan's Survey Research Center indicated that only 34 percent of the husbands polled had favorable or qualifiedly favorable attitudes toward working wives in spite of the fact that 38 percent of the wives in the study were working at least part-time. Another survey, carried out by Leland Axelson in 1961, found that the husband's attitude depended very strongly on whether his wife was working or not.[10] Although it is impossible to say whether the husband's feelings are cause or consequence of his wife's employment, the latter interpretation seems more consistent with the relatively small change in attitude in spite of a radical change in the facts.

The polls also show that the major reason for people's disapproval of employment for married women revolves around the family responsibilities of these women—but a significant minority also believes that women who do not need to support themselves should not compete with men for scarce jobs.

Home Work

Although more and more women are seeking paid employment, the majority of the female population of working age is still engaged in keeping house. It has been estimated that married women spend an average of forty hours per week on housework while their husbands spend about four hours per week. When aggregate hours of work in the home are added to aggregate hours of market work, we find that women end up doing a slightly higher proportion of society's total work (paid and unpaid) during a given year than men.[11]

Juanita Kreps calculates that the 1960 GNP would have increased by $105 billion (or by over one-sixth) if all wives without jobs (aged eighteen and over) and without preschool children had been employed in the market economy. Although she does not claim that these women would make any greater productive contribution in the market than they do in the home, she does suggest that our failure to include the value of housewives' services in the national income may have important consequences for the social status attached to this occupation: "Despite our protests that growth in income is not to be equated with improvements in welfare; that society places a high value on the services of wives in the home and in the community; that the absence of a price tag on a particular service does not render it valueless— despite these caveats, the tendency to identify one's worth with the salary he earns is a persistent one. This tendency is not peculiar to men who earn salaries; it pervades as well the thinking of women who work at unpaid jobs."[12]

Although the increased availability of laborsaving devices and commercial goods for use within the home would appear to have "automated" the housewife out of a job—or at least out of a full-time job—what little evidence there is suggests that there has been surprisingly little reduction in the hours devoted to work in the home.[13] This may reflect (1) the substitution of quality (for instance, higher standards of cleanliness) for quantity; (2) the rather small improvement in productivity possible in the home due to the small scale of operations and the limited prospects for substituting capital for labor where many services, especially child care, are involved; and (3) the tendency for work (reported or actual) to fill the time available.

Rewards for Working

The Earnings Differential

The differences in the earnings of men and women are astonishingly large. In 1971, among year-round, full-time workers, men earned an average of $9,399 while women earned $5,593 (or only 60 percent as much).

One cannot conclude from the existence of an earnings gap that there is unequal pay for equal work (where the latter is defined as performing the same duties on the same job in the same establishment). The fact is that women workers are concentrated in the lowest-paying jobs and are rarely found doing the same work as men. What we see instead is separate labor markets, where jobs are socially labeled for "men only" or "women only."

The resulting sexual division of labor is pervasive. In one study, more than half of all working women were found in "female" occupations in 1960 (that is, those jobs in which more than 70 percent of the workers were women). And this underestimates the extent of segregation due to the nature of the census statistics used.[14] Women become secretaries, nurses, schoolteachers, waitresses, and department-store saleswomen. Men become plumbers, doctors, engineers, school administrators, and automobile salesmen. Once such a division of labor becomes established, it tends to be self-perpetuating, since each sex is socialized, trained, and counseled into certain jobs and not into others.

The particular division of labor that emerges has little economic rationale. What is "men's work" in one period or place may become "women's work" under different circumstances. For example, schoolteaching and clerical work were once male occupations in the United States. Only recently have the occupations of bank teller and school crossing guard been feminized. In the Soviet Union, 79 percent of the doctors, 37 percent of the lawyers, 32 percent of the engineers, and 76 percent of the economists are female.[15] And in western Europe, one finds women dispersed throughout the occupational structure to a much greater extent than in the United States. Thus, cross-cultural and historical situations suggest that the present occupational structure does not reflect basic and unchanging differences in temperament or ability between the sexes.

What is responsible, then, for the occupational segregation and, ultimately, the lower earnings of women? Are women in some way less qualified for the better-paid positions? In attempting to answer these questions, social scientists have carefully examined the existing data.[16] Their studies have shown that there are no important differences between working men and women where schooling, age, race, and geographical distribution are concerned. Such factors as unionism and excessive absenteeism play a very minor role, if any, in explaining the lower earnings of women. It is true that many married women work intermittently and thus fail to accumulate the on-the-job experience that men have, but several studies have shown that women who do work continuously are not much better off than those who don't. It is the *quality* rather than the *quantity* of their work experience that holds their earnings down. They seldom work in the kinds of occupations that would enable them to acquire valuable skills and advance to more responsible positions.

In short, there appears to be at least a 30 percent gap in the earnings of men and women even after adjustments have been made for differences in educational background, years of experience, and similar factors. The only way in which one can "explain" this gap is to adjust for differences in occupational composition by sex. But this does not settle the question of why women are relegated to the lower-paying, less demanding jobs, why their actual contribution to the economy is far below what they could reasonably be expected to produce on the basis of their education, ability, and work experience. In other words, the occupational status of women is not consistent with their capabilities; it represents the major symptom of an opportunity structure that is much more limiting for women than for men.

In a further probe into the causes of existing occupational segregation by sex, two factors appear to be of some importance. First, because of the intermittent nature of their employment, women are often assigned to occupations in which there is virtually no on-the-job training or "learning while earning" which so often provide career progression for men. As a result, their earnings do not increase as they gain additional experience; the male-female earnings gap widens with age. Even more surprising is the fact that this kind of flat age-earnings profile is almost as characteristic of career-oriented women who work continuously as it is for those with more limited work experience. Apparently, career-oriented women suffer a kind of "guilt by association" with other women or are subjected to "statistical discrimination" as females. In short, employers do not hire women for jobs for which there are significant training investments because of their fear that women will leave before the training costs are recouped.

Data on turnover rates and job tenure by sex reveal that these fears are not entirely unjustified. In 1968, monthly quit rates averaged 2.2 percent for males and 2.6 percent for females in manufacturing industries, while median years on current jobs in all industries were 4.8 for males and 2.4 for females. The higher quit rates for women are in part a consequence of their lower occupational status, however, and adjustment for this fact reduces the turnover differential substantially.[17] The remaining differences appear to be related to the home responsibilities of women, and, in the absence of a revolution in sex roles, female employees will continue to be a "poor risk," although not as poor as some employers seem to believe.

The second, more important factor confining women to low-paying occupations is cultural in origin and is related to deeply held views about "women's sphere" and the functions that they have traditionally performed. Many of the occupations in which women are found are closely linked to their homemaking role; others to their socialization as male helpmates. Conversely, occupations from which women are excluded tend to be those that involve "nonfeminine" pursuits or that necessitate supervision of other employees. The result of this cultural discrimination is to crowd women into a limited number of jobs, and the pressure of excess supply lowers wages below the level that would otherwise prevail.[18]

Public Policy on Sex Discrimination

The principal laws and executive orders dealing with sex discrimination in employment include (1) the Equal Pay Act of 1963, requiring equal pay for equal work on the same job in the same establishment; (2) Title VII of the Civil Rights Act of 1964, prohibiting discrimination in hiring, promotion, and all other aspects of employment; (3) Executive Order 11246, as amended by 11375 (1968), prohibiting discrimination by federal contractors and requiring that affirmative action programs be developed and carried out under the threat of contract cancellation; and (4) Executive Order 11478 (1969), prohibiting discrimination in covered positions in the federal government. These laws and executive orders are supplemented by additional legislation at the state and local levels.

The potential usefulness of these measures depends, of course, upon the way they are enforced, but even with maximum utilization and enforcement they may not be fully effective, for the reasons that follow.

Equal pay laws do not get at the root of the problem and may actually have adverse consequences. As the evidence above shows, discrimination usually leads to job segregation, not to unequal pay. Even before passage of the Equal Pay Act, there were few cases of women being paid less than men on the same job, and such practices explained only a very minor proportion of the total earnings differential.[19] Moreover, equal pay laws may actually increase job segregation and crowd women into dead-end jobs because they prevent employers from creating a wage differential to offset the added risks of hiring women in more responsible jobs. Young women are being penalized not so much from being *underpaid* as from being *underutilized*. In short, this legislation tends to have largely symbolic rather than practical value (although one would not want to forget about the $17,415,811 paid in back wages to 51,160 persons as of May 20, 1970, as a result of this legislation).[20]

Equal employment opportunity legislation is clearly of much greater significance, especially when it involves affirmative action programs requiring employers to take the initiative in recruiting and promoting women for all types of work, prohibits sex-segregated want ads, and concentrates on discriminatory patterns and practices. These measures help to break down some of the cultural barriers to equal opportunity. Additional programs should be designed to cope with *institutional* sexism, not just *individual* prejudice. Many of our present laws and court procedures help to protect women and minorities from overt acts of exclusion but are of little use in eliminating customary patterns of behavior and cultural stereotypes which limit opportunities for all but the most aggressive members of these groups.

In the meantime, those faced with enforcing existing laws have the choice of increasing the probability of apprehension or of increasing the cost to those apprehended, since the "expected cost" of ignoring the law is the product of these two factors. Given the difficulties (and costs) of detecting the prohibited behavior, the latter route seems somewhat more promising.

Education is also important. The role of work in the lives of women is expanding enormously, yet employers and women alike continue to behave as if it is not a permanent feature of American life. The increase in the life expectancy of women from forty-eight years in 1900 to seventy-three years today, combined with earlier marriage and childbearing, means that today's young women must find new activities to fill out their later years and that they must be made aware of the need to plan for new life-styles in their adult years.[21]

As women's commitment to work becomes greater, employers will be more willing to provide them with on-the-job training and to advance them to more responsible, higher-paying positions. This, in turn, will encourage female workers to stay in the labor force longer. Employers need to be made aware of the way in which job opportunities affect a woman's commitment to the labor market. As noted above, the excessive turnover of female employees and their more tenuous attachment to the labor force are in part a function of the kind of work they typically do.

Social Consequences of Changes in Economic Status

Government efforts to eliminate discrimination in employment are commonly justified on the grounds that such discrimination is contrary to the American creed of equality of opportunity and thus is morally wrong. Yet, as Milton Friedman astutely observes, legislation in this area may constitute an interference with free preferences—an interference as inimical to a democratic society as curbs on freedom of speech. He argues that the appropriate recourse of those of us who believe that a particular criterion such as sex or color is irrelevant is to persuade our fellows to be of like mind, not to use the coercive power of the state to force them to act in accordance with our principles.[22]

What the Friedman view of the world ignores is that more than a question of legislating morality is involved. The existence of discriminatory practices has specific consequences for social and economic welfare. In particular, sex discrimination has adverse consequences for (1) the distribution of income, (2) the level of economic output, (3) the achievement of a noninflationary, full-employment level of income, and (4) the rate of population growth. In general, it could be argued that a discrimination-free society would have many public good qualities (ones that entail social benefits) that should not be ignored in formulating public policy. However, because greater equality for women in the working world would undoubtedly increase the labor force participation of women dramatically, and because it is difficult to forecast and evaluate the consequences of this for home and family life, personal welfare, and the relationship between the sexes, any such conclusion would have to be made in a gingerly and tentative fashion. In any case, one is still left with the ideal of equal opportunity as a rationale for moving in this direction.

Distribution of Income

As noted above, a great many studies have documented the fact that discrimination is a significant factor in reducing female income and, as such, contributes to a more unfavorable distribution of income and a greater incidence of poverty among female-headed families. In 1967 almost one-third of such families were living in poverty.[23] Moreover, in recent years the proportion of the poor in households headed by a woman has been *increasing*. Higher earnings and more job opportunities for this group would entice more of them into the labor force and provide a more adequate standard of living for the families of those already working.

Given the inverse relationship between husband's income and wife's labor force participation rate, higher earnings for women would tend to redistribute family income to those at the lower end of the income scale, especially in the lower-middle income brackets, where female participation is highest. This conclusion will be weakened to the extent that higher earnings for women are offset by lower earnings for men. (As Barbara Bergmann has suggested, nonworking wives may actually benefit from discrimination against women since it tends to increase their husbands' incomes.)[24] More research is needed before these distributional impacts can be estimated with any accuracy.

Level of Output

Economists are fond of pointing out that discrimination creates a loss of output (a lower GNP) for the economy as a whole. This occurs because resources are allocated by criteria other than "best person for the job" and because the productive contribution of certain groups is limited by discriminatory practices. Empirical studies indicate that the potential gains in efficiency from the elimination of racial discrimination are probably quite small.[25'] Although there are no comparable studies in the area of sex discrimination, the direct economic gains from eliminating this form of discrimination are probably small as well. On the other hand, there could be important second-order effects on the GNP, or on its rate of growth. For example, following a reduction in discrimination, women would have greater motivation to seek education and training if their earnings would be more nearly equal to those of men, and this increase in the efficiency of the labor force would have a positive effect on the total output of the economy.

Achievement of Full Employment without Inflation

Women face substantially higher unemployment rates than men, and the gap has been widening in recent years. (The 1972 rates were 6.6 and 4.9 percent respectively.) Economists have shown that the greater the dispersion of unemployment rates in an economy, the more difficult it is to achieve an acceptable trade-off between inflation and unemployment. The inflationary consequences of low unemployment rates for one group (in this case males) are not fully offset by the deflationary impact of high unemployment rates for another (in this case females). Thus, any policy that reduced this dispersion (even if it did not change the *average* unemployment rate) would decrease the rate of inflation associated with that level of unemployment.

It is sometimes suggested or implied that unemployment among women is less serious than it is among men, and that if the overall unemployment rate increases as women become a larger proportion of the labor force, it is not especially worrisome. But it must be remembered that women's status as "secondary workers" is largely the *result* of their lower earnings. Ironically, if there were less sex bias in employment opportunities, women's income would less frequently be the "marginal income," and there would probably be greater concern about their unemployment rates. In addition, self-supporting women, female family heads, and families dependent on the wife's earnings would be in a much less precarious position economically than they are now.

Rate of Population Growth

The U.S. Commission on Population Growth and the American Future recently recommended that "this nation should welcome and plan for a stabilized population."[26] The commission also proposed that "in order to neutralize the legal, social, and institutional pressures that historically have encouraged childbearing, as well as to equalize opportunities generally, we should eliminate discrimination based on sex by adopting the proposed Equal Rights amendment to the Constitution."[27] It is beyond the purview of this paper to discuss the pros and cons of population stabilization, but assuming that the nation wishes to move in the direction suggested by the commission, it is worth looking at the extent to which the social and economic status of women affects the birth rate. There is no question that women who work have fewer children than those who do not, although we are less sure what is cause and what is effect.[28] Moreover, the overall reduction in fertility during the 1960s may well have been at least partially caused by expanding opportunities for women. As Patsy Mink has suggested:

There have been encouraging signs over the past few years that people are having fewer children—accompanied by shifting social patterns of great interest to women. We are beginning to realize that the age-old tradition of keeping women "in the home" is not only destructive of equality, but may be the major contributor to excess population growth. Obviously, if a woman's only choice is to stay at home all day, for all of her life, she may as well have numerous children to occupy her time. If, on the other hand, we encourage policies which will permit women to choose other roles, many will leave the home and thus decide to have fewer children.[29]

Family Life
No assessment of the consequences of women's working would be complete without some mention of the implications for home and family life. More market work for women *could* lead to such outcomes as

• Less total home work (smaller families, smaller houses, greater substitution of commercial goods and services for home-produced items)
• Less leisure for women (or other family members)
• More home work on the part of men or other family members (and less market work)
• Deterioration in the quality of home work (lower housekeeping standards, "neglected" children)

Although from present trends it would seem that the first two alternatives are more likely, it is difficult to predict these outcomes at the present time. We do know that studies of the impact of maternal employment on the welfare of children have not found any significant effects.[30] Similarly, women who work report that they spend less time on housework and that much of what they did when they were full-time housewives was not essential.[31] As Betty Friedan has suggested, "housewifery" tends to expand to fill the time available. Finally, there appears to be some evidence that the domestic role has a negative effect on women's mental health.[32] For all of these reasons, fuller participation of women in the world outside the home can probably be encouraged without fear of adverse consequences.

Perhaps the more interesting question is what will happen to the division of labor between the sexes. Is the outcome of "more home work on the part of men" a realistic alternative? Many of those who are committed to women's liberation believe that it is an essential condition for real equality. As long as women have the primary responsibility for home and children, their contribution outside the home will be restricted and their sphere of influence circumscribed. This view of the world is held not only by the New Feminists but also by the Swedish government, which, in its 1968 report to the United Nations on the status of women in Sweden, suggested that "no rapid advancement of women in employment and the professions, politics, trade union activity, etc. is possible as long as men fail to assume that share of the work of the home which falls to them as husbands and fathers."[33]

If society were to move in this direction, there would be important ramifications for the working world. Hours of work would need to be modified. Moreover, the single-minded devotion of time and energy to a career that men are currently able to make might not be possible in a society where women did not provide the domestic and social infrastructure for such activities.

But perhaps the overriding issue that must be faced is the extent to which present arrangements provide real freedom of choice. Can women freely choose to work? Can men freely choose *not* to work? Clearly, cultural expectations rather than economic necessity have a way of predetermining the answers to such questions.

Notes

1. Lester C. Thurow, "The American Economy in the Year 2000," *American Economic Review* 62, no. 2 (May 1972): 443.

2. Stanley Lebergott, "The Pattern of Employment since 1800," in *American Economic History*, ed. Seymour E. Harris (New York: McGraw-Hill, 1961), p. 299.

3. Valerie K. Oppenheimer, *The Female Labor Force in the U.S.*, Institute of International Studies, Population Monograph no. 5 (Berkeley: University of California, 1970).

4. Data on the characteristics of female workers are from U.S. Department of Labor, *1969 Handbook on Women Workers;* Abbott L. Ferris, *Indicators of Trends in the*

Status of American Women (New York: Russell Sage Foundation, 1971); J. N. Hedges, "Women Workers and Manpower Demands in the 1970's," *Monthly Labor Review* 93, no. 6 (June 1970): 19–29.

5. This section draws heavily on work done by John D. Durand, *The Labor Force in the United States, 1890–1960* (New York: Social Science Research Council, 1948); Clarence D. Long, *The Labor Force under Changing Income and Employment* (Princeton: Princeton University Press, 1958); Glenn Cain, *Married Women in the Labor Force* (Chicago: University of Chicago Press, 1966); Jacob Mincer, "Labor Force Participation of Married Women: A Study of Labor Supply," in *Aspects of Labor Economics* (Princeton: Princeton University Press, 1962); Oppenheimer.

6. Oppenheimer, pp. 187–188.

7. Francine Blau Weisskoff, "Women's Place in the Labor Market," *American Economic Review* 62, no. 2 (May 1972): 162.

8. G. B. McNally, "Patterns of Female Labor Force Activity," *Industrial Relations,* May 1968; William G. Bowen and T. A. Finegan, *The Economics of Labor Force Participation* (Princeton: Princeton University Press, 1969); Oppenheimer.

9. *1969 Handbook on Women Workers,* p. 205.

10. These surveys are summarized in Oppenheimer.

11. James N. Morgan et al., *Productive Americans,* Survey Research Center Monograph 43 (Ann Arbor: University of Michigan, Institute for Social Research, 1966), p. 102; Juanita Kreps, *Sex in the Marketplace: American Women at Work* (Baltimore: Johns Hopkins Press, 1971), p. 69; Jessie Bernard, *Women and the Public Interest* (New York: Aldine, 1971), p. 74.

12. Kreps, p. 74.

13. Bernard, p. 74.

14. Weisskoff, p. 163.

15. Norton T. Dodge, *Women in the Soviet Economy: Their Role in Economic, Scientific, and Technical Development* (Baltimore: Johns Hopkins Press, 1966).

16. See Isabel V. Sawhill, "The Economics of Discrimination against Women: Some New Findings," *Journal of Human Resources,* summer 1973, for a review of this literature. The major studies have been done by James N. Morgan et al., *Income and Welfare in the United States* (New York: McGraw-Hill, 1962); Malcolm S. Cohen, "Sex Differences in Compensation," *Journal of Human Resources,* fall 1971; Victor Fuchs, "Differences in Hourly Earnings between Men and Women," *Monthly Labor Review,* May 1971; Ronald Oaxaco, "Sex Discrimination in Wages" (paper presented at a conference sponsored by the Woodrow Wilson School of Public and International Affairs, Princeton University, October 1971); Larry E. Suter and Herman P. Miller, "Components of Income Differences between Men and Career Women" (paper presented at the American Statistical Association Meetings, September 1971); Henry Sanborn, "Pay Differences between Men and Women," *Industrial and Labor Relations Review,* July 1964.

17. Sawhill, "Economics of Discrimination."

18. See Barbara R. Bergmann, "The Effect on White Incomes of Discrimination in Employment," *Journal of Political Economy,* March/April 1971, for a theoretical discussion of this crowding hypothesis.

19. Isabel V. Sawhill, "The Relative Earnings of Women in the United States" (Ph.D. diss., New York University, 1968).

20. Elizabeth O. Koontz, "Women as a Minority Group," in *Voices of the New Feminism,* ed. Mary Lou Thompson (Boston: Beacon Press, 1970), p. 83.

21. President's Commission on the Status of Women, *American Women* (Washington, D.C., 1963), p. 6.

22. Milton Friedman, *Capitalism and Freedom* (Chicago: University of Chicago Press, 1962), p. 115.

23. *1969 Handbook on Women Workers,* p. 31.

24. Barbara R. Bergmann, "The Economics of Women's Liberation," mimeographed (September 1971).

25. See, for example, Bergmann, "The Effect on White Incomes."

26. "Population: The U.S. Problem, the World Crisis," *New York Times,* April 30, 1972, supplement, p. 8.

27. Ibid.

28. Bernard, p. 168.

29. "Population," p. 10.

30. F. Ivan Nye and Lois W. Hoffman, *The Employed Mother in America* (Chicago: Rand McNally, 1963).

31. Ibid., p. 27.

32. Bernard, p. 75.

33. "Report to the United Nations, 1968: The Status of Women in Sweden," in *Voices of the New Feminism,* ed. Mary Lou Thompson (Boston: Beacon Press, 1970).

5 Middle Management

Emanuel Kay

The term "middle manager" is used widely but has no precise definition. It refers generally to those managers who are somewhere between the top executives of an organization and the first-level supervisors. For the purposes of this paper, I will call middle managers those who manage managers, supervisors, or professional and technical people and are not vice-presidents of functional or staff areas or general managers (that is, they have no profit and loss responsibilities).

This definition distinguishes middle managers from the top executives, who primarily set policy and deal with the total resources of the organization, and from the first line of supervision, which is often made up of people who are closely related to the employees they supervise in terms of background and experience. This definition tends to more clearly identify a group of managers who are responsible for the following activities:

• *Interpretation and implementation of organization policies and goals.* Middle managers interpret and translate the intentions of the top executives in terms of specific activities within their respective areas.

• *Management of subfunctional and staff specialties.* Basically they are specialists in their functional areas and manage a portion of the total function. For example, in a manufacturing operation they would be the managers of production, methods, and quality control. They are expected to provide an

This paper is a summary of a book, "The Crisis in Middle Management," to be published by the American Management Association.

area of expertise through their own knowledge and performance and through the persons they manage.

• *Lateral coordination.* They coordinate their efforts with each other to provide the smoothest and most efficient realization of their organization's goals.

The need to define this population and to study it in more depth stems from growing but nonsystematic evidence of managerial dissatisfaction. The popular literature, along with a great deal of personal experience in the last several years, strongly suggests to me certain problems in this group. Very little data have been collected about middle managers in terms of the above or any other specific definition. I will make use of all the data that are available, however, and attempt to draw some inferences.

One of the first statistical problems is to determine how many middle managers there are in our work force today. *Employment and Earnings,* a report of the U.S. Department of Labor, lists a category called "managers and administrators, except farms," and under this category there are further breakdowns into salaried workers, self-employed workers in retail trade, and self-employed workers except retail trade.[1] For our purposes, the middle managers would appear to fall into the salaried workers category. But since this category includes all managers at all levels, some correction is needed in order to estimate the number of middle managers in that population. In order to do this, I used the definition of middle management as given above to analyze positions on the organizational charts of ten institutions in aerospace, banking, retail sales, pharmaceuticals, electrical manufacturing, and tire manufacturing. I found that approximately two-thirds to three-quarters of the managers in these organizations fell into my definition of middle management. Using this as a rough guideline and applying it to the population of all managers, I have estimated that there are approximately 4.1 to 4.6 million middle managers in a total managerial work force of 6.2 million. In terms of the total work force of 80 million people, approximately 5.0 percent of the total work force are middle managers.

An examination of the 1971 *Manpower Report of the President* shows that the overall management population and, by deduction, the middle management population, remained a fairly constant proportion of the work force from 1958 to 1970.[2] This is in contrast to some rather significant growth in other occupational groups. In order to show the stability of the middle management population during those years, I computed the ratios of the 1970 statistics to the 1958 statistics for various occupational groups.

Table 5.1. Ratio between 1970 and 1958 Work Forces

Occupational Group	Ratio
Total employed	1.25
White-collar (total)	1.42
Professional and technical	1.60
Managers, officials, and proprietors	1.22
Clerical	1.50
Sales	1.22
Blue-collar (total)	1.19
Service (nonhousehold)	1.48
Service (household)	.79
Farm	.58

From the ratios shown in table 5.1, we see that significant growth has taken place in certain occupational groups (total white-collar, professional and technical, clerical, and nonhousehold service). The managerial group grew at approximately the same rate as the total work force. In effect, many new nonmanagerial positions were created in the 1958–1970 period without an increase in the percentage of managers in the work force who were managing these workers.

The importance of the middle management population is not in terms of their numbers, but rather in terms of what they do and where they are situated in the organization. In effect, we have 5 percent of the work force interpreting and implementing the intent of the top executives, coordinating day-to-day operations, providing functional expertise, and managing the productive functions of the organization.

If middle managers are experiencing a high degree of dissatisfaction with their situation, then we can only assume that their attitudes and actions in relation to the rest of the work force have negative consequences: the problems of middle managers are the problems of a portion of the work group whose effect goes far beyond their relatively small number.

Complaints of Middle Managers

In 1969 we began to get our first indication of discontent in the middle management ranks. The early statements of dissatisfaction stemmed from the change in values that middle managers saw in our society. They started to question the value of their work and the meaning of their jobs in their lives. In effect, they were responding to the values being expressed by younger employees. In 1970–71 another set of complaints were heard which related to the effects of the recession. After the expanding job market of the late 1960s, middle managers suddenly found themselves confronting a very harsh market. As might be expected, the dissatisfaction expressed during this period was more negative and was expressed more bitterly.

My analysis of middle management dissatisfaction is supported by a number of sources[3] and by my personal experience in industry. Using Frederick Herzberg's terms to categorize a variety of not always comparable data, I would argue that the perceived problems of middle managers generally fall into two categories. One category includes "hygiene" factors such as pay, security, and benefits. The second includes "motivators" such as job content, opportunities for growth and development, and responsibility.

Pay Compression

The most bitter hygiene complain of middle managers is that they receive inequitable salary treatment. This feeling generally is a result of what is referred to as "the compression effect"—the fact that the differential in salaries between longer-service and shorter-service employees has been narrowing over a period of many years. There are many reasons for this phenomenon, but in the case of middle managers two factors appear to be the most important:

(1) The individual's annual rate of salary increase tends to be highest early in his career and then to level off for a number of years (and, in some cases, actually to taper off toward the end of his career). It is not uncommon to find that the annual rate of increase starts to level off at about age thirty-five or forty. What this means is that older employees get smaller percentage increases than newer employees and that the larger percentages given to newer employees compress the differential between these two groups.

(2) In the late 1960s, salaries of starting employees were going up at a significantly higher rate than the annual increases given to employees already on the payroll. (This situation is generally attributed to the greater competition for recent college graduates during those years.) The compression caused by the higher starting rates themselves was compounded because they formed the base on which higher annual increases were given to a person early in his career—the dollar gap between older and newer employees being lessened at a much faster rate.

I have data from one major industrial corporation that illustrates the compression effect during the 1960–70 period. This organization is within the top twenty of the Fortune 500 List and is large enough and diversified enough to be fairly representative of American industry. The average annual rates of salary increase for this decade for individuals with various years of service were: 3.3 percent (twenty years), 3.7 percent (fifteen years), 4.2 percent (ten years), 4.4 percent (five years), 4.8 percent (one year), and 5.6 percent (less than one year). The rate of salary increase is thus inversely related to years of service, and the salaries of newer employees are compressed against the salaries of longer-service employees, the differential in salary decreasing over the years.

In a recent survey of 536 managers in departments not directly concerned with personnel or employee relations activities, researchers at the American Management Association found that salary inequity was the most significant complaint of middle managers.[4] Middle managers pointed not only to the erosion of their position relative to recent college graduates but also to the relatively large and well-publicized increases received by members of various unions in recent years. Pay is an important hygiene factor which, if not satisfactory, will arouse discontent. In the case of middle managers, the salary issue appears to have produced a strong negative effect already.

Job Insecurity

During unfavorable economic conditions like those of 1970–71, top management is forced to make difficult decisions concerning which employees should be terminated. The unemployment rate for middle managers went from slightly under 1 percent during 1966–69 to approximately 1.5 to 1.6 percent during 1970–71. This is a dramatic increase in the unemployment rate of a numerically stable group that traditionally has not experienced much unemployment.[5]

Much has been said about the length of time required for reemployment of middle managers, particularly those in their middle forties or older. There do not appear to be any statistics to support the contention that middle managers have to wait longer between jobs than other groups, but there is evidence that older people generally spend more time unemployed before they find their next job,[6] and to the extent that it is representative of the total work force we can say that older middle managers experience more difficulty than younger middle managers in terms of time needed to get another position. The significant thing about the 1970–71 recession with respect to middle managers is that they suddenly went from a traditionally low unemployment rate to a relatively high one. For the first time in many years, they felt threatened with the loss of a job. This experience and its attendant publicity will be a source of continuing concern for many middle managers for years to come. To them it is grim evidence that they are not in a uniquely favored and protected position just because they are the echelon immediately below the top executives.

Another aspect of job insecurity for middle managers relates to business mergers. I cannot find any statistics that deal with the specific effects of mergers on middle manager tenure, but from my extensive personal experience with middle managers I would say that a significant number believe that mergers have a negative effect. This may be one of the myths that has crept into the management folklore, but from the perspective of dissatisfaction, this perception is a "fact" that must be dealt with and is perhaps as important as the actual statistics.

Forced Early Retirement

Forced early retirement means that one is pressured, subtly or otherwise, to give up his job earlier than he had anticipated. During economic declines, some organizations resort to early retirements as a means of reducing the work force. In some cases, incentives such as supplemental benefits are offered to make early retirement more attractive; in others, employees are simply pressured. Forced early retirement generally is directed at older employees, who are within striking distance of normal retirement. The likelihood of their obtaining employment if they are forced to retire is low. They are nudged out of the work force, sometimes quite suddenly, before they have had an opportunity to prepare themselves psychologically.

The Boxed-in Feeling

An individual feels confined when he has almost no opportunity to move from his present job, when the only position for which he is considered qualified is the job he currently holds. The chain of events leading to this boxed-in feeling among middle managers is often as follows:

• The middle manager is hired as a college graduate in a functional specialty such as engineering, manufacturing, or finance.

• During his early years he is not rotated out of his functional area to broaden him and to test his interests.

• He is appointed as a manager because of his demonstrated functional competence.

• Over the years, particularly the earlier years, his salary is increased as a reflection of both his service and demonstrated performance.

• When he has been a middle manager for a number of years and feels the need for a change, he finds that it is difficult for him to move laterally (assuming that he is not going to move up) because (1) he lacks experience in other areas and (2) his salary is too high for his experience level in other functions or subfunctions.

He becomes vulnerable for a number of reasons:

• He is using "old skills" on an "old job" and has limited incentive to develop—unless it is for a promotion.

• He starts to develop a guarded and protective attitude about his job, defending its existence rather than adapting it and himself to changing conditions.

• During economic declines and mergers his position is risky, for he may be seen and dealt with as a rather narrow functional specialist.

Lack of Authority

One of the more common references to "motivators" that runs through the conversations of middle managers is: "We have responsibility but not authority." What they appear to be saying is that they are expected to produce results but that they have little influence over the policies and events that determine these results. Some extensive personal probing of middle managers about what they mean when they say they lack authority revealed a number of different elements:

• *Formal restrictions.* Every organization has limits on the authority of *all* ranks of managers. Formal restrictions usually cover such matters as levels of capital investment, adherence to pay and benefit systems, and recommendations for promotions. Middle managers typically will accept and be responsive to such restrictions if there are not too many, they make sense, and they are administered equitably.

• *Uncertainty.* Many middle managers indicate that they are not sure of the boundaries of their authority and that they usually define them through trial and error. The more venturesome ones step out and test the limits and occasionally are burned in the process. The less courageous ones play it safe, the result sometimes being that they do not exert as much authority as they should. Either way, their uncertainty creates problems both for them and for their organization.

• *Access to the decision-making process.* While they recognize the right and necessity for top management to make certain decisions and to promulgate policies, middle managers feel that their input is not solicited and perhaps not valued, and this often makes it difficult for them to support the decisions of their superiors.

● *Contingency.* Another concern has to do with their inability to act until someone else has acted, usually their boss. Middle managers have to wait until their manager makes a decision or takes some action, and the time delays by the other party create problems.

● *Lateral relations.* Middle managers usually cannot exert direct authority over each other. This is particularly troublesome when one middle manager is causing a problem for another. (This is a common situation since middle managers are called upon to coordinate the operations of an organization.)

Attitudes toward Middle Managers

The View of Superiors

Top management is aware, or is becoming aware, of discontent in the middle management ranks. Its typical reaction, perhaps conditioned by the 1970–71 recession, is to look upon it with disfavor.

● "Middle managers are unrealistic about their environment." Top executives tend to see middle managers as being impractical in their requests for facilities, personnel, and new or expanded programs. They feel that not everyone can always get everything he wants and that middle managers should realize this when their requests are turned down. (And they shouldn't complain so much.) They say that middle managers are not aware of the factors against which their proposals are weighed. And that, of course, is the problem. Middle managers are left to their own devices to rationalize turndowns.

● "They are unrealistic about their roles." Top executives attach considerable importance to their own roles as decision makers. They tend to strongly resist incursion by others on this prerogative. They see middle managers as meddling and at times feel they have to make it clear to middle managers "who makes decisions around here." There seems to be little desire to share decision-making powers with middle managers.

● "They don't realize that top executives have been under increased pressure in recent years." Top executives are under considerable stress to produce results for their organizations. They would like to enlist the aid of middle managers, and when they are unable to, they tend to become decidedly negative toward them. This negativism is at times reflected in an attitude of "If you don't like the way this company is run, then go elsewhere." While this is an understandable human reaction, the effect on middle managers can be damaging. In this type of environment, the better middle managers will in all probability take up the offer and leave, while those who remain behind will tend to withdraw—take fewer risks and propose fewer ideas. A harsh take-it-or-leave-it attitude of top management generally produces a more conforming and mediocre middle management.

● "They are obsolete, unambitious, and resistive to change." Top executives often react to symptoms without fully understanding the reasons for the behavior. Frequently they assume that the poor job performance of middle managers is the result of poor selection. They then look to younger employees as their hope for the future, thinking that they were selected by "better" techniques. But what they fail to recognize and deal with is the fact that the systems for organizing and designing jobs and developing people are at fault—that they tend to produce narrow, inflexible, and obsolete employees. They also fail to recognize that these systems will in time have the same effect on newer and younger employees.

In summary, top executives appear to recognize the symptoms of discontent. From what little evidence we have it appears that they are reacting in an unproductive manner, however. They seem somewhat defensive about middle managers and frustrated in their attempts to deal with them. There also seems to be a built-in conflict between the role of the top executive and the role of the middle manager—particularly as it relates to the exercise of influence. The role of the former has traditionally been one of decision and policy making. There is little or no evidence at this point to indicate that he is willing to share more of this influence with the middle manager. And such a willingness would be one of the key solutions to the problems facing the middle manager.

The View of Subordinates

There is another set of perceptions of middle managers that not only affect them personally but also affect the significance and desirability of their jobs. This is the view that their subordinates have of them. There are not even any "soft" sources to support my contentions about how subordinates view middle managers; what follow are my impressions based on experiences in a large number of business organizations over the last three years. These observations are included because middle managers regard their subordinates' perceptions as quite important.

• "Middle managers have no influence." Subordinates feel that middle managers have little weight with top executives. Many of the things that middle managers go to top management for involve subordinates (pay increases, facilities, equipment, money for new programs, additional help). And subordinates can readily see the results of their manager's attempts to get approval. In many instances he is not even able to provide a good reason for a refusal because he has not been given one.

• "They're indecisive." Many middle managers give the impression of being indecisive because, in fact, they are not in a position to decide. The need to take matters elsewhere for approval usually involves time and conveys the impression that the manager is not capable of making up his mind. It also gives organizations a highly bureaucratic overtone, and the middle manager is seen as just one more cog.

• "They're inflexible." One of the key roles assigned to middle managers is to implement organizational policies and practices. They are at times put in the position of having to apply a policy in a manner that does not make great sense to subordinates. In these cases, loyal and conscientious middle managers will attempt to defend the policy and its application. This only serves to strengthen the perception on the part of subordinates that the manager is acting in a bureaucratic manner.

• "They have an undesirable job." Subordinates, particularly the more sophisticated ones, develop a fairly good perception of the middle manager's role and the bind he is in. What they see causes them to view the job as one not to be aspired to. This may create a situation in which less talented people are attracted to middle management jobs. (We already have ample evidence that this is what is happening at the first level of supervision. Many blue-collar employees no longer see the foreman's job as desirable or worthwhile and turn down opportunities for such positions. In my judgment, it is just a matter of time before the same thing will happen to middle manager jobs.)

How Middle Managers Cope

Much of human behavior is an attempt by people to deal adequately with their environment to satisfy their needs and to maintain a reasonable psychological equilibrium. It is not surprising, therefore, to find a pattern of coping mechanisms among middle managers with respect to their work environment. Some of these mechanisms are individually oriented while others represent a potential for group action.

Job and Career Changes

Many who see their jobs as unfulfilling attempt to correct the situation either by changing jobs or by changing careers. Others change jobs because their company has been relocated or because they have been terminated. If someone changes jobs on a panic basis, he can very quickly be put back into a situation similar to the one he left. In part this is because most companies do not vary significantly from each other. Someone who changes his job in his late thirties or early forties and who does not get a net improvement in his opportunity to grow and develop is in a more difficult position to make another change. Job hopping at this age is extremely difficult unless the economic circumstances are very favorable. Job changes at this age also force one to give up certain security factors, such as service perquisites and vested rights in pension programs.

Dale Hiestand provides some systematic data about people over thirty-five who attempt to change their careers.[7] His limited data is based on a sample of seventy individuals who were pursuing graduate education at Columbia University. Those in full-time graduate study were there because (1) they felt their skills were obsolete, (2) they had developed new interests, (3) new professions had emerged since their graduation from college and they were interested in these new professions, or (4) they had unsatisfied career aspirations, that is, they were entering a field that they could not enter earlier in their careers. Hiestand cites several significant factors that caused or enabled these people to seek career changes. Some had already raised their families, and their children had left home. This tended to reduce their financial burden and give them the economic resources as well as the time to pursue further education. For many of the older students, the economics of the situation were quite good. Some, such as retired military officers, had pensions that supported their educational activities. Others, who had lost their jobs, had enough personal resources as well as severance pay to support an educational effort. Hiestand also cites some data from other universities that give us an indication of the number of people seeking mid-career changes. For example, in 1966, 16.5 percent of the professional and graduate students at New York University (full- and part-time) were over thirty-five, at Columbia University 20.4 percent, and at the University of Chicago 8.7 percent.

Hiestand feels that the number of part-time students over thirty-five will increase, although he offers no estimate of the rate of increase. To support this contention, he points out the growing acceptability in our society for people in their middle years to make a career change, the greater felt need on the part of individuals in this age bracket to make a change, and the generally favorable trend of economic circumstances (both individually and nationally) that promises a financial basis of support for continuing education. One of the significant barriers to this trend, he says, is the attitude of the administrators in educational institutions toward older students. On the average, educational administrators expressed a *negative* attitude toward older students. They generally felt that older students did not complete the programs they started. When pressed, however, they could not present any concrete data to support this notion. The only evidence comes from medical schools and shows that the dropout rate is a function of the age at which a student starts his training. It would appear that if career changes are to take place through educational effort by the individual, some work will have to be done in universities with regard to the attitudes held by educational administrators toward older students. In passing, I might add that administrators' attitudes toward older women students appeared to be more negative than those toward older men students.

At this point, we can only guess at the number of middle managers who are contemplating a career change via an educational effort or the number who might actually benefit from a move of this type. What we are able to see is that it is possible to make such a move.

We should not assume that additional education is the only route to a second career. I have been following seven people who shifted from technical or professional careers in business organizations to second careers as entrepreneurs where additional education was not pursued or was only peripheral to the change. While it would be foolhardy to attempt to generalize from these cases, there are two factors that all the cases have in common. (1) All developed what was to be their second career on a part-time basis over a period of four or five years while they were pursuing their first career. (2) They did not start to engage in the activities of the second career with the specific intent of switching to it full-time at a later date. The full-time switch was more by happenstance than by deliberate intent. In some cases it was precipitated by the loss of a job during the 1970–71 recession and gloomy reemployment prospects. In other cases the switch was precipitated by the success of the second career activities. In other words, the secondary activity became so successful that they could move into it on a full-time basis with a high degree of confidence.

Those who made the shift express greater satisfaction with what they are doing now than with their former jobs. They cite feelings of greater independence and accomplishment and use of a wider range of skills in their new endeavors. One person returned to his former employer after his business failed. Of interest here is that the skills he acquired as a small businessman were recognized by his former employer, and he was rehired to perform a broad business function rather than his previous narrow technical function.

We know very little about second careers and how to effectively counsel individuals who want to make this transition. It would appear that there are at least three common routes to mid-career change: additional education for those careers that have specific educational requirements, direct transfer of similar skills from one environment to a significantly different environment (for example, from controller in a business organization to controller in a university), and entry into small-scale entrepreneurial activities.

Redirection of Effort

A job or career change is often not possible for psychological or economic reasons. A middle manager may see himself as having to give up too much to make a change, or he may not feel that he has enough to offer another company or another career. Someone who must keep an unrewarding job has the option of finding fulfillment off the job. There are no precise statistics on the number of people who cope with dead-end situations in this way, but I have a very strong impression from my consulting work in industry and government that many middle managers are choosing this route. This approach solves two problems for the person. First, he keeps his job and the benefits associated with it. Second, he uses activities away from the job to help him develop and grow as an individual and find more meaning in his life. In effect, the job supports his outside activities. Outside activities that are often cited as meaningful are recreation, hobbies, community work, and campaigns for local political office. This represents a good adjustment for the individual in that he can maintain his basic security needs while participating in fulfilling activities. For the organization, this type of adjustment usually means that the individual's *best* efforts are being applied elsewhere. This entails a significant and hidden loss to the organization, one that we are unable to measure at this time.

Stagnation and Obsolescence

One of the ways middle managers cope with their environment is apathy. In this case, we can expect a process of stagnation and obsolescence to set in. Some years down the road, these are the individuals who will be referred to as "deadwood" and who will become prime candidates for forced early retirement.

Five aspects of obsolescence have been identified which illustrate the forms managerial obsolescence may take.[8]

• *Technological.* An engineering manager fails to keep up with the new knowledge in his specific field since his graduation from college.

• *Interpersonal.* A manager no longer possesses the interpersonal skills required for his job. Thus he may find that he is supervising younger workers and that the interpersonal skills he found effective with older workers are not appropriate.

• *Cultural.* A manager has certain values that conflict with current cultural norms and values. He may feel that employees should show a high degree of respect for persons in authority. This value runs counter to the attitudes of younger employees, who are more open and egalitarian toward persons in authority. He may regard younger people as disrespectful, and in this sense his attitude toward authority is culturally obsolete.

• *Political.* A manager is obsolete politically in terms of the internal politics of his organization. Thus, over the years, he has been identified with a group that had power and influence and that for various reasons has gone out of favor. To this extent, he also is out of favor and is seen as lacking power and influence within the organization regardless of his ability.

• *Economic.* A manager's aspirations for achievement do not meet the aspirations of his organization. In an organization that is setting high goals for itself for what it considers to be good reasons, the economically obsolete manager does not identify with these goals, or he considers them unrealistically high in the light of past levels of achievement that were expected from him. A manager of this type is seen as having lost his open "drive" and is removed from his position or set aside somewhere.

We have no hard data about how many middle managers are regarded as obsolete according to the above criteria. Later I will make some assumptions about the number of obsolete managers—and the extent to which they are obsolete—to provide an estimate of the "hidden" costs of obsolescence and poor performance on the part of middle managers. They are hidden in that they cannot be measured in direct units of production. The effects of obsolete managers are seen more clearly in terms of poor decisions, poorly timed decisions, a lack of innovative or creative effort, and a negative impact on the organization that they supervise.

The coping techniques mentioned thus far—job and career changes, redirection of effort, and stagnation and obsolescence—are individually based. They are things that individuals elect to do for various reasons. In an examination of these individual coping mechanisms, we see a number of interesting points begin to emerge. Job and career changes and redirection of effort in all probability are positive and healthy responses for the individual. They offer prospects of new activities which presumably could lead to continued growth and development. Stagnation and obsolescence have a different result—diminution of skills and interests. We really do not know why some individuals cope one way and some the other way, but it is clear that the organization does not benefit whichever way the individual elects to cope.

Those who seek a positive solution leave their organization—physically or psychologically—while those who stay and stagnate become serious personnel problems. Either way the organization loses.

Manager Unions

Talk of unions for middle managers is a relatively recent phenomenon and is probably a reflection of the insecurity felt in the 1970–71 recession and the pay inequities that many middle managers are experiencing. An American Management Association report on manager unions gives us some fairly specific data.[9] Its recent survey of 536 middle managers found that one out of three would join or would consider joining a managers' union if one were available. Those who responded to the questionnaire felt that the union would provide them with better job security, wages, and health and fringe benefits. They did not feel that union membership would satisfy their need for greater fulfillment in their jobs. In this respect, their appraisal of what a union would and would not do for them appears to be quite realistic. Unions have traditionally dealt with the so-called bread-and-butter or "hygiene" issues. These tend to be significant sources of dissatisfaction for all employees, and middle managers appear to have some interest in satisfying these basic needs through rather traditional approaches, that is, through unions that would bargain for them. If middle managers were to form unions, it is conceivable that their security, pay, and benefits needs would be satisfied and, to this extent, their situation would be significantly improved. This would still leave the problems of satisfying needs having to do with achievement, growth, and a feeling of responsibility. Unions might actually prevent the satisfaction of these needs. While they usually do a good job of satisfying basic needs, the work rules that generally come with unions (promotion by seniority, not working out of one's job classification) might hinder serious attempts at making the work of middle managers more meaningful.

Manager unions represent a group approach to coping, but there are certain obstacles that appear to be preventing middle managers from following this route. The first is legal. The law allows managers to organize but does not require management to recognize or to bargain with their unions. Thus middle managers who organize take a risk. Management can ignore them or retaliate against them with impunity. I have documented one case in which, after middle managers set up a picket line, management retaliated by firing the leaders and telling the others to come back to work by a certain time, which they did.

The second factor is that at the present time middle managers lack militancy. They are not an identifiable constituency and do not seem to have made their needs known within or without their organizations.

Lateral Relations

One of the things middle managers have to learn to do is to cope with each other. Although they are part of a total management process, they tend to focus on their subfunctional specialties and the goals associated with their own activities. Quite frequently they create problems for each other and resort to various mechanisms to facilitate the achievement of their own goals. These mechanisms have been described by George Strauss in reference to a centralized purchasing organization.[10]

• *Rule orientation.* The middle manager will establish rules, particularly as to how work is introduced into his organization if he is performing a centralized service function. The rules typically are designed to enable *him* to rule his organization efficiently. If he controls the input, he can assign the work within his organization in an efficient manner. His desire for efficiency may, however, conflict with the needs of the people who rely on him for a service. Their priorities may run counter to his internal scheduling needs.

• *Rule evasion.* Once the rules are set up, managers become experts at evading them. Some of the evasion represents "end-runs"—that is, getting the work done without going through the normal channels. In some instances, priority appeal procedures are set up that enable a manager to go to the front of the line. These systems usually involve approval from higher levels of management.

• *Personal alliances.* Some middle managers find it to their mutual advantage to make deals—"you help me and I'll help you." This trading may help the managers involved but may distort the fine priorities in the organizations.

• *Education.* Some middle managers resort to "educating" other middle managers about their organization and how it operates. This is done in the expectation that it will influence the behavior of their clients.

• *Empire building.* Some middle managers deal with "difficult" lateral relationships by justifying the taking over of the troublesome organization. The rationale for this is obvious—"if we have direct control over them, they no longer will be a problem to us."

If one were to examine a typical organization, one would find these lateral coping mechanisms in operation, because they seem to work reasonably well. But an atmosphere of win/lose competition can be harmful both to the manager and to the organization. Edward Schein has written that this type of competition usually results in a high level of distrust among different parts of the organization and very poor communication among different segments.[11] Over long periods, this competitive environment can result in the development of stereotypes among different parts of the business— "We're the good guys and they're the bad guys." Most interactions within the organization then become attempts to support the stereotype held about "the other guy," and the real needs and the real issues of the organization are never adequately dealt with. Significantly, such interpersonal relationships and communications develop in the part of the organization that has the responsibility for coordinating the operation of the management system.

Normal Mid-Life Crises

The attempts of middle managers to cope with their environment must be viewed against what typically happens to individuals in mid-life. Many people, particularly men, starting in their early thirties and peaking about age forty, go through a period of reevaluating their aspirations, values, and lives. This reevaluation, which has been referred to as the "destination crisis," occurs more frequently among those with higher levels of education because they tend to have higher expectations. This period is often a troubling one. The individual is forced to confront and cope with certain unpleasant realities, such as plateaued career, physical changes, obsolete job skills, dissatisfaction with one's personal life. He is trying to answer the question "What do I do with the rest of my life?" And the decisions he makes while resolving his destination crisis have a significant effect on the remainder of his career and his life. While he is answering this question, he is apt to be quite troubled because he is experiencing a considerable degree of conflict about the choices he sees as available. The symptoms of the conflict may manifest themselves in lowered effectiveness on the job.

Once the individual has resolved his crisis he is usually quite content. The particular form of adjustment for which he has opted is seen as satisfying his needs, and he probably is happier than he has been at any other time in his life. The point that I am making here is that many people show maladaptive coping techniques at this age regardless of their work situation, but the crises natural at this age are frequently exacerbated by the work environment of middle managers.

Alcoholism

Alcoholism, which is a complex disease, generally is regarded as a maladaptive coping technique. We do not have any statistics on alcoholism that are specific to middle managers, but we can make some conservative estimates about the extent of the problem from fairly reliable national work force data. Estimates based on data from the National Council on Alcoholism indicate a minimum of 5.3 percent frequency of alcoholism on the national level.[12] The incidence of alcoholism in the work force is constant at 5.3 percent for *all* segments of the work force. What that means is that the incidence of alcoholism among middle managers is the same as that among blue-collar workers. We can use the national incidence level to estimate the number of visible alcoholics in the middle manager population. If we assume a 5 percent incidence rate, there are approximately 200,000 visible alcoholics in the middle manager ranks at any given time. These are alcoholics at the later stages of the disease, when the effects on the individual's behavior and his work performance are more visible. (This figure does not include those whose drinking problem is so severe that they are unemployable, those who are working in marginal occupations because of it, or those who have gone to skid row environments.) Again, based on NCA estimates, we should assume that 10 percent of the 200,000 are under active treatment and will be cured. This nets out to approximately 180,000 visible alcoholics in the middle manager ranks today.

Do work-related factors "cause" drinking problems? We do not know the answer to this question. The causes of alcoholism are extremely complex and not completely understood, and it is important that we imply no cause-and-effect relationship between work experiences and alcoholism. The safest approach is to treat alcoholism as a symptom.

A recent comparison of the drinking behavior of people in college to their drinking behavior after they entered the work force provides some suggestive evidence about the link between work and alcoholism.[13] Over five hundred members of Alcoholics Anonymous were the subject of this study. In general, the drinking problems of these people—one quarter of whom were managers or professionals—were not evident in college. The drinking patterns that ultimately developed into alcoholism became evident at the point when they started to develop a commitment to a specific organization and to a very specific role or career path within the organization. In other words, in college and early in their careers when occupational choices were unclear and when they still felt they had flexibility and choice, most were normal social drinkers. The choice and the elimination of alternatives could be regarded as triggering the problem. Once these workers were boxed into a job, they had to find a way to cope with the consequences of success or failure in a rather permanent work role.

Those college graduates who had severe drinking problems in college (approximately 14 percent of the total sample) seem never to have achieved professional or managerial standing. They typically wound up in semi-professional or semiskilled occupations and thus did not fully utilize their college degrees. What we see here, perhaps, is that severe drinking problems in college may prevent people from getting into the more demanding occupations. All the data in this study are highly suggestive and prove nothing. But the study does indicate that the relationship between work and alcoholism deserves further research.

Divorce

Divorce is regarded by some as a maladaptive behavior, but others argue that it is a positive solution to a bad situation. Regardless of which way one would argue, it does not seem possible even to make an estimate of the frequency of divorce among the middle manager population. But it is my impression that the divorce rate at about age forty (which is our best estimate of the median age of middle managers) is rising very rapidly. I believe that the following are important factors in what I assume is a growing frequency of divorce among middle-aged middle managers:

• This age coincides with the peak of the destination crisis.

• This is the age at which children have left home or are close to leaving home; feelings about staying married for the sake of the children are no longer good rationalizations.

• Divorce is more acceptable today as a solution to marital problems.

• The economic consequences of divorce, while still significant, can be born by the relatively more affluent middle managers.

• New divorce laws make divorce easier.

The only piece of data that even remotely supports this hypothesis is the increase in the median years of marriage at the time that divorce takes place. This number is increasing, and this would seem to suggest that more people are getting divorced after having been married for longer periods of time. For example, in 1950 the median length of marriage at the time of divorce was 5.3 years, while in 1968 (the latest year for which data are available) the median length of marriage at the time of divorce was 7.0 years.[14] Again, as in the case of alcoholism, we should assume no cause-

and-effect relationship between work-related factors and divorce.

The Costs of Coping

As might be assumed from the nature of the data available about middle managers, it is not possible to make very accurate estimates of the costs of the coping methods used by middle managers and the benefits that might be realized in solving some of their problems. We can, however, make some assumptions that at least give us some very rough ideas about these costs and possible benefits.

Career Changes

At a minimum, there are two things we would want to estimate in the area of career changes. First, how many people are involved, and second, what the costs of a career change are and what benefits accrue from it. I don't think we can assume that every individual wants a career change or would benefit from one. Our best guideline of how many individuals are actively seeking career changes (or a significant upgrading in their skills to pursue their present careers) comes from Hiestand's data about people over thirty-five who are pursuing additional education. If we assume that there are approximately 6 million students enrolled in colleges in the United States today and that approximately 10 percent of them are over thirty-five (using a round median of Hiestand's enrollment data), then we are talking about 600,000 such individuals. We are talking about less than 1 percent of the total work force who are actively involved in an educational upgrading endeavor of the type described by Hiestand. Let us asume that it was made easier for individuals to do this and that this would result in a tripling of the number of people who would have such interests. We would be talking about 1.8 million individuals who might use education or reeducation as a means of changing their careers or significantly upgrading their skills for their present jobs. This would represent a little more than 2 percent of the total work force and, of course, not all of these individuals would be middle managers. These numbers have to be regarded as speculative. They do not include individuals who are getting additional education through company-sponsored programs such as the Harvard or M.I.T. graduate school programs that attract people from industry.

Now, what would it cost to reeducate a person for a second career? Here I think we can make an estimate with a bit more confidence. If we assume that the average middle manager is making $20,000 a year and that it would take two years for such a program, we then need to talk about a salary replacement cost of approximately $40,000. In other words, $40,000 to support this individual, assuming he would be supported at the same level he was back in his job, would have to come from somewhere. And let's also assume that two years of tuition under some program at $2,500 a year would come to $5,000. Then we would be talking about a total reeducation cost, including salary and tuition, of $45,000 per manager.

Let's take a look at what we would get back in return for this $45,000. We will assume that we are dealing with an obsolete manager—and for the purposes of our discussion we will define one as obsolete who is only contributing at 50 percent of his capacity. We are still paying him the same $20,000 a year but every year in which he works during which he is obsolete we are losing, in effect, $10,000. Now if we were to invest $45,000 to get him up to 100 percent of capacity, we would not be losing $10,000 a year, so it would take us 4.5 years after we have reeducated him to get back our $45,000.

The numbers here are arbitrary, but the reasoning is important. We should keep in mind that the costs of obsolete managers tend to be hidden. They do not show up as lost units of production but they turn up in poor and untimely decisions and lack of innovation and creativity, and the effect multiplies through the people that the managers work with. A poor judgment on the part of a middle manager can have a very severe and significant negative impact on those further down in the organization. This would argue in favor of making such investments for the reeducation of middle managers.

Who would pay for the reeducation? I think different arguments can be advanced for payment by at least three parties. These are the company employing the manager, the manager himself, and the government. We might argue that the company exposed him to a management system that made him obsolete and that therefore it should incur a significant portion of the costs for his reeducation. We could also argue that the manager allowed himself to be exposed to such a system without taking steps on his own to prevent his obsolescence and that therefore he also should be required to pay part of the costs for his reeducation. And finally we might argue that the manager represents a valuable national resource and that if he is to continue to be valuable then the government should have some interest in providing for his reeducation. One formula for cost sharing might be for the employing company and government to share the salary cost and for the manager to pay his tuition costs.

Alcoholism

According to the National Council on Alcoholism, a conservative approach to computing the costs of alcoholism is to assume that it represents 25 percent of the individual's salary.[15] In the case of a middle manager, where we assume an annual salary of $20,000, this would represent an annual hidden loss of $5,000, plus effects on people elsewhere in the organization. The costs of curing alcoholism do not appear to be significantly high. Some companies have internal programs that are primarily geared toward identifying the alcoholic and motivating him to seek help. The help usually is provided by an outside organization such as Alcoholics Anonymous and does not result in any direct cost to the employing organization. The only costs that would seem to be incurred are those involved in training managers and supervisors to deal with the alcoholic employee. These are minimal when compared to the total cost involved in alcoholism and would be not more than the losses resulting from three or four alcoholic employees. The cost/benefit ratios in curing alcoholism are extremely high because of the low direct costs incurred by the organization.

Recommendations

It is not possible in this paper to treat the approaches to solving middle management problems in any great detail, but the broad directions that the solutions might take can be specified.

There is some evidence of increasing alienation between top and middle management. This alienation, if it continues, can only lead to stereotyping and lack of communication. Top management and middle management should be engaging in face-to-face dialogues in order to share their mutual perceptions of each other, to identify key problem areas, and to work together toward solutions. There is no way that the problems will simply disappear, and it is important that both groups learn to see them and deal with them from each other's point of view.

Middle managers work with each other in a complex network of lateral relationships. As we have seen, they learn to cope with each other through rules, rule-evasion tactics, political alliances, education, and power plays. While these mechanisms are useful to them, they may prevent them from giving the right priorities and maximal efforts to important matters. Too much inefficiency results from the coping mechanisms cited above. Middle managers should engage in dialogues where they openly discuss the problems they cause for each other and then develop a means for working more effectively with each other.

Feeling boxed in is the major problem for middle managers. They reach a point when they perceive no alternatives within their organizations, and they withdraw physically or psychologically, or they stay and tend to stagnate. Either way the organization loses. Among the opportunities that should be made available are second careers within the organization, educational sabbaticals, planned early retirement, and planned job rotation.

There are two techniques of job enrichment that are revelant to middle managers. The first is to enrich jobs by adding activities that represent opportunities for increased responsibility, growth, and development. The second is to remove from the middle manager job those elements that tend to represent lower-order work. The advent of computers, mini-computers, remote terminals, and lower-level programming languages offer significant opportunities in this respect. Much of the work flow and coordination among middle managers concerns such things as forecasts, matching production schedules to forecasts, updating, setting priorities, and dealing with emergencies. These activities typically are supported by clerical routines and a flow of paper in which the middle manager inevitably gets involved. Many of these routines can be computerized to free him to do some creative problem solving and more decision making.

Middle managers have been subjected to a very serious pay squeeze. This is a serious source of dissatisfaction, and it must be corrected before other positive steps can be taken. If middle managers, like most other people, are dissatisfied about their pay, then they will not be very receptive to more positive motivational improvements in their work environment. The solution to the equity problem is not just one of giving middle managers higher salaries, but rather one of developing a basis whereby middle manager salaries can continue to grow for valid business reasons. For example, if middle manager positions were to be broadened and enriched, we would have a more defensible basis for increasing the salary ranges of these jobs—which, in turn, would give middle managers greater growth opportunities in salary terms. If middle managers were to be reeducated and were to develop an up-to-date set of skills, their value to the company would be enhanced considerably. Not only would they have the advantage of new technology, but they would have the additional advantage of many years of on-the-job experience. These two factors in combination should provide a reason for paying middle managers higher salaries in comparison to younger and newer employees.

Notes

1. U.S. Department of Labor, Bureau of Labor Statistics, *Employment and Earnings* 18, no. 10 (April 1972).

2. U.S. Department of Labor, *Manpower Report of the President: 1971* (Washington, D.C., 1971).

3. "The Revolt of the Middle Managers," *Dun's Review* 94, no. 3 (September 1969); "Young Managers Want Share of Power," *Employee Relations Bulletin,* National Foreman's Institute, November 25, 1970; "Executives in Ferment," *Dun's Review* 97, no. 1 (January 1971); "Managers Militant . . . Revolt or a Bill of Rights?" *Industry Week,* March 22, 1971; Roger D'Aprix, "Coping with Company Power," *Industry Week,* May 31, 1971; William J. Constandse, "A Neglected Personnel Problem," *Personnel Journal,* February 1972.

4. American Management Association, *Manager Unions* (New York, 1972).

5. U.S. Department of Labor, *Employment and Earnings.*

6. Ibid.

7. Dale L. Hiestand, *Changing Careers after Thirty-Five* (New York: Columbia University Press, 1971).

8. L. M. Cone, Jr., "Society's Latest Disease—M.O.," *Marketing Review* 24 (1969): 15–17.

9. American Management Association.

10. George Strauss, "Tactics of Lateral Relationship," *Administrative Science Quarterly* 7, no. 2: 161–186.

11. Edward H. Schein, *Process Consultation: Its Role in Organization Development* (Reading, Mass.: Addison-Wesley, 1969).

12. National Council on Alcoholism, *Labor-Management Services Bulletin,* March 18, 1971.

13. H. M. Trice and J. A. Belasco, "The Aging Collegian: Drinking Pathologies among Executive and Professional Alumni," in *The Domesticated Drug: Drinking among Collegians,* ed. G. L. Maddox (New Haven: College and University Press, 1970).

14. U.S. Bureau of the Census, *Statistical Abstracts of the United States: 1971,* 92d ed. (Washington, D.C., 1971).

15. National Council on Alcoholism.

III Work and Health

6 Work and the Health of Man

Bruce L. Margolis and William H. Kroes

Most people would agree that the professional athlete has an enviable job, filled with excitement and opportunities for personal satisfaction. The assembly-line worker, on the other hand, is considered to have a boring, tedious job and is rarely envied. There are a number of people who, like the athlete, consider their own job enjoyable or a source of personal satisfaction. Others, like the assembly-line worker, have no expectation of obtaining satisfaction from what they do. No matter what the differences in job satisfaction, however, people who work for a living tend to have some things in common: they invest time and energy in a function called the "job," and in return they expect money, some measure of self-esteem, and an opportunity for mental or physical activity. Money, of course, enables the worker to obtain material goods necessary for his survival and well-being. The very fact of having a job (versus being unemployed), provides some self-esteem, though one's level of self-esteem can be affected by the nature of the job. Activity, whether mental or physical, is something people appear to need and to continually seek when it is absent. (Some psychologists believe it to be a basic need of man.) The job provides standard and often regularly scheduled periods of activity. Simply stated, it gives people something to do. Indeed, work is so central to our culture that a person who does not work is often considered "sick" or "bad."

Generally, all three functions of work—money, self-esteem, and activity—

are essential to the worker, but sometimes people work for only one. For example, some may work simply to satisfy the need for activity—as is the case for retired individuals who are living quite satisfactorily on pensions. One well-to-do gentleman in Miami was working as an usher in a movie theater, earning very little money. His explanation for working was simple: "If I don't work, what else will I do?" There are also mental and physical health consequences associated with need satisfaction and psychological stress that derive from one's work. These consequences vary considerably. Two examples may provide an idea of the extent and intensity of the problem.

The first example comes from George Albee, past president of the American Psychological Association, who tells the following story about a high-powered, successful business executive. This man, let's call him Mr. Winter, single-handedly ran an operation that nobody else in his company fully understood. As Mr. Winter reached his sixty-fourth birthday, a bright and talented younger man was assigned as an apprentice to learn the complex set of activities so that he could take over the operation and the old master could benefit from a well-deserved retirement. Mr. Winter objected, claiming that he did not want to retire. But the company had rules. Not long after his forced retirement, a substantial change in Mr. Winter took place. He began to withdraw from people and to lose his zest for life. Less than a year after his retirement, this once lively and productive businessman was hospitalized, diagnosed as suffering from senile psychosis. Friends from work and even his family soon stopped coming to visit him because they could evoke no response. Mr. Winter was a vegetable.

About two years after the apprentice assumed his new position of responsibility, this young man suddenly died. The company found itself in a serious predicament. The function that was vacated by this untimely death was essential to company operations, yet nobody within the company could effectively fill in. A decision was made to approach Mr. Winter to see if he could pull himself together enough to carry on the job and train somebody to take over. Four of his closest coworkers were sent to the hospital. After hours of trying, one of the men finally broke through. The idea of going back to work brought the first sparkle in Mr. Winter's eyes in two years. Within a few days, this "vegetable" was operating at full steam, interacting with people as he had years before. Again, a bright young man was called in to apprentice under the old master. When the young man was trained and ready to take full responsibility, the company once again retired Mr. Winter. Within six months he was in the hospital, never to leave.

Another example of the impact of the job upon the worker comes from a paper-bag manufacturing plant. The workers running the machines were generally poorly educated and unskilled, and they badly needed the jobs they had. Management was suspicious of these employees, feeling "They are always trying to get away with something." The factory floor was noisy, dingy, hot in summer and cold in winter. Rules were plentiful and strictly enforced. Suspicion and open dislike of management for worker and worker for management was evident. Several years ago, a factory worker died of a heart attack while working at his job. As the news of his death circulated around the plant, several women employees became ill or fainted. A few weeks later, a strong odor leaked into a section of the plant through sewage pipes and a few employees were overcome and had to leave work for the day. Though the odor problem was eliminated, the employees began complaining of dizziness, nausea, malaise, headaches, and other symptoms. A team from the Public Health Service was called in, but no toxic agents could be identified. After thorough examinations and laboratory tests, medical doctors could find nothing wrong with any of the complaining workers. One of the authors was then brought into the plant. Having looked at all the evidence, he concluded that this was a case of industrial hysteria—a physical reaction to severe psychological stress brought about by the job. He offered to make suggestions to ameliorate some of the problems and warned that if no steps were taken things could get worse. No action was taken. Less than a year later the plant was burned to the ground. Newspapers reported that arson was likely.

These anecdotes do no more than illustrate the scope of the problem. Other examples of specific work-related causes of poor mental and physical health have been offered in research studies.

• Workers in heavy industry who describe their foreman as one who does not check on them, does not keep them informed about what is going on around the plant, and does not let them know where they stand report more "nervousness" on the job than workers with a foreman who provides this information.[1]

• Foremen, who are often called the "men in the middle" because of their tenuous position between labor and management, have been found to have ulcer rates about seven times higher than those for first-level workers.[2]

• Workers in a power plant who felt they had insufficient training for their jobs were more anxious than those who felt their training was adequate.[3]

A recent article on the effects of psychological stress on the worker concluded that "there is impressive evidence that the chronic ailments afflicting middle-aged Americans have less to do with fatty diet, cigarette smoking, and lack of exercise than with workaday anger and tensions." [4] This statement points out the importance of work stress as a major cause of a broad range of serious health problems. As evidence accumulates that psychological factors in work produce health problems, scientists have begun to search for the culprit. Thus far, two factors have been identified: (1) frustrations from failure to satisfy basic needs and (2) work-related psychological stress. The first is based upon the concept that unfulfilled psychological needs may trigger physical or mental problems; the second is based upon the notion that work can be so psychologically stressful that even when psychological needs are met physical or mental health problems may arise.

Psychological Factors

Unfulfilled Needs
Most social scientists agree that there are basically three sets of needs that are common to all of mankind, although their specific manifestations may vary from culture to culture:

• "Maintenance needs." The need for food, shelter, and activity is derived from man's physiology. Work provides the means to obtain physical objects which permit satisfaction of these needs. In some cultures work does not satisfy these needs very well, but in most Western countries satisfying maintenance needs is seldom a problem for those who are able to work.

• "Social needs." The need for companionship, recognition, and a feeling of belonging is derived from society. Work can often be a major source of satisfaction of these needs. Serious problems do arise, however, when men are socially isolated because of the requirements of their work. The man on the noisy and continually demanding assembly line is typical of those in our work force who may be in physical proximity to fellow workers but are unable to interact socially. Health consequences may derive from failure to meet social needs.

• "Growth needs." The need for self-actualization and the development of competence and mastery over one's environment is derived from man's psychology. Satisfaction of this need is often characterized as attainment of positive mental health. Failure to satisfy this need can lead to frustration and self-doubt, which in turn can lead to serious physical or mental health problems.

Unfortunately, for those interested in the health consequences of work, there has been a dearth of empirical research to determine the extent to which unfulfilled needs at work result in health problems. Philosophizing psychologists, psychiatrists, sociologists, economists, and others have for years described the plight of the worker. Newspapers have been describing almost daily the dehumanizing effects of work and resulting worker unrest. We must document these social commentaries and determine the specific cause-and-effect relationship between needs unfulfilled at work and any consequent status of the worker's physical and mental health. In no other way can these problems be effectively resolved.

Job Stresses

The second way in which work impinges upon physical and mental health parallels the well-known situation of the gentleman and his femme fatale. She provides satisfaction of many important personal needs but makes substantial demands as well. The fur coats and diamonds he must buy may not bother this apparently satisfied gentleman, but his bank account is slowly being dissolved. Likewise, the apparently satisfied worker may hardly notice the stress under which he is working until his health has been ruined.

Prior to the 1950s there was very little systematic research into the effects of job stress on mental and physical health. One of the first research organizations to be concerned with this problem was the Institute for Social Research at the University of Michigan. Since 1957, this group has been working continuously toward identification of job stresses and their relationship to health. They believe that the following stresses are correlated with coronary heart disease:

● "Role Ambiguity." Having unclearly defined objectives, being unable to predict what others expect of one, only vaguely understanding the scope of one's responsibilities

● "Role Conflict." Being torn by conflicting demands, feeling pressure to get along with people, having differences with one's supervisor

● "Role Overload." Having too much or too little to do, or too difficult or too easy a level of work assignment

● "Responsibility for People." Feeling responsibility for the health and well-being of others, for their work performance, career development, and job security

● "Poor Relations with Others." Not getting along with supervisors, peers, or subordinates

● "Participation." Having influence on decision-making processes in one's organization.

Other significant occupational stresses that have been identified include changing work shifts, unnatural work-rest regimens, frequent geographic moves, and inequities in pay and job status.

Consequences

Physical Health

Although research examining the effects on physical health of psychological stress and unmet psychological needs at work has been fragmented, a number of interesting findings have been reported. Some of the studies were undertaken over twenty years ago, but they are still relevant. For example, in 1948 Carey P. McCord wrote in *Industrial Medicine:* "A lifetime friendship with a train dispatcher may be a short affair—about 15 years. . . . Few are aware that the train dispatcher who starts his duties at age 35, after years of preparation as a telegrapher or tower operator parts company with this troubled globe near the age of 50.1 years. . . . Premature heart disease is the greatest single factor in establishing the average age at death of train dispatchers at 50.1." [5]

At the time McCord wrote, train dispatchers were asked to make approximately five decisions a minute over an eight-hour day, six days a week. These decisions involved life or death for train passengers and crews. After observing one such dispatcher, McCord concluded that "no human mind can carry out such a load without going berserk." Though this problem was identified in 1947, the current president of the American Train Dispatchers Association has indicated that "most of the things Dr. McCord wrote about are still applicable today." [6]

In the 1950s studies were conducted to evaluate the effects of other job stresses.[7] Such stresses as deadlines, intense competition, long hours, or second jobs were found to be associated with higher levels of serum cholesterol and increased risk of coronary heart disease. (Serum cholesterol, one of several factors in the blood that increases with stress, is associated with the onset of coronary heart disease.) Later studies have implicated low job satisfaction as a factor in increased levels of serum cholesterol and coronary heart disease.[8]

A study recently commissioned by the Federal Aviation Agency found that there was (1) "compelling" evidence that the stresses under which air traffic controllers work (in many ways similar to those of train dispatchers) result in increased risk of hypertension, (2) "moderately strong" evidence linking work stress to peptic ulcer, and (3) "suggestive" evidence connecting diabetes to work stress.[9]

Other diseases such as rheumatoid arthritis and various forms of skin problems have been implicated as consequences of job stress, but systematic data are lacking. As is typical in the behavioral sciences, anecdotes are far more plentiful. For example, Sidney Cobb reports a case of rapid onset of alopecia areata (patchy loss of hair) in one employee soon after the announcement that the plant in which he was working was going to be terminated. The plant remained open for two years before actually closing, whereupon the same individual, as well as a coworker, developed the disease again. The close temporal relationship to the stressful situation in both cases argues strongly that stress was the cause or was at least implicated in the development of the disease.

Mental Health

Any discussion of the effects of work on mental health will be strongly influenced by one's definition of mental health. There are two basic definitions: (1) Mental health is the absence of mental illness. (2) Mental health is the optimal level of psychological functioning that an individual can attain; it is a desired state of psychological well-being. Scientists have studied the impact of work using both definitions.

Studies of the mental illness consequences of occupational stress tend to be highly anecdotal, involving descriptive case studies of individuals. Systematic research into the effects of occupational stress has focused upon worker productivity or measures of worker errors rather than on worker health problems. On the other hand, there is research on those aspects of work that contribute to positive mental health. Job restructuring to provide greater opportunity for communication and direct training of workers and supervisors to communicate more effectively have been shown to increase worker morale, job satisfaction, and self-esteem.

In the mid-1950s the industrial psychologist Arthur Kornhauser directed an intensive study of the mental health of automobile workers. In his subsequent book, *Mental Health of the Industrial Worker,* he reported that mental health was poor among factory workers and lower-skilled persons with less responsible jobs. Kornhauser noted that the men's prejob background and personality did not account for the differences and concluded that "jobs in which workers are better satisfied are conducive to better mental health."[10]

Studies by other industrial psychologists have consistently found that the more responsible, higher-level positions tend to provide more need satisfactions than lower-level jobs. Job enrichment programs in which worker responsibility and opportunity for achievement are increased and the task itself is made intrinsically more interesting have resulted in improved job satisfaction, morale, and, inferentially, better worker mental health.

Individual Differences

Why is it that job stress affects people in different ways? Some lose their hair, others develop coronary heart disease or ulcers or become generally depressed and unhappy, while still others show no significant ill effects. The question has not been answered adequately, although possible explanations are beginning to take shape. For example, it is known that the autonomic nervous system is made up of a sympathetic system that energizes the body so that man can respond to stress by acting with strength and speed (as when fighting or fleeing). The parasympathetic system restores equilibrium by counteracting the impact of the sympathetic system through lowering the state of excitation of the body. Current research has indicated that in some individuals the sympathetic response to stress is dominant, while in others the parasympathetic is dominant. The levels and corresponding differences in kinds of nervous activity result in different levels of impact upon such organs of the body as the heart and stomach. Another possible explanation is that specific organs of certain individuals are weak and are most vulnerable to breakdown under stress. But overall, although we know that individual physiological differences exist, the details of these differences are unclear.

Another source of individual differences is personality. Meyer Friedman and Rey H. Rosenman have postulated that "type A" workers (who are characterized by intense drive, aggressiveness, ambition, and competitiveness and who create pressure for getting things done and have a habit of pitting themselves against the clock) are highly prone to coronary heart disease, whereas the more easygoing, patient, less competitive workers ("type B") are less likely to succumb to the effects of job stress. Most people have a little of each type in them, but it is the extent to which one type is dominant that determines risk of heart disease.[11]

Another important aspect of individual differences involves the "fit" of the person and his work environment. Some people find certain kinds of activities stressful while others find the same activities pleasant and comfortable. Research conducted at the University of Michigan strongly suggests that the "person-environment fit" is of great importance in determining the extent to which a job will be stressful for any given worker.[12]

General Well-Being

What are the real differences between physical and mental health? Certainly, physical health refers to visible effects on the body, while mental health describes the status of that subjective and elusive entity known as the mind. However, there is no doubt that the body affects the mind, that the mind affects the body, and that one's job can affect both to a considerable degree.

A study of the NASA Goddard Space Flight Center found that administrators were under more work stress than scientists and engineers. The administrators had higher pulse rates, systolic blood pressure, and smoking rates (all considered risk factors in coronary heart disease). John R. P. French and Robert Caplan, who conducted the study, attributed high levels of "responsibility for people" as the key stress affecting coronary heart disease risk in these administrators.[13] They also found that administrators, engineers, and scientists with high levels of role ambiguity had lower job satisfaction, greater feelings of job-related threat to their mental and physical well-being, and lower utilization of intellectual skills and knowledge. Those with high levels of work overload had higher job-related tension and lower self-esteem. Specific job stresses can thus produce negative effects on both mental and physical health. In a more recent study at the flight center, it was found that there was a noticeable increase in mental problems, major chronic diseases, and hypertension during times of peak stress such as the first lunar orbit and the first two manned landings.

The effects of one's job do not occur in a vacuum. It stands to reason that what happens at home impinges on work activities, and vice versa. A supportive home and social life helps to buffer the effects of job stress by enabling one to recover during nonworking hours. An unfulfilling or stressful home life, in addition to any impact it may of itself have upon mental and physical health, certainly exacerbates the impact of an unfulfilling or stressful job. Thus, to gain meaningful understanding of the health problems of workers, nonwork variables should be considered.

Conclusion

In what we have said thus far, scientific research has been mixed with anecdote and opinion. When asked by the most hard-nosed scientists, "What do you know about the effects of work upon health?" we must become a bit more conservative. We know that work serves a positive function for mankind. People have needs that are to a greater or lesser degree met by work, and the greater the extent that the individual's needs are met, the happier the individual. We know that high levels of psychological stress are produced at the workplace, that some jobs are more stressful than others, and that specific aspects of jobs are particularly stressful. We know that individuals differ in their abilities to handle stress.

Beginning with these basic points of knowledge, it can be inferred that psychological stress produced by the job results in physiological, behavioral, and/or emotional responses which in turn produce health consequences. Psychological stress produced in the laboratory clearly produces physiological, behavioral, and emotional responses, but there is not enough research in the work setting to prove a cause-and-effect relationship between job stress and bad health. But practitioners dealing with health problems on a day-to-day basis generally feel that the correlational, case history, and anecdotal evidence is convincing.

We also believe we have the knowledge to provide remediation programs that can substantially increase human need satisfactions or resolve psychological stress problems at work. Such techniques as job enrichment, participatory methods, training, selection, and behavior modification can be used to improve worker need satisfaction and reduce psychological stress.

The potential effectiveness of some of these techniques can be illustrated by a study conducted at Texas Instruments.[14] One of the major objectives of this study was to find out what would happen in a large manufacturing department if the causes of anxiety among new employees were reduced. Traditionally, a two-hour orientation briefing was given to all new employees. In this experiment, an additional six hours of training specifically aimed at reducing anxiety was introduced. Four points were emphasized:

- The individual's opportunity to succeed on the job was quite high.
- A new employee should disregard "hall" talk.
- A new employee should take the initiative in communication.
- A new employee should get to know his supervisor.

From this simple program, the company reported that

- Training time was shortened by one-half.
- Training costs were lowered to one-third of previous levels.
- Absenteeism and tardiness dropped to one-fifth of previous levels.

- Waste and rejects were reduced to one-fifth of previous levels.
- Costs were cut from 15 percent to 30 percent.

Anxiety having been reduced the workplace became more attractive to the employees. Unfortunately, such innovative techniques have not been used on a large scale, and the profit motive, not worker health, has been the primary reason for their use. Such techniques need tailoring to health problems to improve their effectiveness.

It is clear that we remain largely ignorant of the causal chain linking job stress to illness. Apparently there are substantial individual differences that make some workers vulnerable to the effects of stress and others seemingly resistant. At present we can only guess what the bases are for these differences. Some stresses seem to be more potent than others in producing health problems. Why do these stresses have their particular effect? How do psychological defense mechanisms and nonwork activities serve to reduce the effects of job stress? What is the biochemical chain linking psychological stress to physical health problems? How much does work stress affect the nonwork activities of the stressful worker? Which jobs are most stressful, and which produce the most frequent or most severe health problems? We just do not know the answers to these questions.

One major obstacle to the progress of research into psychological factors in occupational mental and physical health has been poor communication. This derives in part from the fact that researchers in this area come from diverse academic disciplines. Research results appear in various professional journals, but medical doctors often don't read psychology journals, psychologists often don't read business journals, businessmen don't read biology journals, and so on. In order to coordinate efforts, a central information source is needed.

Once communication has been coordinated, interdisciplinary attempts to study the causal chain from unfulfilled needs or job stress to ill health should be made. This causal chain can and should be viewed from sociological, psychological, biological, and biochemical perspectives with understandings at one level lending insights to understandings at another.

With new knowledge and increasing data supporting the effectiveness of existing techniques, remediation programs must be developed and applied. These programs can then be evaluated on a scientific basis to determine which techniques work best and under what circumstances they are most effective. Only a battery of such experiments will take us from the point of thinking we know something to actually knowing something.

Notes

1. Robert G. Neel, "Nervous Stress in the Industrial Situation," *Personnel Psychology* 8, no. 4 (winter 1955): 405–416.

2. P. G. Vertin, "Bedryfsgeneeskundige Aspecten van het Ulcus Pepticum" [Occupational Health Aspects of Peptic Ulcer] (thesis, University of Groningen, Netherlands, 1954).

3. Floyd C. Mann and L. R. Hoffman, "Individual and Organizational Correlates of Automation," *Journal of Social Issues* 12 (1956): 7–17.

4. Walter McQuade, "What Stress Can Do to You," *Fortune,* January 1972.

5. Carey P. McCord, "Life and Death by the Minute," *Industrial Medicine* 17, no. 10 (October 1948).

6. Charles R. Pfenning, President, American Train Dispatchers Association, personal communication to the authors.

7. Meyer Friedman, Rey H. Roseman, and Vernice Carroll, "Changes in Serum Cholesterol and Blood Clotting Time of Men Subjects to Cyclic Variations of Occupational Stress," *Circulation* 17 (1958): 852–861; Scott M. Grundy and A. Clark Griffin, "Effects of Periodic Mental Stress on Serum Cholesterol Levels," *Circulation* 19 (1959): 496–498.

8. Steven Sales and James House, "Job Dissatisfaction as a Possible Risk Factor in Coronary Heart Disease," *Journal of Chronic Disease* 23 (1971): 861–873.

9. Sidney Cobb and R. Rose, "Hypertension, Peptic Ulcer, and Diabetes in Air Traffic Controllers," *Journal of the American Medical Association,* 1973, no. 4, pp. 489–492.

10. Arthur Kornhauser, *Mental Health of the Industrial Worker* (New York: Wiley, 1965), p. 89.

11. Meyer Friedman and Rey H. Rosenman, "Overt Behaviour Pattern in Coronary Disease: Detection of Overt Behaviour Pattern A in Patients with Coronary Disease by a New Psychophysiological Procedure," *Journal of the American Medical Association* 173 (July 1960).

12. John R. P. French, Jr., Willard Rodgers, and Sidney Cobb, "Adjustment as Person-Environment Fit," unpublished (Ann Arbor: University of Michigan, Institute for Social Research, 1971).

13. John R. P. French, Jr., and Robert Caplan, "Organizational Stress and Individual Strain," in *The Failure of Success,* ed. A. J. Marrow (New York: American Management Association, 1972).

14. Earl R. Gomersall and M. Scott Myers, "Breakthrough in On-the-Job Training," *Harvard Business Review* 44, no. 4 (August 1966).

7 The Effects of Occupational Stress on Physical Health

James S. House

In the last thirty to fifty years the centrality of work to individual well-being and health, both physical and mental, has been increasingly recognized by social and medical researchers and by many in business, government, and unions. Work is no longer seen as a means to mere survival but rather as an "almost irreplaceable" element in establishing a person's sense of self and personal worth.[1] It is clear that early social and psychological theorists such as Sigmund Freud and Karl Marx recognized this fact, but systematic empirical evidence has come only with recent developments in medical and social research.

The purpose of this paper is to summarize what is known about the effects of the social and psychological aspects of work on physical health and to suggest implications of this evidence for government action in research and social policy. The social and psychological aspects of work include the social characteristics of work environments and the psychological responses of individuals to them. The relationship of mental health and job performance to these factors has received considerable attention; physical health, on the other hand, has been considered mainly in relation to *physical*

The author is grateful for the helpful comments and suggestions of the following people on an earlier draft of this paper: Sidney Cobb, John R. P. French, Jr., Elizabeth Harkins, George Maddox, James O'Toole, Erdman Palmore, and Thomas Regan. The final responsibility for the analysis and conclusions is his.

characteristics of work environments—physical demands, radiation, quality of air, equipment, and lighting, and so forth.

It has been difficult to establish that improvements in the "quality of life and work" such as increased life and job satisfaction and decreased social and psychological stress result in either short-term or long-term gains in job performance, efficiency, or productivity.[2] Moreover, the evidence that increasing satisfaction or decreasing stress makes people happier and mentally healthier has not always seemed compelling to those with the power to institute change. In part this is because of the difficulties of defining happiness and mental health and in demonstrating tangibly the economic and social benefits of states of mind.

In contrast, to the extent that work or life dissatisfaction and stress produce *physical* disease, there are direct and measurable economic costs to the individual and to the organization, community, and society to which he belongs. (Some of these costs will be noted below.) It is not necessary to justify all social research or planned social intervention and change in economic terms, but if the gains of such research or change can be assessed in economic as well as social or psychological terms, the case for them is strengthened.

The Complex Nature of Stress

People who study it have found stress virtually impossible to define in any but the most general terms.[3] Most see it as something that occurs when an individual confronts a situation in which his usual modes of coping or behaving or insufficient—for example, when demands are made that exceed his abilities or when there are clear obstacles to fulfilling his strong needs or values.[4] Such problems as job dissatisfaction, excessive work load and responsibility, interpersonal conflict, unemployment, and job termination can all be considered as forms of stress.[5] More explicit definitions often lead to confusion between stress itself and the situations that are stressful or the responses produced by stress. One researcher has suggested that it may be more fruitful to talk about "stress research" rather than "stress" as a concept.[6] Stress researchers, then, should consider the following interrelated factors:

- The objective conditions of work conducive to stress
- Individual perceptions of work situations as stressful
- Individual responses to perceived stresses

- Outcomes of perceived stress
- Individual or social situational characteristics that condition the relationships among the first four factors.

Initially, most people interested in the effects of work on health ascertain whether objective conditions of work are related to physical health. For example, are men whose jobs involve high levels of work load or responsibility more prone than others to heart attacks, ulcers, or hypertension? As we shall see, there is evidence suggesting that this is the case. On the other hand, not all men in such jobs incur such diseases, nor are all men whose jobs involve less work load or responsibility immune to such diseases. This is, of course, an obvious fact, but it suggests that the relationship between objective conditions of work and physical health is more complex than it might seem at first glance.

In addition to the variety of genetic and physiological factors that may account for the differences in the way the same situation affects a group of individuals, there are a variety of social and psychological factors, which, if taken into account, can significantly improve the accuracy of prediction or explanation. People with different abilities react differently to the same level of work load or responsibility—some finding it pleasantly challenging, others quite stressful. One person considers working with people very satisfying, while another considers it a source of stress or dissatisfaction because of his lower need for human affiliation. The experience of stress is thus a subjective response that results from a *combination* of particular objective conditions of work and particular personal characteristics (abilities and needs). Characteristics of the social situation (such as a high level of competition among peers) may also combine with the conditions of work (such as a heavy work load) to produce stress. In sum, we can predict the outcomes of given conditions of work much more accurately if we know other relevant individual or social situational characteristics as well.

Even if a number of people report the same amount of subjective stress in their work, they seldom all incur the same type or degree of physical illness. How a person responds to a situation is crucial. In the face of a heavy work load, one person may successfully reorganize his style of work, gain new skills, or call on others for help, while another will flounder along, unable to alleviate the stress, and will eventually suffer a heart attack. To predict whether a person will cope well or poorly under stress requires knowledge of the individual and the characteristics of the work environment that deter-

mine what a person can do (or is likely to do) in response and how successful he will be.

There has been some research on the relationship of objective work conditions and subjective perceptions of stress to physical health, and some
attention has been paid to selected individual and social characteristics
which specify for whom or in what situations objective conditions or subjective perceptions are most likely to affect health. Unfortunately, very little is
known about how people cope with or respond to stressful work situations.

This brief discussion is intended to alert the reader to the complexity and
challenge inherent in attempts to collect and interpret data on how occupational stress affects physical health. It is very important to recognize that
what we commonly call stress is a product of the relationship between individuals and their job situations. Hence the outcomes of such stress are the
result of a complex interplay between the individual and his environment.[7]
High-quality research on the effects of occupational stress on health and intelligent social action can only come when we recognize that stress and its
outcomes (such as physical illness or death) are a consequence of (1) characteristics of the individual, (2) characteristics of the job environment, and
(3) the interaction between these two sets of characteristics. Alleviating
stress in order to improve physical health may require attempts to change
individuals, job environments, or, most likely, the relations between individuals and their environments.

The Pertinent Diseases
In planning for future research and social policy concerning work and health,
primary emphasis should go to diseases that are the greatest sources of
mortality and disability, especially in the working-age population. In regard
to both mortality and disability, cardiovascular diseases, coronary heart disease in particular, dwarf all others. The epidemic proportions of heart disease and related circulatory disorders in modern societies have made them
the focus of most research on the effects of work on physical health. In 1900,
cardiovascular diseases accounted for only 20 percent of all deaths in the
United States, but this figure rose to 55 percent by 1955 and has remained at
that level. These diseases are also the leading cause of disability, accounting for 12 percent of all time lost from work.[8] Elimination of cardiovascular
diseases as causes of death would increase life expectancy by 10.9 years—

more than four times the gain that would be achieved by elimination of any other cause of death. The direct economic cost to the nation of cardiovascular disease in terms of medical expenses and losses in labor output was estimated at $32 billion in 1963 (or 6 percent of the Gross National Product).[9]

Among the cardiovascular diseases, coronary heart disease (CHD), or heart attack, is by far the most serious problem; it accounts for one-third of all deaths (and three-fifths of those due to cardiovascular diseases). CHD is the leading cause of death among males from age thirty-five on. The second leading cause of mortality from cardiovascular disease is cerebrovascular disease, or stroke, accounting for 11 percent of all deaths and 20 percent of all cardiovascular mortality. In general, there are many similarities in the medical factors (for example, high blood pressure, cholesterol, and smoking) that predispose people to both CHD and stroke, but the problem of stroke is less acute at younger ages. The most prevalent form of cardiovascular disease is hypertension or high blood pressure, but its importance derives largely from its role as a precursor of CHD and stroke.[10]

Cancer is the other major source of mortality among adults, accounting for about 17 percent of all deaths among persons over twenty-five. There is little evidence, however, of social or psychological precursors of the disease. Accidents are the next largest cause of mortality but account for at most 5 percent of all deaths.[11] Although some research is beginning to be done on social and psychological factors in accidents, it cannot be adequately reviewed here.

Thus, in terms of both mortality and disability, heart disease is an appropriate focus for this paper. We have more research knowledge of the relationship between heart disease and work than between other diseases and work, but since arthritis and rheumatism rank second and gastrointestinal diseases fourth as sources of disability, they will receive brief note. But aside from that on heart disease, the literature on occupational stress and physical health is rather sparse.

Two kinds of evidence suggest the important role of work-related stress in determining physical disease. First, there are standard epidemiological studies that compare morbidity or mortality rates for different demographic categories such as race, sex, age, occupation, education, and region. Such data are useful in developing hypotheses about the effect of occupational stress on physical disease. A second, more focused type of research can relate specific types of stress to disease and show that the differential distribution of stress across demographic categories accounts, at least in part, for observed differences in mortality or morbidity among groups.

The review of evidence presented here is organized in terms of three major physical health outcomes: overall mortality, morbidity, and longevity; heart disease; and peptic ulcer and rheumatoid arthritis. In each case, both broad demographic comparisons and more focused studies of occupational stress will be considered. The discussion of the more focused studies will present the major evidence relating objective work conditions and subjective perceptions of stress to the relevant health outcome. In the case of heart disease, there is also a discussion of the role of individual and social situational characteristics in the relationship between objective conditions and/or subjective perceptions and health outcomes.

Work and Overall Mortality, Morbidity, and Longevity

Demographic Comparisons

In general, we know that women, whites, and persons of higher educational or social status live longer and have lower age-adjusted mortality rates for many, though not all, diseases.[12] The social-status differential is greater among women than men and larger for communicable diseases than for major chronic diseases such as ulcer, stroke, arthritis, cancer, and heart disease.[13] These data suggest that social-status and race differentials stem more from poor living conditions and medical care or from social stress outside of work than from occupational stress.

There are, of course, occupational differences in the incidence of most diseases, but the reasons for them remain unclear. But the difference in longevity between males and females suggests a central role of work in the genesis of disease. Although physiological, hormonal, and hereditary differences between men and women are also possible explanations of this phenomenon, the different social experiences of males and females may contribute to the longevity differential—and the greater occupational involvement of men is one of the clearest of such differences. Unfortunately, most research on the effects of work on physical health has considered men only. The increasing pressure for greater equality of men and women in the realm of work and elsewhere provides a good opportunity for looking at the effects of work on health in females as well as males. If social and psychological factors in work are important determinants of the male-female differences in mortality and longevity, then such differences should decline with greater equality of the sexes. I shall return to these issues in discussing heart disease.

Focused Studies

The best evidence we have that stress and satisfaction in life and work determine mortality and longevity comes from Erdman Palmore's analyses of data from the Duke Longitudinal Study of Aging, a panel study of 268 volunteers aged sixty to ninety-four (median age seventy) at the time of their initial interview and physical examination.[14] Although the sample was not random, the distribution of the volunteers by sex, race, and occupation approximated that of the area from which they were drawn. The dependent variable was a longevity quotient—the number of years a person actually lived beyond the initial examination divided by the actuarially expected number of years of life remaining at the time of the initial examination.

In the total sample, a measure of "work satisfaction" was the strongest predictor of the longevity quotient,[15] and it remained one of the three strongest predictors for all sex, age, and racial subgroups of the sample except blacks. The second best predictor of longevity in the total sample was a rating of the respondent's overall "happiness" made by the interviewing social worker. What is most notable in these results is that these two sociopsychological measures (1) predicted longevity better than either a rating of overall physical functioning by the examining physician or a measure of tobacco use and (2) remained strong predictors even when these physical variables were statistically controlled.

From this evidence, it appears that satisfaction in work (or lack of dissatisfaction and stress) may be an important determinant of general health and longevity, especially in males. In Palmore's study, work satisfaction was a function both of being able to engage in some form of productive work and of enjoying whatever work one was doing. As we will see below, both of these factors are linked to changes in health status, and especially to heart disease, for younger members of the labor force as well as for older people.

Work and Coronary Heart Disease

Demographic Comparisons

The most striking fact about the distribution of coronary heart disease in America is the degree to which it afflicts young and middle-aged males and spares young and middle-aged white females. Throughout the period of peak occupational endeavor (ages twenty-five to sixty-four) the male mortality rate from CHD among whites is from 2.75 to 6.50 times greater than the female rate, while among nonwhites, males die from CHD at a rate 1.35 to 1.91 times greater than the female rate. Among females, those who are black or who have lower social status run a greater risk of death from CHD. Among males, there are no such sizable or consistent race or status differences.[16]

Interestingly, few people have speculated on the possibly critical role of occupational stress in producing these sex differences. One group of researchers discounts the possibility that the unique hormonal makeup of females prior to menopause can account for the difference because there is no noticeable increase in the female death rate soon after menopause.[17] These authors suggest that we look only to differences in diet, physical activity, and smoking as explanations; they make no mention of occupational stress at all. Earlier it was noted that if occupational stress is a factor in explaining the sex differences in both overall and CHD mortality, there should be evidence of a declining sex difference as female employment and equality increase. In fact, since the late 1950s the male rate seems to have leveled off, while the female rate (for ages thirty-five to fifty-four) is rising.[18]

Also pointing to the possible importance of occupational stress as a factor in heart disease is the wide occupational variation in rates of CHD morbidity and mortality.[19] In a number of studies cited below, occupations involving "greater stress" are shown to have higher susceptibility to heart disease. This kind of occupational comparison has not, on the whole, produced interpretable results, since little effort has been made to specify the types of stress that vary across occupations. As several researchers have suggested, any effort to establish work-related stress as a precursor of heart disease must identify specific kinds of stress and consider how these are differentially distributed across occupations.[20] Demographic comparisons can suggest the potential relevance of occupational stress to CHD, but only more focused studies can demonstrate this relevance.

Focused Studies

Studies of the social and psychological aspects of work in relation to CHD constitute the largest and thus far most productive area of research on the effects of work on physical health. The studies reviewed here use essentially two measures of health: (1) actual disease entities like heart attacks and (2) behavioral and physiological factors that are known to increase the risk of such disease (high levels of cigarette smoking, obesity, blood sugar, blood pressure, cholesterol, etc.).[21] Studies using actual disease as the dependent variable are of two types, retrospective and prospective. In a *retrospective* study, people who have already developed heart disease are matched with a control group who are healthy or have other diseases, and measures of occupational stress and satisfaction are taken. The danger in such an approach is that differences between the groups may be a *result* of heart disease rather than a cause of it. In a *prospective* study, people without disease are interviewed about their lives and work and are followed up until some develop heart disease. Here the evidence is more convincing that the socio-psychological characteristics that differentiate those who incur the disease from those who do not may, in fact, be causes of the disease.

Studies utilizing the "risk factors" of heart disease as dependent variables are usually cross-sectional in design and are occasionally prospective. In a *cross-sectional* study, measures of occupational satisfaction or stress and measures of heart disease risk factors are taken at about the same time, and the association between these factors is then determined. There are problems in ascertaining the direction of causality in such studies, but in most cases it is more plausible to assume that, for example, job satisfaction affected blood pressure than vice versa. In a number of studies, longitudinal or experimental data allow us to see clearly that changes in work-related variables preceded changes in risk factors. But looking at all of this data, what is most convincing is not the results of any single study but the overall patterns that emerge from a variety of studies.

Job satisfaction. A number of retrospective studies in the United States and other countries have found that people with coronary disease report significantly more dissatisfaction with aspects of work (tediousness, lack of recognition, poor relations with coworkers, poor working conditions) than healthy workers, and they report more work "problems" and "difficulties."[22] An analysis of three different samples of occupations showed that those occupations with high average rates of dissatisfaction also had high rates of heart disease mortality. (These relationships were strongest for measures of intrinsic job satisfaction and among white-collar, as opposed to blue-collar, occupations.)[23] Further, no relationship was found between average levels of job dissatisfaction and mortality from a variety of other causes (tuberculosis, cancer, diabetes, influenza, pneumonia, and accidents). In a study that I conducted, a generally consistent pattern of results indicated that men aged forty-two to sixty-five who were more dissatisfied with their work were likely to be higher on a variety of heart disease risk factors (high blood pressure, cholesterol, and blood sugar and obesity). That the same relationship did not occur for younger men indicates that middle-aged and older men may be particularly susceptible to the effects of occupational stress on health.[24]

Closely related to job satisfaction is a man's sense of self-esteem in his work. In the same study, I found that low self-esteem in work was associated with elevated heart disease risk, again primarily for middle-aged and older men, and even more strongly than in the case of job satisfaction. But self-esteem did not relate to heart disease risk among blue-collar men, whereas job satisfaction did. Stanislav Kasl and Sidney Cobb have reported results of a longitudinal study of blue-collar workers who lost their jobs because of the closing of several factories.[25] They found that low self-esteem was associated with high levels of (or increases in) heart disease risk factors. (Self-esteem declined with loss of job and rose with the finding of a new job.) Thus unemployment is one social factor contributing to low self-esteem and hence poorer health prognosis.

An earlier study found strong evidence that men with low self-esteem at work visited their company dispensary much more frequently—perhaps low self-esteem predisposes men to a wider variety of illnesses than just heart disease.[26] Similarly, strong evidence was found that men who felt their jobs were dull and boring made more dispensary visits. In contrast to these studies, it should be noted that others have found no clear, direct relationship between self-esteem and heart disease risk in studies of professional workers.[27] But on balance, these seems to be increasing evidence that low job satisfaction and low self-esteem in work predispose men to heart disease and perhaps other diseases as well.

Job pressures. More closely related to what people normally think of as occupational stress are the effects of high levels of work load, responsibility, and conflict or ambiguity in occupational roles—what will be termed here job "pressures." A series of studies have found that feelings of work overload are associated with elevated heart disease risk in a variety of populations. Work overload refers to a person's feeling that the demands of his job are greater than he can handle, given his available time, resources, and abilities. Deadlines are a frequent source of overload.

Among 104 university professors, men who felt overloaded had significantly higher cholesterol and significantly lower self-esteem.[28] In an unpublished study of twenty-two white-collar employees of the National Aeronautics and Space Administration (NASA), feelings of overload were associated with higher levels of heartbeat rate and cholesterol,[29] although a later study on a larger sample in the same organization failed to replicate this finding.[30] These studies also found significant positive correlations between subjective reports of work overload and more objective measures (ranging from wives' reports of the number of hours their husbands worked to direct observational measures of the demands made on men by others in the organization). These objective measures were also associated with elevated heart disease risk, but the results suggest that the effects of objective job conditions are mediated through the person's subjective experience of overload or stress.

These data are in line with earlier studies relating work load and job pressures to changes in heart disease risk factors. A seminal investigation found marked increases in serum cholesterol in tax accountants as the April 15 deadline for filing federal income tax returns approached.[31] A number of studies have found significantly higher levels of cholesterol in medical students on the day before exams as compared with times when they were not facing exams.[32] It is plausible that these changes are attributable to increased work load. They highlight what it is about work *overload,* as opposed to sheer work load, that makes it stressful—the feeling that one does not have enough time or ability and hence may fail.[33]

Responsibility for the work of others has recently been implicated as a correlate of selected heart disease risk factors and possibly other illnesses. It has been found that managers, scientists, and engineers in NASA who spent a higher percentage of their time on such responsibilities smoked more cigarettes and had higher diastolic blood pressure.[34] Studies showing high levels of heart disease risk among executives might also support this responsibility hypothesis.[35]

Further support for the role of occupational stress in heart disease risk was obtained in my recent study of 288 men in a wide variety of both white-collar (the focus of most of the previous research) and blue-collar jobs.[36] A composite measure of job pressures (including work overload, responsibility, and role conflict) was associated with significantly greater heart disease risk in virtually the whole range of occupations. Like the findings on job satisfaction and self-esteem in this study, the effects of occupational stress were much more pronounced among middle-aged and older men.

Several studies have documented a relationship between occupational pressure or stress and actual coronary heart disease. One researcher asked a number of practicing professionals to rank several categories of practice within the fields of medicine, dentistry, and law in terms of the amount of "occupational stress" involved in each specialty.[37] Regardless of the specific profession involved, the individuals in "high stress" categories of practice reported a higher incidence of coronary disease. In a study of 100 young coronary patients compared to an equal number in a control group, it was found that "prolonged emotional strain associated with job responsibility" preceded the heart attacks of 91 percent of the patients, while such strain was evident in only 20 percent of the control group.[38] Further, this difference between the groups was greater than differences in family history of heart disease, diet, obesity, smoking, and physical exercise. A similar study found that 50 percent of heart disease patients (but only 12 percent of a control group) reported working long hours with few vacations prior to the onset of their diseases.[39]

Thus there is consistent evidence that job pressures—such as work overload, responsibility, and conflicting demands from others—play a significant role in increasing levels of heart disease risk and actual coronary heart disease. Further corroboration of these results will be seen when we turn to data on personality and social situational factors.

Incongruity and change. A final set of factors seems important as a source of occupational stress leading to heart disease, although their exact social and psychological meaning is unclear. A variety of accumulating evidence indicates that a life history of occupational mobility or rapid change in occupational environment predisposes men to heart disease. Researchers point to the "complexification" (or the rate at which things change or become increasingly complex) of the occupational environment as a form of work overload which taxes a person's ability to adapt to new demands.[40] People who are occupationally or geographically mobile (hence exposing themselves to change, complexity, and new demands) and people whose environment changes rapidly around them seem to experience greater heart disease and greater illness of all kinds.[41] The growing evidence that those whose status is incongruent (for example, men with low education in high-status jobs) are more prone to heart disease may, in fact, reflect effects of work overload (their job demands exceed their capacity) rather than "status incongruity.[42]

Conditioning personal characteristics. So far we have considered the direct relationships between objective and subjective aspects of work situations and heart disease. Where the evidence is based on subjective reports of dissatisfaction or occupational stress, it is probable that these subjective reports are the outcome of interactions between objective characteristics of the situation and the characteristics of the person (his motives, needs, abilities, etc.), but attempts to document this empirically are just beginning.[43]

What is more important, there is a large and growing body of literature indicating that men with a certain type of "behavior pattern" are most prone to coronary heart disease. This behavior pattern has been extensively investigated by the physicians Meyer Friedman and Rey Rosenman and the psychologist David Jenkins. Labeled the "Type A behavior-pattern," it is characterized by ". . . excessive drive, aggressiveness, ambition, involvement in competitive activities, frequent vocational deadlines, [and] an enhanced sense of time urgency. . . . The converse . . . pattern, called Type B is characterized by the relative absence of this *interplay of psychological traits and situational pressures.*"[44]

In a series of studies (including an ongoing prospective study of 3400 men now in its eighth year) the Type A man (relative to the Type B) has been shown to be significantly more likely (by a factor of 1.4 to 6.5) to have an actual heart attack.[45] His risk of recurrent and fatal heart attacks has also been shown to be higher. Other investigators have found results in line with those of Friedman, Rosenman, and Jenkins.[46] It is worth noting that in several studies the Type A variable has been shown to have significant predictive power, even when levels of a whole range of standard physiological risk factors are statistically controlled.

The meaning of these results remains unclear, however, since the Type A pattern reflects "an interplay of psychological traits and situational pressures." To some extent these results may be a further demonstration of the importance of work overload and other job pressures discussed above. What role is played by psychological traits? One possibility is that the Type A person possesses personality traits (such as impatience, ambition, competitiveness, and aggressiveness) which cause him to self-select himself into jobs involving greater "stress" ("time urgency," "frequent vocational deadlines," etc.).[47] No direct empirical test of this proposition has been made, however.

It may be that the key psychological trait of the Type A man is his "desire for social achievement" (reflected in ambition, competitiveness, aggressiveness).[48] This trait would appear to be closely related to status seeking or extrinsic motivation for working (desire for money, status, recognition) as opposed to intrinsic motivation (desire for interesting, satisfying work). One study I conducted predicted that persons with extrinsic motivations for working were more likely to select themselves into jobs involving greater occupational stress and hence to experience heart disease. Contrariwise, intrinsically motivated persons would avoid highly stressful work and hence avoid heart disease. Considerable support for these hypotheses was found among white-collar workers, but among blue-collar workers it was intrinsic motivation that was associated with reports of occupational stress and higher levels of heart disease risk. As with other results from this study, these findings indicate that it is difficult to generalize from the predominant type of study in this field (involving white-collar, often professional workers) to men in all types of jobs.

In research on professionals in NASA, it was found that under conditions of occupational stress Type A persons are more prone to manifest increases in heart disease or its risk factors.[49] If this is true, the dramatic and consistent results derived from the Friedman, Rosenman, and Jenkins research may be due to the fact that the classification of a man as Type A indicates that he both possesses certain personality traits *and* experiences greater situational pressures. The role of personality in leading men into situations of stress and/or accentuating the effects of such situations deserves further study.

Conditioning social characteristics. Just as personality factors may determine whether a person experiences stress and how he reacts to it, so may other characteristics of the work situation. I have already noted that social and organizational change are likely to increase stress. For example, those in positions that involve great contact with external environments (and hence more varied and perhaps changing social situations) suffer greater emotional strain[50] and heart disease risk.[51] Alternatively, the work environment may provide resources that mitigate the effects of stress on the individual. Prescriptive theories of work organizations suggest that social support from peers, superiors, and subordinates improves the ability of men to cope with job stress and hence should enhance physical and mental health.[52]

Among professionals in NASA who report high levels of social support from coworkers, there is little relationship between perceived occupational stress and heart disease risk, while among those who report low levels of social support, occupational stress clearly increases heart disease risk.[53] Similar results have been obtained in studies of industrial work groups using measures of mental health as the relevant outcome.[54] And it has been hypothesized that the low rate of heart disease in Japan is due *not* to the presence of less occupational stress but rather to the structure of Japanese work and social organizations, which provide greater support for the individual in face of stress.[55]

As the populations studied in heart disease research have increased in variety, evidence is emerging that stresses that relate to heart disease or its risk factors in some groups may not in others. I have already pointed out differences among age and occupational groups in this regard. The results suggest that personality or environment differences among the groups are proximate causes of the differential in susceptibility to disease. As these findings are explored further, other personality and social situational variables may well be recognized as important conditioners of the relationship between objective or subjective indicators of stress and heart disease.

Work and Other Diseases

Peptic ulcer and rheumatoid arthritis, two other diseases in which social or occupational stress may play a role, provide a framework for examining heart disease. Although there are commonalities of these diseases and heart disease in terms of distribution across demographic groups and associated stress factors, there are also significant differences. Rheumatoid arthritis is second only to heart disease as a cause of disability and days lost from work, while peptic ulcer and other gastrointestinal diseases rank fourth. These diseases are insignificant in terms of mortality, however.[56]

Peptic Ulcer

Although the data are fairly sparse, the distribution of peptic ulcer and some of its occupational correlates shows marked similarities to that of heart disease. Peptic ulcer, like heart disease, is several times more common (in terms of mortality and morbidity) in males than females and is especially frequent in white males. As with heart disease, there has been a decrease in peptic ulcer in males since 1957, while rate of peptic ulcer in younger women has been rising. But unlike heart disease, mortality from this disease is clearly more frequent in lower social classes.[57] Again, sex differences and trends suggest the relevance of occupational factors, and the status differences are congruent with findings reported below.

There have been a variety of studies of differences among occupational groups in terms of peptic ulcer rates. Most suggest that jobs involving greater levels of responsibility and/or interpersonal tension and conflict pre-dispose men (such as foremen and executives) to ulcer.[58] Home responsi-bilities on top of job responsibilities seem to increase the risk of ulcer. Ulcers are more common in men with more children,[59] and younger women who both work and have family responsibilities have been found to be more prone to ulcers than women who have responsibilities in only one domain.[60] (The relationship of responsibility to ulcers is intriguingly collaborated by an experiment with "executive" monkeys. In this experiment, ulcers were in-duced in monkeys who had responsibility for pushing a button to prevent themselves and a powerless partner from receiving a shock.)[61] That inter-personal conflict may also contribute to the above findings is suggested by results showing a higher rate of peptic ulcer in males who experience such conflict in their marriages.[62] These scattered data suggesting that responsi-bility and interpersonal conflict contribute to the development of ulcers are consistent with numerous clinical reports that ulcer patients evidence neu-rotic conflict in regard to aggressiveness and dependency impulses.[63]

The greater prevalance of ulcer in lower-status groups deserves note. Robert L. Kahn and John R. P. French report a set of findings showing that self-esteem in work decreases with decreasing social status, while occur-rence of peptic ulcer rises as self-esteem declines.[64] Thus low self-esteem (often resulting from low status) may predispose people to ulcer as well as to heart disease.

These data suggest that interpersonal conflict, responsibility for others, and self-esteem in work influence the development of peptic ulcer. The strong similarities between the findings on ulcer and those on heart disease raise the intriguing question of why these diseases do not occur more often in the same persons.

Rheumatoid Arthritis

The evidence on rheumatoid arthritis presents quite a different picture from what we have encountered thus far. First, the disease is more common in women than men, at least in its mild to moderately severe forms. (No clear sex differences exist at severe and disabling levels.) Like many diseases, rheumatoid arthritis is more prevalent in lower social strata, but in contrast to most other diseases this is more true for males than females.[65]

Studies relating occupational factors to rheumatoid arthritis are almost nonexistent. What data are available suggest that, in line with what the greater prevalence in women might lead us to expect, occupational stress may be a relatively less important factor in rheumatoid arthritis than in heart disease or peptic ulcer. Interpersonal conflict in family settings has been most clearly shown to relate to increased prevalence of rheumatoid arthritis.[66] Personality research shows that people with rheumatoid arthritis tend to be sensitive and inhibited in expressing anger and hence are likely to harbor resentment in the face of conflict.[67] There is no reason that such conflicts at work as well as at home might not produce rheumatoid arthritis in people with this type of personality, but no clear evidence exists.

Only a few studies bear even tangentially on the role of occupational stress in this disease, although an increase in symptoms of arthritis have been detected among a group of men who had recently lost their jobs.[68] Arthritis has also been found to be more common in people whose incomes are much lower than one would expect on the basis of their education (a possible source of job dissatisfaction?).[69] Even these effects, however, may be due to the effects of the occupational situation on family life rather than directly on the person.

Assessment of Research Findings

On the whole, there is already considerable evidence that occupational stress is a factor that increases morbidity and mortality from physical disease, especially heart disease.[70] The complexity of this evidence suggests that different forms of occupational stress may have differential effects on various subgroups of the total population defined in terms of standard characteristics (such as age, occupation, and sex), personality (such as "Type A"), or social situation (such as social support). These results suggest the need for further research and the potential fruitfulness of it. Some specific suggestions for directions of future research are made below.

The direct policy implications of these results are more problematic. Many medically oriented professionals tend to be unimpressed by such evidence and contend that it is premature to consider social and psychological variables in programs of disease prevention and control. In response, a number of points should be made. First, the power of known medical causes or risk factors in predicting disease is not great. For example, in the area of heart disease even the best combinations of risk factors (such as high levels of smoking, blood pressure, and cholesterol) probably provide at most only fair predictions of the actual incidence of disease.[71] Various forms of occupational stress have been shown both to be associated with these medical risk factors and to make an independent contribution to predicting incidence of disease even when known medical risk factors are implicitly or explicitly controlled. Where explicit statistical controls are employed, as noted above, the stress variables often predict the incidence of disease as well as or better than the known medical risk factors. Thus, one of the main contributions of the type of research reviewed here is to suggest additional factors that improve our ability to predict disease (and ultimately control it) over and above the known medical risk factors.

Second, it appears that the status of the social and psychological variables identified here as "causes of disease" is at least as strong as, if not stronger than, the status of a number of variables manipulated in disease control programs (such as diet and exercise in heart disease control programs). Further, certain of the stress variables (or the personality and social situational conditioners of their effects) often are no harder to manipulate than diet or exercise.

Policy Implications

The policy implications of these results are twofold. First, what we have learned so far suggests the need for further research and the development of competent social scientists and medical researchers to do such work. Second, there is good reason to begin experimentation with disease prevention programs that include efforts to manipulate relevant occupational stresses. These tasks of research and experimentation are, of course, complementary. Research will help to identify the most relevant socio-psychological factors contributing to disease; field experiments will test both the feasibility of manipulating these factors and the effects of manipulating. Such field experiments are crucial to establishing causality and estimating the magnitude of the effects of social and psychological variables on physical health.

Research strategies. The kinds of populations included in research on occupational stress and disease need to be broadened. The bulk of existing research derives from studies of white, male, white-collar workers in specific occupations or organizations. Within specific occupations or organizations blue-collar workers, women, and blacks should be increasingly studied. To learn more about these groups and to understand the degree to which our knowledge from studies in specific organizations can be generalized, a limited number of studies in representative populations should be encouraged. The National Health Survey physical examination program could also be coordinated with a program of interviews on life stress and satisfaction. These large-scale studies should focus on testing the generalizability of conclusions from more limited studies of specific organizations or groups. The large-scale studies also provide a natural vehicle for assessing the degree to which given types of stress relate to one versus many disease entities. Since assessments of multiple diseases are routinely made in these studies, extra costs for collecting such information would be eliminated.

The more limited studies should serve as the crucial area for refining our theoretical knowledge about the nature of occupational stress and its effects on individuals. The complex interplay between the person and his environment, including processes of coping with stress, especially deserve attention. Increasing effort must be directed toward longitudinal or experimental designs.

The theoretical framework developed at the beginning of this paper in conjunction with the findings reviewed here suggest clear focuses for future research. Essentially, future studies should seek to deal with at least two of the classes of social and psychological variables discussed above *in addition to some outcome* (physical health variable). Assessment of objective conditions of work, subjective perceptions of stress, and individual and/or social situational characteristics can produce answers to the following kinds of questions:

• Are certain kinds of people (for example, Type A or extrinsically motivated individuals) more likely to seek out objective conditions conducive to stress; and are they more likely to perceive a given objective situation as stressful?

• Are given objective conditions (such as levels of work load and responsibility) more likely to be perceived as stressful under some conditions (such as competition, nonsupportive relationships with coworkers, inequalities of power or status) than others (such as supportive relations with coworkers, more equal power and status)?

• To what degree are the effects of objective conditions of work mediated through subjective perceptions of stress? Does this depend on other individual or situational characteristics?

Consideration of individual responses to stress (coping processes) in conjunction with measures of other individual or social situational characteristics, objective conditions of work, and subjective perceptions thereof can produce answers to the following kinds of questions:

• What sorts of coping or adaptation responses mitigate the effects of stress on health, and which exacerbate these effects?

- Are certain kinds of coping responses effective only for certain kinds of stresses, persons, or situations?
- Which individual and social characteristics determine the kind of strategy a person chooses for coping with given stresses?

Finally, research on social stress and physical disease will require increased collaboration of social and medical scientists. Such cooperation is not always easy. Interdisciplinary training programs may be useful in increasing the supply of talent capable of such endeavors.

Intervention strategies. It would be rash to assert that our present knowledge of the effects of occupational stress on health offers clear guides to social intervention strategies. Further, efforts to reduce disease, prolong life, reduce stress, and increase satisfaction should not be undertaken without consideration of the costs (easily unanticipated) as well as benefits of such strategies. Nevertheless, two kinds of opportunities for experimentation with social or occupational stress should be considered.

First, for reasons other than improving physical health, efforts to increase job satisfaction and reduce or mitigate the effects or selected occupational stresses are likely to be made to reduce social conflict, improve productivity, etc. Where such efforts are being made, resources should be found to assess their effects on a full range of social indicators including physical health. The effects of such changes on physical health may provide some of the strongest and clearest evidence about their individual and social benefits.

Second, some organizations and small communities are likely to be receptive to experimental efforts to reduce the incidence of physical disease through alterations in life or job satisfaction and stress. Increasing job satisfaction or reducing occupational stress is not an easy matter. As we have seen, those factors in the person and his environment that contribute to stress are complexly interrelated. Nevertheless, let me outline how one might proceed with such a study given a willing population:[72]

- Efforts should begin with diagnostic procedures to make sure that the variables to be manipulated (such as job satisfaction, work overload, responsibility, social structure or group relations, and personality characteristics) do in fact bear a clear relationship to one or more indicators of physical health in the population under study.
- Based on the diagnostic procedures, priorities should be established among the most important factors to be altered. These may be (1) characteristics of the person (such as task and coping abilities, motives or needs, and styles of responding to situations); (2) characteristics of the environ-

ment or social structure (such as levels of work load, responsibility, social support, degree of competition versus cooperation, and participation in decision making); or (3) both kinds of characteristics simultaneously. Ultimately the aim is to improve the "fit" of the person and his environment, since stress may be most generally conceived of as a lack of fit.

• Careful consideration should be given to the efficacy and ethics of proposed means of initiating change. Considerable social research and theory suggests that planned forms of both personal and social change are most likely to succeed when the individuals to be affected have *meaningfully* participated in the decision. Such a strategy also is congruent with evolving social concerns about the ethics of experimentation involving human subjects. Such a procedure for instituting change is itself a major structural innovation.

• The above review suggests some initial kinds of experimental programs. At the level of the individual, efforts can be made to modify, or at least make the individual aware of, personality and behavioral traits that may threaten his health (somewhat analogous to efforts to change patterns of diet, smoking, or exercise). Attempts may also be made to train individuals to cope better with stresses that they confront. At the level of the social environment, efforts can be made to alter levels of work load, responsibility, or interpersonal conflict through modifications of social structures (for example, dividing responsibility among several people; altering patterns of communication and authority relationships). Structural arrangements also may be created with increased levels of social support in the face of stress. Finally, job selection and placement procedures offer a means of increasing the "fit" of individuals and job environments.

• Careful evaluation and utilization of these findings is of course essential.

It now appears likely that the federal government will support research and intervention programs aimed at ameliorating the current "epidemics" of chronic diseases (especially cancer and heart disease). Both research and disease control programs should adequately recognize the role of social and psychological factors in the causation of these diseases. Prevention is a more promising route to disease control than treatment, and the evidence that I have suggests that occupational stress must be central in any heart disease prevention program. Even within existing levels of expenditures much could be gained from judicious promotion of research and field experimentation in this area.

The accumulating evidence that various forms of occupational stress (such as job dissatisfaction, or "alienation," and job pressures) contribute significantly to increased rates of physical diseases as well as other social problems argues strongly for efforts to improve the "quality of work" in American society. The data on variation in disease by social and employment status lend support to already proposed efforts to increase job and income security in the United States (through guaranteed income and/or employment programs, for example). Work remains the main source of income and community status for individuals in American society, and income and status importantly determine exposure to nonwork stress and adequate medical care.

But we also need to go further and attempt to alter the nature of work to make it more satisfying and less stressful. Such efforts should produce gains in physical health as well as in other social indicators. In many ways the effects of occupational stress on physical health most clearly document the economic and human price this nation is paying for having emphasized too long (in business, government, and even labor unions) the physical and economic nature of work at the expense of its social and psychological components. When we begin to envision change in work environments of the types suggested above, we are in fact talking about major social change in our economic and social structure. The evidence is at hand to suggest the utility of limited structural changes for evaluation purposes. Such experiments must be undertaken with a serious commitment to improving the quality of work, even if it means breaking with old practices and traditions.

Notes

1. Robert S. Weiss and David Riesman, "Work and Automation: Problems and Prospects," in *Contemporary Social Problems,* 2d ed., ed. Robert K. Merton and Robert A. Nisbet (New York: Harcourt, Brace and World, 1966).

2. Victor H. Vroom, "Industrial Social Psychology," in *Handbook of Social Psychology,* 2d ed., vol. 5, ed. Gardner Lindzey and E. Aronson (Reading, Mass.: Addison-Wesley, 1968).

3. J. E. McGrath, ed., *Social and Psychological Factors in Stress* (New York: Holt, Rinehart & Winston, 1970); Sol Levine and Norman A. Scotch, *Social Stress* (Chicago: Aldine, 1971); "Social Stress and Cardiovascular Disease," *Milbank Memorial Fund Quarterly* 24, no. 2, pt. 2 (1967).

4. John R. P. French, Jr., and Robert Caplan, "Organizational Stress and Individual Strain," in *The Failure of Success,* ed. A. J. Marrow (New York: American Management Association, 1972); McGrath.

5. C. D. Jenkins, "Psychologic and Social Precursors of Coronary Disease," *New England Journal of Medicine* 284 (1971): 244–255, 307–317.

6. McGrath.

7. R. S. Lazarus, *Psychological Stress and the Coping Process* (New York: McGraw-Hill, 1966).

8. J. S. Felton and Robert Cole, "The High Cost of Heart Disease," *Circulation* 27 (1963): 957–962.

9. I. M. Moriyama, D. E. Krueger, and Jeremiah Stamler, *Cardiovascular Diseases in the United States* (Cambridge: Harvard University Press, 1971).

10. Ibid.

11. Evelyn M. Kitagawa and P. M. Hauser, "Education Differentials in Mortality by Cause of Death: United States, 1960," *Demography* 5 (1968): 318–353.

12. Kitagawa and Hauser; Erdman Palmore and Frances Jeffers, *Prediction of Life Span* (Boston: Heath Lexington, 1971).

13. Kitagawa and Hauser; Monroe Lerner, "Social Differences in Physical Health," in *Poverty and Health: A Sociological Analysis*, ed. John Kosa, A. Antonovsky, and I. K. Zola (Cambridge: Harvard University Press, 1969).

14. Palmore and Jeffers; Erdman Palmore, "Physical, Mental, and Social Factors in Predicting Longevity" and "Predicting Longevity: A Follow-up for Age," *The Gerontologist* 9 (1969): 103–108 and 247–250.

15. Because of the age of the sample, if respondents asked what was meant by work it was defined to include any useful activity including housework, gardening, etc. Questions in the measure asked about being able to do useful work in a competent way. This variable is therefore not precisely analogous to "job satisfaction" in an employed population. Nevertheless, it does reflect a general satisfaction derived from working. Further, the measure of work satisfaction shows its strongest relationship to longevity in that subgroup of the sample (males sixty to sixty-nine) who were most likely to be gainfully employed at the time of their initial examination and interview.

16. Moriyama, Krueger, and Stamler, chap. 4; Renee Marks, "Factors Involving Social and Demographic Characteristics: A Review of Empirical Findings," *Milbank Memorial Fund Quarterly* 45 (1967), no. 2, pt. 2: 51–108; A. Antonovsky, "Social Class and the Major Cardiovascular Diseases," *Journal of Chronic Diseases* 21 (1968): 65–108; Jenkins.

17. Moriyama, Krueger, and Stamler.

18. Ibid.

19. Lillian Guralnick, "Mortality by Occupation and Cause of Death among Men 20 to 64," *Vital Statistics Special Reports* 53 (1963), no. 3.

20. Jenkins; E. A. Suchman, "Factors Involving Social and Demographic Characteristics: Appraisal and Implications for Theoretical Development," *Milbank Memorial Fund Quarterly* 45 (1967), no. 2, pt. 2: 109–116.

21. Note that critically high levels of CHD risk factors are generally diseases in their own right: hypertension (high blood pressure), diabetes (high blood sugar), obesity, hypercholesteremia (high cholesterol).

22. Jenkins.

23. Steven Sales and James S. House, "Job Dissatisfaction as a Possible Risk Factor in Coronary Heart Disease," *Journal of Chronic Diseases* 23 (1971): 861–873.

24. James S. House, "The Relationship of Intrinsic and Extrinsic Work Motivations to Occupational Stress and Coronary Heart Disease Risk" (Ph.D. diss., University of Michigan, 1972).

25. Stanislav V. Kasl, Sidney Cobb, and G. W. Brooks, "Changes in Serum Uric Acid and Cholesterol Levels in Men Undergoing Job Loss," *Journal of the American Medical Association* 206 (1968): 1500–1507; Stanislav V. Kasl and Sidney Cobb, "Blood Pressure Changes in Men Undergoing Job Loss: A Preliminary Report," *Psychosomatic Medicine* 32 (1970): 19–38.

26. Stanislav V. Kasl and John R. P. French, Jr., "The Effects of Occupational Status on Physical and Mental Health," *Journal of Social Issues* 18 (1962): 67–89.

27. Robert Caplan, "Organizational Stress and Individual Strain: A Social-psychological Study of Risk Factors in Coronary Heart Disease among Administrators, Engineers, and Scientists" (Ph.D. diss., University of Michigan, 1971); John R. P. French, Jr., John Tupper, and Ernst Mueller, *Work Load of University Professors,* U.S. Office of Education, Cooperative Research Project No. 2171 (Ann Arbor: University of Michigan, 1965).

28. Ibid.

29. Robert Caplan and John R. P. French, Jr., "Final Report to NASA," unpublished (University of Michigan, 1968).

30. Caplan.

31. Meyer Friedman, Rey H. Rosenman, and Vernice Carroll, "Changes in the Serum Cholesterol and Blood Clotting Time of Men Subjects to Cyclic Variation of Occupational Stress," *Circulation* 18 (1957): 852–861.

32. S. M. Sales, "Organizational Roles as a Risk Factor in Coronary Heart Disease," *Administrative Science Quarterly* 14 (1969), no. 3: 235–336.

33. Albert Pepitone, "Self, Social Environment, and Stress," in *Psychological Stress,* ed. Mortimer H. Appley and Richard Trumbull (New York: Appleton-Century-Crofts, 1967).

34. Caplan.

35. H. J. Montoye et al., "Serum Uric Acid Concentration among Business Executives with Observations on Other Coronary Heart Disease Risk Factors," *Annals of Internal Medicine* 66 (1967): 838–850.

36. House.

37. H. I. Russek, "Emotional Stress and Coronary Heart Disease in American Physicians, Dentists, and Lawyers," *American Journal of Medical Science* 243 (1962): 616–625.

38. H. I. Russek, "Stress, Tobacco, and Coronary Heart Disease in North American Professional Groups," *Journal of the American Medical Association* 192 (1965): 189–194.

39. H. W. H. Miles et al., "Psychosomatic Study of 46 Young Men with Coronary Artery Disease," *Psychosomatic Medicine* 16 (1954): 455–477. Also see H. E. S. Pearson and Joyce Joseph, "Stress and Occlusive Coronary-Artery Disease," *The Lancet* 1 (1963): 415–418; Edward Weiss et al., "Emotional Factors in Coronary Occlusion," *Archives of Internal Medicine* 99 (1957): 628–641.

40. Caplan; Shirley Terreberry, "The Organization of Environments" (Ph.D. diss., University of Michigan, 1968).

41. T. H. Holmes and R. H. Rahe, "The Social Readjustment Rating Scale," *Journal of Psychosomatic Research* 11 (1967): 213–225; Thomasina Smith, "Sociocultural Incongruity and Change: A Review of Empirical Findings," *Milbank Memorial Fund Quarterly* 45 (1967), no. 2, pt. 2: 17–46.

42. Jenkins.

43. French and Caplan; Caplan; M. R. Blood and C. L. Hulin, "Alienation, Environmental Characteristics and Worker Responses," *Journal of Applied Psychology* 51 (1967): 284–290.

44. C. David Jenkins, Rey H. Rosenman, and Meyer Friedman, "Development of an Objective Psychological Test for the Determination of the Coronary-prone Behavior Pattern," *Journal of Chronic Diseases* 20 (1967): 371–379.

45. Jenkins; S. M. Sales, "Differences among Individuals in Affective, Behavioral, Biochemical, and Physiological Responses to Variations in Work Load" (Ph.D. diss., University of Michigan, 1969); idem, "Organizational Roles."

46. Jenkins.

47. Sales, "Organizational Roles."

48. House.

49. Caplan.

50. Robert L. Kahn et al., *Organizational Stress: Studies in Role Conflict and Ambiguity* (New York: Wiley, 1964).

51. Caplan.

52. Rensis Likert, *The Human Organization: Its Management and Value* (New York: McGraw-Hill, 1967).

53. Caplan.

54. Stanley Seashore, *Group Cohesiveness in the Industrial Work Group* (Ann Arbor: University of Michigan, Institute for Social Research, 1954).

55. Y. S. Matsumoto, "Social Stress and Coronary Heart Disease in Japan: A Hypothesis," *Milbank Memorial Fund Quarterly* 48 (1970): 9–31.

56. Sidney Cobb, *The Frequency of the Rheumatic Diseases* (Cambridge: Harvard University Press, 1971); Albert Mendeloff and James P. Dunn, *Digestive Diseases* (Cambridge: Harvard University Press, 1971).

57. Ibid.

58. Mervyn Susser, "Causes of Peptic Ulcer: A Selective Epidemiologic Review," *Journal of Chronic Diseases* 20 (1967): 435–456.

59. P. G. Vertin, "Bedryfsgeneeskundige Aspecten van het Ulcus Pepticum [Occupational Health Aspects of Peptic Ulcer] (thesis, University of Groningen, Netherlands, 1954).

60. Mendeloff.

61. J. V. Brady, "Ulcers in the 'Executive' Monkeys," *Scientific American* 199 (1958): 95–105.

62. Sidney Cobb et al., "The Intrafamilial Transmission of Rheumatoid Arthritis: VII. Why Do Wives with Rheumatoid Arthritis Have Husbands with Peptic Ulcer?" *Journal of Chronic Diseases* 22 (1969): 279–294.

63. Susser.

64. Robert L. Kahn and John R. P. French, Jr., "Status and Conflict: Two Themes in the Study of Stress," in *Social and Psychological Factors in Stress,* ed. J. E. McGrath (New York: Holt, Rinehart & Winston, 1970).

65. Cobb.

66. Sidney Cobb, M. Miller, and M. Wieland, "On the Relationship between Divorce and Rheumatoid Arthritis," *Arthritis and Rheumatism* 2 (1959): 414–418; Stanislav V. Kasl and Sidney Cobb, "The Intrafamilial Transmission of Rheumatoid Arthritis: V. Differences between Rheumatoid Arthritis and Controls on Selected Personality Variables" and "VI. Association of Rheumatoid Arthritis with Several Types of Status Inconsistency," *Journal of Chronic Diseases* 22 (1969): 239–258 and 259–278.

67. Cobb.

68. Cobb.

69. S. H. King and Sidney Cobb, "Psychosocial Factors in the Epidemiology of Rheumatoid Arthritis," *Journal of Chronic Diseases* 7 (1958): 466–475.

70. The focus of this paper on occupational factors affecting health does not imply that measures of satisfaction and stress in other aspects of the person's life are not also important contributors to physical disease. Preliminary evidence suggests that they are. The interplay between satisfaction and stress in work and other roles deserves further study.

71. Jenkins.

72. See also French and Caplan.

8 Work and Mental Health

Stanislav V. Kasl

If a review of evidence is to serve as a basis for policy planning and recommendations, one must begin by stating its objectives and boundaries and by indicating the particular perspective from which it is written. The aim of this review is to organize, summarize, and evaluate the recent empirical evidence (from American studies) that links variations in mental health to differences in the work environment, the primary focus being on studies that permit causal inferences.

Excluded from this review is a large body of occupational mental health literature that is not relevant to its aims.[1] Some of this literature deals with the link between work and mental health from a reversed causal perspective: that is, what the impact is of an employee's mental health problems on his job performance and on his organization, and how the organization can modify this inpact. Other literature is concerned with the selection and placement of employees and with the role of personality traits and vocational interests in predicting subsequent job performance and work adjustment. Omitted also is the literature that deals with metatheoretical issues[2] or with preliminary hypotheses based on clinical intuition or informal observations.

The perspective of this review is a broad sociopsychological one, with an eclectic approach to mental health.[3] Most of the studies discussed utilize self-report methodology, such as structured and standardized interviews or questionnaires.

Since mental health is a particularly troublesome variable, I shall elaborate on the approach I have taken to handling the concept. Basically, variations in approach, definition, and measurement in mental health are the rule rather than the exception. Recent searching examinations of the issue of the conceptual definition and measurement of mental health and mental illness have been plaguing this field.[4] Those studies have failed, however, to provide convergence of opinion—except to emphasize the necessity for multiple definitions and multiple measures. Indeed, it is quite clear that any single measure (such as hospitalization in a mental institution or a psychiatrist's rating) is always going to be both too narrow and too broad. It will be too narrow because it will not reflect all of the underlying dimensions that have been proposed as indicative of mental health. And it will be too broad because it will be contaminated by such influences as reporting biases in questionnaires and the readiness for self-referral in treatment-based indices.

It is possible to group the many partial indicators of mental health into four categories:

• Indices of functional effectiveness or role performance reflect a sociological orientation,[5] and their measurement focuses on quantifying the extent to which a person is unable to perform his usual duties and activities, especially those connected with primary social roles. Hospitalization, absence from work, quitting a job, and deserting a spouse are some examples of this class of mental health criteria.

• Indices of well-being include affective measures (depression, resentment), symptomatic measures (tension, jitters), and the various measures of self-evaluation and satisfaction (self-esteem, job satisfaction, life satisfaction, need satisfaction).

• Indices of mastery and competence, which are emphasized by those with a humanistic orientation to mental health, are positive criteria that include growth and self-actualization, adequacy of coping, use of valued skills, and attainment of valued goals.

• Psychiatric signs and symptoms include dimensions that are not readily classified into one of the other categories and yet are considered to be clinically significant by the discipline of psychiatry. One is the perception of reality.

Taken together, these categories of indicators constitute a working definition of mental health. Their very multiplicity indicates that one index is *not* an adequate substitute for another. Moreover, a useful index of mental health is *not* generated by averaging all the separate indices. We should be interested in the empirical *association* among them. For example, there are several community follow-up studies of discharged mental hospital patients that indicate a very low correspondence between symptomatology and psychosocial functioning.[6] Using a variety of criteria should alert us to the difficulties of interpreting some of the traditional behavioral measures. For example, absenteeism from work may be seen as an indication of inadequate role performance, but it may also reflect coping with some job stress and thus contribute positively to mental well-being.

The Meaning of Work

Defining work seems easier than defining mental health, perhaps partly because the vernacular term *job* is seldom substantially modified by the social scientist in order to create a useful construct. Many writers have discussed the criterial characteristics of work and the structural features of the work setting.[7] From a broad perspective, however, the current definition of work appears to be culture-bound and time-bound and does not particularly fit such roles as those of the housewife or the volunteer worker. Moreover, as Robert Kahn points out, our current notion of work may be an "eroding definition" in an affluent, technologically advanced society—which, apparently, cannot provide employment for everyone who wishes it.[8] What may be needed is a greater fusion of the work role and the leisure role.[9]

It would be difficult to find writers who have not described the work role as a critical one in our society or as a central life activity. Work takes up a large part of the worker's time and effort and is the major source of income. For the individual, it is probably the chief means of contact with the society at large,[10] and it has a major influence on shaping his self-concept or self-identity.[11] These are sweeping generalizations which have presumably been intended to characterize primarily the male role in our society. Even though they are too broad and too vague to be tested directly, they need to be examined because the uncritical acceptance of them at this point might lead to a later reluctance to examine without prejudice the relationship between work and mental health.

There are two major lines of evidence regarding "the meaning of work"· studies of motivation for work and studies of retirement. In a national sample of employed men, 80 percent indicated that they would continue working even if they inherited enough money to live comfortably without working.[12] (Among those who stated that work did nothing for their sense of importance and usefulness, 60 percent still indicated that they would go on working.) Stated reasons for continuing to work were quite revealing: only 9 percent said they enjoyed work, and only another 10 percent indicated that work contributed to their health or self-respect. When asked what they would miss if they didn't work, 9 percent said that they would miss the feeling of doing something worthwhile. One-third said they would miss contact with friends, and a quarter said they would simply feel restless. Other studies suggest that only about a quarter of industrial workers can be called job-oriented because most would not choose "a day's work" as the activity they would miss most.[13] (Many studies have found that work involvement, however measured, increases with the status of the job.)[14]

Turning now to studies of retirement, a Harris poll showed that respondents (especially younger ones) *desire* to retire at an earlier age than they actually *expect* to retire.[15] Although among those already retired 39 percent indicated that retirement failed to fulfill their expectations, less than a quarter of these dissatisfied retirees gave "miss work" as the reason. A study using both a national random sample and a sample of older workers (sixty and over) in the automobile industry has clearly shown that financial considerations are of paramount importance in plans for early retirement and that any attachment to the "work ethic" plays a very small role.[16] When given the opportunity to retire early, one-third of the automobile workers did so, and another third were planning to do so.

Studies of mental health consequences of retirement are not in agreement; some show better morale among elderly men who continue working than among men who retire, others find improvements in reported health after retirement, while still others are unable to attribute any general consequences to retirement.[17] Part of the problem is that cross-sectional comparisons between elderly working individuals and retirees reveal differences that are attributable to either self-selection (that is, who chooses to retire) or to the consequences of retirement. As to which of these is the salient factor, the best guess is that retirement may have adverse consequences only on those who have had a negative prior view of retirement, or who are reluctant retirees, and on those who found intrinsic satisfaction in work. This points out the importance of individual differences among people and among jobs.

Collectively, the studies of the meaning of work and of retirement suggest that low-skilled industrial workers have a rather tenuous attachment to the work role and that their indicated willingness to continue working in the hypothetical absence of financial need reflects not so much the intrinsic satisfaction of work but rather the fact that society has not provided any meaningful alternatives. It is easy to agree with Leonard Sayles and George Strauss that much of the writing on the meaning of work in our society is applicable to workers who do highly skilled or creative work. For those who must perform jobs that are difficult to make intrinsically interesting, a leisure-based culture may be necessary and attachment to the leisure role may be more satisfying.[18]

Mental Health and Job Status

Numerous studies have shown that people from the lowest social class are more likely to be hospitalized[19] and rehospitalized[20] for severe psychiatric illness and to score somewhat higher on interview-based psychiatric symptom checklists than members of higher classes.[21] This evidence might seem to make it rather easy to establish a causal link between low job status and poor mental health, but there are a number of difficulties with such an analysis. One is that social class is a composite index, consisting for the most part of education, occupation, income, and place of residence, and it is difficult to isolate the effect of the occupational dimension. When job level alone is examined with respect to mental illness, the correlation is less consistent than it is with any other of the factors.[22] A more general difficulty with establishing the association between poor mental health and low status is that it has not been possible to reject the hypothesis that people with prior mental health problems experience downward mobility.[23] Thus, while it is plausible to argue that the lower-class environment is characterized by frequent and severe stressful situations that lead to transient and possibly also chronic symptomatology, the work environment itself is not necessarily implicated.

We do find a surfeit of evidence about a positive association between job prestige or status and general job satisfaction, one indicator of mental well-being.[24] Among the components of job satisfaction, those that deal with self-esteem, self-actualization, autonomy, and pay are more closely related to job level than those that deal with work conditions and relations with coworkers or supervisor.[25] Several studies have related occupational level to more general indices of mental health,[26] and we find agreement that people in higher-status jobs have somewhat better mental health (as measured by diverse indices of well-being and of freedom from symptoms). But there are several limitations to this evidence. First, the correlations between job level and job satisfaction or symptomatology, although demonstrated repeatedly in many studies, are rather weak.[27] Second, finer breakdowns of occupation reveal interesting anomalies: for example, male clerical workers appear to have unduly poor mental health[28] and engineers unduly high alienation,[29] given their respective job levels. Third, the higher job satisfaction among respondents in higher-status occupations should not blind us to the fact that these respondents also report more problems at work or worry more about their work.[30] Thus, what may be more closely related to job level is job involvement rather than job satisfaction or some other index of mental health. Finally, it must be noted that in the absence of definitive studies in which the independent variables are fully under experimental control, all associations between job status and mental health variables can receive only a tentative causal interpretation. We cannot impute causality even for such variables as self-esteem, for which a strong theoretical and empirical linkage to job status exists.[31]

Mental Health and Other Dimensions of Work

In addition to job status, many other factors in the work environment have been examined in relation to mental health.

Extensive literature on the subject shows that low job satisfaction is related to the following factors in the work environment:[32]

- *Conditions at work.* The presence of health and safety hazards, unpleasant working conditions (such as fast-paced and physically demanding work), long hours (if forced on the worker), night shifts, unclear tasks, and lack of control over work (such as assembly-line pacing)

- *The activities of the work itself.* Lack of opportunity to use skills and abilities, and highly fractionated, repetitive tasks involving few different operations

- *The work group.* Lack of opportunity to interact with coworkers, large and uncohesive work groups, and nonacceptance by coworkers

- *Supervision.* No participation in decision making, inability to provide feedback to supervisors, lack of recognition for good performance, and inconsiderate or ununderstanding supervisors

- *The organization.* A "flat" organizational structure (with relatively few levels, making career mobility difficult), a staff position (versus a line position), and discriminatory hiring

- *Wages and promotion.* Low financial rewards, perceived inequity in wages, and lack of promotional opportunities.

Additional literature links other indicators of poor mental health with the following factors:[33]

• *Conditions at work.* (Same as those relating to low job satisfaction)

• *The activities of the work itself.* In addition to the characteristics mentioned in relation to low job satisfaction: role overload (both qualitative and quantitative) involving discrepancies among such resources as time, worker's training and skill, machinery, organizational structure, and the demands of the job

• *Shift work.* Fixed afternoon and rotating shifts that affect time-oriented body functions and lead to difficulty in role behavior (that of spouse or parent, for example), particularly for activities that are normally performed during the time of day when the worker is on the shift

• *Supervision.* Job demands that are unclear or conflicting (role ambiguity and role conflicts), close supervision and no autonomy, lack of feedback from supervisor, and problems with one's supervisor

• *The organization.* Working on the fringes of the organization

• *Wages and promotion.* (Same as the characteristics relating to low job satisfaction.)

The obtained relationships to these work factors have been generally stronger for such indicators as life satisfaction, self-esteem, and tension and weaker for indicators based on psychiatric symptoms.

Because of the attention that job enrichment and automation have received, it is worthwhile to discuss these two aspects of the work environment. The relevant literature suggests that job enrichment leads to increased job satisfaction, particularly in the following areas: use of skills and abilities, opportunity to learn new things, perception of work as meaningful (reduced alienation), and amount of responsibility and autonomy.[34] We must distinguish, however, between job *enrichment* (which allows the worker to set his own pace, inspect his own work, set up and repair his own machinery, and so on) and mere job *enlargement* (which only adds elements to the job without altering its quality).[35] There is no evidence that job enlargement has any positive effect on job satisfaction.

To the extent that automation brings about job enrichment, it is a positive influence. But early stages of automation (or, more properly, mechanization) —especially as exemplified by the introduction of new equipment in offices for clerical workers—sometimes represent increased functional specialization and thus lead to *decreased* job satisfaction. Automation may have some other undesirable consequences: the need for closer supervision and a resultant lower satisfaction with supervision; reduced opportunity for social interaction because of constant and close monitoring; greater work pressures because of higher and more rigidly enforced performance standards; reduced job security (as perceived by the worker); and increased feeling that management is impersonal and indifferent.

In evaluating the findings described here, several points have to be kept in mind. First, in many studies the dimensions of the work environment are measured subjectively, that is, they use the worker's perceptions. Therefore, in the cases in which the objective work environment and subjective perceptions of it are only tenuously related, an alteration in the objective work conditions might not have the expected effects on job satisfaction if the subjective perceptions remained unaltered. (For example, in a study by Robert Kahn and his colleagues, an objective measure of role conflict correlated very poorly with a subjective measure.)[36] Second, most of the studies reviewed here are correlational, and causal interpretations of the data are far from obvious. In one study, for example, workers on a rotating shift reported having fewer friends,[37] but does shift work interfere with friendships or do workers who are social isolates opt for this kind of work? Third, many of the dimensions of the work environment correlate with each other (and with job level), and more sophisticated, multivariate analyses are necessary in order to establish which are the crucial dimensions and which others may wash out when statistical controls are applied. And I must emphasize that most of the correlations that have been observed are not very high.[38]

Intercorrelations among Mental Health Indicators

Given that the majority of studies of the work environment have used job satisfaction as the only indicator of mental health, we need to examine the links that can be made between job satisfaction and other mental health indices.

Numerous studies have examined the association of job satisfaction with absenteeism, turnover, and job performance—indices of functional effectiveness.[39] There is reasonable agreement that job satisfaction is negatively correlated with both absenteeism and turnover, but it bears no *uniform* relationship to performance or productivity. Because of these findings, job satisfaction has been interpreted as primarily an index of motivation to come to work. Its possible causal influence on performance appears too complex to lead to a general association. It is more likely that performance has a causal influence on job satisfaction—if good performance is followed by extrinsic (pay and promotion) or intrinsic (use of valued skills) rewards.

Even though absenteeism, turnover, and performance have been the dominant indices of vocational adjustment, they are only partial reflections of functional effectiveness, and they measure only one social role (work). Moreover, they put an exclusive emphasis on compliance with job demands. That vocational adjustment when measured in this fashion can paint a misleading picture about a person's total life is dramatically illustrated by a longitudinal study of women employees of Bell Telephone.[40] In this study, those women who were especially well adjusted, as measured by absences, company dispensary data, and psychiatrist's ratings, were unmarried, led a routine, dull, withdrawn existence, and refused to get involved with other people.

The literature on job satisfaction and other diverse indices of mental health suggests the following:[41]

• Correlations between job satisfaction and indices of personal happiness and life satisfaction are fairly low for men and even lower for women.[42]

• Correlations between indices of vocational adjustment (such as absenteeism) and personal adjustment run somewhat lower, and correlations between job satisfaction and symptom-based indices of mental health are still lower.[43] Among older respondents these correlations are especially low.

• Personal happiness is more closely related to satisfaction with family relationships than with job satisfaction.

• Alienation at work does not seem to generalize to other areas of life, such as intergroup relations or political events. There is no evidence that lack of satisfaction in one area of life is compensated for by particularly strong enjoyment or satisfaction in another—at least in the sense that none of the studies has shown a negative association between a pair of satisfactions or between a pair of mental health indices.

Only limited causal inferences about the relationship of job satisfaction to other indices can be made, however, and these are often in the opposite direction: for example, D. E. Super and J. O. Crites conclude that *prior* personality problems are the most common cause of discharge from work.[44] The safest conclusion, given these relatively weak associations, would be that various aspects of the work environment may have a strong impact on job satisfaction without having much impact on other areas of satisfaction or mental health symptoms. And this conclusion should be further tempered by the suspicion that differences in the generalized tendency to complain or to be defensive have inflated the true association between job satisfaction and other mental health indicators that are also measured by self-report.[45]

Effects of Unemployment

An examination of the consequences of unemployment is a natural extension of this paper's concern with the effects of work on mental health. Unemployment is a major life change; usually it is an involuntary exit from the work environment, and it may tell us much about the meaning of work. At first blush, there appears to be a good deal of suggestive, indirect evidence linking unemployment to poor mental health.[46] A number of studies have shown that high rates of unemployment coexist with, or are shortly followed by, high rates of suicide and psychiatric hospitalization. This global analysis of data leads to many problems, however. For example, the observed link between unemployment and suicide[47] is not always replicated,[48] and case analyses of attempted or actual suicides have not succeeded in pinpointing the role of unemployment.[49] Moreover, rates of psychiatric hospitalization are a very crude, impure index of incidence of mental illness, and the role of other variables, notably financial insecurity, is not at all clear. In short, these associations are ambiguous; we must turn to studies that focus on the experience of unemployment at the level of the individual.

Much of the work on unemployment has been done from the labor-economic viewpoint and is concerned with such issues as factors affecting reemployment, geographical and occupational mobility, the process of finding a new job, and financial difficulties.[50] The literature on mental health consequences, on the other hand, is quite limited.

Many of the relevant unemployment studies date from the late thirties and early forties and are characterized, unfortunately, by such methodological shortcomings as subjective and nonquantifiable data, absence of control groups, and failure to use optimal design (prospective-longitudinal).[51] In addition, the role of other pertinent variables, such as financial difficulties, is seldom examined systematically. One may highlight their findings as follows:

- The employment-unemployment-reemployment cycle was not associated with strong disruption of family structure, personality, or attitudes, except perhaps in families or individuals who were allegedly unstable from the start.
- The best-documented effects of unemployment were in the area of self-esteem, self-respect, depression, and life satisfaction, but it is not clear how long these effects lasted.
- In a great many instances, the men who became unemployed blamed themselves, both in superficial and profound ways, for the loss of their jobs.

• There is no doubt that financial difficulties profoundly altered family life (in terms of leisure activities and daily routines, for example) and that going into debt had additional adverse effects on self-esteem and psychological depression, but the effects of lack of money are difficult to disentangle from the effects of lack of a job.

More recent correlational surveys have shown that, compared to employed men, unemployed men are more unhappy,[52] have higher rates of psychiatric disorder,[53] and believe that their lives are controlled by outside forces rather than by themselves.[54] These findings, of course, are ambiguous regarding the direction of causality. A study of Packard employees after a permanent plant shutdown, though a retrospective account of their experience, does represent a careful analysis of the data.[55] In this study, neither life satisfaction nor alienation was found to be significantly related to length of unemployment. On the other hand, an index of economic deprivation was significantly related to both these mental health variables, which suggests that financial difficulty rather than absence of work is the more powerful variable.

There is, apparently, only one longitudinal investigation into the effects of job loss on mental health.[56] The final results of this study are not yet available, but it appears that men who lost their jobs because of a permanent plant shutdown did not particularly blame themselves for the job loss. Even though some reacted with depression, lowered self-esteem, anger, or anxiety-tension, such reactions were not frequent, and none of these variables were significantly different from those found in a control group.[57] On indices of self-reported health and on physiological variables the unemployed men *did* show the expected stress effects of not working, but these effects were no larger than those associated with the anticipation of the coming plant shutdown that were measured when they were still working.[58] The various indices of mental health did play an indirect role, however: the stress effects on self-reported health and physiological variables were particularly large among men who were poorly adjusted and who found the job loss experience particularly stressful. Variables reflecting community support tended to alleviate the stress.

Individual Differences
A review of this kind would be incomplete without a consideration of how individual traits affect the relationship between work and mental health. Even though the relevant findings come from scattered studies rather than

from a systematic approach to the issue, they point to important limits to the generalizations that have been adduced so far. These studies also suggest conditions under which generalizations hold or do not hold.

There is evidence that individual differences in achievement motivation and aspiration play a crucial role in job satisfaction and mental health. For example, some researchers have concluded that people with high need for achievement will be more dissatisfied, regardless of how high a job level they have reached.[59] There is evidence that the association between job level and job satisfaction is modified by workers' aspirations and that men who fail to achieve the occupational level of their fathers or brothers have lower satisfaction.[60] Robert Kleiner and Seymour Parker have proposed a general theory which links frustrated aspirations to mental disorder,[61] and their findings in a study of urban Negroes support it.[62] The discrepancy in an individual between high educational level and relatively low occupational level has been interpreted as one indicator of frustrated aspirations and has been linked to poor mental health.[63]

Age is one of the demographic characteristics most frequently examined for its role in work and job satisfaction.[64] Older workers (1) are more satisfied with their job, have a better attendance record and less turnover, and identify themselves more strongly with management and its policies, (2) are less concerned with advancement and less worried about keeping their jobs, and (3) have a less positive attitude toward retirement (since work takes on more significance while spare time decreases in significance).

A number of studies have been concerned with the role of various personality variables in modifying the effects of the work environment. Victor Vroom has shown that the effects of participation in decision making on satisfaction and job performance depend very much on the worker's need for independence and the degree of his authoritarianism.[65] Robert Kahn has shown that the effects of role conflict and role overload on tension and job satisfaction are modified by differences in individual flexibility versus rigidity and the resultant differences in the amount of communication with others.[66] Charles Hulin and Milton Blood have shown that individual differences in susceptibility to monotony and boredom play an important role in the effects of job enrichment on satisfaction, absenteeism, and turnover and that beneficial effects of job enrichment can be expected only for workers who are not alienated from middle-class work norms.[67] Rural and small-town workers are apparently less alienated from middle-class work norms than large-city workers; the former reveal greater satisfaction with jobs that involve them personally, while the latter are more satisfied with jobs that are less personally involving.[68] Vroom's reviews offer many other examples of studies in which individual differences in personality characteristics play an important modifying role in job satisfaction.[69]

There is one area that apparently can be ignored: individual differences in importance attached to various aspects of job content and job context. Two studies have concluded that there is no point in weighting job satisfaction scores by the rated importance of each dimension to the respondent.[70]

Complex interactions, such as those between differences in occupational setting and differences in worker characteristics and personality, have sometimes been found. For example, Robert Quinn reports that the association betwen job satisfaction and mental health is stronger among those who are locked into their jobs (that is, those who don't see much of a chance of finding better employment) than among those who are not.[71] Walter Neff has listed a number of differences in occupational setting which he feels may affect the generality of statements about work: (1) degree to which output is under control of the individual worker, (2) extent to which horizontal and vertical mobility is realistically possible, (3) scope of standards of performance, and (4) relative importance of various norms, such as achievement.[72]

Conclusions

This review has thus far been concerned with evidence bearing on the mental health effects of the work environment. Now, in raising the broader and considerably vaguer issue of the implications of this evidence, we need some theoretical framework. The most appropriate appears to be field-theoretical,[73] with particular emphasis on the person-environment (P-E) fit model.[74] This model integrates several elements and processes: (1) the dimensions of the work environment that are job demands (requirements) and those that are resources (need satisfiers), (2) the dimensions of the person that are his abilities (resources) and those that are his needs, (3) the relation, in particular the discrepancies, between the demands and the resources in the environment on the one hand and the needs and the abilities of the person on the other, and (4) the consequences of these discrepancies, including attempts to alter them. Within the P-E model, it is useful to distinguish between objectively measured and subjectively perceived (or misperceived) dimensions of P (self) and E (environment) and between coping that alters dimensions of E and coping that alters dimensions of P.

The P-E model is only a very general and rather abstract perspective from which to view the issue of work and mental health. One consequence of adopting this perspective is the realization that while the dimensions of job requirements and of the corresponding abilities in the person have been frequently studied in the traditional vocational fitness literature (especially for selected low-skilled, blue-collar jobs), the dimensions of the person that represent his needs and the dimensions of the job environment that represent resources (satisfiers of needs) have been neglected. Most of the effort has gone into trying to establish the dimensions of job satisfaction, and there is reasonable agreement on a basic list of job satisfaction areas: pay and other material rewards, work itself, working conditions, immediate supervision, company and management, promotion, and coworkers.[75] In contrast, the writings on human needs relevant to the work environment are largely speculative.[76] And some of the empirical studies of work motivation have been involved in sterile controversies, such as those over the Herzberg two-factor theory of motivation[77] and the importance of economic rewards versus content of work in overall job satisfaction.[78]

Another consequence of the P-E fit perspective is the recognition that job satisfaction measures are interaction measures and do not reflect the dimensions of either the person or the environment alone. They do not allow the person to indicate separately what his needs are and how well these needs are met by the work environment. Interestingly, the two studies in which there was a separate measurement of personality variables (needs or valued dimensions of self-image) and of the work environment (satisfaction of needs or congruence with self-image) failed to replicate the most stable finding we have—the link between occupational level and job satisfaction.[79] Since people at different occupational levels appear to have different needs and expectations, it is likely that measures that reflect the discrepancy between strength of those needs and their satisfaction will relate much less to occupational level than traditional job satisfaction measures do.[80] What we might find, then, is that what primarily differentiates high- and low-status occupations is the degree of ego-involvement or commitment to work.

This perspective also forces us to pay more attention to the dimension of time and to the process of coping with various types of P-E "misfits." Job satisfaction measures are too static and, in fact, tend to disguise and distort the whole process of man's adapting to, and coping with, the discrepancy between his needs and satisfaction of those needs by the work environment. For example, the best interpretation of the higher job satisfaction found among older workers is in terms of a process of gradual retrenchment of goals and aspirations: they are more satisfied because they have fewer expectations and have come to terms with the limitations of their jobs. This is somewhat like the process of "disengagement" described in the literature of social gerontology.[81]

The best description of coping by limiting one's aspirations comes to us from a classical study of automobile workers.[82] The men had very few ambitions, even regarding the rather realistic possibility of becoming a foreman. Their chief notion of a better job was something off the assembly line, but still only a low-level, blue-collar job in the same plant. They dreamed of leaving the factory but never took any realistic steps in this direction, and job security really expressed all of their "mobility" aspirations. Only in their hopes for their offspring (that is, a white-collar job) could one see an expression of their own aspirations, albeit displaced.

The almost limitless plasticity and adaptability of some workers is seen in studies that suggest that even very repetitive and routine work can be satisfying; apparently some workers prefer mechanically paced, highly structured jobs and find some satisfaction in their very rigidity and mindless but predictable triviality.[83]

These findings pose a dilemma, well expressed by Arthur Kornhauser: "The unsatisfactory mental health of working people consists in no small measure of their dwarfed desires and deadened initiative, reduction of their goals and restriction of their efforts to a point where life is relatively empty and only half meaningful."[84]

Kornhauser discusses the two dead-end options for the automobile worker: he can maintain high expectations from work, which leads to constant frustration, or he can limit his expectations, which leads to a drab existence.

There is a lot of suggestive and indirect evidence linking work and mental health: low socioeconomic status relates to high rates of psychiatric hospitalization and symptomatology; periods of high unemployment are closely followed by periods of higher rates of suicide and psychiatric hospitalization; there is a positive association between job satisfaction and other indices of mental health. A precise *causal* interpretation of this evidence is difficult, however, and the more convincing evidence comes from focused comparisons of mental health of men in different jobs and from the findings of relatively poor mental health among workers in low-skilled and unskilled jobs. This is particularly true of some indices of mental health (low job and life satisfaction, poor self-concept and self-evaluation) and less so of others (psychiatric signs and symptoms). In addition, there appears to be evidence that men in low-level jobs adapt by limiting their aspirations and their expectations and that, in effect, the greatest mental health deficit suffered by these men is in the area of job involvement and, consequently, self-actualization.

Thus, while low job status, with all of its associated work conditions, remains our best lead to understanding mental health among workers, much more remains to be learned before we can pinpoint the particularly noxious elements in these low-skilled jobs. For example, although many writers have emphasized the adverse effects of mechanically paced, repetitive work, Kornhauser (in a more intensive multivariate analysis of data) concludes that these aspects of work do not really affect mental health, except perhaps in a symbolic way when the men equate being on such a job with failure. We have also seen that there are strong individual differences, in particular in alienation from the work norm, that make repetitive work satisfying for some.[85] And we must not forget that low-level jobs have poor pay and generally lower job security and that the influence of these variables is not yet clear but is probably powerful (given the evidence that financial circumstances are crucial in influencing the impact of unemployment or retirement).

We also have the issue of the extent to which the various elements of the work environment are modifiable. In general, it would appear that the variables that Herzberg calls "dissatisfiers"[86]—such as working conditions, salary, job security, supervision, and company policy—are more easily modified than "satisfiers"—such as achievement, growth, and the work itself. For example, physically hazardous conditions, like those encountered by mine workers, have documented consequences for mental health and are, in principle, correctable.[87] Similarly, in low-status jobs frequently associated with various stressful life changes (layoff, unemployment, plant relocation, mechanization and automation, lateral job reassignment) there is increasing documentation of the health consequences of such changes.[88] Public policy needs to be directed toward ways of buffering the individual against such changes or preparing him for surviving them better. Men who lose their jobs because of permanent plant closing also lose medical insurance, seniority, and pensions;[89] clearly there is room for improvement here—portable pensions and continuation of health insurance are two possibilities.

On the other hand, it is difficult to see how routine, repetitive, dull work can be made intrinsically more interesting, challenging, or satisfying. Job enrichment may occasionally be a solution, but more often only job enlargement is feasible; and we have seen that the latter does very little to improve job satisfaction or other aspects of mental health. Perhaps the only reasonable solution is to acknowledge the existence of individual differences among workers and to put more effort into screening employees, that is, to select those who "like" routine work.

It appears reasonable to suggest that Herzberg's "dissatisfiers" are more closely linked with indices of well-being and symptoms, while "satisfiers" are more closely linked with other aspects of mental health—job involvement, growth, self-actualization, and competence. We may expect to make some improvement in workers' mental health in the former area but not in the latter.

The tentativeness of these comments stems, of course, from the large gaps in our knowledge. Two lines of future research seem particularly necessary. One involves more longitudinal studies covering three major areas of investigation: (1) life-cycle studies—socialization into the work role and early career,[90] mid-life career changes and entrance into the labor force (for example, mothers of growing children returning to work), and retirement; (2) before-after studies of various "naturally" occurring events that may be beneficial or stressful: job enlargement and enrichment, promotion and demotion, automation, job reassignment, plant relocation, layoff, and plant closing (unemployment); and (3) before-after studies evaluating effects of particular programs, such as special hiring of the "hard-core" unemployed and job retraining.

The other area of needed research is concerned with interrelationships among life roles, or studies of effects of events and changes that cross several life roles. It has been noted that research on work and the family has been quite segregated, and, indeed, it is quite rare to find a study that focuses on more than one role.[91] What we have at the moment are only a few studies that relate job satisfaction to general life satisfaction and to satisfaction in other roles, and the modest, positive correlations made by these studies are not very illuminating. We must ascertain what effects lack of job involvement and lack of fulfillment (self-actualization) in the work role may

have on performance and well-being in the other life roles, and we need to
know more about how we can narrow the gap between the work role and the
leisure role.

Notes

1. Martin Hamburger and Howard Hess, "Work Performance and Emotional Dis-
order," in *Mental Health and Work Organizations,* ed. A. A. McLean (Chicago:
Rand McNally, 1970), pp. 170–195; Harry Levinson, *Executive Stress* (New York:
Harper & Row, 1964); idem, *Emotional Health: In the World of Work* (New York:
McGraw-Hill, 1964); A. A. McLean and G. C. Taylor, *Mental Health in Industry*
(New York: McGraw-Hill, 1958); A. A. McLean, ed., *To Work Is Human: Mental
Health and the Business Community* (New York: Macmillan, 1967); idem, "Occu-
pational Mental Health," in *Industrial Organizations and Health,* vol. 1, *Selected
Readings,* ed. Frank Baker, Peter J. M. McEwan, and Alan Sheldon (London:
Tavistock, 1969), pp. 164–191.

2. Harry Levinson, "Various Approaches to Understanding Man at Work," *Architec-
tural Environmental Health* 22 (1971): 612–618.

3. Technically, my approach is field-theoretical, with a post-Lewinian orientation.
See J. R. P. French, Jr., and R. L. Kahn, "A Programmatic Approach to Studying
the Industrial Environment and Mental Health," *Journal of Social Issues* 18
(1962), no. 3: 1–47.

4. French and Kahn; David Mechanic, *Mental Health and Social Policy* (Englewood
Cliffs, N.J.: Prentice-Hall, 1969); Marie Jahoda, *Current Concepts of Positive
Mental Health* (New York: Basic Books, 1958); Saul B. Sells, ed., *The Definition
and Measurement of Mental Health* (Washington, D.C.: U.S. Government Printing
Office, PHS Publication No. 1873, 1969); W. A. Scott, "Research Definitions of
Mental Health and Mental Illness," *Psychological Bulletin* 55 (1958): 29–45;
M. B. Smith, "Mental Health Reconsidered: A Special Case of the Problem of
Values in Psychology," *American Psychologist* 16 (1961): 299–306.

5. Talcott Parsons, "Definitions of Health and Illness in the Light of American
Values and Social Structure," in *Patients, Physicians, and Illness,* ed. Gartly
Jaco (Glencoe, Ill.: Free Press, 1958), pp. 165–187.

6. G. W. Brown, "The Experience of Discharged Chronic Schizophrenic Patients in
Various Types of Living Groups," *Milbank Memorial Fund Quarterly* 37 (1959):
105–131; H. E. Freeman and O. G. Simmons, "Mental Patients in the Community:
Family Settings and Performance Levels," *American Sociological Review* 23
(1958): 147–154; John Marks, James C. Stouffacher, and Curtis Lyle, "Predicting
Outcome in Schizophrenia," *Journal of Abnormal Social Psychology* 66 (1963):
117–127.

7. Robert L. Kahn, "The Meaning of Work: Interpretation and Proposals for Mea-
surement," in *The Human Meaning of Social Change,* ed. A. A. Campbell and
P. E. Converse (New York: Russell Sage Foundation, 1972); Victor H. Vroom,
Work and Motivation (New York: Wiley, 1964); Walter S. Neff, *Work and Human
Behavior* (New York: Atherton Press, 1968).

8. Kahn.

9. Leonard R. Sayles and George Strauss, *Human Behavior in Organizations* (Englewood Cliffs, N.J.: Prentice-Hall, 1966); C. G. Wrenn, "Human Values and Work in American Life," in *Man in a World at Work,* ed. Henry Borow (Boston: Houghton Mifflin, 1964), pp. 24–44.

10. E. W. Friedman and R. J. Havighurst, *The Meaning of Work and Retirement* (Chicago: University of Chicago Press, 1954).

11. Erik H. Erikson, "The Problems of Ego Identity," *Journal of American Psychoanalytical Association* 4 (1956): 56–121; D. R. Miller, "The Study of Social Relationships: Situation, Identity, and Social Interaction," in *Psychology: A Study of Science,* vol. 5, ed. Sigmund Koch (New York: McGraw-Hill, 1963), pp. 639–737; D. E. Super, "Vocational Adjustment: Implementing a Self-Concept," *Occupations* 30 (1951): 88–92.

12. N. E. Morse and R. S. Weiss, "The Function and Meaning of Work and the Job," *American Sociological Review* 20 (1955): 191–198.

13. Robert Dubin, "Industrial Worker's Worlds: A Study of the 'Central Life Interests' of Industrial Workers," *Social Problems* 3 (1956): 131–142.

14. Lee Taylor, *Occupational Sociology* (New York: Oxford University Press, 1968); L. H. Orzack, "Work as a 'Central Life Interest' of Professionals," *Social Problems* 7 (1959): 125–132.

15. Louis Harris, "Pleasant Retirement Expected," *The Washington Post,* November 28, 1965.

16. Richard Barfield and J. N. Morgan, *Early Retirement: Decision and the Experience* (Ann Arbor: University of Michigan, Institute for Social Research, 1969).

17. Ibid.; Wilma Donahue, Harold L. Orbach, and Otto Pollak, "Retirement: The Emerging Social Pattern," in *Handbook of Social Gerontology,* ed. Clark Tibbitts (Chicago: University of Chicago Press, 1960), pp. 330–406; Friedman and Havighurst; Matilda W. Riley and Anne Foner, *Aging and Society,* vol. 1, *An Inventory of Research Findings* (New York: Russell Sage Foundation, 1968); G. F. Streib, "Morale of the Retired," *Social Problems* 3 (1956): 270–276; W. E. Thompson and G. F. Streib, "Situational Determinants: Health and Economic Deprivation in Retirement," *Journal of Social Issues* 14 (1958): 18–34; W. E. Thompson, G. F. Streib, and John Kosa, "The Effect of Retirement on Personal Adjustment: A Panel Analysis," *Journal of Gerontology* 15 (1960): 165–169.

18. Sayles and Strauss.

19. B. P. Dohrenwend and B. S. Dohrenwend, *Social Status and Psychological Disorder: A Causal Inquiry* (New York: Wiley, 1969); Marc Fried, "Social Differences in Mental Health," in *Poverty and Health: A Sociological Analysis,* ed. John Kosa, Aaron Antonovsky, and Irving K. Zola (Cambridge: Harvard University Press, 1969), pp. 113–167.

20. Jerome K. Myers and Lee L. Bean, *A Decade Later: A Follow-up of Social Class and Mental Illness* (New York: Wiley, 1968).

21. Gerald Gurin, Joseph L. Veroff, and Sheila Feld, *Americans View Their Mental Health* (New York: Basic Books, 1960); Leo Srole et al., *Mental Health in the Metropolis: The Midtown Manhattan Study*, vol. 1 (New York: McGraw-Hill, 1962).

22. Fried.

23. Fried; Dohrenwend and Dohrenwend; Srole et al.

24. Robert Blauner, "Work Satisfaction and Industrial Trends in Modern Society," in *Labor and Trade Unionism*, ed. Walter Galenson and Seymour Lipset (New York: Wiley, 1960); Victor H. Vroom, "Industrial Social Psychology," in *The Handbook of Social Psychology*, vol. 5, 2nd ed., ed. Gardner Lindzey and Elliot Aronson (Reading, Mass.: Addison-Wesley, 1969), pp. 196–268; Gurin et al.; Arthur W. Kornhauser, *Mental Health of the Industrial Worker* (New York: Wiley, 1965); Kahn; T. S. Langner and S. T. Michael, *Life Stress and Mental Health* (New York: Free Press of Glencoe, 1963); John P. Robinson, "Occupational Norms and Differences in Job Satisfaction: A Summary of Survey Research Evidence," in *Measures of Occupational Attitudes and Occupational Characteristics*, ed. John P. Robinson, Robert B. Athanasiou, and Kendra B. Head (Ann Arbor: University of Michigan, Institute for Social Research, 1969), pp. 25–78; L. W. Porter and E. E. Lawler III, "Properties of Organization Structure in Relation to Job Attitudes and Job Behavior," *Psychological Bulletin* 64 (1965): 23–51; Survey Research Center, University of Michigan, *Survey of Working Conditions* (Washington, D.C.: U.S. Department of Labor, Employment Standards Administration, 1971); Harold L. Wilensky, "The Problem of Work Alienation," in *Industrial Organizations and Health*, vol. 1, *Selected Readings*, ed. Frank Baker, Peter J. M. McEwan, and Alan Sheldon (London: Tavistock, 1969), pp. 550–567; Alvin Zander and Robert Quinn, "The Social Environment and Mental Health: A Review of Past Research at the Institute for Social Research," *Journal of Social Issues* 18 (1962): 48–66; Vroom, *Work and Motivation*.

25. Survey Research Center; Chris Argyris, "Individual Actualization in Complex Organizations," *Mental Hygiene* 44 (1960): 226–237; idem, *Integrating the Individual and the Organization* (New York: Wiley, 1964); Robert Blauner, *Alienation and Freedom: The Factory Worker and His Industry* (Chicago: University of Chicago Press, 1964); Stanislav V. Kasl and J. R. P. French, Jr., "The Effects of Occupational Status on Physical and Mental Health, *Journal of Social Issues* 18 (1962), no. 3: 67–89; L. W. Porter, "Job Attitudes in Management: I. Perceived Deficiencies in New Fulfillment as a Function of Job Level," *Journal of Applied Psychology* 46 (1962): 375–384.

26. Gurin et al.; Langner and Michael; Survey Research Center; Kornhauser.

27. Seldom greater than .30. See Gurin et al.; Langner and Michael; Survey Research Center.

28. Gurin et al.

29. Wilensky.

30. Gurin et al.; Langner and Michael.

31. Kasl and French.

32. Blauner, "Work Satisfaction"; C. P. Alderfer, "Job Enlargement and the Organizational Context," *Personnel Psychology* 22 (1969): 418–426; Kahn, "Meaning of Work"; Vroom, *Work and Motivation;* idem, "Industrial Social Psychology"; Robert Caplan, "Organizational Stress and Individual Strain: A Social Psychological Survey of Risk Factors in Coronary Heart Disease among Administrators, Engineers, and Scientists" (Ph.D. diss., University of Michigan, 1971); Edward Gross, "Work, Organization, and Stress," in *Social Stress,* ed. Sol Levine and Norman A. Scotch (Chicago: Aldine, 1970), pp. 54–110; B. P. Indik, "Some Effects of Organization Size on Member Attitudes and Behavior," *Human Relations* 16 (1963): 369–384; P. E. Mott et al., *Shift Work* (Ann Arbor: University of Michigan Press, 1965); Porter and Lawler; Survey Research Center; Zander and Quinn.

33. Caplan; R. L. Kahn and R. P. Quinn, "Role Stress: A Framework for Analysis," in *Mental Health and Work Organizations,* ed. A. A. McLean (Chicago: Rand McNally, 1970), pp. 50–115; Kornhauser; R. L. Kahn et al., *Organizational Stress: Studies in Role Conflict and Ambiguity* (New York: Wiley, 1964); Mott et al.; Robert G. Neel, "Nervous Stress in the Industrial Situation," *Personnel Psychology* 8, no. 4 (winter 1955): 405–416; Survey Research Center; Zander and Quinn.

34. Alderfer; W. A. Faunce, "Automation in the Automobile Industry: Some Consequencies for In-Plant Social Structure," *American Sociological Review* 23 (1958): 401–407; idem, "Automation and the Division of Labor," *Social Problems* 13 (1965): 149–160; C. L. Hulin and M. R. Blood, "Job Enlargement, Individual Differences, and Worker Responses," *Psychological Bulletin* 69 (1968): 41–55; F. C. Mann and L. K. Williams, "Some Effects of the Changing Work Environment in the Office," *Journal of Social Issues* 18 (1962), no. 3: 90–101; Simon Marcson, ed., *Automation, Alienation, and Anomie* (New York: Harper & Row, 1970); J. M. Shepard, *Automation and Alienation* (Cambridge: MIT Press, 1971); Vroom, "Industrial Social Psychology."

35. Hulin and Blood.

36. Kahn et al. The objective measure was the sum of pressures to change behavior, as reported by the role senders who had formal influence on the respondent, while the subjective measure was the respondent's statement of intensity of experienced conflict.

37. Mott et al.

38. For example, Survey Research Center found that the workers' reports of presence of problems in eighteen areas of Labor Standards concern correlated in the low .30s with two indices of job satisfaction and even less with several other mental health indices.

39. Robert B. Athanasiou, "Job Attitudes and Occupational Performance: A Review of Some Important Literature," in *Measures of Occupational Attitudes and Occupational Characteristics,* ed. John P. Robinson, Robert B. Athanasiou, and Kendra B. Head (Ann Arbor: University of Michigan, Institute for Social Research, 1969), pp. 79–98; Kahn, "Meaning of Work"; E. E. Lawler III, "Job Design and Employee Motivation," *Personnel Psychology* 22 (1969): 426–435; idem, "Job Attitudes and Employee Motivation: Theory, Research, and Practice," *Personnel Psychology* 23 (1970): 223–237; A. R. Martin, "Morale and Productivity: A Re-

view of the Literature," *Public Personnel Review* 30 (1969): 42–45; Vroom, *Work and Motivation;* idem, "Industrial Social Psychology."

40. L. E. Hinkle, Jr., "Physical Health, Mental Health, and the Social Environment: Some Characteristics of Healthy and Unhealthy People," in *Recent Contributions of Biological and Psychosocial Investigations to Preventive Psychiatry,* ed. R. H. Ojemann (Iowa City: State University of Iowa, 1959), pp. 80–103.

41. Norman M. Bradburn, *The Structure of Psychological Well-Being* (Chicago: Aldine Press, 1969); A. H. Brayfield, R. V. Wells, and M. W. Strate, "Interrelationships among Measures of Job Satisfaction and General Satisfaction," *Journal of Applied Psychology* 41 (1957): 201–205; J. O. Crites, *Vocational Psychology* (New York: McGraw-Hill, 1969); Stanislav V. Kasl and Sidney Cobb, "Effects of Parental Status Incongruence and Discrepancy on Physical and Mental Health of Adult Offspring," *Journal of Personality and Social Psychology, Monograph* 7 (1967) (Whole No. 642): 1–15; Kornhauser; Langner and Michael; Survey Research Center; Melvin Seeman, "On the Personal Consequences of Alienation in Work," *American Sociological Review* 32 (1967): 273–285; D. E. Super and J. O. Crites, *Appraising Vocational Fitness,* rev. ed. (New York: Harper & Row, 1962); Joseph L. Veroff, Sheila Feld, and Gerald Gurin, "Dimensions of Subjective Adjustment," *Journal of Abnormal and Social Psychology* 64 (1962): 192–205; W. Wilson, "Correlates of Avowed Happiness," *Psychological Bulletin* 67 (1967): 294–306.

42. They average in the low .40s for men.

43. In the mid .20s.

44. Super and Crites.

45. Shared "method-variance" is also a problem. See D. R. Campbell and D. W. Fiske, "Convergent and Discriminant Validation by the Multitrait-Multimethod Matrix," *Psychological Bulletin* 56 (1959): 81–105.

46. M. H. Brenner, "Economic Change and Mental Hospitalization: New York State, 1910–1960," *Social Psychiatry* 2 (1967): 180–188; idem, "Patterns of Psychiatric Hospitalization among Different Socioeconomic Groups in Response to Economic Stress," *Journal of Nervous Mental Disorders* 148 (1968): 31–38; N. A. Dayton, *New Facts on Mental Disorder* (Springfield, Ill.: C. C. Thomas, 1940); A. F. Henry and J. F. Short, Jr., *Suicide and Homicide* (Glencoe, Ill.: Free Press, 1954); Douglas Swinscow, "Some Suicide Statistics," *British Medical Journal* 1 (1951): 1417–1422.

47. T. R. Brown and T. J. Sheran, "Suicide Prediction: A Review," *Life Threatening Behavior* 2 (1972): 67–98.

48. David Lester, "Suicide and Unemployment," *Archives of Environmental Health* 20 (1970): 277–278.

49. Warren Breed, "Occupational Mobility and Suicide," *American Sociological Review* 28 (1963): 179–188; J. A. Harrington and K. W. Cross, "Cases of Attempted Suicide Admitted to a General Hospital," *British Medical Journal* 2 (1959): 463–467; Peter Sainsbury, *Suicide in London* (London: Maudsley Monograph No. 1, 1955).

50. Harold L. Sheppard and A. Harvey Belitsky, *The Job Hunt* (Baltimore: Johns Hopkins Press, 1966); R. C. Wilcock and W. H. Franke, *Unwanted Workers* (Glencoe, Ill.: Free Press, 1968).

51. E. W. Bakke, *Citizens without Work* (New Haven: Yale University Press, 1940); idem, *The Unemployed Worker* (New Haven: Yale University Press, 1940); Ruth Shonle Cavan and K. H. Ranck, *The Family and the Depression* (Chicago: University of Chicago, 1938); Eli Ginzberg, *The Unemployed* (New York: Harper and Brothers, 1943); Mirra Komarovsky, *The Unemployed Man and His Family* (New York: Dryden Press, 1940).

52. Bradburn.

53. Fried.

54. D. W. Tiffany, J. R. Cowan, and P. M. Tiffany, *The Unemployed: A Social-Psychological Portrait* (Englewood Cliffs, N. J.: Prentice-Hall, 1970).

55. Michael Aiken, L. A. Ferman, and H. L. Sheppard, *Economic Failure, Alienation, and Extremism* (Ann Arbor: University of Michigan Press, 1968).

56. Sidney Cobb et al., "The Health of People Changing Jobs: A Description of a Longitudinal Study," *American Journal of Public Health* 56 (1966): 1476–1481.

57. Stanislav V. Kasl and Sidney Cobb, "Some Physical and Mental Health Effects of Job Loss," *Pakistan Medical Forum* 6 (1971): 95–106.

58. Sidney Cobb et al., "Urinary Nor-Epinephrine in Men Whose Jobs Are Abolished," *Psychosomatic Medicine* (in press); Stanislav V. Kasl, Sidney Cobb, and Susan Gore, "Changes in Reported Illness and Illness Behavior Related to Termination of Employment: A Preliminary Report," *International Journal of Epidemiology* 1 (1972): 111–118; Stanislav V. Kasl and Sidney Cobb, "Blood Pressure Changes in Men Undergoing Job Loss: A Preliminary Report," *Psychosomatic Medicine* 32 (1970): 19–38; Stanislav V. Kasl, Sidney Cobb, and G. W. Brooks, "Changes in Serum Uric Acid and Cholesterol Levels in Men Undergoing Job Loss," *Journal of American Medical Association* 206 (1968): 1500–1507.

59. Joseph L. Veroff and Sheila Feld, *Marriage and Work in America: A Study of Motives and Roles* (New York: Van Nostrand Reinhold, 1970).

60. William H. Form and James A. Geschwender, "Social Reference Basis of Job Satisfaction: The Case of Manual Workers," *American Sociological Review* 27 (1962): 228–237; Zander and Quinn.

61. Robert J. Kleiner and Seymour Parker, "Goal Striving, Social Status, and Mental Disorder," *American Sociological Review* 28 (1963): 189–203.

62. S. Parker and R. J. Kleiner, *Mental Illness in the Urban Negro Community* (New York: Free Press, 1966).

63. E. F. Jackson, "Status Consistency and Symptoms of Stress," *American Sociological Review* 27 (1962): 469–480; Stanislav V. Kasl and Sidney Cobb, "Physical and Mental Health Correlates of Status Incongruence," *Social Psychiatry* 6 (1971): 1–10.

64. K. W. Back and K. J. Gergen, "Personal Orientation and Morale of the Aged," in *Social Aspects of Aging,* ed. I. H. Simpson and J. C. McKinney (Durham, N.C.: Duke University Press, 1966), pp. 296–305; H. Melzer, "Mental Health Implications of Aging in Industry," *Journal of Genetic Psychology* 107 (1965): 193–203; Riley and Foner; Robinson.

65. Victor H. Vroom, *Some Personality Determinants of the Effects of Participation* (Englewood Cliffs, N.J.: Prentice-Hall, 1960).

66. Kahn et al., *Organizational Stress.*

67. Hulin and Blood.

68. A. N. Turner and P. R. Lawrence, *Industrial Jobs and the Worker: An Investigation of Response to Task Attributes* (Cambridge: Harvard University Press, 1965).

69. Vroom, *Work and Motivation;* idem, "Industrial Social Psychology."

70. R. B. Ewen, "Weighting Components of Job Satisfaction," *Journal of Applied Psychology* 51 (1967): 68–73; Robert P. Quinn and T. W. Magione, "Evaluating Weighted Models of Measuring Job Satisfaction: A Cinderella Story," unpublished (Ann Arbor: University of Michigan, Institute for Social Research, 1972).

71. Robert P. Quinn, "Locking-in as a Moderator of the Relationship between Job Satisfaction and Mental Health," unpublished (Ann Arbor: University of Michigan, Institute for Social Research, 1972).

72. Neff.

73. Morton Deutsch, "Field Theory in Social Psychology," in *The Handbook of Social Psychology,* vol. 1, ed. Gardner Lindzey and Elliot Aronson (Reading, Mass.: Addison-Wesley, 1968), pp. 412–487.

74. R. V. Dawis, G. W. England, and L. H. Lofquist, *Minnesota Studies in Vocational Rehabilitation,* vol. 15, *A Theory of Work Adjustment* (Minneapolis: University of Minnesota, Industrial Relations Center, 1964); John R. P. French, Jr., Willard Rodgers, and Sidney Cobb, "Adjustment as Person-Environment Fit," unpublished (Ann Arbor: University of Michigan, Institute for Social Research, 1971); L. H. Lofquist and R. V. Dawis, *Adjustment to Work* (New York: Appleton-Century-Crofts, 1969); F. M. Carp, "Person-Situation Congruence in Engagement," *The Gerontologist* 8 (1968): 184–188.

75. Frederick I. Herzberg et al., *Job Attitudes: Review of Research and Opinion* (Pittsburgh: Psychological Service of Pittsburgh, 1957); Daniel Katz, "Survey Research Center: An Overview of the Human Relations Program," in *Groups, Leadership, and Men,* ed. Harold Guetzkow (Pittsburgh: Carnegie Press, 1951), pp. 68–85; Survey Research Center; Patricia C. Smith, Lorne M. Kendall, and Charles L. Hulin, *The Measurement of Satisfaction in Work and Retirement: A Strategy for the Study of Attitudes* (Chicago: Rand McNally, 1969); Vroom, *Work and Motivation.*

76. Richard Centers and Daphne E. Bugental, "Intrinsic and Extrinsic Job Motivations among Different Segments of the Working Population," *Journal of Applied*

Psychology 50 (1966): 193–197; Frederick I. Herzberg, *Work and the Nature of Man* (Cleveland: World, 1966); Levinson, "Understanding Man at Work"; C. M. Lichtman and R. G. Hunt, "Personality and Organization Theory: A Review of Some Conceptual Literature," *Psychological Bulletin* 76 (1971): 271–294; McLean and Taylor, *Mental Health in Industry;* R. H. Schaffer, "Job Satisfaction as Related to Need Satisfaction in Work," *Psychological Monographs* 67 (1953), no. 14 (Whole No. 364).

77. Frank Friedlander and Eugene Walton, "Positive and Negative Motivations to Work," *Administrative Science Quarterly* 9 (1964): 194–207; Frederick I. Herzberg, Bernard Mausner, and Barbara Snyderman, *The Motivation to Work* (New York: Wiley, 1959); Nathan King, "Clarification and Evaluation of the Two-Factor Theory of Job Satisfaction," *Psychological Bulletin* 71 (1970): 18–31.

78. Mitchell Fein, "The Real Needs and Goals of Blue Collar Workers," *The Conference Board Record,* February 1973, pp. 26–33; N. Q. Herrick, "Who Is Unhappy at Work and Why," *Manpower,* January 1972.

79. Argyris, "Individual Actualization"; Harold L. Wilensky, "Varieties of Work Experience," in *Man in a World at Work,* ed. Henry Borow (Boston: Houghton Mifflin, 1964), pp. 125–154; idem, "Problem of Work Alienation."

80. T. B. Armstrong, "Job Content and Context Factors Related to Satisfaction for Different Occupational Levels," *Journal of Applied Psychology* 55 (1971): 57–65; Franklin P. Kilpatrick, Milton C. Cummings, and M. Kent Jennings, *The Image of the Federal Service* (Washington, D.C.: Brookings Institution, 1964); Taylor.

81. B. L. Neugarten, "Adult Personality: Toward a Psychology of the Life Cycle," in *Middle Age and Aging,* ed. B. L. Neugarten (Chicago: University of Chicago Press, 1968), pp. 137–147.

82. Ely Chinoy, *Automobile Workers and the American Dream* (Garden City, N.Y.: Doubleday, 1955).

83. Hulin and Blood; W. P. Sexton, "Industrial Work: Who Calls It Psychologically Devastating?" *Management of Personnel Quarterly* 6 (1968): 2–8.

84. Kornhauser, p. 270.

85. Hulin and Blood; Sexton; Turner and Lawrence.

86. Herzberg, Mausner, and Snyderman.

87. Abraham Zaleznik, Jack Ondrack, and Andrew Silver, "Social Class, Occupation, and Mental Illness," in *Mental Health and Work Organizations,* ed. A. A. McLean (Chicago: Rand McNally, 1970), pp. 116–142.

88. M. A. Jacobs et al., "Life Stress and Respiratory Illness," *Psychosomatic Medicine* 32 (1970): 233–242; E. S. Paykel, B. A. Prusoff, and E. H. Uhlenhuth, "Scaling Life Events," *Archives of General Psychiatry* 25 (1971): 340–347; R. H. Rahe, "Subjects' Recent Life Changes and Their Near-Future Illness Susceptibility," and A. H. Schmale, "Giving Up as a Final Common Pathway to Changes in Health," in *Advances in Psychosomatic Medicine,* ed. Z. J. Lipowski, vol. 8,

Psychosocial Aspects of Physical Illness (Basel: S. Karger, 1972), pp. 2–19 and 20–40; George Strauss, "The Set-Up Man: A Case Study of Organizational Change," *Human Organization* 13 (1954): 19–27.

89. Sidney Cobb and Stanislav V. Kasl, "Some Medical Aspects of Unemployment," in *Employment of the Middle-Aged,* ed. G. M. Shatto (Springfield, Ill.: C. C. Thomas, 1972), pp. 87–96.

90. D. E. Super, "The Definition and Measurement of Early Career Behavior: A First Formulation," *Personnel and Guidance Journal* 41 (1963): 775–780.

91. Robert Rapoport and Rhona Rapoport, "Work and Family in Contemporary Society," *American Sociological Review* 30 (1965): 381–394.

IV The Redesign of Jobs

9 The Work Module: A Proposal for the Humanization of Work

Robert L. Kahn

A proposal for the humanization of work involves a number of assumptions, the obvious one being that work today is not fully "humanized," if it ever was. A more subtle assumption is that work continues to be of central importance for individuals and for the society at large.

That importance is basically instrumental: work is engaged in primarily for the sake of its product, the goods and services that it generates. But it is no less true that work is often valued for its own sake, that for many people it meets the need for meaningful activity, as defined by others and as experienced by themselves. For many others, however, the work experience is unpleasant and is marked with severe disadvantages. These people persist at work only because they see no alternative way to meet basic needs. If this is both obvious and undesirable, it follows that we should be concerned with ways to make work more meaningful and satisfying, and to do so without paying an unacceptable social price in terms of diminished quantity or quality.

These goals may not be wholly compatible. We must explore their compatibility under present conditions and discover the conditions under which their compatibility would be maximized. That exploration and discovery should be the common responsibility of government and business, labor unions and universities. It is the kind of effort implied by "the humanization of work."

The "humanization of work," a phrase admittedly more inspiring than precise, implies some criticism of the present, some set of values on which that criticism is based, and some program by means of which the goal of humanization can be attained; it ignores the possibility that tedious and monotonous work may be necessary to avoid starvation.

For present purposes, we can define the humanization of work as the process of making work more appropriate, more fitting for an adult human being to perform.

- Work should not damage, degrade, humiliate, exhaust, stultify, or persistently bore the worker.
- It should interest and satisfy him.
- It should utilize many of the valued skills and abilities he already possesses and provide opportunity for him to acquire others.
- It should enhance, or at least leave unimpaired, his interest and ability to perform other major life roles—as husband or wife, parent, citizen, and friend.
- It should fulfill the instrumental purpose of getting a living, in terms acceptable to him.

Measures of the Humanization of Work

No satisfactory set of measures has yet been devised for the dimensions listed above, nor is there agreement about the best way to measure them. As with other new and developing fields, the need is to utilize various approaches and to keep selecting the more promising of them. Two will be discussed here: measurement in terms of satisfaction-dissatisfaction and measurement in terms of person-environment fit (that is, the goodness-of-fit between the motives and abilities of the person on the one hand and the opportunities and demands of the job situation on the other).

Satisfaction

Measurement in terms of satisfaction and dissatisfaction proceeds on the simple assumption that work has been humanized when human beings report that they are satisfied with it. This research approach has been used more than any other in studying people at work, and most of what we know about the meaning of work has been developed in these terms.

Moreover, this approach has by no means been played out. I expect that reported satisfaction with the major aspects of work will continue to be important in guiding efforts to improve the quality of jobs. Certainly, the experience of satisfaction or dissatisfaction is subjective and is therefore a product of the objective situation and the unique individual who is responding to it. In that sense, satisfaction responses are "soft" data, not wholly understandable in terms of the objective situation and not wholly to be optimized by changes in that situation. But in another sense the statement of satisfaction or dissatisfaction is the ultimate datum; it refers to the experience of the individual, and it is the quality of that experience that humanization is all about. There is ample evidence that workers distinguish among the satisfying and dissatisfying components of their jobs and that their responses are rooted in the real world, modified in the light of their personalities, their expectations, and their previous experiences.

The last point is, of course, a limitation, and it reminds us not to infer too much from responses of satisfaction. If a person has experienced little, he tends to be satisfied with little—more than he has, but still little. Life at an earlier time has been described in a classic phrase as "solitary, poor, nasty, brutish, and short," but it is most unlikely that the people who endured that life would have described it so.[1]

Satisfaction, then, should be one measure of the humanization of work, but it should not be the sole criterion. Objective measures are needed as well. We recognize that a satisfying diet is not necessarily nourishing and healthful. Satisfying television programs may be uninformative or, if some of the research on violence is confirmed, may even be damaging. Similarly, we can differentiate between the objective and the subjective aspects of a job, and we will understand them best when both are measured on the same dimensions. For example, a worker can be asked whether he feels that his job is hazardous, and the hazardousness of the job can also be measured in terms of the frequency of accidents and injuries.

Goodness-of-Fit

Several of my colleagues at the University of Michigan have proposed that the basic concept for understanding the relationship of a worker to his job should be "goodness-of-fit" between his personal characteristics and the properties of his environment, and that these characteristics and properties should be measured both as he sees them (that is, subjectively) and as they "really" are (that is, objectively).[2] They illustrate this approach by means of a hypothetical example involving a typist and a copy-typing job. Keeping up with the work requires a typing speed of fifty words per minute; this is an objective characteristic of the job. The typist, however, is able to type only thirty words per minute; this is an objective measure of her ability. The difference between the two objective scores is fifty minus thirty, or twenty words per minute, and this is an objective measure of the goodness-of-fit between person and job.

The subjective situation may be quite different, of course. The typist may overestimate her ability, in the comforting fashion that people often do. She may believe that she can type forty words per minute. She may also underestimate the demands of the job, perhaps as a defense against feeling overloaded, and report that the job requires a typing speed of only forty words per minute. Thus, the subjective goodness-of-fit (forty minus forty) would be perfect, but the objective goodness-of-fit (fifty minus thirty) would be poor.

Finally, we can compare the objective and subjective reports, both regarding the job requirement (a property of the environment) and regarding the typist's ability (a property of the person). These comparisons provide measures of accuracy of report, which in the present example show an error of ten points (fifty minus forty) in the typist's report of her environment, and another error of ten points (thirty minus forty) in her report of her personal attribute or ability.

In recent research, goodness-of-fit has been measured along such dimensions as independence, affiliation, achievement, responsibility, self-utilization, and self-development—the last two referring to the use of one's existing skills and to the development of new skills, respectively. Among high school students, for example, goodness-of-fit on some of these dimensions is related to such outcomes as self-esteem, emotional states (such as depression, anxiety, or resentment), and reported probability of dropping out of school. Among employees in a government agency, goodness-of-fit was measured on a large number of dimensions and was found to be related to such psychological outcomes as job satisfaction and to such physiological outcomes as cholesterol level. The pattern of these findings, however, is not strong. The goodness-of-fit approach appears promising, but its value remains to be fully demonstrated. At present, the best indicator of the quality of work—human or less than human—is the satisfaction or dissatisfaction of the people performing it.

Determinants of Job Satisfaction

Hundreds of studies have been done to discover the factors that make jobs satisfying for workers in particular plants and companies. At least a dozen studies have been done on representative populations, usually within a single community. Recently the Department of Labor supported a nationwide study of working conditions and job satisfaction conducted by the Survey Research Center of the University of Michigan.[3]

These studies do not share any single approach to the measurement of job satisfaction. Some of them ask direct questions about satisfaction and dissatisfaction; others infer satisfaction from the person's expressed willingness to go into the same line of work if he were starting over, to advise young people to take up his own line of work, or to continue working even if he had no economic need to do so. These differences in measurement represent a further complication to the fact that most studies of job satisfaction have been done on unrepresentative populations, omit any mention of factors found not to be related to satisfaction or dissatisfaction, and have never been replicated.

Given these problems, it is impressive that several persistent themes emerge and that we can claim the following factors to be highly probable causes of satisfaction and dissatisfaction at work: occupation, status, supervision, peer relationships, job content, wages, promotion, and physical conditions of work.

Occupation and Status

Almost everyone who has studied job satisfaction across any considerable array of occupations has found significant differences among them. People in different kinds of jobs are not equally satisfied with them. Moreover, the differences in satisfaction that are characteristic of different occupations are strongly related to status: the higher the status of the occupation, the more satisfied are the people who engage in it. This relationship holds regardless of whether one thinks of status in terms of the general social opinion that one occupation is more desirable than another or whether one defines status solely in terms of the socioeconomic characteristics of the job. Table 9.1 illustrates the magnitude of the status-satisfaction relationship. It is synthesized from several studies, each of which used as a measure of job satisfaction the proportion of persons in an occupation who said they would try to get into the same line of work if they were to begin their careers again.

The table is remarkable for the range of response—from 93 percent of university professors to 16 percent of unskilled auto workers who say they would seek the same type of work again. The sharpest break comes between professional and nonprofessional jobs, although there is an overall differ-

Table 9.1. Percentage of Workers Saying They Would Choose Similar Work Again

Occupation	Percent	Occupation	Percent
Professional and white-collar		**Skilled trades and blue-collar**	
Urban university professors[b]	93	Skilled printers[a]	52
Mathematicians[a]	91	Paper workers[a]	42
Physicists[a]	89	Skilled auto workers[a]	41
Biologists[a]	89	Skilled steelworkers[a]	41
Chemists[a]	86	Textile workers[a]	31
Firm lawyers[b]	85	Blue-collar workers[b]	24
School superintendents[c]	85	Unskilled steelworkers[a]	21
Lawyers[a]	83	Unskilled auto workers[a]	16
Journalists (Washington correspondents)[a]	82		
Church university professors[b]	77		
Solo lawyers[b]	75		
White-collar workers (nonprofessional)[b]	43		

Note: For related versions of this table and full descriptions of the population samples on which it is based, see John P. Robinson, Robert B. Athanasiou, and Kendra B. Head, eds., *Measures of Occupational Attitudes and Occupational Characteristics* (Ann Arbor: University of Michigan, Institute for Social Research, 1967); Robert Blauner, *Alienation and Freedom* (Chicago: University of Chicago Press, 1964); Harold Wilensky, "Varieties of Work Experience," in *Man in a World at Work,* ed. Henry Borow (Boston: Houghton Mifflin, 1964); and Neal Gross, Ward Mason, and W. A. McEachern, *Explorations in Role Analysis: Studies of the School Superintendency Role* (New York: John Wiley & Sons, 1958).
[a] Data from a study of 3,000 workers in sixteen industries conducted by the Roper organization and reported by Blauner
[b] Data from a study of Detroit workers and professionals by Wilensky
[c] Data from a study of school superintendents in Massachusetts by Gross, Mason, and McEachern

ence between white-collar and blue-collar jobs in favor of the former. But that difference is not so great as the differences associated with skill and status levels in blue-collar jobs, and with clerical and sales versus professional work in white-collar jobs. Indeed, there is some overlap between blue-collar and white-collar jobs, with the skilled trades showing a larger proportion of satisfied workers than the sales and clerical jobs.

Studies that compare occupations in terms of responses to more direct questions about satisfaction show a similar pattern but with some reduction in the differences among occupations. It seems likely that this reflects a combination of wish and realism that is evoked by such questions. The researcher asks the worker if he is satisfied with his job and leaves him to provide his own frame of reference—his own comparison group, his own range of accessible occupations, his own assessment of his talents and the opportunities of the labor market. To the extent that he has made a "successful adjustment," he reports some degree of satisfaction. The occupation-status-satisfaction pattern is not limited to the United States. A study of six other nations high in industrial development,[4] another of twenty-three countries in different stages of industrial development,[5] and a random sample of Leningrad workers under the age of thirty [6] all report similar results.

There are few findings so consistent as these, and it is interesting to speculate on the reasons for the consistency. Many authors have proposed explanations in terms of prestige, control over conditions of one's own work, cohesiveness of one's work group (if any), ego-gratification from the challenge and variety of the work itself, and other factors.

A somewhat different, although not incompatible explanation would begin by regarding an occupation as a role that is defined in terms of certain expected activities and certain rewards for their performance. Each occupation comprises a unique cluster of satisfaction-giving and dissatisfaction-imposing activities and a unique set of extrinsic rewards and penalties. When occupations are ordered according to status (as reported in survey data), we are simply asking people to tell us which occupation-defined sets of activities and rewards are best and which are least attractive. If we subsequently find that these rankings correspond to expressions of satisfaction or dissatisfaction on the part of individuals actually performing the different occupational roles, we have only demonstrated that the norms about what makes jobs good or bad are widely shared, irrespective of one's own occupation.

If we find, as we do, that these rankings also correspond to less subjective measures of status, such as the socioeconomic measures of the Census Bureau, we have demonstrated that in the particular culture under study the financial rewards of jobs and the education required for access to them generally follow and thus intensify the pattern of other rewarding characteristics.

The importance of status as a determinant of job satisfaction can be overstated, of course. Satisfaction varies within occupations, and various aspects of jobs make them good or bad in the eyes of men and women. These points are well illustrated in table 9.2, which shows the results of a nationwide study of the Survey Research Center, based on a sample of 1,244 adults (aged nineteen to sixty-five) residing in urban areas throughout the United States.

Table 9.2. Average Ratings of Various Aspects of Job

Occupation	Pay	Job Security	Kind of Work-Place	Chance to Use Skills	Kind of People	Freedom to plan	Chance to Learn
Professional							
People-oriented							
Artist, musician	3.40	3.80	1.80	2.00	1.25	1.80	3.00
Professor, librarian	2.75	1.57	1.75	1.25	1.13	1.63	1.63
Advising profession	2.08	1.63	1.60	1.20	1.37	1.26	1.43
School teacher	2.59	1.74	1.94	1.15	1.65	1.50	1.35
Other medical	2.53	1.73	1.67	1.47	1.71	1.73	2.00
Data-oriented							
Scientist, physician	1.75	2.06	1.25	1.56	1.50	1.69	1.56
Accountant, auditor	1.94	1.31	2.25	1.62	1.85	1.62	1.69
Engineer	1.97	1.58	1.84	1.72	1.58	1.58	1.79
Technician	2.73	2.12	1.91	1.79	1.82	2.03	2.09
Managerial							
Self-employed (large firm)	2.52	1.83	1.95	1.43	1.64	1.26	1.65
Self-employed (other)	2.91	2.47	2.00	1.62	2.03	1.47	1.91
Salaried	2.14	1.57	1.72	1.46	1.68	1.62	1.87
Clerical							
Bookkeeper	3.06	2.06	2.17	1.56	1.56	1.94	2.06
Secretary, typist	2.59	1.87	2.04	1.90	1.66	2.14	2.57
Other clerical	2.61	2.18	2.00	2.46	1.74	2.43	2.78
Sales							
High status (goods)	2.91	1.91	1.78	1.64	1.36	1.64	1.45
High status (services)	2.55	1.82	1.73	1.18	1.73	1.27	2.00
Sales clerk	3.33	2.43	1.93	2.25	1.71	2.64	3.04
Other sales	2.86	2.59	2.50	1.95	1.58	1.59	2.49
Skilled							
Self-employed	3.13	3.38	2.50	1.88	1.86	2.25	2.50
Foreman	2.18	2.15	2.28	2.05	2.24	2.13	2.34
Other	2.54	2.41	2.22	1.93	1.95	2.67	2.60
Semiskilled							
Operatives	2.72	2.49	2.32	2.71	1.93	3.34	3.34

Table 9.2 Average Ratings of Various Aspects of Job (continued)

Occupation	Pay	Job Security	Kind of Work-Place	Chance to Use Skills	Kind of People	Freedom to plan	Chance to Learn
Service							
Protective	3.14	1.29	2.19	2.33	1.52	2.85	2.76
Armed forces	3.00	1.33	1.78	2.67	1.89	2.33	2.67
Household	3.50	2.79	2.09	2.75	1.81	1.83	3.50
Other service	3.16	2.12	1.91	2.44	1.83	2.35	3.13
Unskilled							
Laborer	3.10	2.31	2.27	2.72	1.83	2.97	2.93
Overall Average							
Men	2.63	2.19	2.12	1.53	1.79	2.30	2.51
Women	2.73	2.13	1.91	2.11	1.63	2.27	2.72
Standard Deviation	1.33	1.34	1.17	1.36	.90	1.48	1.58

Source: Robinson, Athanasiou, and Head, *Measures of Occupational Attitudes and Occupational Characteristics.*
Note: Range is from 1 (= very good) to 5 (= poor).

In this study the occupations of artist and musician are highly rated, and so is the occupation of teacher, but the pattern of rating is not the same. Being an artist or musician gets a high rating for kind of people, kind of workplace, and freedom to plan one's own work; it gets a relatively low rating for pay and job security. Indeed, on the latter point no other occupation is as low. School teachers, rated similarly to artists and musicians on many aspects of the job, rate considerably higher on job security and somewhat higher on pay. Unskilled labor, understandably enough, is rated relatively low in most respects—but perhaps not so low as one might have guessed from the objective characteristics of the job. For the unskilled, pay is rated lowest of all aspects of the job, and the kind of people with whom one works rates highest. Indeed, there is a great deal of stability in this aspect of the job across most occupations, although foremen and self-employed in small business are rated lower in it. The differences are insignificant, however, and are worth mentioning only because of the suggestion that they reflect the responsibilities of direct supervision under difficult circumstances.

Although these data remind us that the several components by which jobs are judged are rated quite independently, there is a persistent demand placed upon researchers to summarize, combine, and speak in terms of overall satisfaction and dissatisfaction. The demand is not wholly unreasonable, given that individual choice and experience occur within such combinations of facts. The person encounters the job as a whole, and though he can distinguish its satisfying aspects from those that frustrate him, he can seldom alter them singly to suit his needs. Within what are usually rather narrow limits, he accepts the demand and reward pattern of his occupation, or he contemplates a change in occupation—a prospect that may have about it more illusion than reality.

Table 9.3 presents schematically an interpretation of the research results on occupation, status, and satisfaction. Since it is a composite of many unrepresentative and incompatible studies, it is best regarded as a set of hypotheses.

Job Content

The data of table 9.2 remind us that people do distinguish among the various aspects of a job and can make separate evaluative judgments about them. Nevertheless, it is difficult to sort out the independent effects of these components on overall satisfaction. For example, it is difficult to separate the effects of job content in itself from the status, prestige, and other characteristics included in a real-life occupation or job-in-organization. The occupational structure of society is not arranged in accordance with the requirements of experimental design, and jobs that are interesting and varied in content tend also to be well rewarded. Intrinsic and extrinsic advantages go together, more often than not.

If one risks interpretation, it appears that the intrinsic characteristics of the work have substantial effects on satisfaction and dissatisfaction. Direct questions to workers about sources of satisfaction and dissatisfaction, or about elements that make jobs good or bad, show that job content is among the several most important aspects of work.[7] Moreover, the aspects of job content that appear most consistent in their effects are fractionation and lack of control or, to put it in positive terms, variety and autonomy.

Most observers of industrial development would agree that jobs tend to become more atomized and repetitive as technology becomes more sophisticated, in the current sense of that term. The doctrines of Frederick Winslow Taylor,[8] F. B. and Lillian Gilbreth,[9] and the succeeding generations of time-study engineers have been explicit about the productive advantages of simplicity and repetitiveness and specialization in industry. This view has been

Table 9.3. Hypothesized Occupational Differences in Job Satisfaction

Occupation	Most Satisfied	Very Satisfied	Satisfied	Ambivalent	Slightly Dissatisfied	Somewhat Dissatisfied
Professional-Technical	Professor Librarian School teacher (female)	Public Adviser Other people-oriented Nurse Artist	Scientist Accountant	Engineer School teacher (male)	Technician	
Managerial	Salaried (upper management)	Salaried (other)	Self-employed (large firm)		Self-employed (other)	
Sales			High-status	Sales clerk (female)		Sales clerk (male)
Clerical			Secretary Bookkeeper	Miscellaneous clerical		Repetitive clerical
Skilled			Foreman	Craftsman	Skilled	
Semiskilled				Higher	Middle	Repetitive
Unskilled						Laborer
Service		Protective	Armed	Household Other (female)		Other (male)
Farmer		Owner (large)	Owner (small)			Laborer

Source: Robinson, Athanasiou, and Head, Measures of Occupational Attitudes and Occupational Characteristics.

supported and implemented actively by industrial management, and it has been largely unchallenged by organized labor. The critics of extreme specialization have, for the most part, been social scientists. In studies from forty years ago[10] to the present, they have provided a consistent and substantial body of evidence that highly fractionated and repetitive tasks are performed by dissatisfied workers.

Job rotation and job enlargement are counterproposals to conventional time study and work simplification: definitive evidence of their effects is not yet available, although the reported experience of several companies is encouraging.[11] It seems likely that the positive effects of job enlargement will depend very much on the properties of the enlarged job and that they can be assessed in the same terms we would apply to any other job. To the extent that enlargement brings significant improvement in variety, opportunity to use valued skills, and the chance to acquire new skills, we would expect it to be successful in increasing job satisfaction. We badly need a set of objective measures to characterize job content in commensurate terms across a wide range of occupations. These could then be used to establish base lines and trends within job categories, to make comparisons between jobs, and to determine experimentally the effects of changing job content.

Proponents of an uncritical use of time study, work simplification, and fractionation sometimes defend the monotony of fractionated jobs by asserting that they are en route to automation. The route, however, can be very long and the prospect correspondingly displeasing to the individual. Moreover, the question of whether automation reduces dissatisfying repetitiveness in factory jobs is also unsettled, although it may tend in this direction.[12]

The problems of fractionation and repetition are closely related to those of autonomy and control. For example, the assembly line, which has come to be regarded as the epitome of industrial work, not only defines the job in simplified and repetitive terms, but it stipulates the exact method by which the job must be done and the pace at which it must be performed. Fewer studies have been made of the effects of these characteristics on satisfaction, but those that have been made show a negative relationship, especially between control of work pace and satisfaction. Workers on assembly lines express dissatisfaction about the mechanical pacing;[13] comparisons of factory worker satisfaction under mechanically controlled and self-controlled conditions show substantial differences in favor of the latter;[14] and workers in all occupations rate self-determination highest among the elements that define an ideal job.[15]

Supervision

That the characteristics of supervisory behavior are related to worker satisfaction is undeniable: many studies attest to the relationship, and none present contrary evidence. Theoretical schemes and measures have been proposed to describe the relevant behaviors of supervisors and the responses of those supervised. Most of the research depends upon reports of individual workers both for evidence of satisfaction and for description of the supervisory behaviors that satisfy or dissatisfy—a weak basis for inference. There are conspicuous exceptions, however. Several studies measure supervisory behavior independent of worker satisfaction, and other studies measure changes in satisfaction after changes have been induced in supervision.[16]

The effects of the supervisor's interpersonal behavior are better documented than his planning, execution, or technical skills. High worker satisfaction is associated with behavior that is considerate of employees and is employee-centered.[17] Satisfaction is associated also with supervisory behavior that shares decision-making power and accepts influence from subordinates. Evidence of the effects of such behavior, sometimes described as delegation and sometimes as participative or consultative management, has accumulated from experiments over the last thirty years.[18]

Peer Relationships

Most people are more satisfied to work as members of a group than in isolation. To be more precise, this statement should be qualified by other factors, particularly those of personality and those referring to the quality of interaction in the group. Nevertheless, most research has not taken such "third factors" into account but has sought and found direct relationships between interaction and satisfaction: workers prefer jobs that permit interaction, are more likely to quit jobs that prevent peer interaction, and cite congenial peer relationships as among the major characteristics of good jobs.

In addition to the studies showing positive effects of peer interaction, peer accessibility, and limited physical distance, a number of studies in the laboratory and a few in the field show the importance of acceptance by the group. It is likely that the consistent pattern of research results on peer interaction reflects a general norm of acceptance within work groups. Little research has been done on the conditions under which such a norm develops, but at least one researcher has emphasized the importance of similarity of attitudes,[19] and others have stressed the existence of shared goals under conditions in which cooperation is rewarded.[20]

Wages and Promotion

High pay and high satisfaction with work tend to go together, but in most studies that have come to this conclusion other factors have varied. As a result, it is difficult to be sure of the extent to which high wages in themselves produce sustained high levels of satisfaction and the extent to which the higher levels of satisfaction typical of higher-paid jobs reflect the variety, substantive interest, and autonomy that are also typical of such jobs. A major and important exception to this uncertainty is provided by E. E. Lawler and L. W. Porter,[21] who found that wage level was related to job satisfaction among 2,000 managers, even when managerial level was held constant. Other recent studies have suggested that the effect of wage level on satisfaction depends on frame of reference, perception of equity, or cognitive dissonance.[22]

It seems likely that the overall relationship between pay and satisfaction will hold. In any monetary culture in which wages and salaries constitute for most people the major or only source of income and the means of access to almost all goods and services, it is difficult to imagine that wages will not be a determinant job satisfaction. About the variations and qualifications of that statement, however, we still have much to learn.

Promotional opportunities are considered by some authors as distinct from wages and other extrinsic rewards, although some factor analyses do not support the distinction.[23] Studies of promotional opportunities are not numerous, and those that have been done are limited to the individual's perception of his own opportunities. Such studies show the perceived likelihood of promotion to be positively related to satisfaction with the job.

The *Survey of Working Conditions,* sponsored by the Department of Labor, provides for the first time nationwide data on problems and opportunities for promotion from the worker's point of view.[24] More than half of all workers in this study said it was "very important" to them that the chances for promotion be good, and another quarter answered "somewhat important." This is a strong response, although some factors were rated still more important— among them, having interesting work, enough resources to do the job, good pay, and adequate job security. These other factors, however, are hardly separable from promotion. Indeed, one of the inherent difficulties in interpreting the relationship between promotion and satisfaction is the complexity of promotion as a concept. It is by definition a change of status, a change of job, and, not infrequently, a change of occupation. On this basis alone, the concept of promotion is subject to all the confounding and merging of variables we have already discussed in considering problems of status and occupation. In addition, promotion constitutes a major means of recognition for work done, a means of showing approval and acceptance. It also introduces variety (as in job rotation) and, presumably, the challenge of expanded or more difficult activities. It would require a major effort to isolate the separate effects of these components of promotion on satisfaction, and there is no present sign that such an effort is being made.

Certainly one would predict a strong positive relationship between promotional opportunities and job satisfaction, given the obtained relationship between status and satisfaction. Since status ranking is an ordering of jobs according to their desirability, and promotion is by definition an increase in status (and therefore satisfaction), promotional opportunity becomes an instrumental value in a job and a source of satisfaction itself. The 1969 *Survey of Working Conditions* shows this relationship for both men and women. (More than 60 percent of all job discrimination reported by women referred to problems of promotional opportunity.)

Working Conditions

The physical conditions of work and the hours required are difficult to assess in terms of overall job satisfaction. Extremely bad working conditions (long hours, high temperature, poor ventilation, and the like) can make any job literally unbearable. In the range ordinarily encountered, however, such conditions are prevented by law, union contract, and the norms of the larger society. As a result, working conditions emerge as a separate and identifiable factor but affect satisfaction less than the other factors we have considered.[25] Frederick Herzberg considers working conditions incapable of satisfying although quite capable of dissatisfying.[26] Other research finds them very low on the list of things that make a job either ideal or "worst possible."[27]

Shift work is an exception. Studies of shift work typically (but not always) show significantly lower levels of satisfaction among employees who must work at night, and still lower satisfaction levels for those who must change from one shift to another. A large and intensive study of shift workers explains this effect in terms of the individual's pattern of other valued activities (marriage, child-rearing, friendship, and others) and the extent to which shift work interferes with them.[28]

These, then, are the themes that emerge in answer to the question of what makes work satisfying. They are persuasive and not very mysterious. Improve or increase comfort, challenge, pay, and the opportunity for interaction with coworkers, and you will increase the satisfaction of workers with their jobs. That, it can be argued, is a good in itself, but for many years it has been argued that job satisfaction is also an instrumental good—that it should be valued for what it leads to.

Job Satisfaction and Productivity

If the question, "Does job satisfaction lead to improved productivity?" could be answered with an unqualified yes, many troubles, practical and theoretical, would be over. Managers, by making workers more satisfied, would also motivate them to become more productive. By doing good, management would also do well. It is an attractive idea. Indeed, it is a managerial dream. It is not, so far as research can tell us, a complete reality. The evidence indicates that satisfaction is related to productivity in some circumstances and not in others, and that these circumstances have yet to be fully defined. Past work has included many theoretical arguments in favor of the satisfaction-productivity hypothesis.[29] There are also a substantial number of studies that have tested the relationship between job satisfaction and productivity within single organizations under unspecified social and technical conditions, and there are a few that have gone deeper.

In ordinary industrial situations the satisfaction-productivity relationship seems, on the average, to be negligible. In an extensive review of the literature, A. H. Brayfield and W. H. Crockett come to the decision that there is no such relationship.[30] Frederick Herzberg reviewed twenty-six studies, including some of those assessed by Brayfield and Crockett, and found evidence for a positive satisfaction-productivity link in fourteen studies, none whatsoever in nine, and a negative relationship in three.[31] Victor Vroom reviewed twenty studies in which the magnitude of the satisfaction-productivity relationship was given and found a correlational range from $-.21$ to $+.86$, with an excessively modest mean of $+.21$.[32]

Rensis Likert proposes that there is an inherent tendency for low satisfaction to be expressed in low productivity but that several factors obscure or counteract this tendency.[33] One such factor is the pace-determining constraints and demands which, particularly on the assembly line, determine the rate of production almost regardless of the emotional and motivational state of the worker. Another is the inadequacy of productivity criteria—for example, their failure to take account of the costs of conflict, retraining, recruitment, and the like. A third is the neglect of duration; the effects of low satisfaction may not be immediately manifest.[34]

These are plausible arguments, but they are not settled beyond doubt. It does seem clear that two rather contradictory trends have been apparent in American managerial practice for several decades. One is increasing concern with worker satisfaction, often with the accompanying justification that such concern leads to increased productivity. The other is an increasing reliance on forms of technology and production controls that minimize the effects of worker attitudes on the organizational product.

There is some oblique evidence for the success of the latter trend. Evidence is consistent, if not rich, with respect to the association of satisfaction with other measures of job-relevant behavior, including absence, turnover, and accidents. Least in quantity, but impressive in their implications, are those studies that show a relationship between job satisfaction and the success with which the individual functions in other life roles.[35] It is possible that the costs of the frustration of work, particularly when the technical and supervisory controls are effective, are paid elsewhere—in the home and the community. Several researchers have begun to document such costs in terms of individual health, but less has been done at the level of family and community.[36] Problems of causality are extremely difficult to resolve in this connection, and we badly need studies that resolve them.

I conclude that there are many paths to productivity, as there are to the evocation of any other human behavior. Some of them, like the fear of the gun, can induce great effort, but also great dissatisfaction, potential conflict, escape, or rebellion. Others can, within limits, create gains in both satisfaction and productivity.

We need to learn much more about those limits and about the conditions under which both satisfaction and productivity can be enhanced. Likert, summarizing a great deal of research on the subject, emphasizes the following methods that promote both productivity and satisfaction:

• Use of ego motives as well as economic motives. (Ego motives refer to the desire of the individual to achieve and maintain a sense of personal worth and importance, to grow and achieve in terms of his own goals, and to receive recognition and approval for so doing.)

- Group participation and involvement in setting goals, improving methods, appraising progress, and establishing compensation systems
- Intensive communication among individuals and groups, directed upward and laterally in the organization as well as downward, and initiated at any point in the organization
- Extensive personal interaction in setting goals and exerting influence on organizational matters, both within the organization itself and via labor unions
- Decision making primarily by "organizational families" (supervisor and immediate subordinates), linked throughout the organization
- Goal setting by group participation in such "families," except in emergencies
- Influence and control widely distributed and substantial.[37]

This, of course, is one interpretation of the available research on the social and psychological aspects of organization. Consistent with the interpretations of several other researchers,[38] it describes an overall prescription for organizations, rather than suggesting that different modes of leadership may be appropriate under different circumstances[39] or under different technologies.[40] Despite differences in interpretation and in research emphasis, all serious reviews of organizational research indicate that wide ranges of productivity and satisfaction are compatible. The relationship between these two major criteria of organizational functioning is ultimately a matter of choice and design, not an inevitable law of human behavior. To put it more positively, many organizational characteristics that are associated with high productivity are at least compatible with the increased humanization of work.

An Experimental Approach

If we are committed to the humanization of work, there are a number of things that we should do. We should begin by recognizing the magnitude of the problem. The task is not to discover some formula that simultaneously maximizes productivity and satisfaction under all circumstances. I doubt that such a formula exists. Instead, we should do research that will teach us what our options are in the humanization of work, and what the costs are that attach to those options.

When we know more about those possibilities, we must choose among them. Such choices are expressions of values, and they involve decisions on national policy, corporate policy, and union policy. Such decisions are made continually, of course. They are reflected, for example, in the drastic reduction of hours of work since the turn of the century and in the increasingly comprehensive legislation regarding health hazards on the job. It seems likely that more dramatic issues will emerge and more difficult questions will be raised—Do we want more consumer goods or more leisure, more consumption in the short run or a longer life on this planet?

The humanization of work, if we were to enunciate it as a major national goal, would require that each technological innovation be assessed not only in terms of its potential addition to productivity but also in terms of its addition to or subtraction from the satisfaction and self-actualization of the people engaged in the productive process. Such issues would become part of the law and part of the negotiations between management and union.

Moreover, to treat the humanization of work as a goal implies that we do not know enough about it to accomplish such a transformation instantly. Yet if the goal is to be made real, it implies a commitment and a willingness to learn and to keep on learning. And that means, in Donald Campbell's exciting phrase, the decision to become an experimenting society—not merely in the sense of trying new things but in terms of trial and careful evaluation under circumstances that we can afford and measure.[41] This is the very opposite of sweeping, unevaluated fad and reform, as it is the opposite of rockbound resistance.

Such an experimental approach is novel only in its application to problems of social policy. In other sectors of life, it is as familiar as the design and trial of a pilot plant. It waits only to be tried with respect to the social arrangements of work as well as the technical. Outside the realm of work, examples of such experiments have begun to appear. The experiment on the negative income tax may settle ancient ideological battles about what people do when the threat of poverty is removed: Do they become more or less active in the search for employment and the development of increased earning capacity? The experiment with educational vouchers, to be spent by parents for the educational arrangements of their choice, may help discover ways of increasing parental influence without at the same time increasing intergroup conflict. And the proposed experiment with rent subsidies may answer equally difficult questions about the upgrading of housing and the stimulation of the housing supply.

It is tempting to imagine a series of major field experiments on the humanization of work. One such experiment that seems to hold considerable promise involves the development and trial of the work module.[42]

The Work Module

There has been some research and a great deal of speculation on the problem of goodness-of-fit between people and jobs. A good deal of this work has concentrated on the process of selection. This approach tends to accept without question the properties of the task role and looks to invent ways of identifying in advance persons who can perform the task competently for a sustained period. Other research has centered on processes of training and counseling, which can be regarded as ways of changing people in order to improve goodness-of-fit after they have been assigned to a particular job. More recently, some researchers have attempted to examine the possibility of changing the requirements of the job itself—for example, by enlarging the content of routine jobs or by increasing the decision-making function of all jobs in an organization.

None of this work has begun with the simple premise that the individual could maximize, or at least improve, his goodness-of-fit with the job if he were permitted to define his own role—to construct his own job, so to speak. Yet the evidence to support this premise is large and varied. For example, occupations in which such opportunity for role definition or role elaboration is great are characteristically high in intrinsic job satisfaction. This is true of professors, research scientists, and farmers, all of whom tend to work quite independently. It is true also of high government officials, business executives, and self-employed heads of businesses, all of whom occupy positions near the top of some hierarchy and have the freedom of choice implied by that fact. These jobs are different in many other respects, but the people who hold them show high levels of satisfaction and work involvement, express a wish to go on working even in the absence of economic need, and say that they would advise a son or daughter to follow the same career line.

The work module experiment is a way of discovering the extent to which the individual choices characteristic of such jobs can be introduced into other jobs without impairing organizational effectiveness. The concept of the work module itself is simply that of a time-task unit—the smallest allocation of time to a given task that is sufficient to be economically and psychologically meaningful. We will assume that unit to be two hours, and for the present discussion we will define a work module to be two hours of work at a given task—operating a punch press, manning an assembly-line station, or using a typewriter.

It is obvious that a conventional job consists of four such modules (eight hours) per day, five days a week, forty-eight or fifty weeks a year. It is slightly less obvious that the work activities of any organization can be thought of as consisting of some unique pattern of modules of time-task units. Moreover, the number and variety of such units that happen to define a work role are culturally determined and subject to change. For example, in most factories the machine operator's job consists of twenty modules per week at the same task. The self-employed farmer's job consists of more modules and a variety of tasks.

Such prescriptions change across cultures and over time. Forty hours a week would have been considered part-time work not many years ago and would still be considered so in some places. Other prescriptions, however permanent they seem, are also subject to change—the age at which young people enter the labor force, the age and manner in which older people abandon the work role, the basis on which people may have access to one or another kind of work, and the relationship between work and nonwork roles. It is usual, however, to find these aspects of work set by tradition or statute and prescribed with some uniformity for most jobs.

The introduction of the work module (two hours at a particular task) would substitute individual choice (within organizationally acceptable limits) for the less flexible methods of definition and allocation just described. The individual would construct his job from the work modules available that he is qualified to perform.

As a simple example, let us imagine a stock man in a supermarket, whose present job consists of stamping prices on food containers and placing the items on the shelves. He stamps prices and stocks shelves eight hours a day, five days a week; this time-task pattern defines his job. It was offered in those terms, and he could take it or leave it. But if the work of the supermarket were thought of in terms of two-hour modules, the stock clerk might choose to spend two modules a day at that task, perhaps one at the cash register, and one learning inventory control. Or he might wish to change the time pattern of his work to reduce the number of days a week by increasing the number of modules worked each day.

Operating problems. The first point is that the work module approach potentially removes rigid constraints of time and fractionated tasks by treating such factors as variables, and as variables over which the individual has major influence. The second point, equally important, is that this increase in individual choice must occur within the operating constraints of an ongoing organization. Such constraints are not negligible, and a good deal of experimentation will be required in order to discover and invent ways of acknowledging them within the framework of the modular approach to defining jobs. The emergent pattern of individual preferences that is invited in response to the modular approach must be reconciled with the pattern of activities needed to transact the basic business of the enterprise. If the technology of steel production requires that blast furnaces operate twenty-four hours a day and seven days a week, some people must work nights and weekends. If no one prefers the work modules defined by those tasks and times, some compromise of preferences will be necessary. If compromise is required, some set of decision rules and some procedure must be agreed upon. One could imagine settling such differences on any of a number of bases—seniority, management prerogative, pay differentials, rotation, and the like. But whatever the principle, the procedure must be developed and put into practice.

Moreover, the modular allocation of work within an organization is a continuing or at least a recurring process; it cannot be done once and for all. The requirements of the organization change with changes in market conditions and technology, and the preferences of the work force change in response to turnover, aging, and other individual considerations. The process of modular choice and allocation must therefore be repeated. How often it must be repeated is likely to be a compromise between chaos and rigidity. One can imagine a semiannual or annual "election" or polling of workers, but perhaps more continuous procedures could be developed.

Other organizational constraints are of lesser importance in principle but will be no less difficult to work out in practice. Some system of rated experience and training must be used to determine which tasks lie within the competence of an individual; the assembly-line worker who would prefer to spend two modules a day as a tool-and-die maker must be qualified for the position before his preferences can be acted on. The union, if there is one, must be seriously involved in the whole process, since the allocation of tasks on the modular basis includes many decisions that lie within the bargaining agreement. The computation of wages will become more complex as workers are assigned to several tasks that have different pay rates. These complications, however, are less formidable under existing procedures of timeclocks and computer-prepared payrolls. One can foresee also some complications in reconciling the modular allocation of work with federal and state statutes; an individual may want to work fifty-six hours a week for three weeks and take the fourth week as vacation, but the law says he must be paid overtime after forty hours, and management may be unwilling to pay a premium in order to give the worker his choice of hours. To some extent, the working through of these issues can be thought of as variations on the main experimental theme of the work module itself; to some extent each organization must be regarded as presenting a unique set of constraints and requirements within which the experiment must take shape.

Conversion. In addition to the questions of operation confronting the modular scheme, there is the difficulty of the changeover: how to get from here to there, so to speak. One can imagine a sequence something along the following lines. Management and union make an initial agreement to try out modular work allocation, perhaps for a period of one year, with continuation to depend upon both having judged the experiment to have been successful. Agreement is next reached regarding all jobs to be included in the modular allocation process and those to be excluded. For example, all supervisory positions, and nonsupervisory positions requiring rare skills, may be excluded. As a third step, the requirements of training and experience are stipulated for each job to be included in the experiment; these decisions define the workers eligible to bid for each task. At about the same time, agreement must be reached on the process of matching individual preferences to organizational needs. This procedure may be centralized or decentralized, done by staff or representatives, by management or management-union committees. Management must now stipulate the organizational requirements; that is, the conventional jobs must be restated in modular terms. (This process, if no other changes are introduced at the same time, is merely arithmetic. Requirements for given tasks or skills are stated in terms of the number of hours or modules required each day.)

At this point a job market of modular units has been created. Workers are asked to state their preferences. These statements are then matched to the organizational requirements, in accordance with procedures already agreed upon, and work proceeds on the new basis of task allocation. At the end of the first term or trial peiod, perhaps six months, the procedure is repeated with whatever improvements are suggested by the initial experience.

One can imagine many variations on this basic theme. Coverage may be very limited (to certain unskilled and semiskilled jobs, for example) or very broad. The rights of a worker to his original job may be treated as absolute, so that any individual preference for the status quo is granted before the modular allocation process begins, or all job activities may be included in the market of modules. The allocation of tasks and hours may be considered fixed for substantial periods or subject to change at any time on the basis of individual preferences and available modules. A series of experiments will be needed to discover which of such variations are appropriate under particular circumstances.

Results. The work module experiment is proposed as a means of improving goodness-of-fit between the individual and the job. To the extent that it does so, its first effects should be increased satisfaction with work. Secondary individual effects should include increases in reported self-utilization (use of valued skills and abilities) and self-development (acquisition of new skills and abilities). Ramifying effects on other life roles—as spouse, parent, friend, citizen—are less predictable, but they should be explored. It is at least plausible that major improvements in the work role will have positive results in other sectors of life. Effects on physical health should also be positive, since an improvement in goodness-of-fit means a reduction in job stress and the accompanying physical and psychological strains.

Most difficult to measure, perhaps, are the effects of the work module experiment on the larger community. They might be negligible in the case of a single plant, but if the modular allocation of work were to be given a more widespread trial in a community, the effects could be substantial. For example, the labor force could be enlarged by the addition of people who do not need or cannot accept full-time jobs. Young people enrolled in school or college, women with particular responsibilities for child care, and older people who cannot or need not work full-time might be attracted to work some number and pattern of modules. We could expect also to see some increase in employment stability, because individuals would not need to quit their jobs in order to get some change in work pattern, and organizations would not need to terminate workers in order to get some adjustment to market fluctuations.

We could expect positive effects at the organizational level as well as at the individual level. Absence and turnover can be regarded in part as behavioral responses to unsatisfactory work situations. To the extent that the modular allocation of work better meets the needs of the individual, he has less reason to leave the job temporarily or permanently. The organization also gains in innovative capacity, because information and experience are more widely held; such gains might be visible in terms of suggestions for technical improvement. The broader acquisition of experience might also increase the organizational reserves for replacement and promotion and in this way reduce its costs of recruitment and training.

The predicted organizational gains from the modular allocation of work, even if they should be realized, would not be cost free. Certainly time will be required to plan and execute the changeover from conventional to modular assignments. Some of that time can be regarded as a one-time cost, but some of it will be a continuing charge of modular allocation and reallocation of tasks. It is likely that some conflicts will arise over matters of equity and the inability of the organization to meet individual preferences; how difficult and how costly the resolution of such differences will be remains to be seen. Bookkeeping and payroll computation will surely become more complex, and even computers respond to increased complexity with increased costs. The involvement of workers in several tasks may conceivably result in some loss of expertise and some corresponding increase in error, especially during the initial phase of a new allocation of tasks. Finally, if the modular allocation of work involves an increase in the number of workers employed in an organization, it may involve some increases in those fringe costs of employment that are associated with individuals rather than hours of work.

To what extent these and unforeseen costs will materially reduce or obliterate the organizational gains from the work module remains to be seen. Only trial and evaluation will resolve such questions.

Conclusion
Whether the work module is a useful idea can be determined by trying it. If it is successful, so much the better; if it is unsuccessful, other proposals are needed. The major issue is not the work module itself, but the dilemma of industrial society to which it is an attempted response—the humanization of work. That dilemma, I believe, can be resolved by the process of innovation, trial, and evaluation, and by no other means.

We have had too much of assumption and stereotype. Managements have accepted too long, for example, the assumption that every increment of fractionation in a job represents a potential increment of production. Unions have assumed too long that they could prevent workers from being exposed to unreasonable hazards or physical strains but not from being bored to death. And the larger society has assumed too long that there was no such thing as sociopsychological pollution—that the effects of monotonous or meaningless jobs were sloughed off as the workers went through the plant gates to home and community.

The experimenting society will approach the humanization of work by replacing such assumptions with facts and by arriving at such facts through the familiar and unavoidable process of trial and evaluation. In this process, government, industry, unions, and universities can collaborate to the benefit of all.

Notes

1. Thomas Hobbes, *Leviathan* (New York: Oxford Press, 1947), pt. 1, chap. 13. The quotation and the accompanying comment were suggested by Philip Converse.

2. John R. P. French, Willard Rodgers, and Sidney Cobb, "Adjustment as Person-Environment Fit," mimeographed (Ann Arbor: University of Michigan, Institute for Social Research, 1971).

3. Survey Research Center, University of Michigan, *Survey of Working Conditions* (Washington, D.C.: U.S. Department of Labor, Employment Standards Administration, 1971); Neal Q. Herrick and Robert P. Quinn, "The Working Conditions Survey as a Source of Social Indicators," *Monthly Labor Review,* April 1971, pp. 15–24.

4. Alex Inkeles, "Industrial Man: The Relation of Status to Experience, Perception, and Value," *American Journal of Sociology* 66 (July 1960): 1–31.

5. Robert W. Hodge, Donald J. Treiman, and Peter H. Rossi, "A Comparative Study of Occupational Prestige," in *Class, Status, and Power,* ed. Reinhard Bendix and S. M. Lipset (New York: Free Press, 1966).

6. A. Zdravomyslov and V. Iadov, "An Attempt at a Concrete Study of Attitude toward Work," *Soviet Sociology* 3 (1964): 3–15.

7. Frederick I. Herzberg, Bernard Mausner, and Barbara Snyderman, *The Motivation to Work* (New York: Wiley, 1959); Gerald Gurin, Joseph L. Veroff, and Sheila Feld, *Americans View Their Mental Health* (New York: Basic Books, 1960); Franklin P. Kilpatrick, Milton C. Cummings, Jr., and M. Kent Jennings, *The Image of the Federal Service* (Washington, D.C.: Brookings Institution, 1964).

8. Frederick W. Taylor, *The Principles of Scientific Management* (New York: Harper & Row, 1911).

9. F. B. Gilbreth and Lillian M. Gilbreth, *Fatigue Study* (New York: Macmillan, 1919).

10. S. Wyatt, *Incentives in Repetitive Work,* Industrial Health Research Board, report no. 69 (London: H. M. Stationery Office, 1934).

11. H. Bruce Duffany, paper read before the American Association for the Advancement of Science, Philadelphia, December 1971.

12. Floyd C. Mann and L. R. Hoffman, *Automation and the Worker* (New York: Holt, 1960).

13. Charles R. Walker and Robert H. Guest, *The Man on the Assembly Line* (Cambridge: Harvard University Press, 1952).

14. J. Walker and R. Marriott, "A Study of Some Attitudes to Factory Work," *Occupational Psychology* 25 (1951): 181–191.

15. Kilpatrick, Cummings, and Jennings.

16. Nancy C. Morse and Everett Reimer, "The Experimental Change of a Major Organizational Variable," *Journal of Abnormal and Social Psychology* 52 (1956): 120–129; idem, *Satisfactions in the White-Collar Job* (Ann Arbor: University of Michigan, Institute for Social Research, 1953); Alfred J. Marrow, David G. Bowers, and Stanley E. Seashore, *Management by Participation: Creating a Climate for Personal and Organizational Development* (New York: Harper & Row, 1967).

17. J. K. Hemphill and A. E. Coons, "Development of the Leader Behavior Description Questionnaire," in *Leader Behavior: Its Description and Measurement,* ed. Ralph M. Stogdill and A. E. Coons, Bureau of Business Research Monograph no. 88 (Columbus: Ohio State University, 1957), pp. 6–38; Rensis Likert, *New Patterns of Management* (New York: McGraw-Hill, 1961).

18. Kurt Lewin, Ronald Lippitt, and Ralph K. White, "Patterns of Aggressive Behavior in Experimentally Created 'Social Climates,' " *Journal of Social Psychology* 10 (1939): 271–299; Arnold S. Tannenbaum, ed., *Control in Organizations* (New York: McGraw-Hill, 1968).

19. T. M. Newcomb, "The Prediction of Interpersonal Attraction," *American Psychologist* 11 (1956): 575–586.

20. Muzafer Sherif and Carolyn W. Sherif, *Groups in Harmony and Tension: An Integration of Studies on Intergroup Relations* (New York: Harper, 1953); Morton Deutsch, "An Experimental Study of the Effects of Co-Operation and Competition upon Group Process," *Human Relations* 2 (1949): 199–231; S. C. Jones and V. H. Vroom, "Division of Labor and Performance under Co-operative and Competitive Conditions," *Journal of Abnormal and Social Psychology* 68, March 1964: 313–320.

21. E. E. Lawler and L. W. Porter, "Perceptions Regarding Management Compensation," *Industrial Relations* 3 (1963): 41–49; idem, *Pay and Organizational Effectiveness* (New York: McGraw-Hill, 1971).

22. Robert B. Athanasiou, "Opinion Formation through Dissonance Reduction" (thesis, Rensselaer Polytechnic Institute, 1965); Elliott Jaques, *Equitable Payment* (New York: Wiley, 1961); Martin Patchen, *The Choice of Wage Comparisons* (Englewood Cliffs, N. J.: Prentice-Hall, 1961); J. S. Adams, *Wage Inequities, Productivity, and Work Quality* (Berkeley: University of California, Institute of Industrial Relations, 1964).

23. Survey Research Center.

24. Ibid.

25. Ibid.

26. Herzberg, Mausner, and Snyderman.

27. Kilpatrick, Cummings, and Jennings.

28. Paul E. Mott et al., *Shift Work: The Social, Psychological and Physical Consequences* (Ann Arbor: University of Michigan Press, 1965).

29. Douglas McGregor, *The Human Side of Enterprise* (New York: McGraw-Hill, 1960); Likert, *New Patterns of Management.*

30. A. H. Brayfield and W. H. Crockett, "Employee Attitudes and Employee Performance," *Psychological Bulletin* 52 (1955): 396–424.

31. Frederick Herzberg et al., *Job Attitudes: Review of Research and Opinion* (Pittsburgh: Psychological Service of Pittsburgh, 1957).

32. Victor H. Vroom, *Work and Motivation* (New York: Wiley, 1964).

33. Rensis Likert, *The Human Organization* (New York: McGraw-Hill, 1967); idem, *New Patterns of Management.*

34. Ibid.

35. Gurin, Veroff, and Feld; Mott et al.

36. John R. P. French, Jr., and Robert D. Caplan, "Organizational Stress and Individual Strain," in *The Failure of Success,* ed. A. J. Marrow (New York: American Management Association, 1972); Sidney Cobb, *The Frequency of the Rheumatic Diseases,* Vital and Health Statistics Monographs (Cambridge: Harvard University Press, 1971).

37. Likert, *Human Organization;* idem, *New Patterns of Management.*

38. Chris Argyris, *Personality and Organization* (New York: Harper & Row, 1957); idem, *Interpersonal Competence and Organizational Effectiveness* (Homewood, Ill.: Dorsey Press, 1962); idem, *Integrating the Individual and the Organization* (New York: Wiley, 1964); McGregor.

39. Fred E. Fiedler, *A Theory of Leadership Effectiveness* (New York: McGraw-Hill, 1967); John R. P. French, Jr., "The Social Environment and Mental Health," *Journal of Social Issues* 19 (1963), no. 4: 39–56.

40. Joan Woodward, *Industrial Organizations* (London: Oxford University Press, 1965).

41. Donald T. Campbell, "Methods for the Experimenting Society," *American Psychologist* (in press).

42. This approach to the humanization of work has developed over a long period and has benefited from the reactions and suggestions of many colleagues. It was first proposed in a conversation with Dr. Leslie Kish.

10 Alienation and Innovation in the Workplace

Richard E. Walton

Managers don't need anyone to tell them that employee alienation exists. Terms such as "blue-collar blues" and "salaried dropouts" are all too familiar. But are they willing to undertake the major innovations necessary for redesigning work organizations to deal effectively with the root causes of alienation? My purpose in this article is to urge them to do so, for two reasons: (1) The current alienation is not merely a phase that will pass in due time. (2) The innovations needed to correct the problem can simultaneously enhance the quality of work life (thereby lessening alienation) and improve productivity. In the first part of the article, I shall risk covering terrain already familiar to some readers in order to establish the fact that alienation is a basic, long-term, and mounting problem. Then I shall present some examples of the comprehensive redesign that I believe is required.

I also hope to provide today's managers with a glimpse at what may be the industrial work environment of the future, as illustrated by a pet-food plant which opened in January 1971.

This paper appeared in *Harvard Business Review,* November-December 1972, under the title "How to Counter Alienation in the Plant." Reprinted, with changes, by permission of the author and the publisher. Copyright 1972 by the President and Fellows of Harvard College; all rights reserved. The author is grateful to Andy Miller of the *Harvard Business Review* for his substantial editorial improvements.

In this facility, management set out to incorporate features that would provide a high quality of work life, enlist unusual human involvement, and result in high productivity. The positive results of the experiment to date are impressive, and the difficulties encountered in implementing it are instructive. Moreover, similar possibilities for *comprehensive* innovations exist in a wide variety of settings and industries.

The word "comprehensive" is important because my argument is that each technique in the standard fare of personnel and organization development programs (job enrichment, management by objectives, sensitivity training, confrontation and team-building sessions, participative decision making) has grasped only a limited truth and has fallen far short of producing meaningful change. In short, more radical, comprehensive, and systemic redesign of organizations is necessary.

Anatomy of Alienation

There are two parts to the problem of employee alienation: (1) the productivity output of work systems and (2) the social costs associated with employee inputs. Regarding the first, U.S. productivity is not adequate to the challenges posed by international competition and inflation; it cannot sustain impressive economic growth. (I do not refer here to economic growth as something to be valued merely for its own sake—it is politically a precondition for the income redistribution that will make equality of opportunity possible in the United States.) Regarding the second, the social and psychological costs of work systems are excessive, as evidenced by their effects on the mental and physical health of employees and on the social health of families and communities.

Employee alienation *affects* productivity and *reflects* social costs incurred in the workplace. Increasingly, blue- and white-collar employees and, to some extent, middle managers tend to dislike their jobs and resent their bosses. Workers tend to rebel against their union leaders. They are becoming less concerned about the quality of the product of their labor and more angered about the quality of the context in which they labor.

In some cases, alienation is expressed by passive withdrawal—tardiness, absenteeism and turnover, and inattention on the job. In other cases, it is expressed by active attacks—pilferage, sabotage, deliberate waste, assaults, bomb threats, and other disruptions of work routines. Demonstrations have taken place and underground newspapers have appeared in large organizations in recent years to protest company policies. Even more recently, employees have cooperated with newsmen, congressional committees, regulatory agencies, and protest groups in exposing objectionable practices.

These trends all have been mentioned in the media, but one expression of alienation has been underreported: pilferage and violence against property and persons. Such acts are less likely to be revealed to the police and the media when they occur in a private company than when they occur in a high school, a ghetto business district, or a suburban town. Moreover, dramatic increases in these forms of violence are taking place at the plant level. This trend is not reported in local newspapers, and there is little or no appreciation of it at corporate headquarters. Local management keeps quiet because violence is felt to reflect unfavorably both on its effectiveness and on its plant as a place to work.

Roots of Conflict

The acts of sabotage and other forms of protest are overt manifestations of a conflict between changing employee attitudes and organizational inertia. Increasingly, what employees expect from their jobs is different from what organizations are prepared to offer them. These evolving expectations of workers conflict with the demands, conditions, and rewards of employing organizations in at least six important ways:

• Employees want challenge and personal growth, but work tends to be simplified and specialties tend to be used repeatedly in work assignments. This pattern exploits the narrow skills of a worker, while limiting his or her opportunities to broaden or develop.

• Employees want to be included in patterns of mutual influence; they want egalitarian treatment. But organizations are characterized by tall hierarchies, status differentials, and chains of command.

• Employee commitment to an organization is increasingly influenced by the intrinsic interest of the work itself, the human dignity afforded by management, and the social responsibility reflected in the organization's products. Yet organization practices still emphasize material rewards and employment security and neglect other employee concerns.

• What employees want from careers, they are apt to want *right now.* But when organizations design job hierarchies and career paths, they continue to assume that today's workers are as willing to postpone gratifications as yesterday's workers were.

• Employees want more attention to the emotional aspects of organization life, such as individual self-esteem, openness between people, and expressions of warmth. Yet organizations emphasize rationality and seldom legitimize the emotional part of the organizational experience.

• Employees are becoming less driven by competitive urges, less likely to identify competition as the "American way." Nevertheless, managers continue to plan career patterns, organize work, and design reward systems as if employees valued competition as highly as they used to.

Pervasive social forces. The foregoing needs and desires that employees bring to their work are but a local reflection of more basic, and not readily reversible, trends in U.S. society. These trends are fueled by family and social experience as well as by social institutions, especially schools. Among the most significant are:

• *The rising level of education.* Employees bring to the workplace more abilities and, correspondingly, higher expectations than in the past.

• *The rising level of wealth and security.* Vast segments of today's society never have wanted for the tangible essentials of life; thus they are decreasingly motivated by pay and security, which are taken for granted.

• *The decreased emphasis given by churches, schools, and families to obedience to authority.* These socialization agencies have promoted individual initiative, self-responsibility and self-control, the relativity of values, and other social patterns that make subordinacy in traditional organizations an increasingly bitter pill to swallow for each successive wave of entrants to the U.S. work force.

• *The decline in achievement motivation.* For example, whereas the books my parents read in primary school taught them the virtues of hard work and competition, my children's books emphasize self-expression and actualizing one's potential. The workplace has not yet fully recognized this change in employee values.

• *The shifting emphasis from individualism to social commitment.* This shift is driven in part by a need for the direct gratifications of human connectedness (for example, as provided by communal living experiments). It also results from a growing appreciation of our interdependence, and it renders obsolete many traditional workplace concepts regarding the division of labor and work incentives.

I believe that protests in the workplace will mount even more rapidly than is indicated by the contributing trends postulated here. The latent dissatisfaction of workers will be activated as (1) the issues receive public attention and (2) some examples of attempted solutions serve to raise expectations (just as the blacks' expressions of dissatisfaction with social and economic inequities were triggered in the 1950s and women's discontent expanded late in the 1960s).

Revitalization and Reform

It seems clear that employee expectations are not likely to revert to those of an earlier day. And the conflicts between these expectations and traditional organizations result in alienation. This alienation, in turn, exacts a deplorable psychological and social cost as well as causes worker behavior that depresses productivity and constrains growth. In short, we need major innovative efforts to redesign work organizations, efforts that take employee expectations into account.

Over the past two decades we have witnessed a parade of organization development, personnel, and labor relations programs that promised to revitalize organizations:

• *Job enrichment* would provide more varied and challenging content in the work.

• *Participative decision making* would enable the information, judgments, and concerns of subordinates to influence the decisions that affect them.

• *Management by objectives* would enable subordinates to understand and shape the objectives toward which they strive and against which they are evaluated.

• *Sensitivity training* or *encounter groups* would enable people to relate to each other as human beings with feelings and psychological needs.

• *Productivity bargaining* would revise work rules and increase management's flexibility with a quid pro quo whereby the union ensures that workers share in the fruits of the resulting productivity increases.

Each of the preceding programs *by itself* is an inadequate reform of the workplace and has typically failed in its more limited objectives. While application is often based on a correct diagnosis, each approach is only a partial remedy; therefore, the organizational system soon returns to an earlier equilibrium.

The lesson we must learn in the area of work reform is similar to one we have learned in another area of national concern. It is now recognized that a health program, a welfare program, a housing program, or an employment program alone is unable to make a lasting impact on the urban-poor syndrome. Poor health, unemployment, and other interdependent aspects of poverty must be attacked in a coordinated or systemic way.

So it is with meaningful reform of the workplace: we must think "systemically" when approaching the problem. We must coordinate into the redesign the way tasks are packaged into jobs, the way workers are required to relate to each other, the way performance is measured and rewards are made available, the way positions of authority and status symbols are structured, and the way career paths are conceived. Moreover, because these types of changes in work organizations imply new employee skills and different organizational cultures, transitional programs must be established.

A Prototype of Change

A number of major organization design efforts meet the requirements of being systemic and comprehensive. One experience in which I have been deeply involved is particularly instructive. As a recent and radical effort, it generally encompasses and goes beyond what has been done elsewhere.

During 1968, General Foods was planning an additional plant at a new location, Topeka, Kansas. The existing manufacturing facility in Illinois was then experiencing many of the symptoms of alienation that I have already outlined. There were frequent instances of employee indifference and inattention that, because of the continuous-process technology, led to plant shutdowns, product waste, and costly recycling. Employees effectively worked only a modest number of hours per day, and they resisted changes toward fuller utilization of manpower. A series of acts of sabotage and violence occurred.

Because of these pressures and the fact that it was not difficult to link substantial manufacturing costs to worker alienation, management was receptive to basic innovations in the new plant. In mid-1968 Lyman Ketchum, operations manager for pet foods, became committed to the idea of designing the plant to both accommodate changes in the expectations of employees and utilize knowledge developed by the behavioral sciences.

Key Design Features

The early development of the plant took more than two years. This involved planning, education, skill training, and building the nucleus of the new organization into a team.

During this early period, Ed Dulworth was selected to assume overall responsibility for the Topeka facility. Dulworth was an engineer by training and experienced in the manufacturing processes to be employed in the Topeka plant; his past performance left no doubt about his technical competence. He had in the past established effective and close relationships with his immediate subordinates. Dulworth soon selected two subordinates —a manufacturing services manager and a production manager—who in turn selected an assistant production manager. The project team that took on the responsibility for designing the new plant organization over the next year and a half was comprised of these four managers and me. Lyman Ketchum occasionally met with the team and made substantive contributions.

We met with behavioral science experts and visited other industrial plants that were experimenting with innovative organizational methods. Thus the managers were stimulated to think about departures from traditional work organizations and given reassurance that other organizational modes were not only possible but also more viable in the current social context. While the consultations and plant visits provided some raw material for designing the new organization, the theretofore latent knowledge of the five managers played the largest role. Their insights into the aspirations of people, and basically optimistic assumptions about the capacities of human beings, were particularly instrumental in the design of the innovative plant. In the remainder of this section, I shall present the nine key features of this design.

Autonomous work groups. Self-managed work teams are given collective responsibility for large segments of the production process. The total work force of approximately seventy employees is organized into six teams. A processing team and a packaging team operate during each shift. The processing team's jurisdiction includes unloading, storing materials, drawing ingredients from storage, mixing, and then performing the series of steps that transform ingredients into a pet-food product. The packaging team's responsibilities include the finishing stages of product manufacturing— packaging operations, warehousing, and shipping.

A team is comprised of seven to fourteen members (called operators) and a team leader. Its size is large enough to include a natural set of highly interdependent tasks, yet small enough to allow effective face-to-face meetings for decision making and coordination. Assignments of individuals to sets of tasks are subject to team consensus. Although at any given time one operator has primary responsibility for a set of tasks within the team's jurisdiction, some tasks can be shared by several operators. Moreover, tasks can be redefined by the team in light of individual capabilities and interests. In contrast, individuals in the old plant were permanently assigned to specific jobs.

Other matters that fall within the scope of team deliberation, recommendation, or decision making include:

● Coping with manufacturing problems that occur within or between the teams' areas of responsibilities
● Temporarily redistributing tasks to cover for absent employees
● Selecting team operators to serve on plant-wide committees or task forces
● Screening and selecting employees to replace departing operators
● Counseling those who do not meet team standards (for instance, regarding absences or giving assistance to others).

Integrated support functions. Staff units and job specialties are avoided. Activities typically performed by maintenance, quality control, custodial, industrial engineering, and personnel units are built into an operating team's responsibilities. For example, each team member maintains the equipment he operates (except for complicated electrical maintenance) and housekeeps the area in which he works. Each team has responsibility for performing quality tests and ensuring quality standards. In addition, team members perform what is normally a personnel function when they screen job applicants.

Challenging job assignments. While the designers understood that job assignments would undergo redefinition in light of experience and the varying interests and abilities on the work teams, the initial job assignments established an important design principle. Every set of tasks is designed to include functions requiring higher-order human abilities and responsibilites, such as planning, diagnosing mechanical or process problems, and liaison work.

The integrated support functions just discussed provide one important source of tasks to enrich jobs. In addition, the basic technology employed in the plant is designed to eliminate dull or routine jobs as much as possible. But some nonchallenging, yet basic, tasks still have to be compensated for. The forklift truck operation, for example, is not technically challenging. Therefore, the team member responsible for it is assigned other, more mentally demanding tasks (such as planning warehouse space utilization and shipping activities).

Housekeeping duties are also included in every assignment, despite the fact that they contribute nothing to enriching the work, in order to avoid having members of the plant community who do nothing but menial cleaning.

Job mobility and rewards for learning. Because all sets of tasks (jobs) are designed to be equally challenging (although each set comprises unique skill demands), it is possible to have a single job classification for all operators. Pay increases are geared to an employee mastering an increasing proportion of jobs first in the team and then in the total plant. In effect, team members are payed for learning more and more aspects of the total manufacturing system. Because there are no limits on the number of operators that can qualify for higher pay brackets, employees are also encouraged to teach each other. The old plant, in contrast, featured large numbers of differentiated jobs and numerous job classifications, with pay increases based on progress up the job hierarchy.

Facilitative leadership. Team leaders are chosen from foreman-level talent and are largely responsible for team development and group decision making. This contrasts with the old plant's use of supervisors to plan, direct, and control the work of subordinates. Management feels that in time the teams will be self-directed and so the formal team leader position might not be required.

"Managerial" decision information for operators. The design of the new plant provides operators with economic information and managerial decision rules. Thus production decisions ordinarily made by supervisors can now be made at the operator level.

Self-government for the plant community. The management group that developed the basic organization plan before the plant was manned refrained from specifying in advance any plant rules. Rather, it is committed to letting these rules evolve from collective experience.

Congruent physical and social context. The differential status symbols that characterize traditional work organizations are minimized in the new plant. There is an open parking lot, a single entrance for both the office and plant, and a common decor throughout the reception area, offices, locker rooms, and cafeteria.

The architecture facilitates the congregating of team members during working hours. For example, rather than following the plan that made the air-conditioned control room in the process tower so small that employees could not congregate there, management decided to enlarge it so that process team operators could use it when not on duty elsewhere. The assumption here is that rooms which encourage ad hoc gatherings provide opportunities not only for enjoyable human exchanges but also for work coordination and learning about others' jobs.

Learning and evolution. The most basic feature of the new plant system is management's commitment to continually assess both the plant's productivity and its relevance to employee concerns in light of experience. I believe pressures will mount in this system with two apparently opposite implications for automation. On the one hand, people will consider ways of automating the highly repetitive tasks. (There are still back-breaking routine tasks in this plant; for example, as fifty-pound bags pile up at the end of the

production line, someone must grab them and throw them on a pallet.)
On the other hand, some processes may be slightly deautomated. The
original design featured fully automated or "goof-proof" systems to monitor
and adjust several segments of the manufacturing process; yet some employees have become confident that they can improve on the systems if they
are allowed to intervene with their own judgments. These employees suggest that organizations may benefit more from operators who are alert and
who care than from goof-proof systems.

Implementation Difficulties

Since the plant's beginning in January 1971, a number of difficulties have
created temporary, and in some cases enduring, gaps between ideal
expectations and reality.

The matter of compensation, for example, has been an important source
of tension within this work community. There are four basic pay rates:
starting rate, single job rate (for mastering the first job assignment), team
rate (for mastering all jobs within the team's jurisdiction), and plant rate.
In addition, an employee can qualify for a "specialty" add-on if he has
particular strengths (in electrical maintenance, for example).

Employees who comprised the initial work force were all hired at the
same time, a circumstance that enabled them to directly compare their
experiences. With one or two exceptions on each team, operators all received their single job rates at the same time, about six weeks after the
plant started. Five months later, however, about one-third of the members
of each team had been awarded the team rate.

The evaluative implications of awarding different rates of pay have stirred
strong emotions in people who work so closely with each other. The individual pay decisions had been largely those of the team leaders, who were
also aware of operators' assessments of each other. In fact, pay rates and
member contributions were discussed openly between team leaders and
their operators as well as among operators themselves. Questions naturally
arose:

• Were the judgments about job mastery appropriate?

• Did everyone have an equal opportunity to learn other jobs?

• Did team leaders depart from job mastery criteria and include additional
considerations in their promotions to team rate?

Thus the basic concepts of pay progression are not easy to treat opera-
tionally. Moreover, two underlying orientations compete with each other and

create ambivalences for team leaders and operators alike: (1) a desire for more equality, which tends to enhance cohesiveness, and (2) a desire for more differential rewards for individual merit, which may be more equitable but can be divisive.

Similar team and operator problems have also occurred in other areas. Four of these are particularly instructive:

• The expectations of a small minority of employees did not coincide with the demands placed on them by the new plant community. These employees did not get involved in the spirit of the plant organization, participate in the spontaneous mutual-help patterns, feel comfortable in group meetings, or appear ready to accept broader responsibilities. For example, one employee refused to work in the government-regulated product-testing laboratory because of the high level of responsibility inherent in that assignment.

• Some team leaders have had considerable difficulty in *not* behaving like traditional authority figures. Similarly, some employees have tried to elicit and reinforce more traditional supervisory patterns. In brief, the actual expectations and preferences of employees in this plant fall on a spectrum running from practices idealized by the system planners to practices that are typical of traditional industrial plants. They do, however, cluster toward the idealized end of the spectrum.

• The self-managing work teams were expected to evolve norms covering various aspects of work, including responsible patterns of behavior (such as mutual help and notification regarding absences). On a few occasions, however, there was excessive peer group pressure for an individual to conform to group norms.

Scapegoating by a powerful peer group is as devastating as scapegoating by a boss. The same is true of making arbitrary judgments. Groups, however, contain more potential for checks and balances, understanding and compassion, reason and justice. Hence it is important for team leaders to facilitate the development of these qualities in work groups.

• Team members have been given assignments that were usually limited to supervisors, managers, or professionals: heading the plant-safety committee, dealing with outside vendors, screening and selecting new employees, and traveling to learn how a production problem is handled in another plant or to troubleshoot a shipping problem. These assignments have been heady experiences for the operators but have also generated mixed feelings among others. For example, a vendor was at least initially disappointed to be dealing with a worker because he judged himself in part by his ability to get to higher organizational levels of the potential customer (since typically that is where decisions are made). In another case, a plant worker attended a corporation-wide meeting of safety officials where all other representatives were from management. The presence and implied equal status of the articulate, knowledgeable worker were at least potentially threatening to the status and self-esteem of other representatives. Overall, however, the workers' seriousness, competence, and self-confidence usually have earned them respect.

Management, too, has been a source of difficulty. For example, acceptance and support from superiors and influential staff groups at corporate headquarters did not always come easily, thus creating anxiety and uncertainty within the new plant community.

Management resistance to innovative efforts of this type has a variety of explanations apart from natural and healthy skepticism. Some staff departments feel threatened by an experiment in which their functions no longer require separate units at the plant level. Other headquarters staff who are not basically threatened may nevertheless resist an innovation that deviates from otherwise uniform practices in quality control, accounting, engineering, or personnel. Moreover, many managers resent radical change, presuming that it implies they have been doing their jobs poorly.

Evidence of Success

While the productivity and the human benefits of this innovative organization cannot be calculated precisely, there have nevertheless been some impressive results:

• Using standard principles, industrial engineers originally estimated that 110 employees should man the plant. Yet, the team concept—coupled with the integration of support activities into team responsibilities—has resulted in a manpower level of slightly less than seventy people.

• After eighteen months, the new plant's fixed overhead rate was 33 percent lower than in the old plant. Reductions in variable manufacturing costs (92 percent fewer quality rejects and an absenteeism rate 9 percent below the industry norm) resulted in annual savings of $600,000. The safety record was one of the best in the company and the turnover was far below average. New equipment is responsible for some of these results, but I believe that more than one-half of them derive from the innovative human organization.

• Operators, team leaders, and managers alike have become more involved in their work and also have derived high satisfaction from it. For example, when asked what work is like in the plant and how it differs from other places they have worked, employees typically replied: "I never get bored," "I can make my own decisions," "People will help you; even the operations manager will pitch in to help you clean up a mess—he doesn't act like he is better than you are." I was especially impressed with the diversity of employees who made such responses. Different operators emphasized different aspects of the work culture, indicating that the new system has unique meaning for each member. This fact confirms the importance of system-wide innovation. A program of job enrichment, for example, will meet the priority psychological needs of one worker but not another. Other single efforts are similarly limited.

• Positive assessments of team members and team leaders in the new plant are typically reciprocal. Operators report favorably on the greater influence that they enjoy and the open relations which they experience between superiors and themselves; superiors report favorably on the capacities and sense of responsibility that operators have developed.

• While the plant is not without the occasional rumor that reflects some distrust and cynicism, such symptomatic occurrences are both shorter-lived and less frequent than those that characterize other work organizations with which I am familiar. Similarly, although the plant work force is not without evidence of individual prejudice toward racial groups and women, I believe that the manifestations of these social ills can be handled more effectively in the innovative environment.

• Team leaders and other plant managers have been unusually active in civic affairs (more active than employees of other plants in the same community). This fact lends support to the theory that participatory democracy introduced in the plant will spread to other institutional settings. Some social scientists, notably Carole Pateman, argue that this will indeed be the case.[1]

• The apparent effectiveness of the new plant organization has caught the attention of top management and encouraged it to create a new corporate-level unit to transfer the organizational and managerial innovations to other work environments. Lyman Ketchum, the line manager responsible for initiating the design of the innovative system, was chosen to head this corporate diffusion effort. He can now report significant successes in the organizational experiments under way in several units of the old pet-food plant.

What It Cost

I have already suggested what the pet-food manufacturer expected to gain from the new plant system: a more reliable, more flexible, and lower-cost manufacturing plant; a healthier work climate; and learning that could be transferred to other corporate units.

What did it invest? To my knowledge, no one has calculated the extra costs incurred prior to and during start-up that were specifically related to the innovative character of the organization. (This is probably because such costs were relatively minor compared with the amounts involved in other decisions made during the same time period.) However, some areas of extra cost can be cited:

Four managers and six team leaders were brought on board several months earlier than they would otherwise have been. The cost of outside plant visits, training, and consulting was directly related to the innovative effort. And a few plant layout and equipment design changes, which slightly increased the initial cost of the new plant, were justified primarily in terms of the organizational requirements.

During the start-up of the new plant, there was a greater than usual commitment to learning from doing. Operators were allowed to make more decisions on their own and to learn from their own experience, including mistakes. From my knowledge of the situation, I infer that there was a short-term—first-quarter—sacrifice of volume, but that it was recouped during the third quarter, when the more indelible experiences began to pay off. In fact, I would be surprised if the pay-back period for the company's entire extra investment was greater than the first year of operation.

Why It Works

Nine factors facilitated the success of the new plant:

• The particular technology and manufacturing processes in this business provided significant room for human attitudes and motivation to affect cost; therefore, by more fully utilizing the human potential of employees, the organization was able to both enhance the quality of work life and reduce costs.

• It was technically and economically feasible to eliminate some (but not all) of the routinized, inherently boring work and some (but not all) of the phys-ically disagreeable tasks.

• The system was introduced in a new plant. It is easier to change employ-ees' deeply ingrained expectations about work and management in a new plant culture. Also, when the initial work force is hired at one time, teams can be formed without having to worry about cliques.

• Favorable conditions existed in the available work force at Topeka. Local supply of labor was not tight at the time of hiring. The recruiting effort em-phasized job challenge and the innovative character of the work organiza-tion, and management tried to screen for employees likely to be effective. They were able to review over six hundred applicants to hire less than seventy.

• The physical isolation of the pet-food plant from other parts of the com-pany facilitated the development of unique organizational patterns.

• The small size of the work force made individual recognition and iden-tification easy.

• The absence of a labor union at the outset gave plant management greater freedom to experiment.

• The technology called for and permitted communication among members of the work teams.

• Pet foods are socially positive products, and the company has a good image; therefore, employees were able to form a positive attitude toward the product and the company.

I want to stress that these are merely facilitating factors and are *not* pre-conditions for success. For example, while a new plant clearly facilitates the planning for comprehensive plant-wide change, such change is also possible in ongoing plants. In the latter case, the change effort must focus on a limited part of the plant—say, one department or section at a time. Thus, in the ongoing facility, one must be satisfied with a longer time horizon for plant-wide innovation.

Similarly, favorable labor supply conditions make it more likely that one can draw a work force that will have not only work-relevant skills but also attitudes that make them potentially responsive to the challenge and variety built into the work. For example, studies have suggested that rural workers are more likely than urban workers to respond positively to increases in job challenge and complexity. Nevertheless, I believe that the labor-supply conditions could have been considerably less favorable than they were at Topeka without affecting the results.

The presence of a labor union does not preclude innovation, although it can complicate the process of introducing change. To avoid this, management can enter into a dialogue with the union about the changing expectations of workers, the need for change, and the nature and intent of the changes contemplated. Out of such dialogue can come an agreement between management and union representatives on principles for sharing the fruits of any productivity increases.

One factor I do regard as essential, however, is that the management group immediately involved must be committed to innovation and able to reach consensus about the guiding philosophy for the organization. A higher-level executive who has sufficient confidence in the innovative effort is another essential. He or she will act to protect the experiment from premature evaluations and from the inevitable, reactive pressures to bring it into line with existing corporate policies and practices.

Management and supervisors must work hard to make such a system succeed—harder, I believe, than in a more traditional system. In the case of the pet-food group, more work was required than in the traditional plant, but the human satisfactions were also much greater.

The Other Innovators

While the pet-food plant has a unique character and identity, it also has much in common with innovative plants of such U.S. corporations as Procter & Gamble and TRW Systems. Moreover, innovative efforts have been mounted by many foreign-based companies—Shell Refining Co., Ltd.

(England), Northern Electric Co., Ltd. (Canada), Alcan Aluminium (Canada), and Norsk Hydro (a Norwegian manufacturer of fertilizers and chemicals). Related experiments have been made in the shipping industry in Scandinavia and the textile industry in Ahmedabad, India. Productivity increases or benefits for these organizations are reported in the range of 20 percent to 40 percent and higher, although I should caution that all evidence on this score involves judgment and interpretation. All of these experiments have been influenced by the pioneering effort made in 1950 in the British coal-mining industry by Eric Trist and his Tavistock Institute colleagues.[2]

Procter & Gamble has been a particularly noteworthy innovator. One of its newer plants includes many of the design features employed in the pet-food plant. High emphasis has been placed on the development of "business teams" in which organization and employee identification coincides with a particular product family. Moreover, the designers were perhaps even more ambitious than their pet-food predecessors in eliminating first-line supervision. In terms of performance, results are reportedly extraordinary, although they have not been publicized. In addition, employees have been unusually active in working for social change in the outside community.[3]

Progressive Assembly Lines

Critics often argue that experiments like those I have discussed are not transferable to other work settings, especially ones that debase human dignity. The automobile assembly line is usually cited as a case in point.

I agree that different work technologies create different opportunities and different levels of constraint. I also agree that the automotive assembly plant represents a difficult challenge to those who wish to redesign work to decrease human and social costs and increase productivity. Yet serious experimental efforts to meet these challenges are now under way both in the United States and overseas.

To my knowledge, the most advanced projects are taking place in the Saab-Scandia automotive plants in Södertälje, Sweden. Consider, for example, these major design features of a truck assembly plant:

• Production workers have been included as members of development groups that discuss such matters as new tools and machine designs before they are approved for construction.

• Workers leave their stations on the assembly line for temporary assignments (for example, to work with a team of production engineers "rebalancing" jobs on the line).

• Responsibility for in-process inspection has been shifted from a separate quality-inspection unit to individual production workers. The separate quality section instead devotes all its efforts to checking and testing completed trucks.

• Work tasks have been expanded to include maintenance care of equipment, which was previously the responsibility of special mechanics.

• Individuals have been encouraged to learn several jobs. In some cases, a worker has proved capable of assembling a complete engine.

Encouraged by the results of these limited innovations, the company is applying them in a new factory for the manufacture and assembly of car engines, which was opened in January 1972. In the new plant, seven assembly groups have replaced the continuous production line; assembly work within each group is not controlled mechanically; and eventually the degree of specialization, methods of instruction, and work supervision will vary widely among the assembly groups.

In effect, the seven groups fall along a spectrum of decreasing specialization. At one end is a group of workers with little or no experience in engine assembly; at the other end is a group of workers with extensive experience in total engine assembly. It is hoped that ultimately each group member will have the opportunity to assemble an entire engine.[4]

In addition to the improvements that have made jobs more interesting and challenging for workers, management anticipates business gains that include: (1) a work system less sensitive to disruption than the production line (a factor of considerable significance in the company's recent experience); and (2) the twofold ability to recruit workers and reduce absenteeism and turnover. (The company has encountered difficulty in recruiting labor and has experienced high turnover and absenteeism.)

Another Swedish company, Volvo, also has ambitious programs for new forms of work systems and organization. Especially interesting is a new type of car assembly plant being built at Kalmar. Here are its major features:

• Instead of the traditional assembly line, work teams of fifteen to twenty-five men will be assigned responsibility for particular sections of a car (such as the electrical system, brakes and wheels, steering and controls).

• Within teams, members will decide how work should be divided and distributed.

• Car bodies will be carried on self-propelled carriages controlled by the teams.

• Buffer stocks between work regions will allow variations in the rate of work and "stockpiling" for short pauses in the work flow.

• The unique design of the building will provide more outside windows, many small workshops to reinforce the team atmosphere, and individual team entrances, changing rooms, and relaxation areas.

The plant, scheduled to open in 1974, will cost 10 percent more than a comparable conventional car plant, or an estimated premium of $2 million. It will employ six hundred people and have a capacity to produce thirty thousand cars each year. Acknowledging the additional capital investment per employee, with its implication for fixed costs, Volvo nevertheless justifies this experiment as "another stage in the company's general attempt to create greater satisfaction at work." [5]

Question of Values

The designers of the Procter & Gamble and pet-food plants were able to create organizational systems that both improved productivity and enhanced the quality of work life for employees. It is hard to say, however, whether the new Saab-Scandia and Volvo plants will result in comparable improvements in both areas. (As I mentioned earlier, the assembly line presents a particularly difficult challenge.)

In any event, I am certain that managers who concern themselves with these two values will find points at which they must make trade-offs—when they can enhance the quality of work life only at the expense of productivity, or vice versa. What concerns me is that it is easier to measure productivity than to measure the quality of work life, and that this fact will bias how trade-off situations are resolved.

Productivity may not be susceptible to a single definition or to precise measurement, but business managers do have ways of gauging changes in it over time and comparing it from one plant to the next. They certainly can tell whether their productivity is adequate for their competitive situation.

But we do not have equally effective means for assessing the quality of work life or measuring the associated psychological and social costs and gains for workers.[6] We need such measurements if this value is to take its appropriate place in work organizations.

Conclusion

The emerging obligation of employers in our society is dual: (1) to use effectively the capacities of a major natural resource—namely, the manpower they employ—and (2) to take steps to both minimize the social costs associated with utilizing that manpower and enhance the work environment for those they employ.

Fulfillment of this obligation requires major reform and innovation in work organizations. The initiative will eventually come from many quarters, but I urge professional managers and professional schools to take leadership roles. There are ample behavioral-science findings and a number of specific experiences from which to learn and on which to build.

Furthermore, the nature of the problem and the accumulating knowledge about solutions indicate that organizational redesign should be systemic; it should embrace the division of labor, authority and status structures, control procedures, career paths, allocation of the economic fruits of work, and the nature of social contacts among workers. Obviously, the revisions in these many elements must be coordinated and must result in a new, internally consistent whole.

This call for widespread innovation does *not* mean general application of a particular work system, such as the one devised for the pet-food plant. There are important differences within work forces and among organizations. Regional variances, education, age, sex, ethnic background, attitudes developed from earlier work experiences, and the urban-rural nature of the population all will influence the salient expectations in the workplace. Moreover, there are inherent differences in the nature of primary task technologies, differences that create opportunities for and impose constraints on the way work can be redesigned.

Notes

1. Carole Pateman, *Participation and Democratic Theory* (Cambridge: Cambridge University Press, 1970).

2. Eric L. Trist et al., *Organizational Choice* (London: Tavistock, 1963).

3. Charles Krone, Internal Consultant, Procter & Gamble, personal correspondence to the author.

4. For a more complete description of this plant, see Jan-Peter Norstedt, *Work Organizational and Job Design at Saab-Scandia in Sodertalje* (Stockholm: Swedish Employers' Confederation, Technical Department, December 1970).

5. Volvo offices, Gothenburg, Sweden, press release, June 29, 1972.

6. For the beginning of a remedy to this operational deficiency, see Louis E. Davis and Eric L. Trist, "Improving the Quality of Work Life: Sociotechnical Case Studies," chapter 11 of this book.

11 Improving the Quality of Work Life: Sociotechnical Case Studies

Louis E. Davis and Eric L. Trist

A high degree of industrialization and technology has been accompanied in many countries by the alienation of workers from their jobs. Many business, union, and government leaders have come to accept alienation as an inevitable consequence of an advanced industrial society and feel that little, if anything, can be done about it. But there are growing indications that the quality of working life can be improved, and alienation from the job reduced, if certain changes are made in the workplace. In the last twenty years, following innovations in the British coal industry,[1] research has uncovered many effective technological alternatives to the current design of work that substantially increase productivity and decrease worker alienation,[2] and there is a rapidly growing literature on this subject.[3]

Experiments in work redesign began on a small scale with individual jobs and then grew plant-wide and eventually firm-wide. In Norway the commitment to work redesign experiments is nationwide in scope, and a similar situation is developing in Sweden.

Work is also being restructured in Japan, although the approach there is quite different from the one used in Scandinavia.

These diverse developments are best understood in the light of a body of theory having its base in the systems approach.[4] One part of this theory is concerned with the analysis and design of the interacting technological and social dimensions of organizations. It has become known as sociotechnical theory.

Briefly, sociotechnical theory rests on two premises. The first is that in any purposive organization in which men are required to perform activities (when work is to be done and human beings are required as actors in it) the desired output is achieved through the actions of a social as well as a technical system. These systems are so interlocked that the achievement of the output becomes a function of their joint operation. The important concept is "joint," for it is here that the sociotechnical idea departs from more widely held views—those in which the social system is thought to be completely dependent on the technical. "Joint optimization" is also crucial to this theory: It is impossible to optimize for overall performance without seeking to optimize jointly the correlative but independent social and technological systems.

The second premise is that every sociotechnical system is embedded in an environment that is influenced by a culture, its values, and a set of generally acceptable practices. This environment permits certain roles for organizations, groups, and the individuals in them. To understand a work system or an organization, one must understand the environmental forces that are operating on it. This emphasis suggests, correctly, that socio-technical theory falls within the larger body of "open system" theories. Stated simply, this means that there is a constant interchange between what goes on in a work system or an organization and what goes on in the environment. The boundaries between the environment and the individual systems are highly permeable. What goes on outside affects what goes on inside. When something significant occurs in the general society, it will inevitably affect the organizations within it. There may be a period of cultural lag, but sooner or later the societal tremor will register on the organizational seismographs.

Sociotechnical theory provides a basis for analysis and design that overcomes the greatest inhibition to development of organization and job strategies in a growing, turbulent environment. It breaks through the long-standing separation between the worlds of those who plan, study, and manage social systems and those who plan, study, and manage technological systems, because it rejects the notion that in purposive organizations the technology is unalterable and must be accepted as given; that is, it rejects technological determinism. Until recently, only the variables and relationships that are not influenced by technology were examined and altered. But unless technology, which considerably determines the structure of work and thus the demands placed on individuals in an organization, is included in the analysis of work, only peripheral relations can be studied. Sociotechnical theory rejects the "technological imperative," which is the position of engineers, economists, and managers who consider psychological and social requirements as constraints on technological systems. That a substantial part of technological design includes social system design is not usually understood or appreciated.

Sociotechnical analysis provides a basis for determining appropriate boundaries of systems containing men, machines, materials, and information. It considers the operation of such systems within the framework of an environment that is itself made an overt and specific object of study. It concerns itself with spontaneous reorganization or adaptation, with control of system variance, with growth, and with self-regulation. These aspects of social systems are becoming increasingly important as organizations are required to develop strategies that focus on adaptability and commitment. For these reasons, sociotechnical theory offers one of the best current approaches to meeting the challenge of enhancing the quality of working life.

This paper discusses some of the many work redesign experiments that have been conducted in various parts of the world and in different industries. The studies are arranged according to the type of work setting and change strategy. The early developments were British and American in origin; they spread to Norway, Canada, Holland, India, and Japan. Studies are now also available from Sweden, France, Italy, and Australia.

Some of the cases are only described briefly because they are well known. Others are treated in more detail either because they are unfamiliar or because the special requirements for change or diffusion warrant expanded discussion. Most of the cases selected for detailed reporting are ones in which the authors participated themselves or ones which they have discussed with those who were directly involved.

Experiments in Traditional Production Methods

Primary Work Group Reorganization
The earliest of the long-term, empirical sociotechnical studies began in 1948 in an English colliery and continued for ten years.[5] It is unique in that mining technology and physical environment sharply display the effect of

organizational design on sociopsychological relations—an effect which in other technologies is frequently masked by compensatory management action. Quite aside from mechanical devices, individual skills, and wage payment systems, the design of the work organization and its effect on all participants stand out as a major factor contributing to system performance and personal satisfaction.

For economic reasons it was necessary to reintroduce longwall working into a particular area of the coal mine under study. For some time, this area had been worked with short faces where "composite" work groups customarily shared all tasks. Improved roof control made longwalls feasible, but the men did not want to go back to the one-man, one-task jobs traditional on longwalls. While union representatives and management arrived at a settlement regarding wages, the workers arranged a scheme whereby they could share tasks and shifts among themselves. Goals were set for the performance by the overall group of the entire three-shift cycle, and inclusive payments were made to the group for the completion of all the required tasks, plus an incentive for output. Such payment placed responsibility on the entire group for all operations, generating the need for individuals performing different tasks, over interdependent phases of the cycle, to interrelate positively rather than negatively, as they had done under the conventional mode of organization. Equal earnings required equal contributions from the cycle group's members, which led to the spontaneous development of self-directed interchangeability of workers according to need. Interchangeability required multiskilled face workers (which most were from their shortwall experience) and permitted a sharing of the fund of underground skill and identity.

Work was arranged to maintain task continuity. Each shift picked up where the previous shift left off, and when an activity group's main task was done, it redeployed itself to carry on with the next task to prevent "cycle lag." Teams worked out their own systems for rotating tasks and shifts, thereby taking over regulation of deployment and affording the opportunity for equalizing good and bad work times. Each team was large enough so that enough men were available to perform the tasks that arose on the shift.

The autonomous cycle group thus integrated the differentiated activities of longwall mining by internal control through self-regulation. By contrast, the integration practices used in conventional longwall mining were those of indirect external control through specialization of tasks with fixed assignments, wage incentive bargaining for each task, and unsuccessful attempts at direct supervision.

Some objective indicators of the appropriateness of composite organization for longwall mining were positive changes in absence rates, cycle progress, and productivity. Face work puts many stresses on miners, particularly when difficulties arise; changing tasks, shifts, or workplaces helps to reduce these stresses. Table 11.1 shows the variety of work experience possible under each method of organization. When changing or sharing difficult tasks was not possible (under the old method), there was high withdrawal and absence from work. Table 11.2 shows the difference in absence rates under the two systems. It may be inferred that absence rates had an effect on cycle progress and productivity, which are shown in tables 11.3 and 11.4.

As so frequently happens with innovations before they become "ideas in good currency," the new organizational design did not spread. It threatened existing arrangements by being too productive for unions and requiring management to make radical changes in organizational form and supervision.

Assembly-Line Modification

A manufacturing department producing a line of small plastic medical appliances in a unionized West Coast firm was the setting of the first controlled experiment on the shop floor to manipulate the configuration of technology (as interpreted in task design and assignment) as jobs.[6] The specific purpose of the experiment was to explore the conditions under which improvement in productivity could be expected from changes in job content. The major criteria used to evaluate the effectiveness of the modifications were quantity and quality of output; worker attitudes and satisfaction were also measured. Modifications were introduced through the department manager. Two experimental job designs were compared with the existing assembly-line job design: (1) Group job design. The conveyor and pacing were eliminated, and workers rotated among nine individual stations using a batch method of assembly. Other conditions were the same as for the existing design. (2) Individual job design. All nine operations, final inspection, and securing of materials were combined into one job and performed by workers at individual work stations.

The experiment showed that greater variety of tasks and responsibility for methods, quality, pacing, and product completion led to higher productivity, quality, and satisfaction. Under the group job design (no pacing by conveyor), the productivity index fell to an average of 89, compared to the

Table 11.1. Variety of Work Experience (Averages for Whole Team)

Aspect of Work Experience	Conventional Longwall	Composite Longwall
Main tasks	1.0	3.6
Different shifts	2.0	2.9
Different activity groups	1.0	5.5

Source: E. L. Trist et al., *Organizational Choice* (London: Tavistock, 1963).

Table 11.2. Absence Rates (Percentage of Possible Shifts)

Reason for Absence	Conventional Longwall	Composite Longwall
No reason given	4.3	0.4
Sickness and other	8.9	4.6
Accident	6.8	3.2
Total	20.0	8.2

Source: Trist et al., *Organizational Choice*.

Table 11.3. State of Cycle Progress at End of Filling Shift (Percentage of Cycles)

State of Cycle Progress	Conventional Longwall	Composite Longwall
In advance	0	22
Normal	31	73
Lagging	69	5
All cycles	100	100

Source: Trist et al., *Organizational Choice*.

Table 11.4. Productivity as Percentage of Estimated Face Potential

	Conventional Longwall	Composite Longwall
Without allowance for haulage system efficiency	67	95
With allowance	78	95

Source: Trist et al., *Organizational Choice*.

assembly-line average of 100, while quality improved. Defects fell from an average of 0.72 percent to 0.49 percent per lot. Under the individual job design, after only six days the average productivity index rose slightly above the original line average. Quality improved fourfold, with defects per lot falling to 0.18 percent.

Interviews with assembly-line workers and a survey of their attitudes and expectations before any changes were introduced indicated that they were satisfied with their jobs, management, and the company and considered the lack of responsibility a positive feature. They were dissatisfied with pacing, the repetitiveness of the work, and the lack of opportunity to do higher-quality work. The identical interviews and survey after individual job design was operating indicated that the same workers were satisfied with their composite jobs and were eager for more responsibility and the opportunity for self-regulation. When asked to compare the composite with the previous assembly-line jobs, they indicated that they would leave the company before going back to the old methods.

Another experiment in assembly-line modification is the enlargement of assembly-line jobs undertaken by a midwestern home laundry manufacturing firm which sought to improve workers' attitudes and increase output and quality.[7] The company felt it might have gone beyond the "optimum" division of labor on its assembly lines, so that increased costs of nonproductive work and line-balance delay exceeded the savings of fractionation. To this company job enlargement meant providing jobs that involved an increased number and variety of tasks, self-determination of pacing, increased responsibility for quality, increased discretion for work methods, and completion of a part or subassembly. For a number of years the company had pursued a deliberate program of transferring work from progressive assembly lines to single-operator work stations; this transfer permitted study of the effects of enlarged jobs on workers' performance and attitudes.

The results indicate that there may indeed be an optimum division of labor on assembly lines. The authors make a case for job enlargement based on reduction of costs of nonproductive work and line-balance delays. Greatly improved quality of output and increased worker satisfaction were obtained —gains perhaps otherwise unobtainable—along with savings in labor costs and greater production flexibility.

Total Departmental Reorganization

The impact of the organizational component of job design on the productivity of work groups is illustrated by a field experiment conducted in a textile plant in India that had recently installed automatic looms.[8] The looms had been studied intensively by engineers for the purpose of laying out equipment and assigning work loads based on "careful" time measurements of all of the job components. Yet the new methods failed to produce quantity and quality levels equal to those when nonautomatic looms were used, let alone attain the improvements expected.

The work to be done in a weaving shed containing 240 looms was divided into twelve one-task jobs:

- A weaver tended approximately 30 looms.
- A battery filler served about 50 looms.
- A smash hand tended about 70 looms.
- A gater, cloth carrier, jobber, and assistant jobber were assigned to 112 looms.
- A bobbin carrier, feeler-motion fitter, oiler, sweeper, and humidification fitter were each assigned to 224 looms.

These occupational tasks were highly interdependent. The utmost coordination was required to maintain continuity of production. However, the worker-machine assignments created organizational confusion. Each weaver had to relate to five-eighths of a battery filler, three-eighths of a smash hand, one-fourth of a gater, one-eighth of a bobbin carrier, and so on. The jobbers who carried out on-line maintenance reported to shed management through a separate supervisory channel from weavers, and there were no criteria to establish whose looms should have priority when breakdowns and other trouble occurred.

To meet these problems, internally led work groups were organized so that a single group became responsible for the operation and maintenance of a specific bank of looms. Geographic rather than functional division of the weaving room produced interaction patterns that made for regularity of relationships among individuals with interrelated jobs. They could now be held responsible for the production of their teams. This reorganization was suggested by the workers themselves as the result of discussions held by the social science consultant with them and the shed supervisors and manager. The consolidated loom groups reported to a single shift supervisor who in turn reported to an overall shed manager.

As a result of these changes, efficiency rose from an average of 80 percent to 95 percent, and damage dropped from a mean of 32 percent to 20 percent after sixty working days. In the adjacent part of the weaving shed, where job design changes were not made, efficiency dropped for a while to 70 percent and never rose above 80 percent, while damage continued at an average of 31 percent. The whole shed was then converted, and the improvements were permanently maintained. When it became clear that there was improvement, a way was found to introduce consolidated loom groups throughout the large number of nonautomatic sheds. A third shift, which had been previously resisted by the union, could then be introduced. Within loom groups, status differences were reduced; the less skilled were given opportunities to learn the roles of the more skilled, so that a promotion path was created. Wages were increased as substantially as costs were decreased.

Experiments in New Production Methods

The Sheltered Experiment

As a novel and valuable strategy for making changes in existing organizations, the sheltered experiment was developed in the Canadian aluminum industry.[9] The experiment lasted twelve months and was sheltered by agreement from management rules and union contracts so that both parties could see concrete results. A growing number of industrial studies reflect the impact of sophisticated automated technology on organizational structure. The semiprocess technology normally used in continuous aluminum casting generated randomly spaced responses by workers. The sheltered experiment called for the introduction of semiautonomous work crews. Within each crew there was interchangeability of tasks, so that roles became larger than jobs. The crews also assumed responsibility for deciding who would perform a certain task and when it would be performed.

The results were: (1) high satisfaction of workers with new roles and the new skills learned; (2) demonstration of a new organizational form (the self-regulated work team); and (3) increased ability of the work crew to meet emergencies. Production of the casting unit increased 12 percent, and productivity attributable to the experiment showed a net gain of 7 percent. The cost per ton of production was reduced by $2.35 compared to the previous period.

New Technology as an Impetus to New Organization

In addition to the sheltered experiment, another project was carried out in the same Canadian aluminum firm[10] which resulted in the formation of a large number of autonomous work groups to look after some 3000 smelting furnaces (or pots). The project shows what adaptive social change can accomplish when a new technology essential for cost-effective operation in an intensely competitive worldwide industry renders obsolete the traditional forms of work organization.

The new technology involved the substitution of solid-state in place of mercury arc rectifiers, increasing the amperage in the pots and leading to higher productivity. The higher amperage required a different level of continuous quality control, made possible by the introduction of on-line computers. The greater heat and frequency of certain operations made it necessary to mechanize a large number of tasks of the pot line operation. Control of the traditional French Canadian work force, whose older members were poorly educated and rural in outlook, had been achieved through close external supervision and a rigid hierarchy of narrow one-man jobs. This form of organization could not handle the new technology.

The divisional management was trained in sociotechnical concepts and analysis at UCLA by the authors. This management, in consultation with supervisors and key workers (after agreement with the union), whom they in turn trained, worked out a new form of organization in which primary, internally led groups of six workers were responsible for a line. In addition, there were extensive changes in the service and maintenance departments. Because the new work organization required considerably fewer men and supervisors, acceptance of the plan was not immediate. Alternative employment had to be found for some; early retirement was given to others. Great care had to be exercised since unemployment in the region was high.

A recent communication from the personnel manager states that the new groups have done well, improving during their two years of existence. Quantitative records of the results are still awaited. This and related experiments have led to similar work arrangements in two new fabrication plants and have attracted wide attention in Canada because of the firm's standing as a leading Canadian enterprise.

The Plant as an Evolving Learning System

Continuous development of all workers in a department can be achieved by moving men and groups to a semiautonomous condition as part of a company-wide program, as was demonstrated at an oil refinery in England.[11] The variety of changes introduced included widespread participation in decision making and the development of new competencies through on- and off-the-job training.

Each machine operator was given a complete subprocess unit to control, including an instrument panel in the main control room. Jobs in the shift teams were flexible, and operators learned each other's units and assisted each other in times of upset. Time clocks were removed, and flexibility of arrival, departure, and time away from work was allowed. (Men were able to make arrangements with the senior operator for competent replacements.) Training was provided in the plant and at a local technical college. Operators covered for each other to take time off for training. Senior operators were given authority to alter plant conditions in order to meet a weekly plan and became able to run the plant safely and efficiently without management intervention.

Everyone participated in planning changes, including redesign of the routing of pipelines. This redesign removed considerable operating problems for the men, and the costs saved paid for the modifications in less than a month. The men were given complete responsibility for test runs and routine testing. As a result, the life of equipment was extended significantly— before repair shutdown and off-plant testing was reduced by 75 percent. Supervisors and foremen had complete discretion about expenditures within the department budget.

The results indicate increased job satisfaction and more effective operations. The sickness-absence rate fell from 5.4 percent to 2.8 percent, and the promotion of senior operators to foremen doubled over the three-year period of the experiment compared to the previous year. Output in the first unit increased by 35 percent and in the finishing unit by 40 percent because of technical improvements suggested within the department. The second and third units, whose outputs limit total plant output, increased by 100 percent because of improvements in manual operations. The entire process plant department achieved a steady operation requiring little management intervention. The men became more satisfied both with their jobs and with management.

The Redesign of Maintenance Roles

Modification of job content and of the organization units of general maintenance craftsmen was undertaken by a West Coast branch plant of a national industrial chemical manufacturing company.[12] Local management was seeking to improve productivity, to eliminate jurisdictional disagreements among various crafts, and to respond to worker demands for more creative activities and opportunities for closer identification with the job. Crucial to the entire undertaking were the presence of a strong industrial union and a long history of mutual trust and respect in union-management relations.

Maintenance crews consisting of broad-spectrum repairmen for general maintenance were assigned to each operating department. Centralized shops, having conventional single-craft jobs, supported the departmental crews by doing work requiring heavy or costly machinery. The jobs of the newly designated maintenance repairmen were enlarged to include general welding, layout and fabrication, pipe fitting, boilermaking, equipment installation, and dynamic machine repair. The additional skills were acquired by means of a formal on- and off-the-job training program. Jobs were then reclassified and wages increased accordingly. To support the crews, two specialist classifications were introduced. Workers in these classifications performed certain special types of welding and machine repair.

The changes in organization and enlargement of jobs produced positive results in a number of criteria of operational effectiveness: quantity and quality of output, lowered costs, and personal relationships and reactions. Before the changes were initiated, the company's total maintenance labor costs had moved upward, paralleling the national index. After reorganization and job enlargement, the labor costs index fell from 130 to 110 in two years (the index was 100 in 1954), while the national index continued to rise, from 110 to 120. The labor costs of the enlarged group of maintenance repairmen, considered separately, fell from an index of 90 to 65 over the same period. When the index of performance (output divided by direct labor costs) was examined, the production departments showed no change over the period, while the maintenance repairmen showed an increase from 150 to 230. Total employment in the firm was reduced from an index of 100 to 95. The ratio of complaints about product quality and packaging to orders shipped, an indirect measure of quality, fell from an index of 100 to 55 over the same period.

Workers with enlarged higher-skill jobs were concerned with the importance of their jobs, control over job content and work methods, variety of assignments, special training, responsibility for quality, and performance of preparatory activities. The responses of this group indicate that they were concerned with matters to which management attaches great importance, possibly foreshadowing the development of identity in objectives between management and workers holding enlarged jobs. Workers indicated that they wished to make contributions to improvements in operations. They related company success to their own and their own advancement to better skills and performance. They identified learning of new skills as a positive value of the job and indicated readiness to accept additional duties to help improve their own and group performance.

The Upgrading of Supervisory Roles

It is difficult to design supervisory roles because there are few good models to follow. These jobs are often complicated by the supervisor's conflicting objectives vis-à-vis workers and management and by conflict between the supervisor's management objectives and his superior's. In addition, supervisors are often uncertain about the behavior required for effective leadership, the implied threat to their status and effectiveness inherent in the authoritarian-participation conflict, and the ambiguity that exists over the discharge of their responsibilities. For purposes of designing supervisory jobs, there is a paucity of information and data apart from generalities concerning leadership behavior.

Two modifications in supervisors' jobs were introduced separately into a number of experimental aircraft instrument shops in the U.S.[13] (Control shops were selected that paralleled these in terms of type of work, style of supervision, worker skills, and past performance.) The changes were undertaken in the industrial facility of a West Coast military aircraft overhaul, repair, and test station. Except for senior executives, all 5900 employees were civilians. The modifications were as follows: (1) *Product responsibility.* The redesigned supervisor's role involved responsibility for all functions required to complete the products processed in the shop. This changed two experimental shops from functional to product organizations, requiring the acquisition of additional knowledge and skills by supervisors and workers. (2) *Quality responsibility.* Inspection was added to the supervisor's functions, including authority for final quality (authority to accept or reject a product). (Some time after the quality control inspectors were withdrawn the supervisors transferred the authority to key workers.)

The objective performance of the supervisors improved. Supervisor behavior became more autonomous and more oriented to the technical problems of producing the product and to worker training. The modifications shortened the quality and process of information feedback loops to workers and concentrated dispersed functional authority. As supervisors moved toward technological aspects of management, giving more time to planning, inspection, control, etc., they had less time to manage the men, who to a much greater extent managed themselves. This change in management style was acceptable to the workers, as judged by their positive attitudes. The attitudes of supervisors were also enhanced in the experimental shops, indicating that the changes satisfied personal needs and helped to develop individuals who were contributing to the organization's viability or health.

Improvements at the Professional and Technical Levels

Complexity and Interface Negotiation

Several of the leading U.S. aerospace firms have made use of behavioral science concepts and methods to improve interpersonal relations, but few have gone on to employ them to change work organization. A recent report, however, describes an action research project in one of the most sophisticated of these firms which took such a step to improve its project and matrix organization.[14]

The "workers" were engineering analysts (with Ph.D.'s) and computer programmers (with M.S.'s) producing software. The interaction between these two groups was too complex to be managed from outside. Status differences and mutual distrust had to be overcome before it could be managed from inside. Moreover, this could not be fully accomplished until new relations had been worked out with the technical supervisors and heads of the functional departments and with the project manager. This set of relations comprised the "nuclear system."

The high degree of uncertainty characterizing the work and the many unanticipated problems encountered led to crisis management that was prodigal in the expenditure of resources without containing cost overruns.

Key groups were often shut up together for several weeks, working overtime, in a place known as the "bat cave" from which they would emerge only when a critical problem had been solved. Correspondingly, project managers could hire any talent they wanted from other departments or from outside on short notice to catch up after delays. They could then dismiss these men as soon as they were no longer needed. This practice was called the "job shop."

The research showed that these customs could be replaced by regular and open dialogue among all concerned. Group meetings were organized that helped develop a shared "cognitive map" of everything that had to be done, and flexible monitoring was initiated which permitted continuous adaptive planning. In fact, a new type of control system was evolved that increased learning and personal satisfaction, while improving results.

Professional Career Development

A leading U.S. aerospace firm was suffering from large cost overruns and time delays in meeting contract requirements for the design and testing of aerospace devices.[15] The nature of the devices (and the contract) called for state-of-the-art design, i.e., invention of new designs along with the use of existing parts or subunits. The firm's management felt the designers were recalcitrant, at worst (or unrealistic perfectionists, at best), spending too much time and money in doing their work.

Analysis determined that these highly skilled and privileged aerospace engineers were rejecting existing designs and proceeding to design *de novo*. In the aerospace industry could they be expected to behave otherwise? Those working in the industry have learned to relate more to the industry as a whole than to the individual firm. As contracts changed, engineers and scientists would move to new contracts, usually in other firms. The crucial aspect in this interfirm movement is the state-of-the-art capability of the scientists and engineers. This is what the firms are looking for and what makes for the difference in value (and income) of the engineers. It is the touchstone of continued employment.

When management understood the basis of the behavior, a solution that embodied both jobs and career needs was developed. Management began to consider how immediate contract needs could be met for the organization while the individual maintained his state of the art. This was accomplished when immediate work was viewed as an intersection in time between two tracks. The first track consisted of a series of tasks or jobs required by the organization; the second track consisted of experiences that advanced or supported an individual's capabilities. This is the same concept as professional career development, and is, of course, essential to the concept of human resource management.

The career needs of the individual and production needs of the organization were considered jointly. This required that management guarantee, through planning, that an individual has career-advancing assignments soon and frequently, although at any one time he may be engaged in more routine assignments. This program provided a new base for the organization and its members to satisfy their different but related needs.

Corporate Strategies for Sociotechnical Change

The Central Mandate

A very great change in management philosophy at Philips, an international electronics and electrical manufacturing firm in Holland, began in the early 1960s and has resulted in extensive restructuring along sociotechnical lines.[16] A leading principle of this new philosophy has been the encouragement of local plant developments. Management selected the Technical and Efficiency Organization (TEO), one of the main staff divisions, as the instrument to carry out the central mandate for change. The importance of this choice cannot be overemphasized, for responsibility for the human and social aspects of work organization was assigned to the group that is also responsible for its technical and efficiency aspects. To have assigned it to the personnel department would have perpetuated the split between the human relations and industrial engineering outlooks. What the board did was to redefine the mission of TEO in sociotechnical terms. This made it incumbent upon TEO to add psychological and social science competence to engineering and operations research competence and to work at the problem of developing an integrated capability.

TEO as a staff division cannot impose its policies on operational management, but acts as an internal resource, supporting and evaluating projects undertaken in different plants and disseminating the findings and experience throughout the concern. A process of organizational learning of the broadest kind was thus set in motion. In 1965 TEO issued a major report entitled "Work Restructuring for Unskilled Workers" which led to a substantial increase in the number of work restructuring projects being undertaken.

The example below illustrates how TEO makes research studies of such projects when invited by the departments concerned. This can only take place when those in charge wish to increase their understanding of the complexities involved through systematic and sustained analysis.

This particular reorganization project concerned an assembly shop. In the original situation, three foremen, five charge hands, and 231 assembly workers and inspectors worked under the department head. The work, carried out in a process- or function-oriented mode, consisted of light assembly work. The personnel consisted mainly of women whose work cycles vary between 5 and 120 seconds. Everyone had his or her own job, with the foreman responsible for arranging the work and individual quality feedback. The wage system consisted of a fixed individual wage plus a performance allowance which depended on the quantity and quality of the work produced and the motivation of the individual concerned.

The most important changes made were:

• Independent groups were formed and made responsible for job allocation, supply of materials, quality inspection within the group, submission to final inspection, and appointment of delegates to talks with departmental management.

• The groups worked on a group job in a product-oriented mode. The job of foreman disappeared, and the three foremen were transferred, after consultation, to jobs outside the department.

• The charge hands, with the new title of group leader, were given more extensive duties involving consultation with and assessment of the personnel in each group.

• The number of random-sample inspectors was decreased in accordance with the number of groups that gradually switched to the new form of organization.

In 1968 the new organization consisted of fourteen group leaders and 282 assembly workers and inspectors under a department head. This represented a considerable saving of lower managerial personnel. In 1967 an investigation undertaken by TEO at the request of management into the consequences of these changes revealed the following:

• Wastage and repairs decreased from 7 percent to 3 percent as a result of faster feedback of faults.

• The pattern of communication with ancillary departments changed as a result of the deverticalization. Far more appeals were made to ancillary departments for the solution of departmental problems.

• The members of semiautonomous groups derived more satisfaction from their work than did workers in the old situation: They felt physically fitter and less harassed, but had a more negative view about the throughput of work. The self-regulating activities were clearly recognized and approved as such by the members of the group. In addition, their attitude to colleagues was more positive than in the case of individual workers.

No answer has yet been given to such important questions as: How stable is the informal leadership in the semiautonomous groups? How often should work be rotated?

This case shows how difficult it is to consider the various changes in isolation from one another. Each change is accompanied by, and related to, others. In this case the cooperation of the lower supervisory personnel was obtained by enlarging their jobs as well. The foremen who were transferred were more than fifty years old. The transfers in this case were arranged with a great deal of care, so that there have been no adverse effects for the foremen concerned.

The whole Philips report is of great value in the wealth of case histories, in the attention paid to failures as well as to successes, and in the learning which has resulted from the analysis and from its feedback to those concerned.

The Innovative Subsidiary

In the early 1960s the refining side of Shell Oil in Britain experienced severe problems of overmanning, chronic difficulties in labor relations, and increasing management frustration.[17] The company decided to make an all-out effort to bring about changes that would make possible a higher level of motivation and commitment to company objectives on the part of all its employees, leading to an enhanced level of performance. The results of this project have been reported by Paul Hill, who led the internal team that developed and implemented the program (which is still in operation). The following paragraphs are condensed from his summary.

A small team was set up to study the company's long-standing motivation problem on a full-time basis and to propose long-term plans for solving it. A collaborative relationship was established between outside social science resource people from the Tavistock Institute and internal resource people from the company. One result was a considerable transfer of knowledge and skills into the organization.

A document was produced that stated explicitly the objectives the company would work toward and the management philosophy, or values, which would be used to guide decision making in pursuing them. Key features of the document were a reconciliation of the company's economic and social objectives and the adoption of the principle of joint optimization of the social and technical systems.

At a residential off-site conference, the top management team of the company, led by the managing director, committed itself to the objectives and philosophy and to seeking commitment to them throughout the organization. The top management team met under similar circumstances at critical decision points in the program to decide and guide the general course it should take. In order to secure this wider commitment a complex dissemination program was developed. Through numerous conferences at each location, large numbers of employees at all levels were able to test the objectives and philosophy for themselves. The remaining employees had an opportunity to do this at departmental meetings; eventually all the employees in the company were included. The dissemination process was dynamic, not stereotyped. Different methods were tried out, and each location developed programs that were best suited to its own refinery situation. The dissemination process achieved considerable success in securing a widespread understanding of, and commitment to, the company's objectives and philosophy. It also produced quite a number of highly enthusiastic employees. They represented the critical mass who led the process of implementation.

With few exceptions, trade union representatives, both outside officials and internal shop stewards, reacted very favorably to the company's intentions and offered their support. The dissemination program developed new skills in many people and created a climate in the company that permitted and encouraged trying out new ideas. Although not all the experiments fully achieved their purpose, they contributed to the overall learning and development and provided a stepping-stone to the next move forward. An important example of this type of innovation was the setting up of joint management-union working parties, whose new role and new frame of reference were accepted by the majority of the shop stewards and by all of the trade union officials. Although they did not fully complete their tasks, the work they did made a valuable contribution to the productivity bargains that followed.

The outcome of the productivity bargaining, after the expenditure of much time and effort, was also very successful. More important than the content of the bargains—significant as that was—was the manner in which they were decided. Both management and union representatives were dedicated to the bargaining's success and shared to a greater extent than ever before the same frame of reference. The level of participation on the part of shop stewards in the formulation of the bargains and the level of effective communication with the shop-floor employees was exceptionally high. The result was commitment to the content and the spirit of the deals, not merely a collection of unenforceable agreements. A more general result of the new climate and the new collaborative working relationships between shop stewards and management was a vast improvement in the industrial relations situation at Shell Haven, where they had been exceedingly bad. General morale improved accordingly.

The other major field where innovation took place was in the design of jobs. Here again, partial success in one venture did not stop progress, but led to the start of another. The process was again dynamic. The pilot projects at Stanlow Refinery created great opportunities for learning and indicated good possibilities for improvement in performance levels. The introduction of two simplified methods of analyzing existing systems provided another great learning experience, in which many people in the company were involved. The application of the methods at Stanlow showed good and promising results. As with the earlier pilot projects, they demonstrated how shop-floor employees could contribute significantly to these results. The nine-step method of sociotechnical analysis was also found valuable, both as a training tool and in its practical application in places outside the company.

The largest-scale application of the philosophy was in the design of the social system at Teesport, the new highly automated refinery. The principle of joint optimization of social and technical systems was consciously and carefully applied, with highly successful results. A wide variety of other implementation measures were all undertaken within the framework of the philosophy. They included changes in the staff appraisal system and in manpower planning, job enrichment projects, and so on.

The development program was subjected to many countervailing pressures, some internal (such as the retirement or transfer of key people, both in management and among the resource people), and others external (such as the disruption of crude supplies by war and the pressures felt at the Teesport refinery to regress to old norms).

Local Experimentation

It is often asserted that effective sociotechnical changes cannot be introduced without the commitment of top management. A number of cases demonstrate that this is not always the case. Small changes can get under way in particular departments, the success of these convincing others, until finally top management conducts a review and becomes convinced enough to give them a "blessing." If good results continue, management may then decide to back the new way of doing things as affirmed corporate policy.

A remarkable case of this kind has been reported from Corning Glass Works.[18] One or two innovations in the research and development department of one plant developed from experimental sociotechnical change with the assistance of behavioral scientists. Other departments were impressed with their success and tried out changes for themselves. Since then, widespread corporate support has been obtained for work redesign based on sociotechnical research.

National Sociotechnical Change

Collaboration between Employers and Unions

The first country to attempt the redesign of work on a nationwide basis is Norway.[19] The program specifically directed at enhancing the quality of working life, the Norwegian Industrial Democracy Project, has given a new dimension to sociotechnical studies by relating them to the crucial questions of value change in society as the postindustrial era is brought nearer by the technologies of the second industrial revolution.

The project began in 1961 and is still proceeding. It grew out of a crisis between the Norwegian Confederation of Employers and the Norwegian Confederation of Labor over a sudden increase in the demand for worker representation on boards of directors of firms, which was proposed as a way of reducing alienation and increasing productivity. It was remarkable that the two confederations (later joined by the government) requested the assistance of social scientists to gain a better understanding of what ordinarily would have been treated as a political problem. A group directed by Einar Thorsrud was established to undertake research relevant to the problems of the two confederations. The group, the Institutes of Work Research, drew from the beginning on the Tavistock Institute's Human Resources Centre as a collaborating organization.

Another remarkable feature of the project is the extent to which research plans have been drawn up in conjunction with representatives of the sponsoring confederations. This was a necessary condition for success, since the objective could not be limited to undertaking isolated sociotechnical experiments. The purpose was first to secure in the leadership of both sides of Norwegian industry an understanding of the relevance of sociotechnical philosophy of work to problems at the national level, and then to establish the conditions that would allow this philosophy to diffuse throughout Norwegian industry.

The first phase of the project consisted of a field study of what actually happened in the five major firms where workers were represented on the boards of directors. These government owned or partly owned enterprises

were obliged by law to have workers' representatives. The results showed
that very little happened except at the symbolic and ceremonial level. There
was no increase in participation by the rank and file, no decrease in work
alienation, no increase in productivity. The overall state of industrial relations
being stable within a stable framework of political democracy, little was
accomplished simply by adding a workers' representative to the executive
board of directors. However, the inclusion of such representatives in trustee
boards representing the public interest in Norwegian industry proved invalu-
able. (A recent law, May 1972, has replaced these boards with bodies exer-
cising wide powers, introducing in all concerns, except the smallest, a political element with consequences impossible to foresee.) These results,
which were compared with experiences in other countries, were widely discussed in both confederations and in the press. The discussions opened the
second phase of the project, to search out ways for securing improved conditions for personal participation in a man's immediate work setting as con-
stituting "a different and perhaps more important basis for the democratization of the work place than the formal systems of representation." This led to
the idea of sociotechnical experiments in selected plants in key industries,
which, if successful, could serve as demonstration models for diffusion purposes. The selections were made by the members of the two confederations
serving on the research committee in consultation with sector committees of
the industries concerned. No pains were spared in developing both understanding and acceptance, at all levels, of the experiments in the proposed
plants. The plants were selected on the grounds that they were respected
organizations which possessed both influence and prestige. They were seen
as foreshadowing the future direction of Norwegian industrial development
without being too far ahead of the field. To obtain this breadth and depth of
sanctioning and centrality of societal positioning was regarded as essential.
Its absence in other contexts had prevented the spread of successful innovations.

The first experiment was carried out in the metal-working industry,[20] a
sector regarded as critical but one which required considerable rehabilitation. A rather dilapidated wiredrawing plant in a large engineering concern
was chosen on the grounds that if improvements could be brought about
there they could be brought about anywhere. Productivity increased so much
that the experiment was suspended; the workers concerned had begun to
take home pay packets in excess of the most skilled workers in the firm. Thus

a very large problem had to be sorted out. Although the experiment confirmed earlier findings regarding what could be accomplished when alienation is reduced, it also revealed, for the first time, the magnitude of the constraints embedded in the wage structures and agreements negotiated according to the norms of the prevailing work culture. The difficulty of changing such a structure, which enjoys an enormous historical accumulation, accounted in considerable measure for the failure of earlier pilot experiments to spread.

The second experiment was in the pulp and paper industry,[21] also regarded as a critical sector, but where the problem was not so much to upgrade performance with old technologies as to gain control over new ones. The sophisticated chemical pulping department was selected in one paper mill where the basic work was information handling—the core task in the technologies of the second industrial revolution. The requisite skills are perceptual and conceptual; the requisite work organization is capable of handling the complex information flows on which controlling the process depends. To do this requires immense flexibility and capability for self-regulation. In the experimental department a number of the key process variances were not being controlled by the social system, nor had some of the most important ones been identified. The research team had to engage those concerned in evolving a form of organization that brought as many of them as possible under the control of the primary work groups. After much resistance and many setbacks, a process of continuous learning was established and maintained as improvements were effected first in one area, then in another.

The model of an action group was established, which consisted of the operators concerned actively using supervisors, specialists, and managers as resources, rather than passively responding to them simply as bosses. This model was then taken up by Norsk Hydro, the largest enterprise in Norway, which manufactures fertilizers, chemicals, and metals for the world market. The model was used first to refashion an old plant and then to develop the entire organization and operating procedures for a new one.[22]

The success of the Norsk Hydro experiments was publicized widely throughout Scandinavia. It marked the beginning of the third phase of the project, which concerned the diffusion process itself. The joint committee that originally sponsored the project was transformed into the National Participation Council, and the new Parliamentary Commission on Industrial Democracy was formed. In Sweden similar developments have recently taken place at the national level, but it will be some time before a critical mass of concrete experience with the new methods can build up. Meanwhile, in Norway, the most significant recent developments have taken place in the shipping industry in the manning of bulk carriers.[23]

Undoubtedly there are features in the culture and the industrial situation of the Scandinavian countries, particularly those of Norway, which have enabled them to act as the world's laboratory in developing a new concept of industrial democracy based on sociotechnical theory. In larger, more authoritarian countries, where the first industrial revolution has left a deeper imprint or the culture is more fragmented, much greater difficulties are to be expected.

The Spread of a Grass-Roots Movement

A remarkable movement involving a new philosophy of work has been spreading in Japanese industry over the last ten years. There is special emphasis on improving product quality by increasing worker involvement and participation in decision making at the shop floor level and encouraging the worker's personal development. This represents a dramatic break with the traditional culture of the Japanese factory and the imported Taylorism which was recently added.

Sony has been a leading exponent of the new philosophy. This company attributes a significant role in its remarkable growth to this philosophy, particularly with reference to the ability of its work force to cope with the rapid technological change in its products. Juran concludes that "the Japanese are headed for world quality leadership" through the development of these methods, and provides the first account in English of the Quality Control Circle (QCC) movement.[24] QC circles can best be described as groups of workers and foremen who voluntarily meet together to solve shop-oriented production quality problems. John Hird[25] has published a report of recent QCC experiences and S. Kobayshi[26] reports the QCC developments at Sony.

The first social innovation is that status in terms of age is in the process of being eliminated. The older generation and the younger generation are beginning to merge into a kind of senior-junior, teacher-pupil relationship performing closely associated jobs in which they assume joint responsibility for the work.

This relationship also extends to the scientist-technician and to people with differing backgrounds and academic disciplines who are brought together to solve problems across technical, business, financial, and political boundaries. In these respects Japanese social structure is beginning to develop into a series of collective partnerships, involving deep relationships and effective teamwork, supported by free-flowing information, responsible judgment, and youthful zeal.

The second social innovation is the mechanism of the teamwork itself. The bulk of the teamwork is carried out through the QC circles, which aim at improving daily work and human relations through what the Japanese describe as the "mutual development of the participants."

Since June 1962, when the first three circles were officially registered with the Union of Japanese Scientists and Engineers, the QCC movement has grown fantastically. The members of the Fourth QC Circle Team that toured the United States in September 1970 reported that there were over 400,000 circles (with over 4,000,000 workers) operating within Japanese industry.

The basic objectives of the QC circles are as follows:

• To encourage first-line supervisors to educate themselves and to develop leadership and supervisory qualities

• To raise the morale of the shop, to carry quality control to the ultimate degree, and to encourage and develop employees' self-awareness of what quality is, what problems may arise, and what to do about them, by including all workers

• To unify company-wide QC activities and provide a nucleus of personnel within each shop to work toward clarifying the understanding of management policy associated with quality, and to stabilize workmanship habits in order to meet quality standards.

The QC circles are active not only when there are particular production quality problems to be solved but continue regularly throughout the year. The QC circles provide for the progressive development of each individual's native intelligence and shrewdness and allow him to gain recognition and prestige for himself through the successes achieved by the group.

An examination of the information that the Japanese Union of Scientists and Engineers (JUSE) has made available shows that the membership in QC circles is voluntary. A circle may have as few as three or as many as twenty members, but generally averages from five to ten. Once a circle is organized, it is officially registered with JUSE and becomes part of a national organization.

The first-line supervisor usually, but not always, acts as the circle leader. The circle members then meet together and:

• Discuss common problems

- Set up strategies for attacking these problems
- Devise ways and means for getting factual data
- Analyze the data they have collected
- Map out plans for bringing about improvement
- Make suggestions and recommendations to management.

   The types of statistical quality control tools the circle members use are:

- Pareto curves
- Frequency histograms
- Control charts (for process studies)
- Cause-and-effect diagrams (fishbone charts)
- Scatter diagrams (correlation)
- Binomial probability charts.

   These are the tools and techniques that for the most part have remained almost exclusively in the hands of quality control engineers in the United States.

   Each member of a QC circle participates in the group's activities and becomes part of the thinking machinery concerned with bringing about improvements in the job. Each person becomes the source of new ideas, and the sharing of these ideas strengthens cohesiveness and comradeship within the group and allows for the cross-pollenization of education and experience. As one man described it, "QC circles serve as nerve cells in the workings of quality control that allow for a smooth funneling of communication between management and the workers."

   Savings have been reported ranging from as little as $250 to a high of $500,000 per case per year. While savings of $100,000 are frequent, the average runs about $56,000.

   A recent survey by JUSE has shown that 32 percent of QC meetings take place during working hours and 44 percent outside, while 24 percent meet under both conditions. When meetings take place outside working hours, compensation in various forms is offered in 71 percent of the cases. While 35 percent of the circles meet once a month, 65 percent meet more often; 80 percent of the meetings are for an hour or more (35 percent for two hours or more).

   Of 1566 companies surveyed, 1424 (91 percent) were using QC circles. These industries produced chemicals, electronics, textiles, general machinery, wood products, and consumer products. The big driving force behind the QC movement is top management, who have placed heavy emphasis on quality control education at all levels in their companies. (This account is based on Hird's report, which also emphasizes the extent to which the Japanese lay stress on a philosophy of happiness and creativity in work.)

Developments

In the United States
More limited developments have been taking place in U. S. firms for a long time, the oldest of which is the job enlargement movement that followed Charles Walker's and Robert Guest's work at General Motors in the early 1950s.[27] This was followed by job rotation, and in the 1960s by job enrichment (as advocated by Frederick Herzberg).[28] Several consulting firms now offer assistance in job redesign in this tradition; one has carried out over two hundred assignments in the last year or two.

A great deal of attention has been given to the experiments at Texas Instruments by Scott Myers in which groups of workers designed their own jobs in electronic component assembly.[29] Cost savings of $300,000 were reported for the first few months by the experimental plant when compared with a traditional plant. Companies such as the Polaroid Corporation, IBM (with some 50 projects under way), Mead Corporation (with innovative automated plant design), Procter & Gamble, and General Foods (with new plant designs) are all making contributions to new work arrangements.

Much of this work has been confined to the individual, though more of it is becoming concerned with the work group. Too little of it has embraced the wider implications from a systems viewpoint, in which the social and technical implications are thoroughly considered over a much larger domain, eventually involving the corporation as a whole. This is now beginning to happen.

A large inventory of cases was prepared for the International Conference on the Quality of Working Life in September 1972 (to be published in 1975 as the conference proceedings). These studies reflect the recent spread of concern with and response to issues of the quality of working life. However, they are very uneven in conception, theory, and outlook. Some are well-intentioned parochial attempts to modify in marginal ways the coercive requirements of bureaucratic and machine theory (or scientific management) organization. Others are frontier developments in design of new organizations on a sociotechnical systems basis. Still others range in between, from routine job enrichment through innovations in social systems.

An important development in connecting the different approaches is under way at the Cryovac Division of W. R. Grace & Co. This undertaking, started at a new California plant, represents a joining together of job enrichment and sociotechnical systems analysis. The plant has sophisticated technology, involving high mechanization and continuous process activities. Beginning with one subprocess, the development is spreading to involve the entire plant. The results of the initial undertaking show again that workers can acquire a wide range of sophisticated process skills, work semiautonomously, and discharge considerable responsibility when given the authority to control and regulate processes. Productivity has increased by 11 percent. A second subprocess development appears to be approaching a 40 percent productivity increase. The latest development has spread to the company's other plants.

A variety of undertakings based on psychological approaches to work organizations as social systems should also be mentioned. General Electric Company has under way a series of experiments to develop semiautonomous work teams aimed at developing alternatives to scientific management and to increase effectiveness. They are taking place in several locations with different manufacturing processes. Preliminary results show much higher levels of satisfaction for supervisors and workers in all cases and in some a doubling of productivity.

At Donnelly Corporation, with the assistance of the Institute of Social Research of the University of Michigan, semiautonomous work teams have been introduced as company policy, and structure and leadership have all changed. Employees are now salaried and participate in departmental problem-solving meetings. Production teams show considerable increase in decision making, coordination, and influence, although the effect on satisfaction is mixed. Productivity in a key division has increased by 48 percent and salaries by 25 percent.

An interesting study of disadvantaged black workers bears on government and industry programs for helping them secure stable employment. One company's programs (supported by government funding) were a dismal failure in stemming the very high rate of turnover among newly hired disadvantaged workers. Turnover was almost entirely attributable to the extraordinarily poor quality of the jobs to which the men were assigned—

a circumstance which no amount of training could mitigate. The training may have been dysfunctional because it raised the men's expectations to a point that increased their intolerance for poor jobs. In this circumstance training to instill in disadvantaged workers the "right attitudes" toward work may be little more than attempts to brainwash the disadvantaged to endure placidly poor jobs to which they are economically subjugated.

In Europe, Australia, and New Zealand
In the last three or four years several leading firms in European countries have taken substantial and widespread steps to improve the quality of work life of their employees.

ICI, the largest firm in Britain, has become convinced that "job enrichment pays off."[30] Initial attempts to secure the cooperation of blue-collar workers and their unions failed, but success attended a thoroughgoing attempt to involve office personnel in redesigning jobs that computerization had made monotonous. Their effort attracted national attention through being reported in the *Economist*. It was followed by a second project on the shop floor that also succeeded. Workers in groups of eight with a supervisor as discussion leader developed their own work methods, salary proposals, etc., and presented them to an outside assessment team which recommended approval or rejection to management. Some 20,000 of a total work force of 64,000 are reported to be involved in some form of self-management.

The Norwegian experience has been taken up in Sweden. Volvo and Saab are beginning to experiment with alternatives to assembly lines for certain operations. The most far-reaching recent developments in Norway have been in large bulk carriers such as tankers. Altogether, some one hundred firms are said to have work design projects under way. Other projects are reported in France and some in the subsidiaries of U.S. firms.

Dr. F. E. Emery, who while at the Tavistock Institute, London, played a leading role in developing sociotechnical studies, reports substantial developments in his native Australia. These involve the Australian subsidiaries of Alcan, Shell, and ICI, but the original projects were carried out in purely Australian enterprises. Arrangements between confederations of employers and labor on the Norwegian pattern have also recently been made in New Zealand, which is pressing forward with the degree and diversity of its industrialization.

Conclusions

Autonomy, Personal Growth, and Participation

The cases we have reviewed indicate that types of organization structure, management methods, and job content can be developed that lead to cooperation, commitment, learning and growth, ability to change, high work satisfaction, and improved performance. When responsible autonomy, adaptability, variety, and participation are present, they lead to learning and behavior that improve the organization and enhance the quality of working life for the individual.

By autonomy we mean that the content, structure, and organization of jobs is such that individuals or groups performing those jobs can plan, regulate, and control their own work worlds. Autonomy implies a number of things, among which are the need for multiple skills within the individual or within a group organized so it can share an array of tasks; and self-regulation and self-organization, which are radical notions in conventional industrial organizations. Under the principle of self-regulation, only the critical interventions, desired outcomes, and organizational maintenance requirements need to be specified by those *managing,* leaving the remainder to those *doing.* Specifically, situations are provided in which individuals or groups accept responsibility for the cycle of activities required to complete the product or service. They establish the rate, quantity, and quality of output. They organize the content and structure of their jobs, evaluate their own performance, participate in setting goals, and adjust conditions in response to work-system variability.

The studies indicate that when the attributes and characteristics of jobs are such that the individual or group becomes largely autonomous in the working situation, then meaningfulness, satisfaction, and learning increase significantly, as do wide knowledge of processes, identification with the product, commitment to desired action, and responsibility for outcomes. These findings supported the development of a job structure that permitted social interaction among jobholders and communication with peers and supervisors, particularly when the maintenance of continuity of operation was required. Simultaneously, high performance in quantity and quality of product or service outcomes was achieved. This has been demonstrated in such widely different settings as the mining of coal, the maintenance of a chemical refinery, and the manufacture of aircraft instruments.

The content of jobs has to be such that individuals can learn from what is going on around them and can grow, develop, and adjust. Slighted, but not overlooked, is the psychological concept of self-actualization or personal growth, which appears to be central to the development of motivation and commitment through satisfaction of the higher-order intrinsic needs of individuals. The most potent way of satisfying intrinsic needs may well be through job design.[31] Too often jobs in conventional industrial organizations have simply required people to adapt to restricted, fractionated activities, overlooking their enormous capacity to learn and adapt to complexity. (Such jobs also tend to ignore the organization's need for its workers to adapt.) In sophisticated technological settings, the very role of the individual is dependent on his adaptability and commitment. With nobody around at a specific instant to tell him what to do, he must respond to the situation and act as needed. The job is also a setting in which psychic and social growth of the individual should take place. Blocked growth leads to distortions that cost the individual, the organization, and the society. Where the sociotechnical system is designed so that the necessary adaptive behavior is facilitated, positive results in economic performance and personal satisfaction have occurred at all levels in the organization.

Man surely has always known, but only lately has it been demonstrated, that part of what a living organism requires to function effectively is a variety of experiences. If people are to be alert and responsive to their working environments, they need variety in the work situation. Routine and repetitious tasks tend to dissipate the individual. He is there physically, but not in any other way. Psychologists have also studied this phenomenon in various "deprived environments." Adult humans confined to stimulus-free environments begin to hallucinate. Workers may respond to the deprived work situation in much the same way—by disappearing (getting them back is another issue). Variety in industrial work has been the subject of study and controversy for fifty years. Recently, considerable attention has focused on the benefits to the individual and the organization of enlarging jobs to add variety.[32]

Another aspect of the need for variety is less well recognized in the industrial setting today, but will become increasingly important in the emergent sophisticated technological environment. Cyberneticist W. R. Ashby has described this aspect of variety as a general criterion for intelligent behavior of any kind. To Ashby, adequate adaptation is only possible if an organism already has a stored set of responses of the requisite variety. This implies that in the work situation, where unexpected things can happen, the task content of a job and the training for that job should match this potential variability.[33]

Participation of the individual in the decisions affecting his work, in development of job content and organizational relations, as well as in planning of changes, is fundamental to the outcome of many of the cases. Participation plays a role in learning and growth and permits those affected by changes in their roles and environments to develop assessments of the affects.

Systemic Properties

Beyond these considerations is the total system of work. We notice that in the cases where tasks and activities within jobs fell into meaningful patterns reflecting the interdependence between the individual job and the larger production system, then enhanced performance, satisfaction, and learning took place. In sociotechnical terms, this interdependence is most closely associated with the points at which variance is introduced from one production process into another. When necessary skills, tasks, and information were incorporated into the individual or group jobs, then adjustments could be made to handle error and exceptions within the affected subsystem; failing that, the variances were exported to other interconnecting systems. Conversely, in "deterministic" systems, the layers on layers of supervisors, buttressed by inspectors, utilitymen, repairmen, and so on absorb the variances exported from the workplace.

Implications and Action Requirements

The most important research on the quality of working life has implications for leaders of business and industry, unions, and government. Some of these will not be easily accommodated, for they require fundamental rethinking of the roles of people in organizations and concomitant modification in organizations, management, labor contracts, and government regulations.

Some of the tentative conclusions are directly contrary to cherished beliefs held at all levels of our society. Widely held beliefs cannot be undermined rapidly—another reason for the slow progress to date. The most significant conclusions and implications can be stated as follows:

- Productivity or efficiency versus the quality of working life is in itself an inappropriate concept. Productivity and quality are not opposite ends of a continuum, but are on two different scales. Enhancing one does not necessarily diminish the other. Under appropriate organizational structure and job design, experience shows that the two are directly related, i.e., both increase together.

• Coercive regulation and control by management begets more coercion. Planning and measuring to achieve and maintain coercive or repressive regulation and control of an organization's members trap both management and unions. They are forced into dead-end situations, with no options for developing suitable social or technical organizations. Urgently required are new ways of measuring outcomes where the social system and its members are considered as resources as much as the technical system and its parts are now. At a national as well as company level, the incompleteness of economic theory and supportive accounting systems relegates these concerns to externalities, removing them from organization design and the management decision process. The effect has inhibited considerations of the quality of working life.

• Regarding flexibility of technology, the indications are that the opposite of technological determinism is the reality. Results of sociotechnical design of factories with sophisticated technology indicate that there is more than enough flexibility on the technological side to suit social system requirements for a high quality of working life. Of course, there are limitations, but the full constraints are not known because almost everywhere engineers are asked to look at and design the technical system independently of any other considerations.

• Self-regulation and control at the workplace through autonomous or semiautonomous jobs and groups yield high levels of satisfaction, self-development, and learning and high performance in output and quality. They form the basis for further organizational design to reduce the repressive and coercive character of organizations and resulting worker alienation.

• In all instances where substantial enhancement of the quality of work life has taken place, it was preceded by a rethinking of management ideology about how organizations and individuals work. The ideology of the first industrial revolution regarded man as unreliable, unmotivated, and responding only to economic inducements. Men were spare parts in organizations and society. This ideology has had to be reassessed and changed. Though spurred on by the requirements of the second industrial revolution, this reassessment is a slow process and a large undertaking.

Support is required at a nationwide level to provide demonstrations, allow sheltered experiments to take place, and disseminate results. Government should aid in these efforts by supporting a new paradigm for productivity: relaxing (under controlled conditions) wage and hour laws; permitting experiments to be undertaken; providing national social indicators on the quality of working life; and not least, as an employer, beginning to redesign its own organizations.

Notes

1. E. L. Trist and K. W. Bamforth, "Some Social and Psychological Consequences of the Longwall Method of Coal Getting," *Human Relations* 4 (February 1951): 3–38.

2. L. E. Davis and R. R. Canter, "Job Design Research," *Journal of Industrial Engineering* 7 (1956): 275.

3. L. E. Davis and J. C. Taylor, eds., *The Design of Jobs* (Baltimore: Penguin Books, 1972).

4. F. E. Emery, ed., *Systems Thinking* (Baltimore: Penguin Books, 1969). See the chapter by F. E. Emery and E. L. Trist, "Socio-Technical Systems."

5. E. L. Trist et al., *Organizational Choice* (London: Tavistock, 1963).

6. Davis and Canter, p. 275.

7. E. H. Conant and M. D. Kilbridge, "An Interdisciplinary Analysis of Job Enlargement: Technology, Costs, and Behavioral Implications," *Industrial and Labor Relations Review* 18 (October 1965): 377; L. E. Davis, "The Coming Crisis for Production Management: Technology and Organization," *International Journal of Production Research* 9 (1971), no. 1: 65–82.

8. A. K. Rice, "Productivity and Social Organization in an Indian Weaving Shed," *Human Relations* 4 (November 1953): 297; idem, *Productivity and Social Organization: The Ahmedabad Experiment* (London: Tavistock, 1958).

9. G. G. Chevalier, "Socio-Technical Experiment in Casting Department," unpublished report (Aluminum Company of Canada, Ltd., 1972); J. T. Archer, "A Case Study of Sheltered Experiment at Aluminum Company of Canada, Ltd.," *Quarterly of Working Life: Cases* (in press).

10. J. J. Gagnon and Edward Blutot, "Autonomous Groups in Aluminum Reduction," unpublished report (1969).

11. D. W. E. Burden, "Participative Approach to Management: Microwax Department," unpublished report (Shell U. K. Ltd., 1972); C. P. Hill, *Toward a New Management Philosophy* (London: Gower Press, 1971).

12. L. E. Davis and R. Werling, "Job Design Factors," *Occupational Psychology* 34 (1960): 109.

13. L. E. Davis and E. S. Valfer, "Supervisor Job Design," Proceedings of the Second International Congress on Ergonomics, *Ergonomics* 8 (1965), no. 1; idem, "In-

tervening Responses to Changes in Supervisor Job Designs," *Occupational Psychology* 39 (1965): 171.

14. D. R. Kingdon, *Matrix Organization* (London: Tavistock, 1973).

15. L. E. Davis, "TRW Systems, Design Test Engineering," unpublished report (1970).

16. Editorial Secretary P.P.M.R., "Work Structuring," Phillips, Eindhoven.

17. Hill.

18. Michael Beer and E. F. Huse, "Systems Approach to Organization Development," *Applied Behavioral Science* 8, no. 1 (January 1972): 79–109.

19. F. E. Emery and Einar Thorsrud, *The Form and Content in Industrial Democracy* (London: Tavistock, 1969).

20. Einar Thorsrud and F. E. Emery, *Mot en Ny Bedriftsorganisasjon* (Oslo: Tanum Press, 1970).

21. P. H. Engelstad, *Teknologi og Sosial Forandring pa Arbeidsplassen* (Oslo: Tanum Press, 1970).

22. Emery and Thorsrud, chap. 5, "Norsk Hydro."

23. Philip Herbst, *Socio-Technical Design* (in press).

24. J. M. Juran, *Industrial Quality Control* (New York: McGraw-Hill, 1967).

25. John Hird, *Professional Engineer,* December 1971.

26. S. Kobayshi, *Creative Management* (New York: American Management Association, 1971).

27. C. R. Walker and R. H. Guest, *The Man on the Assembly Line* (Cambridge: Harvard University Press, 1952).

28. Frederick Herzberg, *Work and the Nature of Man* (New York: World, 1966).

29. M. S. Meyers, *Every Employee a Manager* (New York: McGraw-Hill, 1970); J. R. Maher, *New Perspectives in Job Enrichment* (New York: Van Nostrand Reinhold, 1971), chap. 5.

30. W. J. Paul and K. B. Robertson, *Job Enrichment and Employee Motivation* (London: Gower Press, 1970).

31. E. E. Lawler III, "Job Design and Employee Motivation," *Personnel Psychology* 22 (1969), no. 4: 426–435.

32. L. E. Davis, "Toward a Theory of Job Design," *Journal of Industrial Energy* 8 (1957): 305–309; Herzberg.

33. W. R. Ashby, *Design for a Brain* (New York: Wiley, 1960).

V Education and Work

12 Occupational Bias in Formal Education and Its Effect on Preparing Children for Work

David C. MacMichael

"Society," declares Kenneth Hoyt, "has charged education to teach youngsters *to* work, [and] *about* work and the working world."[1] There is a considerable literature arguing that the American public school system was set up to do nothing more than to provide employers with suitably indoctrinated and docile workers. Indeed, such early apostles of mass public schooling as Horace Mann, William Harris, Elwood P. Cubberley, and David Snedden appealed to businessmen to support education precisely as the means for teaching respect for authority, instilling conformity, inculcating the rewards of effort and obedience, and counteracting the blandishments of labor unions.[2]

The same literature reports businessmen's continual disappointment with the limited success achieved by the schools in meeting this major objective. At the same time, an opposite group contends that the schools have been all too successful in pursuit of the goal—with the result that schools are joyless places that crush aspirations and more than adequately prepare students, or victims, for lifetimes spent in conforming to the will of others.[3] This debate has little to do with the quite distinct matter of whether the schools adequately teach work *skills;* it focuses, rather, on whether they socialize young people appropriately to embrace the work *ethic*.

Schools and the Work Ethic

The question of what the work ethic is has often been overlooked in the agreement that it ought to be transmitted. There is confusion between the bourgeois, self-imposed ethic of frugality, investment, and self-denial as a life-style which was necessary in the establishment of the capitalist system, and the work ethic imposed by the bourgeois on the working class. This later ethic was economically expressed by the British economist David Ricardo in his iron law of wages, which, while necessarily emphasizing frugality (since he considered bare subsistence to be the natural determinant of laborers' wages), effectively denied opportunity for savings and investment to all but those whose metabolism allowed an uncommon amount of room for self-denial in addition to the denial externally imposed. This imposed ethic stressed obedience, conformity, and docility to the will of human masters (virtues that the middle class regarded as appropriate to the relationship between the entrepreneur and God). Thus, the imposed ethic had an entirely different moral character from that of the self-imposed one. The confusion between the two is compounded today by recognition that the Protestant (bourgeois) ethic has less than complete application to the corporate industrial era:

> To teach the work ethic in its original form would cause problems for society and for the school. The present system is better described as consumerism than capitalism, and old-style frugality could wreck it. A part of the youth culture rejects every type of work ethic. The industrial work ethic is eroding, and a postindustrial work ethic has yet to develop. But it seems indefensible not to teach youth that employers do value the traditional work ethic and that major violations of it will lead to discharge.[4]

Also germane to any discussion of this matter is the charge that the educational system has encouraged a false worship of the baccalaureate degree, overemphasizing college preparation, with attendant depreciation of the value of work that does not require a college degree. It may be that this is true, and if so, the cause may be traced to the confusion between middle-class and working-class work ethics. As Colin Greer argues, although schools were charged with (and successfully carried out) the task of selecting and breaking in the future work force in line with the working-class ethic imposed by the middle class, they were also, as middle-class run and staffed organizations, committed willy-nilly to the middle-class ethic and to the achievement of middle-class goals.[5] Very important to this ethic is the notion of deferral of gratification. Remaining in school or going on to college (instead of taking an available job) pays dividends in the ability to secure a higher-status, higher-pay job at a later date. By definition, this depreciates the job that does not require deferred gratification.

Inevitably, too, the standard of accountability that middle-class values impose on schools establishes as "better" or more "successful" those schools that prepare the highest percentage of students for deferred gratification in college. Contrariwise, schools that "fail" are those that have the highest percentage of dropouts—those students who cannot even defer gratification until high school graduation. Thus, a good school is considered to be one oriented toward further education—and good students to be those who are similarly oriented. It is not surprising that parents, many of whom passed through a very similar school system to that which exists today, have similar values and also want to see their children prepared for higher education and higher-status employment.

It might be argued that the American public school system, originally designed to produce factory and office fodder trained in the middle-class-imposed working-class ethic, has failed at least partly because its middle-class personnel are unable to avoid demonstrating their commitment to another ethic, which promises higher rewards. The middle-class teacher, counselor, or school administrator cannot hold out any image of success except that of middle-class achievement. In this way, even leaving out all the other factors socializing the American child toward a middle-class rather than a working-class ethic, the school system necessarily introduces bias toward middle-class occupations and the middle-class means of entering them. This not only encourages more students to make the attempt to reach higher-status jobs but tends to cause those who do not to regard their choice as second-best.[6]

Too much stress should not be placed on the school as the creator of occupational bias. The school, after all, is merely one of society's means of transmitting its cultural preferences; it reflects the values of the society. And American society, like almost every other society in the world, assigns status to various occupations. The most highly valued are middle-class in nature, even when they are not the most highly paid. This attitude is, perhaps, more characteristic of the United States than of Europe because of the absence of a definable working class with its own tradition and political organization.[7] For many years prior to the First World War, the United

States was accustomed to importing most of its highly skilled labor from Europe, and the resulting association of skilled manual labor with foreign-ness necessarily detracted from its desirability. Thus, despite rhetoric to the contrary, the manual occupations (excluding agriculture) have never been honored in America. To expect that a school system that reflects the values of a nation would honor those occupations is to expect the peculiar. There has been a strong interaction between the wholesale adoption of this middle-class ideal by the society at large and its delivery to the young of the society by the schools. Since the school follows society and not the other way round it is clear that the school only reinforces an existing and growing social preference for those occupations socially defined as desir-able and provides socially preferred means (extended education) for entering them. To this extent, the schools do bias occupational choice in favor of white-collar, high-status occupations that require (rationally or not) extended educational preparation.[8]

The accusation leveled by some critics that American schools do not transmit the work ethic effectively can be accepted as correct only if the ethic is defined as the working-class ethic. To the extent that it transmits, instead, the essentially opposed middle-class ethic—especially as that ethic has been modified to meet the norms of corporate capitalism—the public school system defeats one of the major purposes of its establishment in the first place. And the mechanism of transmission of this middle-class ethic is the middle-class teacher.

The Role of the Teacher

The literature on the process of occupational choice persistently identifies the teacher as a key figure.[9] Career-education advocates recognize the situation intuitively when they propose, as a means of reinforcing the work-ing-class ethic, the introduction of representatives of different classes of workers as counselors and teachers in the schools. In this sense, career education represents yet another attempt by the middle-class directors of society to make the schools serve the purpose for which they established them in the first place. They may expect success, however, only to the extent that the people who replace the middle-class teacher as the role model in school are themselves able to (or willing to) transmit the working-class ethic. It is more than likely that they will not want to transmit this now disparaged ethic. Instead, these educators will more probably follow the course of vocational education. Vocational educators strive to implant in their students skills that enable them to bargain more effectively with employers. And, not surprisingly, employers tend to be unhappy with vocational education—largely because it is oriented to skill and not attitude (working-class ethic).[10] (It is significant that present trends in teacher union organization and bargaining tactics may also weaken the limited ability of middle-class teachers to present the model of submissiveness to authority that is part of the desired working-class ethic.)

Rather interestingly, much of the renewed support for Roman Catholic parochial schools offered by the current business-oriented national administration may be attributed to the belief that these institutions, by their very nature, are not likely to transmit the Protestant ethic with its connotation of upward mobility. These schools, traditionally attuned to values of submission and docility, are probably superior worker training schools than public schools. The persistence of Irish, Italian, and Polish Catholics in occupations with lower socioeconomic status, the utilitarian nature of Catholic institutions of higher education, and the tendency of those Catholic parents who have adopted secular, American middle-class goals to abandon the parochial schools, all allow an inference that these nonmainstream schools are less likely than public schools to inculcate middle-class values stressing upward mobility and, in the process, depreciating manual occupations.[11] Lutheran schools may have the same socioeconomic tendencies.

Racial Overtones

As the studies of Colin Greer, David Tyack, Lawrence Cremin, and other revisionists among education historians demonstrate, the early treatment of southern and eastern European immigrant children in American public schools assumed their racial inferiority. Consequently, although the WASP teacher might exemplify an upwardly mobile ethic and life-style, the assumption was that this was not to be adopted by other than WASP or northern European children. (This assertion can be supported through educational statistics that were maintained in terms of national origin.) For some years, the schools were successful in implanting notions of inferiority by the process of picking out the hewers and drawers and pushing them into the labor force at an early age. But for a number of reasons, not the least of which were the demands for national unity imposed by the two world wars, the children of Slavs and southern Europeans began to be urged to adopt the same educational and occupational goals that the schools held out to their American and northern European clientele. Also, the fact that the teaching profession was reasonably easy to enter meant that more and more non-WASP children found their own middle-class ethnic models in the classroom.[12]

The same cannot be said for black pupils. There can be little doubt that the segregated Negro schools of the pre-1954 era definitely served the social purpose of ingraining a subordinate working-class ethic. Indeed, the most influential black spokesman of the early part of this century, Booker T. Washington, never ceased to impress on his hearers the need for black Americans to embrace the working-class ethic as the means for gaining social acceptance. Sights were not to be raised higher than that. It would not be farfetched to speculate that the drive for Negro equality that marked the 1960s and continues today is at least partly a result of school integration and the exposure of black youth to middle-class, aspiration-oriented white teachers.

Research on educational and occupational aspirations among minority youth reflects a peculiar ambivalence. At the same time that a school points to the path upward and encourages black youths to take it, it delivers the unmistakable message that the path will be too steep for them and that lower aspirations would be more realistic. Oddly enough (assuming that there is a demonstrable amount of racially based aspiration discouragement projected consciously or unconsciously by the schools) black students of lower socioeconomic status tend to have higher career and educational expectations than white students of similar background. Nevertheless, black students report a much higher level of felt teacher prejudice against their race. One researcher notes a discrepancy between very high educational aspirations (92 percent of black high school students interviewed were certain they would finish college; 80 percent believed their parents wanted them to finish; but only 49 percent believed their teachers wanted them to finish) and low occupational aspirations. For instance, 30 percent of the students who aspired to a college education did not aspire to a job requiring one. The author of the study speculated that the black students realistically calculated that they would have to be overqualified in terms of education in order to compete with whites even for lower-status jobs.[13] This adds support to the conclusion of Peter Blau and Otis-Dudley Duncan that proportional occupational gains for Negroes through education are less than for whites.[14]

There is a wealth of anecdotal and experiential data to support the proposition that the schools tend to limit the occupational aspirations of minority ethnic groups generally, and of the less academically talented of all groups. This does not mean, however, that the school better prepares these children for work by instilling the working-class work ethic. It may well be that the schools inevitably induce a distaste for lower-status work by too closely relating academic performance and qualification for further education with the types of jobs one can hope for—and, in the case of black students, inducing a negative correlation. This suspicion is not new, of course. There has always been a strong business voice alleging that too much schooling spoils the potential worker.[15] Even such thinkers as Paul Goodman and Eric Hoffer (incompatible as they might otherwise be) agree that younger, minority-group job seekers have lately shown a marked distaste for accepting jobs that not too many years ago were regarded as at least semiskilled. The distaste seems to rest essentially on the ground that once a job is made available to blacks it automatically loses status. Interestingly, since this involves a partial reversal of traditional American attitudes distinguishing between "white man's" and "nigger's" work, the depreciation of status of such jobs as bus driver, highway repairman, telephone operator, and so forth seems to occur more in the eyes of blacks now being allowed entry than in the eyes of whites. One recalls Groucho Marx's refusal to accept membership in a club on the grounds that there must be something wrong with one that would want him.

The New Ethic
Up to this point the discussion has dealt essentially with two different and rather traditional work ethics and their effect on occupational choice. It should be recognized that, as part of the change of values that seems to be affecting large portions of the Western world, these ethics are undergoing significant changes as well. Since schools tend to lag in their ability to adopt newer social values, it is probable that they have played little part in the transmission of the emerging ethical value systems—indeed, as the long hair and dress code controversies indicate (at least superficially), the officialdom of schools has striven mightily to suppress them. The means of transmission of these values appears to be the peer group, the unidentifiable leadership of the youth culture.

An important aspect of the emerging value system as it relates to work involves the discarding of traditional status implications of jobs. The willingness of some of the educationally most favored to take subsistence jobs of little or no status has intrigued those who write of America's greening or bluing. The ethic involved here is certainly not working-class, since it emphasizes anything but subordination and discipline. The work habits and attitudes cultivated are those Michael Piore associates with the secondary job market—irregularity, instability, and tolerance for a variety of appearances, modes of conduct, and levels of performance.[16] Income from such jobs is often pooled to support group living and to allow the working individual or nonworking members of the group to take part in activities outside the cash economy which are regarded as true vocations—politics, ecological action, or plain hedonism.

The Influence of Economics

In retrospect, it is easy to see that the shift from transmission by the schools of working-class values to that of middle-class values coincided with the shift from a manufacturing to a service economy—from blue-collar to white-collar. The emphasis on higher education that is characteristic of the post–World War II era coincided with a tremendous expansion of employment opportunities in white-collar jobs. The middle-class value preferences of the school system were thus reinforced and rationalized by the realities of the job market. The social preferences of the majority, school characteristics, and the development of the economy were, for almost two decades after the war, in a rare state of harmony. It was during this period, one should recall, that serious treatises established that the rate of American economic growth was a function of its public educational inputs.[17] The controversies over American education during the 1950s almost never related to occupational preparation. Attention was directed toward remedying shortcomings in the area of cognitive skills ("Why Johnny Can't Read") and, after Sputnik, teaching science and mathematics.

Postwar assumptions about occupational preparation were summed up in the Life Adjustment Program that grew out of the 1944 Prosser Resolution. Most interestingly, considering that Charles Prosser was the apostle of vocational education in America and the actual author of the 1917 Smith-Hughes Act, it was believed that the jobs of the future would tend to be so dull, routine, and simplified that the average employee could not find his life satisfactions in his work. Hence, the task of the schools was to prepare him for this inevitable occupational fate, not by training him for work but

by exposing him to the actualities of work and encouraging the development of civic, aesthetic, and domestic capabilities through which he could
fulfill himself.[18] While Life Adjustment was destroyed in the name of post-
Sputnik academic excellence, it is certainly possible, despite the absence
of outcry about its effect on labor force preparation, that work as a means of
self-fulfillment was downgraded in the eyes of a generation of school-
children. Surprisingly, though, the school generation of the forties and
fifties was identified with the period of quiet campuses and hardworking,
career-oriented students eager to become organization men and reap the
split-level, tail-finned rewards of modern materialism.

It was not until the early 1960s, when attention began to be focused on
youth unemployment, that much concern for the relationship between
school and work began to be expressed again. Almost immediately, as the
Manpower Development and Training Act began to lodge important youth
job training responsibilities in the Department of Labor, the vocational
educators—upstaged during the academic excellence drive of the late
1950s—began to argue that the fault lay in the schools and the remedies
must be found there. They argued that it had been the overemphasis on
academic preparation for the scientific race with the Soviet Union that had
led to the poor employment situation of youth. A reemphasis on job preparation for the majority of students, those who would not go on to college, was
necessary. But the 1963 Vocational Education Act (and its amendment in
1968) apparently had insufficient effect, and the latest result is the career
education program.

As we have seen, the work ethic transmitted by the school has tended to
be that ethic most appropriate for the existing stage of the economy—
allowing, of course, for the inevitable time lags. An economy changing from
agriculture to industry needed, and got, a school system that endeavored
to teach both Americans and immigrant rural folk the discipline and subordination necessary in the factory. As the employment structure became
white-collar and middle-class in nature, the natural tendency of the schools
to transmit a middle-class viewpoint reinforced and supported economic
and societal needs. In the immediate post–World War II era when the
United States, as the only power to emerge unscathed from the war, truly
dominated the world economy, the expanded opportunities for highly
educated manpower seemed limitless. The rewards for extending the period
of education, both for the individual and the society, seemed demonstrably

so great that it is little wonder that the schools bent every effort to encourage young people to delay entry into the labor force in order to seek higher-status jobs later. It was inevitable that under such circumstances the schools depreciated the value of work not requiring extended education.

Today's emphasis on career education and the open discouragement of extended education ("baccalaureate degree worship") clearly is a reversal of a long trend in American education. It also marks a reversal in the long trend of economic development. The industrialization process that required of the educational system first more and more properly disciplined and subordinated workers, then more highly educated and specialized white-collar workers, and then masses of managers and professionals, seems to be coming to an end.[19] If this is so, there is bound to be both friction and increasing social and individual dissatisfaction with the educational system. This will occur because biases in the educational system for jobs of higher status achieved through deferred entry into the labor market will not be coordinated with national economic and social requirements. If the need for masses of new managers is coming to an end, this is hardly congruent with educational statistics that project enormous increases in the percentage of high school graduates who will go on to college during the 1970s. Assuming that higher education encourages an even stronger bias toward high-status occupations than public school education does, the lack of synchronization will pose very serious social and economic questions about the purpose of education and about the serviceability of either of the traditional work ethics.

Education for the Future

If, as I have postulated, the present educational system can only transmit the middle-class ethic, and if this ethic is unsuitable for the emerging era, then it is clear that the society will not long tolerate the present educational system. I have also noted that an interesting and perhaps important minority of middle-class products of the school system are actively rejecting the middle-class ethic to undertake low-status, subsistence employment in order to support their noneconomic careers. It is significant that their life-style is congruent with the demands of the service economy, and for that reason they may be more realistic than their school counselors. Given their rejection of discipline and subordination, however, it remains to be seen to what extent the economy can tolerate such workers.[20]

Career education seems to be a deliberate attempt to re-create the working-class ethic, particularly in its emphasis on appropriate attitudes. At the same time, it does not appear to differ significantly from the ethic adopted by the Consciousness III types in other important respects. First, there is the deliberate rejection of status as defined by middle-class standards. More subtly, there is recognition of a certain casualness and impermanence in employment as well. (Career education spokesmen emphasize their belief that people must be prepared for frequent changes in occupation during their working lifetimes.) This is a distinct change from the old middle-class belief that an appropriate vocational choice and preparation allowed one to spend a lifetime advancing in skill, experience, and status in his career. The man who had to change jobs had, in an important sense, failed.[21]

Despite charges to the contrary, the American public school system has been vocationally oriented throughout its existence. It is true, of course, that the orientation has been toward middle-class vocations. But it cannot be denied that vocational opportunity during the past half century or more has been expanding rapidly in just those occupations that embraced the middle-class ethic. In personal and economic terms, this educational investment and emphasis on preparation for higher-status occupations has been justifiable and necessary. The coincidence that the educational system transmitted the middle-class values and occupational biases needed in the marketplace made the schools, as they are presently organized and staffed, excellent and efficient vehicles both for occupational training and for guiding students into socially and individually beneficial career paths.

But it seems highly improbable that the economy of the future will provide increased opportunity in those occupational fields regarded as high-status by the middle-class ethic. Furthermore, the characteristics of status embodied in the ethic—long preparation and deferred gratification, hierarchical authority, receipt of deference, emphasis on the development of intellectual and rational faculties, theoretical as opposed to practical skills, lifelong involvement, and, usually, high actual or potential income—may themselves be downgraded. The more desirable occupations may be seen as those for which preparation is not lengthy. Both the exercise of authority and the receipt of deference from others are now being increasingly viewed as embarrassing and to be shunned. Rationality and intellectuality are suspect; intuition and emotion are preferred. Possession of practical skill is preferred to theoretical mastery.[22] (This may appear to contradict the preference for brief preparation. But, for example, the emphasis on the training of paraprofessionals and the demand for shortening formal courses —à la Maoist educational reform in China—exemplify the trend.) One of the more noticeable features of middle-class life in the past decade or so has been the facility and willingness with which many people change careers. (It is interesting that this phenomenon has appeared at a time when teacher organizations have laid heavy stress on security and tenure.) Finally, the present emphasis on income equalization in the United States indicates that possession of a very high income, or one greatly differentiated from that of persons in lower-status occupations, may be losing its force as a desirable social distinction.

The hierarchical, rational-intellectual, extended, theoretically oriented school, whose techniques and disciplines are defended largely as a means of enabling those who submit to them to achieve the distinctions of middle-class status, obviously will have little appeal to that element of society which rejects both the goals and attributes of the school. But it is also clear that the majority of the society today still accepts the middle-class ethic. The prime cause of tension in American education at the present time is the conflict between an advance guard anxious to transform the schools into instruments appropriate to the future they see rushing upon us and a main body devoted to preservation of the schools as bastions of present values. If, as supporters of the middle-class ethic argue, these values are eternal and appropriate to any future, then of course the occupational biases trans-mitted through their inculcation are to be applauded as benefiting both the society and the individual student. If, on the other hand, the values are appropriate only to the particular stage of social and economic development through which we have passed during the last century or so, the transmis-sion through the schools of middle-class occupational aspirations and modes of preparation are bound to have pernicious results. The most pernicious, from the viewpoint of the individual and his economic well-being, could be that he will have been taught in school to aspire for "success" in precisely those fields in which opportunity is diminishing.

The overall social consequences of economically inappropriate educa-tion have been remarked upon frequently in those underdeveloped coun-tries that have adopted the educational models of Europe and the United States. The existence of a relatively large cohort of youth trained to middle-class occupational aspiration paired with the paucity of genuine economic opportunities to accommodate such aspirations leads, as Gunnar Myrdal argues, to the creation of the bureaucratic "soft state" [23] or to the existence of a disaffected lumpen-intelligentsia. The expansion of state and local government employment over the past decade, as well as the rise of such revolutionary groups as Students for a Democratic Society, indicate that both these developments are possible and may already be under way within the United States.

Summary

I have argued that the school supports the American social preference for white-collar, nonmanual employment and that its means are not so much curricular as exemplary. The school as a white-collar institution staffed by middle-class people and held to middle-class standards of accountability necessarily and inevitably biases students toward white-collar occupations and middle-class-approved means for entering them.

Social preference is itself responsible for the transformation of the public school from an institution designed to impose the working-class ethic on the majority of its students to one that, once the selecting-out function was abandoned, could not but transmit the middle-class ethic. And the fact that this coincided with the change in the national economy that saw more and more blue collars exchanged for white ones made the process economically viable. Again, it must be emphasized that because of the historical coincidence of social preference, economic desirability, and institutional propriety, the transmission of middle-class occupational bias to the majority of students has, on balance, been beneficial, especially over the past twenty-five years. Indeed, it is only within the past couple of years, as the historical coincidence seems to have come to an end and social, economic, and institutional complementariness no longer is apparent that the phrase "occupational bias" with its pejorative connotations could have been used to describe encouragement of middle-class aspirations.

I have attempted to demonstrate that the old middle-class ethic and the associated value system may no longer be appropriate to the emerging economy. There is evidence that a new value system is developing, especially among the youth of the American middle class, that is more appropriate, particularly with regard to occupational status. It is questionable whether the school system, which as presently constituted is the institutional embodiment of the traditional middle-class value system, can do other than it has done—that is, encourage "upward" mobility toward "higher-status" jobs through the deferral of gratification in extended education. To the extent that it continues to do so (and it is important to recognize that in a time of transition there will still be areas where, for a considerable period of time, the older values will still be viable and opportunities for status and income by adhering to them will exist) the school system will become less relevant for students and less likely to be supported by the economic system. Unfortunately, this will occur at a time when those groups —blacks, Chicanos, and other low-status ethnics—who have not achieved status within the old order and have been encouraged to believe they will do so through the mechanism of school, are demonstrating their commitment to the middle-class value system. Should the school now seem to conspire to change the rules of the social game just at the time when these groups have been invited to play, their anger and confusion will be great. Black parents have been particularly hostile to attempts to introduce innovations and openness in their schools. They want the same educational medicine that whites have used to cure social ills. For the same reasons, many black leaders are suspicious that career education is Bookerism in modern dress.[24]

Thus, even in a situation where a change in the whole notion of occupational status and the means for achieving it would be socially and economically advantageous, the school may not only find it difficult because of its innate characteristics to transmit the value change but it will be under intense pressure from many different and powerful segments of society not to change. Until such time as the postindustrial economy and society has emerged and its values become felt, the probability is that the school will continue to transmit the present overwhelming bias for white-collar occupations requiring lengthy formal education and certification.

Notes

1. Kenneth B. Hoyt, "Education as Preparation for Employment," Report of the National Commission on Technology, Automation, and Economic Progress, *Technology and the American Economy* (Washington, D.C.: U.S. Government Printing Office), appendix, vol. 4, pp. 91–92.

2. For a good survey see Arthur G. Wirth, "The Vocational-Liberal Studies Controversy between John Dewey and Others, 1900–1917" (Bethesda: ERIC Document

Reproduction Service, #ED 051 002, 1970). For a more strident view, see Colin Greer, *The Great School Legend: A Revisionist Interpretation of American Public Education* (New York: Basic Books, 1972), pp. 59–79.

3. See, for example, Ivan Illich, *Celebration of Awareness* (New York: Doubleday, 1970); Leslie A. Hart, *The Classroom Disaster* (New York: Teachers College Press, 1970); Edgar Z. Friedenberg, *The Vanishing Adolescent* (Boston: Beacon Press, 1959).

4. Kenneth B. Hoyt et al., *Career Education: What It Is and How to Do It* (Salt Lake City: Olympus Publishing Co., 1972), p. 40.

5. Greer, pp. 108–109.

6. Jacob J. Kaufman et al., "The Preparation of Youth for Effective Occupational Utilization: The Role of the Secondary School in the Preparation of Youth for Employment" (Bethesda: ERIC Document Reproduction Service, #ED 011 060, 1967), pp. 12–6–12–7.

7. See George Katona, Burkhard Strumpel, and Ernest Zahn, *Aspirations and Affluence: Comparative Studies in the United States and Western Europe* (New York: McGraw-Hill, 1971), pp. 154–163, for the influence and educational aspirations of such a class in West Germany.

8. Ivar Berg, *Education and Jobs: The Great Training Robbery* (New York: Praeger, 1970).

9. See, for example, N. J. Pallone, F. S. Richard, and R. B. Hurley, *Race, Sex and Social Mobility: An Exploration of Occupation Aspirations among Black and White Youth* (New York: New York University, School of Education, Center for Field Research, 1969); Walter L. Stump, John E. Jordan, and Eugene W. Frieben, "Cross-Cultural Considerations in Understanding Vocational Development," *Journal of Counseling Psychology* 14 (1967): 325–331.

10. Hoyt et al., pp. 24, 46; Frederick Hurbison and Charles Myers, *Education, Manpower and Economic Growth: Strategies of Human Resource Development* (New York: McGraw-Hill, 1964), pp. 160–161.

11. Greer, p. 85; Otto F. Krausheer, *American Non-Public Schools: Patterns of Diversity,* typescript Danforth Foundation study, chap. 6.

12. Friedenberg, pp. 126–131.

13. Michael James Hindelang, "Educational and Occupational Aspirations among Working Class Negro, Mexican-American and White Elementary School Children," *Journal of Negro,* fall 1970, pp. 351–353. For survey of the literature see Zahava D. Blum and Peter H. Rossi, "Social Class Research and Images of the Poor," in *On Understanding Poverty,* ed. Daniel H. Moynihan (New York: Basic Books, 1969).

14. Peter M. Blau and Otis-Dudley Duncan, *The American Occupational Structure* (New York: Wiley, 1967), p. 442.

15. Wirth, pp. 296–297.

16. Michael J. Piore, "Jobs and Training," in *The State and the Poor,* ed. Samuel H. Beer and Richard E. Barringer (Cambridge, Mass.: Winthrop, 1970), pp. 55–62.

17. Gary Becker, *Human Capital* (Chicago: University of Chicago Press, 1964).

18. U.S. Office of Education, "Life Adjustment for Every Youth" (1945).

19. Assistant Secretary of Labor Michael Moskow told the New Jersey Association of College Administration Counselors that job prospects for college graduates will continue to deteriorate throughout the 1970s. He said that there is "a decreasing demand for professionals, diminishing monetary return from degrees, and projected increase in service-produce industries" requiring a lesser proportion of college-educated employees. Hence, "We need to reassess the desirability of exerting strong pressures on high school students . . . to enter college." He concluded his speech by calling for more emphasis on career education (*Wall Street Journal,* May 24, 1972, p. 9).

20. An important economic phenomenon is the growth of agencies that provide casual labor for the growing variety of jobs, some of which—clerical and technical ones especially—represent an admixture of primary and secondary labor market characteristics.

21. Friederich Ben-Ami, "Changing Skill Requirements, Job Training, Motivation, and Mobility," in *Technological Change and Human Development, An International Conference at Jerusalem,* ed. Wayne L. Hodges and Matthew A. Kelly (Ithaca: Cornell University, New York State School of Industrial and Labor Relations, 1970), pp. 99–115.

22. Richard Hofstadter, "The Age of Rubbish," *Newsweek,* July 6, 1970.

23. Gunnar Myrdal, *Asian Drama* (New York: Pantheon Books, 1969).

24. Walter Karp, "Free Schools and Free Men," in "Purpose and Process, Readings in Educational Research and Development, Appendix 2," in *Appendix to Hearings on H.R. 3606 and Related Bills to Create National Institute on Education before Select Subcommittee on Education* (Washington, D.C.: House of Representatives, Education and Labor Committee, 1972).

13 Vocational Education for All in High School?

Beatrice G. Reubens

The proposal that every student leaving high school should have a specific, marketable skill is a key element in the broadly conceived career education program of the U.S. Office of Education.[1] This emphasis on education as preparation for employment is a reaction to adverse features of the current scene: the failure of the general curriculum to ready students either for jobs or higher education, the overvaluation of college education, the nonvocational aspect of much of secondary vocational education, the dropout problem in high schools and colleges, the high youth unemployment rates, the deterioration of work attitudes, and the growing disdain for blue-collar jobs.

At a time when some critics of the schools have been urging solutions that reject many traditional values and activities, the advocates of career education stress smooth entry into the conventional work world, where job requirements often are specified by poorly informed, credentials-conscious employers.[2] Significantly, the career education movement views young entrants to the labor market as full of deficiencies, but it accepts or even ignores unfavorable labor market conditions. As this paper will show,

The author, solely responsible for the views expressed, is grateful for comments by Rupert N. Evans, Eli Ginsberg, Gerald G. Somers, Charles Brecher, Robert Shick, and Alice Yohalem.

the constraints on individual fulfillment and career satisfaction in our labor market are not faced realistically.

While career education has many interpretations, virtually all of its advocates agree that classroom vocational-technical education at the high school level is a vital part.[3] If their arguments are successful, it is possible that half of all high school students would obtain most of their occupational preparation through formal vocational classes.[4] This would be a considerable increase: at present, a little over 25 percent of all high school students are enrolled in vocational programs. (The uncertainty about the precise number arises from double counting, enrollment in optional *courses* as distinguished from a vocational *program,* derivation of statistics only from courses receiving federal financial support, and the dubious vocational status of courses such as homemaking.) [5]

Since the proposed expansion of high school vocational education must build on the existing system, a review of evaluation studies of current programs is warranted. What do we know about the value of vocational education for the segment of the high school population that has been involved? Are those of them who go straight to jobs better off in any measurable sense than comparable students who also go to work right after graduation but who have not followed a vocational high school curriculum? Is the nature of the curriculum the causal or decisive factor? Other important issues include the holding power of the various high school curricula against dropping out and the effect of vocational education on the pursuit of further education.

With this review as a background, it may be possible to confront the issues arising from an extension of vocational education to half or more of the high school population. Specifically, attention can be directed to the needs of particular groups of students, the desirable total size of the vocational program in view of labor market conditions, the forms of vocational education, and the school level where courses should be offered.

Vocational Students

Less is known about secondary school vocational students than researchers and administrators would like. We do know that there are over five million of them and that they represent a lower-middle to low group—unable or unwilling to undertake an academic program, but possibly superior in motivation if not in academic ability to those in the general curriculum (the watered-down academic course). Much overlapping of ability and attitude between these programs exists, of course, and the situation is not uniform from place to place.

Controversy surrounds the socioeconomic background of vocational students. On the basis of a 1969 survey, the U. S. Office of Education concluded that students in vocational classes "were an approximate cross section of the total population of comparable age groups." [6] This finding conflicts with an earlier USOE analysis of 1960 Project Talent data which indicated lower than average socioeconomic background and academic ability for vocational students. The National Planning Association questions the data and conclusions of the 1969 survey, leaning toward the earlier picture painted from Project Talent data—that vocational students are a generally less favored group, though by no means homogeneous. The NPA criticism of the 1969 survey would be more convincing if NPA had not introduced occupational and educational data for the whole labor force, covering both sexes and all ages, as a base of comparison with data on the vocational student's head of household (who, surely, was usually male and thirty-five to fifty-five years old).[7]

If both USOE surveys are actually correct for their periods, we would have the remarkable situation that from 1960 to 1969, while the emphasis in governmental programs shifted to the disadvantaged, the vocational student body changed from disadvantaged to average. Certainly, recent data showing a slight overrepresentation of minority youth in vocational courses lends further confusion.[8]

The most adequate facilities, equipment, and teaching in secondary vocational education are found in small- to medium-sized cities. Suburbs mount high-quality programs but have few courses and students, central cities present the least adequate programs, and rural areas (which often lack a central vocational high school) tend to offer only home economics, agriculture, and office occupations. Most rural students attend vocational high schools in neighboring small cities, reducing the handicap of residence in areas of meager employment opportunities.[9]

A significant aspect of vocational courses is their sex-typing and, particularly, the relegation of girls to the occupations that lead to less favorable labor market outcomes or have no connection to work at all. The five largest programs at the secondary level in 1970 were comprehensive homemaking, typing and related skills, agricultural production, filing and office machines, and stenographic-secretarial; most of these courses are female-dominated or avocational or both.[10]

Evaluating Vocational Programs

The assessment of current high school vocational education is beset with conceptual problems, methodological pitfalls, and statistical limitations. It is not unusual for investigators to devote more space to discussions of these issues and criticism of other studies than to the presentation of their own findings.[11]

Those who consider that much of academic education is also vocational (and that some education classified as vocational does not prepare one for work) question the evaluation of whole programs. These researchers feel that gross comparisons slight the variety and disparities within the vocational curriculum, the differences among students that are not easily quantified, and the doubts about how occupational skills actually are imparted and how people learn.

Another group treat vocational students as consumers of education whose choice of programs should be respected with little regard to labor market demand; they feel that to test the outcomes, especially in monetary terms, would be as unfair as expecting academic students to justify their study of foreign languages by obtaining jobs that utilize them. Vocational students may benefit from their courses in their home lives or leisure activities rather than (or as well as) on the job. These educators think that the only test that should be applied to education, including vocational subjects, is how well the students learn—that neither the costs of teaching nor the economic outcomes for the students should be considered.

Even if the development of occupational skills is accepted as the basic purpose of vocational education, as federal policy and the career educators assume, recognition must be given to the existence of multiple or joint purposes, which sometimes compete with each other.[12] If basic literacy, reduced dropout rates, good work habits, improved social adjustment, greater equality of opportunity and outcomes, educational satisfaction, or lower delinquency and truancy rates are encouraged by vocational education, or if vocational education is peculiarly suited to disadvantaged youth, then separate grounds for supporting the curriculum exist, quite apart from the labor market performance of graduates.[13] It has been suggested that all of the possible objectives of vocational education can be covered under four headings: efficiency, consumption, equity, and socialization.[14]

Beyond the conceptual problems lie the difficulties of methodology and data. Without enumerating these here, it can be said that the effect has been to leave no study thoroughly acceptable. After an exhaustive review of the major studies, Ernst Stromsdorfer, author of the National Planning Association study, recently concluded: "Unfortunately, for a variety of reasons, each of these studies is flawed." [15]

The state of current research and evaluation of vocational education may be gauged from the heartfelt reply of a Wyoming vocational educator to a questionnaire on the problems of occupational education in the 1970s. The pressing need, he wrote, is for "empirical evidence that will prove beyond a shadow of a doubt that our traditional occupational education programs are superior to the so-called academic and general programs insofar as they relate to getting a job, finding a job, keeping a job, being promoted on the job, etc." [16]

But the difficult task is to establish vocational education as the *cause* of observed differences in performance. Variations among students in attitudes, motivation, and other characteristics not subject to precise measurement may invalidate control groups and bias results in favor of vocational education. Better performance of vocational graduates in the labor market may reflect employers' prejudices about credentials rather than the skills brought to the job. Finally, students must be followed up for a number of years after graduation in order to reach a judgment, but it is difficult then to know how much of the variation is attributable to post–high school education or training. Despite the hazards, researchers have boldly sought to provide answers to guide policy.

The findings of a large number of studies will be reviewed here, with emphasis on the labor market performance of vocational and other high school graduates who go to work without taking further vocational education in the first years after school. Some estimates of the proportion in this category can be made. The Ohio State University longitudinal study of full-time employed males fourteen to twenty-four years old who had had twelve years of schooling indicates that 41 percent of whites and 31 percent of blacks obtained some formal vocational education within the first five years after leaving high school.[17]

Another way to look at the subject is to examine the senior class in high school. According to Project Talent data on the 1960 senior class, almost four-fifths of the boys and three-fifths of the girls had either higher education or further vocational education within five years of graduation. The evidence is that these proportions have risen since 1960, especially for girls.[18] If one is testing the effect of vocational versus academic or general high school education, excluding the influence of higher education and postsecondary vocational education, then no more than 25 to 30 percent of the graduating high school class is to be examined. The performance of school dropouts, 15 to 20 percent of the age group, is not considered here except incidentally.

The large body of research on a variety of subjects—the utilization of vocational education on the job, earnings, unemployment, job satisfaction, cost-effectiveness and cost-benefit ratios, the effects on dropping out, and the pursuit of further education—will now be reviewed specifically. Too little data exists to examine such attitudinal issues as job security, job status, nonwork satisfaction, socialization, and other noneconomic or nonmonetary variables. It should be noted that the effects of the Vocational Education Act of 1968 are hardly touched on in the studies covered below.

Utilization of Vocational Education on the Job

The experts differ about how specialized vocational education actually has been in the United States. Their disagreement reflects the diversity of programs from place to place and even within large cities.[19] But it cannot be denied that the broad program divisions commonly used (agriculture, health, technical, office, trade and industry) have given a specific focus to training.

Two tests may be applied to the vocational graduate. Are his first and subsequent jobs in the field for which he trained? Did he get jobs at skill levels consistent with his high school training? More research has been done on the former issue, although the latter may be the more important one.

Field of training. The relation between the field of training and the job is defined differently from study to study, and there is disagreement on the significance of a student's entering an occupation in, say, manufacturing when he has graduated from an agriculture program. Some say that it makes no difference to the nation or the student which industry he enters if he is suitably placed in terms of status and earnings. Others point to a misallocation of vocational education funds if a substantial proportion of graduates are placed in jobs outside their field of training. Thus, the Fleischmann Commission of New York, criticizing the vocational courses of the state's high schools, declared: "No matter how interesting or innovative vocational programs are, if graduates cannot find employment related to their training, that training must be considered useless." [20]

Official records compiled by the Office of Education show that the vast majority of vocational graduates enter training-related jobs, but individual studies report lower percentages. Some studies, particularly Max Eninger's, find that those who enter training-related jobs do better than other vocational graduates in earnings, job security, and job satisfaction, but others disagree. [21]

An extensive analysis of training-relatedness has been made by Gerald Somers, based on a follow-up of a national sample of vocational graduates of 1966 for the first three years after graduation. [22] Just over half of the high school vocational graduates took first jobs that were completely different or only slightly related to their field of training, while less than one-fifth of post–high school and less than one-fourth of junior college vocational graduates were in this category.

The specific vocational program influenced the degree of training-relatedness of the job. Health studies led to the highest proportion of graduates in training-related jobs and agriculture to the lowest. As time passed, subsequent jobs for graduates at every level, and from virtually every program area, diverged from the field of training. Regression analyses established that the level of school, the specific program, the socioeconomic status of the job, and sex are the most important variables in explaining whether the job was related to training. At the high school level, the student's grade point average also assumed statistical significance. [23]

Somers's study reveals that only a fraction of entry jobs utilize specific high school vocational training and provide job satisfaction. These are typically of relatively high socioeconomic status and are obtained by boys with high grade averages.

The shift from the area of training into better-paid fields has been called a rational response. [24] Garth Mangum indicates that the enrollment in many high school vocational courses is so far in excess of the average number of job openings in the fields of training that a regular oversupply would result if many enrollees did not drop out before graduation and many graduates did not take jobs outside their field of training. [25]

Further obstacles to establishing a high degree of correspondence between specific vocational studies and first jobs are: (1) the lack of vocational motives in some students' course choices, (2) the haphazard way that local education agencies decide on course offerings, (3) the inadequacy or inappropriateness of vocational education in particular programs, (4) the lack of local labor market information for planning, and (5) the desire of states to attract new industries by offering a trained labor supply.[26] Somers concludes that ". . . the particular program area was of little significance in the student's post-graduation employment and earnings. . . . The findings support the view that general training in vocational skills is to be preferred to specific training, that clusters of job skills in vocational training are to be preferred to single job skills." [27]

The current enthusiasm for the cluster approach, found widely in Europe as well as in this country, should not conceal the difficulty of defining clusters of job skills that are both usable and sufficiently different from the old program areas.[28] The German Confederation of Trade Unions (DGB), commenting on the current desire of the education authorities to impart broad vocational skills, observed that ". . . the problem of related trades is very difficult to resolve . . . the choice is made on the basis of confused criteria and it is doubtful whether they are very efficient. . . ."[29] Nor is it encouraging to read American documents, which list occupational clusters that seem barely different from existing programs. While the successful adoption of the cluster approach may reduce some of the discussion of training-relatedness in vocational education, it seems likely that issues of fact and interpretation will simply be transferred from the program area to the cluster. The need for planning according to labor market demand is not diminished by the switch to clusters.

Skill level of entry job. If the greater cost per student of vocational education over other high school education is to be justified,[30] the vocational graduate should qualify for a higher-level entry job, advance more rapidly, and have greater job satisfaction than the matched nonvocational graduate. If vocational education is regarded primarily as a method of learning or a means of instilling good work habits, less concern may be shown with the type of work entered, but it must be asked whether cheaper learning methods might not be equally effective and at the same time produce the same or a better distribution of jobs and earnings for vocational graduates.

Few studies directly compare vocational graduates with other graduates on the criterion of the skill level of entry jobs. One survey of nine northeastern urban communities concluded that there was no significant difference among the graduates of the three curricula in broadly measured skill levels, except for a tendency of vocational graduates to find jobs in manufacturing while the academic and general graduates gravitated toward white-collar jobs.[31] The study noted that there was a greater discrepancy between the jobs desired and the jobs obtained by graduates of each curriculum than there was among the actual jobs obtained by the graduates of the three curricula.

Several studies have examined the jobs entered by vocational graduates without a comparison to other high school graduates and have found that a disquieting proportion of vocational graduates enter unskilled or semiskilled jobs requiring little or no prior training.[32] In fact, Somers's national sample of high school vocational graduates showed a fairly high proportion still in such jobs three years after their 1966 graduation. (By 1969 labor markets had tightened and many in the sample had acquired additional education and training.) Substantial variation occurred in job status, according to the specific vocational course in high school. Significantly, the proportions in low-skilled jobs were considerably smaller both at the outset and three years later among graduates of post–high school and junior college vocational programs than among those who had only graduated from high school.[33]

There is a need for a longitudinal national study of various types of high school graduates' first and early jobs, with a detailed occupational classification system revealing skill levels. It would be interesting to test whether changing business conditions affect the entry jobs of graduates of the various curricula in different ways, as the National Planning Association suggests is true of earnings differentials.[34]

It may assist the analysis of vocational graduates if one examines the entire population of high school graduates who go directly to work and do not enter further, full-time education in the first decade of their working lives. Advocates of career education (or expanded vocational education) usually assume that there are a large number of job vacancies for high school graduates with skills. They argue that the production of additional jobs in the right fields and places will automatically open up career ladders to those who might otherwise be unemployed or trapped in low-level jobs. But even a cursory examination of the labor market situation of the young suggests that in fact there is a limited demand for skilled high school graduates.

The annual Special Labor Force Reports of the Bureau of Labor Statistics has a series, *Employment of High School Graduates and Dropouts,* which enables one to analyze for 1959–1971 the full-time jobs held in October by the graduates of the previous June—a reasonable approximation of first jobs.[35] Also, through the data in appendix table C of these reports, a form of longitudinal survey is presented of the jobs held one, two, and three or more years following graduation by high school graduates not attending any type of full-time school. No breakdowns are available by high school curriculum.

Over the entire period 1959–71, the data show a great stability in the small proportion of male high school graduates whose first jobs can be classified as utilizing their school-acquired occupational skills. In fact, it is difficult to label as much as 20 percent of the first jobs as requiring any vocational education at all. The categories of professional, technical, and kindred; managers, officials, and proprietors; craftsmen; foremen and kindred; farmers and farm managers; and the higher-level clerical, sales, and service jobs accounted for about one-fifth of the male entry jobs in an average year. On the other hand, over half of the male graduates took jobs as laborers or operatives each year; at most these jobs require brief on-the-job training. Even higher proportions of dropouts and minority graduates were in these unskilled jobs. In the thirteen-year period, 1959–1971, the unemployment rates of high school graduates ranged from a low of 7.4 percent in 1965 to a high of 19.1 percent in 1963; rates were under 10 percent during four years and 14 percent or over during five years. It appears that the job distribution for high school graduates was more adverse in years of economic recession than in years of "baby boom" impact. Support for some of these conclusions over a more limited period is found in the Ohio State longitudinal survey.[36]

These general findings are duplicated in several studies of individual cities. In New York City a survey of entry jobs in five major industries revealed a substantial number of jobs with no opportunity to utilize school skills. Indeed, there was a stated preference by employers for learning on the job or in evening classes.[37] A small role for traditional vocational education is also indicated in excellent community labor market analyses of Detroit and Kalamazoo.[38] Employers in the survey of nine northeastern cities likewise had need for few vocational high school graduates.[39]

From the annual Special Labor Force Reports one also learns that very little upward occupational mobilitiy occurs in the first years after high school graduation. It is only after they have been out of high school for several years that young men make sizeable shifts toward more skilled occupations. Age, work experience, additional on-the-job training, or part-time study gradually open to some youths the positions that vocational education is unable to obtain for its graduates. Currently, many mature workers (twenty-five to sixty-five) with no more than a high school education have remained in unskilled or semiskilled jobs. Some have advanced along a short career ladder to craftsmen or foremen; only a few have gone beyond.[40] This, then, is the present-day labor market for high school graduates. (And it is slightly worse for those with less than a high school education.)

Contributing to the situation is the fact that teenage workers have high unemployment rates, reflecting a shortfall in the total number of jobs (as well as high turnover rates) that has existed even when there has been no baby boom effect and when the demand for labor generally has been high. A great many of the jobs available to high school graduates or dropouts are low-paid, dead-end, or temporary, and they are also sought as part-time jobs by students. The type of skilled, well-paid work extolled by the vocational educators is not available to most high school graduates, whatever their curriculum.[41]

In explaining the failure of a large number of vocational graduates to enter jobs at suitable skill levels, weight must also be given to deficiencies of both vocational programs and their students:[42]

• It is unfair to charge vocational education with the employment record of students who enroll for nonvocational purposes. Homemaking, agriculture, and typing are the leading programs for such students.

• Some vocational students are adequately prepared for the technical side of their jobs but are deficient in other aspects. Thus, large employers in the New York City area have complained at conferences that typists meet the entry standard for typing but cannot pass the seventh-grade reading and spelling tests—surely a reasonable minimum for a twelfth-grade graduate!

• Vocational courses are offered for some low-level jobs that do not require preentry skill training. For example, hospitals not only prefer to do their own brief on-the-job training for nurse's aide but actually avoid the graduates of the high school vocational course because it predisposes girls to boredom and poor performance on the job.[43] The best that graduates of such courses can do is to get training-related unskilled jobs; otherwise they enter unskilled work in other fields.

• Some vocational graduates do not need their skills on the job, but their access to entry jobs is favorably influenced by their vocational schooling. It should not be a matter for congratulation that some employers prefer vocational graduates over others for their unskilled jobs. Nor should it be cause for celebration that apprenticeship programs sometimes choose vocational graduates—and then make them repeat all of their high school courses.[44] This problem arises, in part, from serious gaps between the conceptions held by vocational educators of the nature and structure of job skills and the reality and variety of the actual jobs (influenced as they are by employers' propensity to overstate skill and education requirements, the size of firm, trade union rules, licensing requirements, and market forces).[45]

• The vocational course may be poorly designed to meet industry's needs or may not actually teach what it purports to teach.[46] A representative of the National Tool, Die and Precision Machinery Association told a Department of Labor conference on apprenticeship research in October 1971 that the four-year high school course in machine shops "is of virtually no use to us."

• Some students do not absorb vocational skills and have no more to offer employers than similar nonvocational graduates.

• Some courses may not prepare students for actual openings in the local labor market, thus forcing them to take unskilled jobs.

• Vocational students in rural areas may take courses locally that do not prepare them for the jobs available in the areas to which they move.

• For some of the better jobs open to high school graduates, employers prefer academic to vocational preparation. A California vocational educator complains that "we strive to provide specific vocational training and then find that the employer is perfectly happy to take a liberal arts graduate and give him on-the-job training. . . ."[47] One researcher reports that job supervisors give academic graduates higher ratings than vocational graduates on the same jobs.[48]

• Some courses prepare students for jobs requiring a specific skill, but often the jobs pay so poorly that unskilled jobs at higher pay are taken in preference.

• Some courses are offered at the high school level, but the actual jobs are only open to those with additional education.

Even if all the faults of vocational education and the deficiencies of its students were corrected, it is likely that many high school graduates would still enter the unskilled or semiskilled ranks. The availability of older, more educated, or experienced workers for the more skilled jobs, the desire of some employers to do their own training, and the limited possibilities for promotion in small firms combine to make many types of vocational education irrelevant to the available entry jobs.[49]

Earnings of Graduates

The benefits of vocational education are, to many, synonymous with monetary advantage. More than any other indicator, differences in wage rates or earnings between vocational and other high school graduates entering the labor market full-time are cited as the critical factor. Earnings are a more comprehensive measure than wage rates, since average earnings reflect hours of work, overtime, and unemployment as well as the wage rate.

Some studies have registered a wage rate or earnings differential in favor of the vocational graduate, but others have discerned little or no difference.[50] Even those who find an initial advantage for the high school vocational graduate discover that the difference tends to disappear in six to ten years (for reasons that are only guessed at).[51]

In its recent work with unpublished data from the national longitudinal survey conducted by Ohio State University, the National Planning Association has uncovered possible cyclical effects of the relationship between earnings and types of educational course.[52] The NPA analysis of out-of-school male youth does not deal exclusively with high school graduates, but the regressions are controlled for educational attainment. They show no significant earnings advantage for vocational curriculum students over those in the college preparatory, commercial, or general curricula in 1966. But two years later, a statistically significant advantage for vocational students appears. It is said to be linked to minor cyclical movements in the unemployment rates of the various groups.

The reported gap in earnings in 1968 as compared with 1966 may reflect fuller work weeks and more overtime pay—factors particularly pertinent to vocational graduates employed in manufacturing industries. Or the larger number of available jobs, upgrading, and rising wage rates may have affected vocational graduates more than others. A final possibility, not to be ruled out until further cyclical readings are taken of the same sample, is that two years of additional experience in the labor market was more favorable to vocational graduates than to others. This revelation of possible cyclical effects raises the interesting question of which period should be chosen to judge the economic return on society's and the individual's investment in education.

On balance, it can be said that an earnings advantage of high school vocational graduates over others has not yet been firmly established. Does it matter which vocational program is followed? A study in three northern cities showed no statistically significant difference in earnings among graduates of different vocational programs (including the commercial program) in the first or sixth year after graduation from a high school vocational program. These results held for the six-year average as well.[53] But in regard to a study still in process, Irwin Herrnstadt and Morris Horowitz have written that "tentatively there seems to be some relative advantage to cooperative work study, at least as measured in terms of wage gains and occupational stability, over a five and one half years period, beginning with mid-1966."[54]

So far as minority youth are concerned, male vocational high school graduates appear to surpass male nonvocational graduates in earnings and other
aspects of employment, but the reverse is true for females.[55] But minority
vocational graduates fare less well than whites with the same educational
background.[56] Scattered evidence suggests that disadvantaged vocational
graduates, white and black, have slightly higher earnings than comparable
graduates from the general curriculum.[57]

Somers's study comparing the earnings of vocational graduates of different school levels indicates that junior college graduates consistently start
with a wage advantage (and continue to have one) over high school and
post–high school vocational graduates; the latter have no advantage over
high school graduates. As regards earnings, higher schooling level, favorable region, urban setting, and good school grades were found to be more
important for high earnings than the particular field of training.[58]

It is significant that earnings levels vary more locally and regionally than
the costs of providing vocational education. Cost-benefit analyses will therefore show that certain locations are more rewarding than others as sites of
vocational programs. Yet this factor cannot be given full weight; the residential patterns of potential students must have an influence on the location
of a school, even if graduates migrate from the area.[59]

Unemployment Rates of Graduates

A common finding has been that vocational graduates find their first jobs
more quickly and subsequently experience fewer and briefer spells of unemployment than others with a high school education.[60] The Ohio national
longitudinal survey reports, however, that those who had completed a vocational program in high school did not have a better unemployment record in
1966 than academic or commercial graduates, although they had less unemployment than general curriculum graduates.[61] Unpublished data for 1968
from the same survey indicate that *employment* rates were higher for those
who had been enrolled in a vocational curriculum in high school than for
those in academic or general curricula. But when regression models are
applied which control for socioeconomic characteristics, no statistically significant differences appear between vocational and other students.[62] Since
this is a well-executed national survey with a low nonresponse rate, its negative findings for vocational education deserve attention.

A national survey of high school graduates of technical-industrial programs found that those who entered training-related jobs had greater em-

ployment security than other graduates.[63] Another national survey reported that high school vocational graduates had higher unemployment rates than junior college or postsecondary vocational graduates.[64]

Two institutional factors may ease the transition to full-time work for vocational graduates in comparison with other students. To a considerable extent, vocational graduates arrange for their first postschool jobs before school ends, often with the employer for whom they have been working while in school.[65] Among high school vocational graduates in Somers's national sample of 1966, those in distributive, trade and industry, and agriculture programs had a higher proportion of prearranged entry jobs than those in technical, office, and health programs.[66] Cooperative education and other work-experience plans also foster prompt entry into jobs. A study of Detroit high school graduates of 1963 showed that 95 percent of those in cooperative education but only 79 percent of other graduates obtained entry jobs promptly; two years later, however, the initial advantage of the cooperative education graduates had disappeared.[67]

A second factor in the employment records of vocational graduates is the greater placement assistance available to them in schools through the official service and individual teachers. It is true that informal sources (such as parents and friends) account for most first jobs at all educational levels, and for all students. But the school's placement service is more important for vocational graduates than for others.[68]

Researchers point to the unreliability of most raw data on unemployment, the lack of proper control groups to take account of the differences in group characteristics, and the difficulties of interpreting lower vocational unemployment rates as evidence of the value of the specific skills taught in school.[69] It is not clear that the alleged lower unemployment rates among vocational graduates reflect the *content* of vocational education as distinguished from the *characteristics* of those selected for vocational education and its auxiliary services.

Job Satisfaction of Graduates

The assumption is often made that those who enter jobs for which they have been prepared feel more satisfied and exhibit lower turnover rates. To the extent that one can rely on the opinions of individuals, it appears that high school vocational education graduates are somewhat more satisfied than other high school graduates, but one researcher reports that the differences are not statistically significant.[70]

It has been found that among technical and industrial vocational graduates, those who enter training-related jobs are more satisfied than others.[71]
Comparisons of vocational graduates of various educational levels show
that at each stage, vocational graduates are more apt to be satisfied than
dissatisfied. Training-relatedness and the socioeconomic level of the job are
significant explanatory variables for the entire sample, but not for high
school graduates separately.[72]

School Dropout Rates

If vocational education prevented dropping out and its attendant problems,
there would be external benefits.[73] But studies are inconclusive about the
extent to which vocational education, as distinguished from other types of
education, can serve this purpose and whether it can provide greater net
benefits than other methods of prevention.[74] Moreover, dropout rates for
vocational programs seem to be higher than those for other high school programs, even when students are controlled for ability and socioeconomic
status.[75]

Somers's 1966 national sample suggests that the records of vocational
schools may overstate the number of dropouts because those who transfer
to another program or geographical area may be listed as dropouts.[76] His
analysis also shows (and this is confirmed by other findings) that in some
vocational programs those classified as dropouts had a wage position superior to that of graduates. Questions are therefore raised about the optimum
length of vocational courses and the economic importance of actually com-
pleting a specific vocational course.[77] Some authorities recommend that
occupational certificates be given to vocational dropouts who achieve minimal competency, both as a signal to employers and as an inducement to
dropouts to return to school for a diploma.[78] Others believe that graduation
may actually be less important than educators and public policy makers
believe.[79]

Advanced Education

The fear that enrollment in high school vocational programs may deflect able
students from the pursuit of higher education has lost much of its force in
the last decade. As postsecondary technical-vocational courses mushroom,
community and junior colleges blanket the nation, and open admissions
policies are announced by colleges, vocational graduates are opting for
further education instead of immediate work almost as frequently as other
high school graduates. Christopher Jencks finds the type of high school cur-

riculum a minor factor in the decision to attend college.[80]

New York City's experience illustrates the general trends that are reinforced there by the relatively high demand for educated personnel, the superior background and ability of vocational students over those in the general curriculum, and the adoption of open admissions by the City University of New York. In 1963 only 12.7 percent of the graduates of public vocational high schools went on directly to full-time further study, but by 1970 the figure stood at 67.0 percent.[81] Another 15.6 percent of vocational school graduates were accepted but did not enroll, 3.4 percent enrolled part-time, and 1.7 percent applied but were not accepted for further education. In all, only 5.6 percent of the 1970 vocational graduates are known *not* to have applied for advanced education in 1970.

The further education record of New York City graduates with vocational diplomas was far superior to that of graduates with general or commercial diplomas, while those with technical diplomas did better or as well as academic graduates. The academic schools as a whole sent 75.0 percent of their 1970 graduates to further education; another 4.8 percent were accepted but did not enroll, 1.6 percent enrolled part-time, and 1.2 percent were not accepted. Some 13.3 percent did not apply, almost twice the percentage for vocational school graduates.

The type of further education elected distinguishes vocational from academic graduates more than the proportions continuing their education beyond high school. While more than three-fifths of the New York City vocational graduates chose two-year colleges, only one-fourth of the academic high school graduates enrolled in this form of higher education.

The progress nationally has been slower but still substantial. Project Talent found that 21.8 percent of the boys and 13.4 percent of the girls who were seniors in vocational programs in 1960 went to college within five years of graduation. For seniors in commercial or business programs, the percentages were 44.3 of the boys and 15.9 of the girls.[82] A national study of three classes of trade and industry graduates of the late 1950s and early 1960s disclosed that 15 percent went to college and 42 percent had some kind of formal post–high school education.[83]

A more recent national survey, by Project Metro, of selected urban secondary vocational programs indicates that a fourth of graduates from both the vocational and general education curricula proceed to college, along with 70 percent of graduates of the academic curriculum.[84] Controlled regression analysis of unpublished data from the 1968 Ohio State national longitudinal survey of young males indicates that the academic curriculum student, whether graduate or dropout, is more likely to be exposed to college education than the vocational student.[85] Vocational graduates choose both the two-year college and terminal postsecondary vocational education to a greater extent than academic graduates, but not necessarily more than general curriculum graduates. More than half of the vocational graduates of 1966 (followed up for three years in Somers's national survey) had some type of additional education by 1969. Thirty percent proceeded directly to further studies from high school. Those who entered two-year vocational courses in community or junior colleges showed a high propensity to transfer to four-year colleges.[86]

Some vocational graduates attend public or private postsecondary technical or commercial schools that offer terminal education. Some 7,000 private schools offer courses to 1.5 million students, mostly after high school graduation. As an alternative to expanding public vocational education in high schools, the Fleischmann Commission of New York has recommended that the state government offer vouchers to eleventh- and twelfth-grade students wishing to attend one of the state's 275 private vocational and technical schools.[87] If this voucher system is established, the operations of these schools and the outcomes for their students should be evaluated and compared with public institutions that offer similar courses.

Whether the trend toward higher education for vocational graduates is welcomed or regretted depends on one's attitude toward education and jobs.[88] It is clear, however, that because of this trend additional support should be given to flexible high school vocational curricula permitting (1) wide options to be exercised both in jobs and further study, (2) a cluster approach to subject matter, (3) a comprehensive school setting, and (4) a heavy stress on academic subjects (and remedial work). Along with high entrance rates to New York's open admissions system have come high dropout rates, which in many cases is due to inadequate preparation in basic communication and computation skills. If vocational courses become primarily feeders to further education, the curriculum will have to be reassessed.

Economic Considerations

Cost-effectiveness and cost-benefit analyses could be useful tools in evaluating various educational and training systems in relation to their costs. These methods could also be used to suggest which educational investments should be expanded or contracted. But the limited number of studies of this nature, few of them national in scope, and the unresolved conceptual, methodological, and statistical problems led Ernst Stromsdorfer to conclude recently: "It is thus still unclear, except at the most gross level of analysis, just what are the private and social costs and returns of vocational educa- tion."[89] Since Stromsdorfer has been closely associated with many economic analyses of vocational and other forms of education at the high school level and has interpreted the work of others, his words carry weight.

There was great hope that his analysis for the National Planning Associa- tion of the unpublished benefit data from the Ohio national longitudinal sur- vey, coupled with the cost data used in several previous analyses, would give a definitive answer about high school vocational education. But he found only that vocational education shows "a small effect on earnings vis- à-vis the secondary academic and general curriculums."[90] This is true both overall and with analyses of individual vocational skills. While he stated that "vocational education apparently yields positive returns to students," he admitted that "no clear judgment can be made as to the amount of resources to shift from the academic and general to the vocational curriculum."[91]

Stromsdorfer, reworking other studies, has compared high school voca- tional education with junior college and postsecondary vocational-technical programs. Terminal postsecondary vocational-technical schooling, usually a one-year course, "pays off" for secondary academic graduates but not for secondary vocational graduates. Economic efficiency considerations seem to indicate that society should not invest in the latter educational sequence.[92] But even if further studies taking account of omitted noneconomic and addi- tional economic benefits show unfavorable results, social and political con- siderations may support the investment in postsecondary vocational-tech- nical education for secondary vocational graduates.

Somers found that under the existing organization of schools and jobs, junior college vocational education pays off better than high school or post- secondary vocational education. But he also found that not all junior college vocational programs pay off to individuals. Moreover, some programs at each school level are worthwhile and important to society, apart from indi- vidual rewards.[93] Stromsdorfer concluded that "the *average* mix of skills and courses taught in the junior college yields a higher rate of return than the *average* mix of skills and courses taught in post-secondary vocational-tech- nical institutions."[94]

There is considerable evidence of the superiority of vocational education in the junior or community college setting for both vocational and nonvocational high school graduates.[95] But it should not be assumed that junior college programs are faultless.[96] The superior performance in the labor market of junior college graduates may reflect differences in ability and background which have not been controlled in studies. In addition, junior college courses are more responsive to the labor market, operate at a higher level than secondary courses, and are relatively scarce for the occupations that require postsecondary but less-than-college training.[97]

Since many students at the lower school levels are not able or willing to attend a junior college, the case cannot be made that all vocational education should be delayed until junior college. But for those with options, the postponement appears profitable. These conclusions are offered as only one input for educational planners and, as Alice Rivlin has pointed out, there is need for caution in using rate-of-return estimates.[98]

A relatively unexplored subject is the direct comparison of marginal cost-benefit ratios for youths trained in vocational schools and for matched groups of apprentices or trainees in industry who did not take vocational courses. Here the additional social issue arises of who should pay for training.[99]

It is, of course, a serious fault of cost-benefit analysis that it tends to play down or ignore altogether the educational, social, psychological, and nonwage costs and benefits.[100] Even economists are not likely to be fully satisfied with cost-benefit analyses of educational systems for some time to come, and it may be still longer before educational planners will be ready to accept such results as a reliable guide to complex decision making.[101]

Conclusions
This review has failed to satisfy the desire of the Wyoming vocational educator mentioned earlier for decisive and irrefutable evidence of the labor market advantage to high school vocational graduates. The most recent findings in the National Planning Association's report, based on the best national data available, give but weak support in this direction.[102]

Researchers still have considerable difficulty in separating the effects of the particular type of education from certain characteristics of, and influences on, the students. And follow-up studies find it hard to control for subsequent formal and informal vocational skill training which may be more significant than the type of high school education. Above all, the studies to date do not indicate how much change should be made in various types of education to reach optimum efficiency and to achieve other educational objectives.

As this review has shown, a substantial number of high school vocational graduates enter unskilled jobs with little promise of further advancement. And vocational education does not seem to be the most effective means of redistributing the good jobs to disadvantaged youth; other more direct methods, such as opening places in apprenticeship programs, might be cheaper and yield better results.[103] One can explain American youth unemployment in terms of the structure of the labor market better than in terms of the lack of vocational skills on the part of the new entrants.

Young labor market entrants in Europe take similar unskilled jobs at an earlier age, without benefit of senior high school education or vocational skill courses, in the expectation that employers will do whatever on-the-job training is required. A recent report by the British Schools Council, *Careers Education in the 1970's*—reflecting the views of educators, representatives of business and labor, and government officials involved in youth employment and training—argues for a good general education rather than vocational education during compulsory schooling. While several grounds are offered, two points are particularly relevant. The report states that "much so-called vocational education in schools is less than truthful because it is offered to children who will undertake unskilled jobs." And "to spend much time in school on teaching industrial or commercial skills closely related to specific employment is to do badly what others can do well. For some time large firms have preferred to train their own employees. . . ."[104]

A statement by the distinguished Swedish educator, Torsten Husén, is also pertinent:

As late as the end of the 1950's, many spokesmen of business and industry contended that the school ought to put prolonged compulsory school attendance to better account by providing marketable vocational training, especially the kind that could be useful in local economies. Today, however, the more progressive members of the business community warmly endorse a solid general education, with particular emphasis on the formation of good study and work habits, as being more essential than the inculcation of specific trade know-how.[105]

It is not irrelevant that these countries have for the most part experienced labor shortages and little youth unemployment since the end of World War II. Perhaps our heavy emphasis on improving the occupational qualifications of the least educated portion of our youth has been a misguided approach to deficiencies in the level and structure of demand.

Two questions are thus raised by the comparative experience: how much of the added education given to young people and the added expense of vocational education is justified by the outcome for graduates and society, and how should the costs of such skill training be divided among society, the students, and the employers?

It may be argued that it is unfair to judge the performance of American vocational education on the basis of studies which do not take account either of the most recent improvements stemming from the Vocational Education Act amendments of 1968 or the innovative proposals of educators for further progress.[106] Substantial reductions in cost for vocational programs vis-à-vis academic ones may be achieved by the shift from individual high school programs to regional or area skill centers, elimination or reduction of the the least productive programs, adoption of the "cluster of skills" approach, substitution of industrial arts for more specific skill courses, greater reliance on work-experience and cooperative education arrangements, and heavier use of employer premises for the practical side of traditional vocational education.

If traditional high school vocational education can be strengthened, should not its potential for giving every high school student a marketable skill be recognized? The answer depends partly on the nature of the future labor market for high school graduates. We assume that the group that will go directly to work without further education will be a distinct minority. Most of these young people will be restricted to the least desirable entry jobs, which require no prior skills. For many, basic literacy and good work attitudes may be more important for employment than occupational skills; an increasing number of employers are looking for these qualities, rather than traditional vocational skills.

A nationwide forecast of the educational needs of new entrants to the labor force in 1967–75 projected that high school vocational education would be sufficient for only 8 percent of the available jobs.[107] A more optimistic view is suggested by the National Planning Association in its analysis of the number of jobs that will be available by 1980 in occupations that require no more than a high school education for which vocational high schools offer courses.[108] The NPA study is misleading, however, since the total number of job vacancies that require only high school education will not be open as *entry* jobs. Many of these jobs will, in fact, be held by older, experienced workers who are high school graduates or less. For the few entry jobs, vocational graduates will be competing with other entrants.

To be sure, there are several fields in which the number of high school vocational students might be increased with a satisfactory employment outcome.[109] But it is not clear that all vocational students presently in school or likely to be enrolled can be accommodated in programs which will place them at the proper skill level.

It is a myth to suggest that most high school graduates who go directly to work could be placed on a real career ladder if they only had vocational education in high school. The American idea that it is important for every youth to be given skills so he can compete for a limited number of openings is damaging to the large number who must fail in the competition and is wasteful of resources that might be better used to improve the employability of young people in other ways—not by giving them occupational skills they cannot use.

While the cluster approach to vocational education is an improvement, it by no means eliminates the basic problem: the labor market can absorb relatively few skilled high school graduates at their proper level. This situation prevailed under the tight labor market of the late 1960s and appears likely to continue even when the number of young entrants declines under demographic and educational influences.

It is the structure and level of demand for young workers that is the problem. It may be possible to alter the nature of labor demand, but it will require an effort independent of measures to improve the youth labor supply. The emphasis of career education and vocational education advocates, like the Manpower program advocates of the 1960s, has been on improving the supply of labor, with little attention to the demand side.[110] Just as Manpower programs in the 1970s have become sensitive to the quantity and quality of jobs, so vocational education must take a hard look at the job situation for those who do not go beyond high school. A false dichotomy has been erected by some vocational educators between the demands of the labor market and the occupational skills needed or desired by the individual; the latter is dependent on the former.

Reservations about traditional vocational education also arise from the persistent difficulties of staffing, fighting vested interests and inertia, keeping courses technologically up to date, obtaining employer support, and making the total curriculum responsive to labor market trends.[111] Interestingly enough, these are precisely the problems reported to the author in several countries with highly developed vocational education programs, Belgium, France, and, to a lesser extent, Holland. Nor is apprenticeship free of these defects. It is worth noting that in the advanced European countries there is a growing tendency to assign practical training to the industrial setting and theoretical education to the schools, whether the base is an apprenticeship system or formal vocational education. This is part of the trend toward an increased school component in total training, the drive to integrate vocational and academic education, and the movement for lifelong or recurrent education.[112]

Sweden, another country with a well-developed vocational education program at the secondary level and virtually no apprenticeships, is more satisfied with its operations. Since 1971 vocational courses have been offered in comprehensive high schools as a practical or technical line, organized in twenty-three occupational clusters. The emphasis is on broad general education in the vocational courses with a reliance on postsecondary education or on-the-job experience for specific skill training. Some complaints from employers have arisen about this new approach because graduates who enter work directly are inadequately prepared.

It is anticipated that vocational students soon will comprise 40 percent of the total upper secondary enrollment, which, in turn, will account for 90 percent of the age group. The Swedish ability to absorb vocational graduates in the fields for which they are trained is, of course, related to persistent labor shortages and reliance on foreign workers to fill a large number of low-level and routine jobs.

Swedish employers, having participated actively in the design of curriculum and courses, and having offered their premises for some of the practical training, accept graduates at an appropriate skill level. Trade unions also participate fully. The equal and cooperative roles of both education and labor market authorities at all levels of government minimize the problems of curriculum responsiveness. Considerable movement of teaching staff between schools and industry is provided. Vocational school premises are used extensively by the labor market training programs, and in other ways the two programs are integrated and noncompetitive. There are opportunities for dropouts and graduates of any level and any type of curriculum to acquire occupational skills. Swedish experience also refutes the idea that vocational education is purely preventive, and labor market training merely corrective, and that an increase in the former may make it possible to reduce the latter.

The advocates of career education and the vocational amendments of 1968 have given the impression that vocational education is inextricably bound to general instruction about, and orientation to, the world of work.[113] Most European countries separate "career" education from the teaching of occupational skills and find it possible to foster one without the other in compulsory education.

The drive for career education in the United States may be hampered by the failure to distinguish between the two aspects. It is possible to press very hard for work orientation studies *without* urging an expanded teaching of occupational skills in high school classes. Among other things, the expectation of career educators that most high school students are ready to make a commitment to a definite career is counter to what we know about occupational choice. One of the chief functions of higher education is to give additional time for maturation and decision making. To repeat what was said earlier, the jobs taken by the vast majority of high school graduates and dropouts who go directly to work should not be confused with careers.

Beyond the general considerations that affect a proposed expansion of traditional vocational education are the factors specific to the several groups of high school students likely to be affected: those in the college preparatory program (50 percent), those in the general curriculum (25 percent), and those in current vocational programs (25 percent).

The Academic Curriculum

It has been established that graduates of four-year and two-year colleges (as well as college dropouts) are at a disadvantage in the labor market if they have no occupational skills. An ability to type, for example, can make a considerable difference to the college graduate with no occupational specialty. But does it follow from this that all college-bound students should be given a marketable skill in high school? The advocates of career education endorse the objective but are vague on the means of accomplishing it.[114] Some educators consider that preparation either for the next stage of education or for work is an adequate achievement for the academic program. But others believe that too many students are under pressure to go to college and that many would feel freer to resist if they could acquire a marketable skill in high school.

It must be recognized that there are two rival approaches to the democratization of education in the United States. One proposes to open higher academic education to all, translating equality of opportunity into equality of outcome. The other seeks to restore a pride in manual skills by diffusing such skills more widely and relieving the pressure on young people to pursue academic studies when their inclinations and abilities lie elsewhere. Something of a compromise is reached in the two-year college that teaches occupational skills and permits transfer to a four-year college.

College-bound youth should be lowest in priority for high school vocational education, considering their white-collar and professional orientation and their need to develop skills in language, mathematics, and analytical thinking. The academic program itself is occupational education for many,[115] and substitution of vocational for academic subjects is contrary to the occupational needs of many college students. Moreover, it can be anticipated that the competitive position of the current type of vocational student will be impaired if a significant number of potential college students are led to seek work right after high school.[116]

From what has been said earlier about the superior offerings, greater variety of courses, and greater economic returns to vocational graduates of junior or community colleges or technical institutes, it would seem more advisable to provide easy transitions to these kinds of expanded and improved forms of vocational education for college dropouts as well as for high school and college graduates than to attempt to give this training to all in high school. Those on the academic track who do not go to college may still be better off to postpone occupational skill training until after graduation. On a voluntary basis, of course, academic students should be free to elect vocational subjects.

The General Curriculum
Not a kind word has been said about the general curriculum, the watered-down academic course, nor should there be. It does not serve its students even passably well. Students in the general curriculum account for two-thirds of high school dropouts. Schools where the general curriculum prevails have the worst attendance, discipline, drug, and crime problems. Their graduates and dropouts have higher unemployment rates than other high

school students, and they have the least desirable jobs.[117] But the situation will not be improved by concealment—for example, by granting all high school graduates the same type of diploma, as New York City has begun to do.

The issue is whether an alternative high school curriculum, heavily vocational, can aid this group, which to a considerable extent encompasses disadvantaged and minority students, especially in large cities. The present situation is not encouraging and raises doubts whether basic literacy can be instilled, let alone occupational skills.[118] As Melvin Barlow puts it, "Students who cannot read or write well, who have failed to achieve occupationally acceptable communications skills including mathematics achievement, and who know little about the world of work and seem to have little inclination to enter the labor force pose special problems for vocational education programs and to vocational educators."[119] Laure Sharp declares that "the disadvantaged high school or post–high school student from a ghetto or rural slum background will often need considerable remedial work in academic subjects before he can succeed in any vocational program. . . ."[120] Dropouts from the general or academic track, as a recent study in Wisconsin indicates, are unwelcome in vocational schools.[121]

A root problem in extending vocational education is the questionable ability of the school to overcome the educational disadvantages brought to the classroom from the family and the community.[122] We may be expecting too much of our schools and placing more blame on them than is warranted.[123] A related question is the elementary schools' policy of sending into the high schools students whose reading, arithmetic, and communication performance has not met elementary school standards. A reconsideration is needed of the place where remedial work should occur—should it be at the level where failure occurs or at some higher level?

Conditions in the urban schools must be radically changed if concepts of good work attitudes and habits are to be transmitted to the students. Classes and lectures devoted to such subjects are completely wasted if the students are aware of disorder in the corridors, illicit trade in the washrooms, unpunished truancy, and diplomas granted simply for attendance. One may ask how automobile workers can be expected to come to work every day after their experience in school, where attendance was occasional, and in the army, where going AWOL was a fairly common experience. It is unrealistic to ignore the general environment and the spirit it communicates. Reliance on lectures or courses to instruct young people in moral virtues seems a weak measure in any case, but such courses surely are hopeless if the full force of everyday life in and out of school contradicts whatever is being taught.

The reported advantages of vocational education as a setting for imparting basic literacy skills should be tested widely and carefully. In fact there is room here for a series of controlled social experiments with different approaches toward basic learning.[124] Such experimental programs would undoubtedly produce better screening processes, with the consequence that some students who are now admitted to vocational or academic programs would be found in need of remedial work.

There is a movement to shorten the total classroom hours of a part of the high school student body in order to ease the passage to adulthood and economic participation. Evidence has been presented that a vocational high school course might be three years instead of four.[125]

A selected group of students from the general curriculum might be directed to classroom vocational education. The rest should be directed toward two variations of vocational education, perhaps beginning in junior high school. These two forms, work-study and cooperative education, are recognized in discussions of career education but are not differentiated as they are here.

Work-study. In a work-study program, the school helps the student to obtain a part-time job, but the job is not necessarily a training situation or one that will develop a skill. The employer has full responsibility for the work side, and the school uses its half day to teach basic subjects which may or may not be related to the job. By participating the school may have a beneficent influence on work conditions and may obtain for this group of students some of the jobs that the more academically qualified currently hold as part-time work for income purposes. At present there are many programs of this type outside of vocational education.[126]

Work-study is best suited to the least able high school students, who may thus be more willing to remain in school, find the transition to full-time work easier, and make a realistic adjustment to the unfavorable labor market situation faced by youth who have no more than a high school education and low academic scores. If the total number of work-study places is inadequate to the need, as it seems likely to be, programs can be initiated by the schools either to create jobs in the school's library, cafeteria, or offices or to secure subcontract jobs at prevailing wages from employers. A major job creation program, with federal financing, may be necessary.

Cooperative education. Although greatly expanded over previous years, cooperative education, in which work and study are related, had only 290,000 participants in 1970, a small fraction of the total vocational education enrollment. A desirable number of cooperative education participants might be 50 percent of all students in high school vocational and general curricula. (Evidence exists that those who might particularly benefit from cooperative education are presently excluded.)[127] Nonprofit and public employers should be canvassed heavily along with private employers.[128] Revision of child labor laws and the cooperation of trade unions as well as massive job creation are required to implement a large-scale cooperative education program.

Cooperative education has cost advantages over traditional vocational education in addition to psychic benefits to school-weary young people. If participants are paid, and if they work summers, the opportunity costs of remaining in school will be reduced. In addition, full-time job placement may be facilitated.[129] The forthcoming study by Herrnstadt and Horowitz should clarify the advantages of this kind of education.

The Vocational Program

The increasing proportion of vocational students who elect higher education might be better served if their programs were more academic or at least remedial in basic communication and computation skills. These students might gain entrance to college more easily and avoid remedial courses there. The idea of teaching academic subjects through vocational means to some of the college-bound should be widely tested through an experimental program. This might be particularly advantageous for those of the college-bound whose capacity for higher academic work is most in doubt, although they and their parents may resent any segregation from the more able academic students.

The least able students in vocational courses, who tend to enter unskilled or semiskilled jobs, might profit from a greater emphasis on basic communication skills and work attitudes. They should be diverted from the more specific skills courses to cooperative education or work-study programs.

Traditional vocational education should be confined to cluster courses that actually permit direct entry into employment above the unskilled or semiskilled level. Nationally, office and business programs appear to be particularly suitable at the high school level, but several other fields, such as dental assistant or technician, also warrant expansion.[130]

The following recommendations emerge from this review:

• The highest priorities in high school education should be the improvement of basic communication and computation skills, inculcation of good work attitudes, and orientation to the work world.

• Work-study and cooperative education programs should be greatly expanded, as a means both of easing the move from school to a full-time job and of making the final years of school more bearable for nonacademic youth. In advocating these programs, one must acknowledge the great difficulty of establishing sufficiently large work-study and cooperative programs through the ordinary employment channels. It seems inevitable that large-scale, federally financed job creation for young people will be needed if this approach is adopted for a substantial segment of the high school population.

• Traditional vocational education in high schools, reorganized along the lines of clusters of skills, should concentrate cn fields in which high school graduates can obtain jobs above the unskilled or semiskilled level. The total enrollment should roughly match the number of local job opportunities, taking account of all sources of entry labor and the dropout rate of vocational students. Occupational skill training should be deferred until high school is completed in the case of students who are preparing for or thinking about entering college.

• Opportunities for academic and vocational high school dropouts and graduates (as well as college dropouts and graduates) to acquire occupational skills at appropriate levels should be integrated with academic education. Area skill centers, private institutes, and junior and community colleges should be further developed to serve these groups in a more organized fashion.

• Carefully controlled experiments should be conducted to test the efficacy of vocational education as a general learning environment.

• There should be further research into and analysis of the outcomes and the costs of various types of education.

Notes

1. Sidney P. Marland, "Career Education: Every Student Headed for a Goal," *American Vocational Journal,* March 1972; *Manpower Report of the President, 1972,* pp. 92–93; "Career Education," *Thrust* [magazine of the Association of California School Administrators] 1, no. 5 (April 1972); Kenneth B. Hoyt et al., *Career Education* (Salt Lake City: Olympus, 1972), p. 2.

2. Ivar Berg, *Education and Jobs: The Great Training Robbery* (Boston: Beacon Press, 1971).

3. Hoyt et al., p. 11; Marland; Grant Venn, *Man, Education and Manpower* (Wash-

ington, D.C.: American Association of School Administrators, 1970); "Career Education."

4. Hoyt et al., pp. 92–95.

5. Sar A. Levitan, G. L. Mangum, and Ray Marshall, *Human Resources and Labor Markets* (New York: Harper & Row, 1972), p. 137; National Planning Association, Center for Priority Analysis, *Policy Issues and Analytical Problems in Evaluating Vocational Education* (Washington, D.C.: U.S. Office of Education, 1972), chap. 3; Gerald G. Somers and J. Kenneth Little, eds., *Vocational Education: Today and Tomorrow* (Madison: University of Wisconsin, Center for Studies in Vocational and Technical Education, 1971), pp. 47–48.

6. U.S. Office of Education, *Vocational Education: Characteristics of Students and Teachers, 1969* (Washington, 1970).

7. National Planning Association, chap. 2, pp. 3–10, tables 2–1, 2–2; John C. Flanagan and Steven M. Jung, *Progress in Education: A Sample Survey (1960–1970)* (Palo Alto: American Institutes for Research, 1971), pp. 22–23.

8. John Shea et al., *Years for Decision,* vol. 1 (Columbus: Ohio State University, Center for Human Resource Research, 1971), p. 20; Herbert S. Parnes et al., *Career Threshholds,* 4 vols. (Columbus: Ohio State University, Center for Human Resource Research, 1969–73), 1: 26; Levitan, Mangum, and Marshall, p. 140; National Planning Association, chap. 12, pp. 11–13; Somers and Little, pp. 270–271.

9. National Planning Association, chap. 3, pp. 16–19; Levitan, Mangum, and Marshall, p. 140; Rubert N. Evans, Garth Mangum, and Otto Pragan, *Education for Employment,* Policy Papers in Human Resources and Industrial Relations, no. 14 (Ann Arbor: University of Michigan, Institute of Labor and Industrial Relations, 1969).

10. National Planning Association, chap. 3, p. 14.

11. Jacob J. Kaufman et al., *An Analysis of the Comparative Costs and Benefits of Vocational versus Academic Education in Secondary Schools* (Philadelphia: Pennsylvania State University, Institute for Research on Human Resources, 1967); Erick L. Lindman, *Financial Support for Vocational Education in the Public Schools* (Washington, D.C.: U.S. Office of Education, Bureau of Research, 1972); Laure M. Sharp and Rebecca Krasnegor, *The Use of Follow-Up Studies in the Evaluation of Vocational Education* (Washington, D.C.: Bureau of Social Science Research, 1966); Ernst W. Stromsdorfer, *Review and Synthesis of Cost-Effectiveness Studies of Vocational and Technical Education* (Columbus: Ohio State University, Center for Vocational and Technical Education, 1972); "Vocational Education," *Journal of Human Resources* 3 (1968), supplement: 38–40; J. Robert Warmbrod, *Review and Synthesis of Research in the Economics of Vocational-Technical Education* (Columbus: Ohio State University, Center for Vocational and Technical Education, 1968); Robert C. Young, W. C. Clive, and B. E. Miles, *Vocational Education Planning* (Columbus: Ohio State University, Center for Vocational and Technical Education, 1972); National Planning Association; Somers and Little.

12. Hoyt et al., p. 95; National Planning Association, app. A; Somers and Little, pp. 222–234; Young, Clive, and Miles, pp. 69–160.

13. Martin Hamburger and Harry E. Wolfson, *1000 Employers Look at Occupational Education,* Occupational Curriculum Project, Report no. 1 (Board of Education of the City of New York, 1969), pp. 124–125, 145–146; Michael K. Taussig, "An Economic Analysis of Vocational Education in the New York City High Schools," *Journal of Human Resources* 3 (1968), supplement: 59–87; U.S. Department of Health, Education, and Welfare, *Vocational Education: The Bridge between Man and His Work,* General Report of the Advisory Council on Vocational Education (Washington, D.C., 1968); Young, Clive, and Miles, pp. 69–71; National Planning Association, chap. 1, pp. 11, 13.

14. National Planning Association, app. A.

15. Ibid., p. 103.

16. Allen B. Moore and Sue J. King, *Problem Areas in Occupational Education for the 1970's,* Center for Occupational Education, Occasional Paper no. 12 (Raleigh: North Carolina State University, 1972).

17. Parnes et al., 4: 73.

18. John C. Flanagan et al., *Project Talent, Five Years after High School* (Pittsburgh: American Institutes for Research and University of Pittsburgh, 1971), chap. 14, p. 3; Flanagan and Jung, pp. 14–15.

19. Rupert N. Evans, "School for Schooling's Sake: The Current Role of the Secondary School in Occupational Preparation," in *The Transition from School to Work,* Princeton Research Report Series, no. 111 (Princeton: Princeton University, Industrial Relations Section, 1968), pp. 198–200; Hamburger and Wolfson, pp. 4–10, app. A, B; Evans et al., p. 58; "Vocational Education," p. 139; Young, Clive, and Miles, pp. 100–102; Taussig, pp. 64–65.

20. New York Commission on the Quality, Cost, and Financing of Elementary and Secondary Education, *The Fleischmann Report on the Quality, Cost, and Financing of Elementary and Secondary Education in New York State,* 3 vols. (New York: Viking, 1973), vol. 2, chap. 7, p. 22; Levitan, Mangum, and Marshall, pp. 138–139; "Vocational Education," p. 127; Young, Clive, and Miles, pp. 94–97; Evans, p. 199.

21. *Education for a Changing World of Work,* Report of the Panel of Consultants on Vocational Education (Washington, D.C., 1963); Max U. Eninger, *The Process and Product of T&I High School Level Vocational Education in the United States: The Product* (Pittsburgh: American Institutes for Research, 1965), chap. 5, pp. 19–24; idem, *The Process and Product of T&I High School Level Vocational Education in the United States: The Process Variables* (Pittsburgh: Educational Systems Research Institute, 1968); Kenneth B. Hoyt, "Transition from School to Work," unpublished paper (Princeton Symposium, 1968), p. 9; Jacob J. Kaufman et al., *The Role of the Secondary Schools in the Preparation of Youth for Employment* (University Park: Pennsylvania State University, Institute for Research on Human Resources, 1967), chap. 6, pp. 18–20; Levitan, Mangum, and Marshall, p. 141: Evans, Mangum, and Pragan, p. 60; Evans, pp. 198–200;

Kaufman et al., *Comparative Costs and Benefits;* Sharp and Krasnegor; Gerald G. Somers, *The Effectiveness of Vocational and Technical Programs* (Madison: University of Wisconsin, Center for Studies in Vocational and Technical Education, 1971), pp. 87–102, 205–209; Somers and Little, pp. 242–244; "Vocational Education," pp. 38–39, 127–128; Warmbrod, pp. 34–37; Taussig, pp. 75–76.

22. Somers, pp. 87–111, 205–208.

23. Somers.

24. Sally T. Hillsman, "Entry into the Labor Market: The Preparation and Job Placement of Negro and White Vocational High School Graduates" (Ph.D. diss., Columbia University, 1970); Somers, pp. 206–208.

25. Somers and Little, pp. 41–47; National Planning Association, chap. 3, pp. 4–11.

26. National Planning Association, chap. 4, pp. 1–2.

27. Somers, pp. 206–208.

28. Hoyt et al., pp. 63, 85, 89–90; Hamburger and Wolfson, pp. 123–125, 130–133; Somers and Little, pp. 108–113; *Manpower Report of the President, 1972,* pp. 92–93; "Vocational Education," pp. 7, 139.

29. International Labor Office, *CIRF Abstracts* 11, no. B47017, March 1972.

30. Authorities agree that vocational programs cost more than other programs but disagree on the amount of the differential, the methods of determining costs, and the variations by vocational skills. See Elchanan Cohn et al., *The Costs of Vocational and Nonvocational Programs: A Study of Michigan Secondary Schools* (University Park: Pennsylvania State University, Institute for Research on Human Resources, 1972); Teh-Wei Hu, Maw Lin Lee, and Ernst Stromsdorfer, *A Cost-Effectiveness Study of Vocational Education* (University Park: Pennsylvania State University, Institute for Research on Human Resources, 1969), pp. 128–131; Evans, p. 197; Kaufman et al., *Comparative Costs and Benefits,* p. 119; Levitan, Mangum, and Marshall, p. 141; Lindman et al.; New York Commission, 2, chap. 7: 22–30; Stromsdorfer; "Vocational Education," pp. 78–97; Warmbrod, p. 18; Young, Clive, and Miles, pp. 111–115.

31. Kaufman et al., *Secondary Schools,* chap. 6, table 6.14; "Vocational Education," pp. 128–129.

32. Charles Brecher, *Upgrading Blue Collar and Service Workers* (Baltimore: Johns Hopkins Press, 1972), pp. 36–38, 54–56, 72–73; Hamburger and Wolfson, pp. 41–42, 68; Hillsman; J. Kenneth Little and Richard W. Whinfield, *Follow-up of 1965 Graduates of Wisconsin Schools of Vocational, Technical, and Adult Education* (Madison: University of Wisconsin, Center for Studies in Vocational and Technical Education, 1970), p. 14; George G. Mallinson, *Characteristics of Non-College Vocationally-Oriented School Leavers and Graduates* (Kalamazoo: Western Michigan University, 1968); Somers, pp. 78–86.

33. Somers, pp. 78–86.

34. National Planning Association, chaps. 1, 6.

35. U.S. Department of Labor, Bureau of Labor Statistics, *Employment of High School Graduates and Dropouts,* Special Labor Force Reports, nos. 5, 15, 21, 32, 41, 54, 66, 85, 100, 108, 121, 131, 145.

36. Parnes et al., 4: 25, 32–40, 75–86, 97–99.

37. Hamburger and Wolfson, pp. 60–79; Hillsman.

38. Fred S. Cook and F. W. Lanhan, *Opportunities and Requirements for Initial Employment of School Leavers with Emphasis on Office and Retail Jobs* (Detroit: Wayne State University, College of Education, 1966); Harold T. Smith and Henry C. Thole, "Secondary and Post-secondary Occupational Education in Kalamazoo County, Michigan," in *Dimensions of Manpower Policy,* ed. Sar A. Levitan and Irving H. Siegal (Baltimore: Johns Hopkins Press, 1966).

39. Kaufman et al., *Secondary Schools,* chap. 7, p. 39.

40. U.S. Department of Commerce, Bureau of the Census, *Educational Attainment: March 1972,* series P-20, no. 243, November 1972, p. 35.

41. University of Wisconsin, Center for Studies in Vocational and Technical Education, *Vocational Education and Training under a Comprehensive Manpower Policy: Proceedings of a Conference* (Madison, 1970), p. 11.

42. Trudy Banta and Patricia Marshall, "Schools and Industry," *Manpower,* June 1970, pp. 25–31; Samuel M. Burt, *Industry and Vocational-Technical Education* (New York: McGraw-Hill, 1967); Arthur Corrazini, *Vocational Education: A Study of Benefits and Costs* (Princeton: Princeton University, Industrial Relations Section, 1966); Brecher; Evans et al.; *Education for a Changing World of Work;* Eninger, *The Product;* idem, *The Process Variables;* Hamburger and Wolfson; Hillsman; Hoyt et al.; Kaufman et al., *Secondary Schools;* Garth L. Mangum, *Reorienting Vocational Education,* Policy Papers in Human Resources and Industrial Relations, no. 7 (Detroit: Wayne State University, Institute of Labor and Industrial Relations, 1968); Moore and King; National Planning Association; "Vocational Education"; Somers and Little; Smith and Thole; Taussig.

43. Hamburger and Wolfson.

44. Kaufman et al., *Secondary Schools,* chap. 7, pp. 32–39; "Vocational Education," pp. 85, 108–109, 137; Brecher, pp. 72–73.

45. Berg; Hamburger and Wolfson; Young, Clive, and Miles.

46. Brecher; Hamburger and Wolfson; Hillsman; "Career Education," p. 54.

47. Moore and King, p. 17.

48. Kaufman et al., *Secondary Schools,* chap. 6, p. 27.

49. Burt; Evans et al., p. 46; Eli Ginzberg, "Vocational Education Is Not the Answer," *Phi Delta Kappan,* February 1971, pp. 369–371; Kaufman et al., *Secondary*

Schools, chap. 4, pp. 21–23, 29, chap. 7, pp. 10–31; *Manpower Report of the President, 1968,* p. 120; *Manpower Report of the President, 1972,* pp. 86–88; Michael J. Piore and Peter B. Doeringer, *Low Income Labor Markets and Urban Manpower Programs* (Cambridge: Harvard University Press, 1969); Smith and Thole, p. 172; U.S. Department of Labor, Bureau of Labor Statistics, *Youth Unemployment and Minimum Wages,* Bulletin 1957, chap. 4.

50. Hoyt, p. 9; Corrazini; Eninger, *The Product;* idem, *The Process Variables;* Evans et al., p. 60; Kaufman et al., *Secondary Schools,* chap. 6, pp. 23–25, 37; Kaufman et al., *Comparative Costs and Benefits,* pp. 121–136; Jacob J. Kaufman and Morgan V. Lewis, *The Potential of Vocational Education* (University Park: Pennsylvania State University, Institute for Research on Human Resources, 1968); Levitan, Mangum, and Marshall, p. 141; Stromsdorfer, pp. 70–71; "Vocational Education," p. 132; Young, Clive, and Miles, pp. 71–79; National Planning Association, chap. 6, p. 12; Taussig; Teh-Wei Hu, Maw Lin Lee, and Ernst W. Stromsdorfer, "Economic Returns to Vocational and Comprehensive High School Graduates," *Journal of Human Resources,* winter 1971, pp. 25–50; idem, *Cost-Effectiveness Study.*

51. National Planning Association, app. A, pp. 81–83, 99; Kaufman et al., *Comparative Costs and Benefits;* Stromsdorfer, pp. 70–71; Eninger, *The Product;* idem, *The Process Variables;* Hu, Lee, and Stromsdorfer, *Cost-Effectiveness Study.*

52. National Planning Association, chap. 1, pp. 12–13; chap. 6, pp. 8–11; app. A, pp. 62–63; app. B, tables 2–5.

53. Stromsdorfer, pp. 89–90; Hoyt.

54. Irwin L. Herrnstadt and Morris A. Horowitz, personal correspondence to the author.

55. Stromsdorfer, pp. 71–73; Hu, Lee, and Stromsdorfer, *Cost-Effectiveness Study;* idem, "Economic Returns."

56. Jeffry Piker, *Entry into the Labor Force* (Detroit: Wayne State University, Institute of Labor and Industrial Relations, 1969), pp. 49–57; Twentieth Century Fund Task Force on Employment Problems of Black Youth, *The Job Crisis for Black Youth* (New York: Praeger, 1971); National Planning Association, chap. 6, pp. 16–19; Stromsdorfer, pp. 71–73; Kaufman et al., *Secondary Schools,* chap. 9; Hillsman, chap. 6.

57. Somers and Little, pp. 272–274.

58. Somers, pp. 117–165.

59. Young, Clive, and Miles, pp. 53–60.

60. *Manpower Report of the President, 1970,* p. 68; "Career Education," p. 4; Somers and Little, p. 242; Evans, Mangum, and Pragan, p. 60; Kaufman et al., *Comparative Costs and Benefits;* Jacob J. Kaufman and M. V. Lewis, *The School Environment and Programs for Dropouts* (University Park: Pennsylvania State University, Institute for Research on Human Resources, 1968); Stromsdorfer, pp. 68, 91; "Vocational Education," p. 39; Taussig, p. 70; Eninger, *The Product;*

New York Commission, vol. 2, chap. 7; Eninger, *The Process Variables;* Hoyt, p. 9; Somers, pp. 71–75, 85–86; Kaufman and Lewis, *Potential of Vocational Education;* Hu, Lee, and Stromsdorfer, *Cost-Effectiveness Study.*

61. Parnes et al., 1: 75, 3: 57–58.

62. National Planning Association, chap. 6, pp. 20–21, app. B, table 11a.

63. Eninger, *The Process Variables.*

64. Somers, pp. 72–75, 86.

65. Ibid., pp. 76–78.

66. Ibid., pp. 68–70, 76–78, 226–228.

67. Cook and Lanhan.

68. Somers and Little, p. 242; "Vocational Education," pp. 129–130.

69. Taussig, pp. 70–72; Alice Rivlin, "Critical Issues in the Development of Vocational Education," in *Unemployment in a Prosperous Economy,* Princeton Research Report Series, no. 108 (Princeton: Princeton University, Industrial Relations Section, 1965), pp. 164–165.

70. National Planning Association, app. A, pp. 46–47; Eninger, *The Product;* idem, *The Process Variables;* Kaufman et al., *Secondary Schools;* Kaufman and Lewis, *Potential of Vocational Education;* Hu, Lee, and Stromsdorfer, *Cost-Effectiveness Study,* p. 236.

71. Eninger, *The Process Variables.*

72. Somers, pp. 103–110.

73. National Planning Association, app. A, pp. 57–58; Taussig.

74. Janet Combs and W. W. Cooley, "Dropouts: In High School and after School," *American Educational Research Journal,* May 1968, pp. 353–354, 359; Levitan, Mangum, and Marshall, pp. 142–143; Warmbrod, pp. 37–38; Young, Clive, and Miles, pp. 80–86; Taussig, pp. 80–82; "Vocational Education," pp. 109–114; Brecher, pp. 36–38; Banta and Marshall; Corrazini; Kaufman and Lewis, *School Environment;* Rivlin, "Development of Vocational Education," p. 161; Evans, Mangum, and Pragan, p. 62.

75. Robert Birnbaum and Joseph Goldman, *The Graduates: A Follow-up Study of New York City High School Graduates of 1970* (New York: City University of New York, Center for Social Research, 1972), pp. 38–41; National Planning Association, chap. 1, p. 14; chap. 6, pp. 25–27; Somers and Little, pp. 272–273; Stromsdorfer, p. 74; Hu, Lee, and Stromsdorfer, *Economic Returns,* p. 140.

76. Somers, pp. 12–13.

77. National Planning Association, chap. 1, pp. 14–15; chap. 6, pp. 27–29; app. B,

table 15; Stromsdorfer, pp. 73–78; Young et al., pp. 83–85; Taussig, p. 76; Somers, pp. 124–128; Hu, Lee, and Stromsdorfer, *Cost-Effectiveness Study,* pp. 234–235.

78. Hamburger and Wolfson, p. 133.

79. National Planning Association, chap. 6, pp. 27–28.

80. Christopher Jencks et al., *Inequality* (New York: Basic Books, 1972), pp. 157–158.

81. Birnbaum and Goldman, tables 4.1, 4.3, 4.11.

82. Flanagan et al., table 9.3a.

83. Eninger, *Process Variables;* Mallinson.

84. Max U. Eninger, *Project Metro—Evaluation Data on Vocational Education Programs in Major Metropolitan Areas,* 3 vols. (Pittsburgh: Educational Systems Research Institute, 1971).

85. National Planning Association, chap. 6, pp. 22–25.

86. Somers, pp. 69, 167–177; Kaufman et al., *Secondary Schools,* chap. 6, pp. 13–17.

87. Harvey Belitsky, *Private Vocational Schools and Their Students* (Cambridge: Schenkman, 1969); Young, Clive, and Miles, pp. 62–65; Hoyt et al., p. 97.

88. Berg; Mark Blaug, ed., *Economics of Education* (Baltimore: Penguin Books, 1968), vol. 1; Venn; National Planning Association, chap. 6, p. 24; U. S. Department of Health, Education, and Welfare; University of Wisconsin.

89. National Planning Association, app. A, p. 103.

90. Ibid., chap. 6, p. 15.

91. Ibid.

92. Stromsdorfer, pp. 54–57.

93. Somers, pp. 178–197.

94. Stromsdorfer, p. 57.

95. National Planning Association, chap. 2; chap. 4, p. 6; chap. 6, pp. 29–34; Little and Whinfield; Brecher, pp. 36–38, 54–56; Smith and Thole; Somers.

96. Hoyt et al., pp. 97–98.

97. Somers and Little, p. 41; National Planning Association, chap. 4, p. 6.

98. Rivlin, "Development of Vocational Education," pp. 156–160.

99. Somers and Little, pp. 58–61, 155–197; Evans, Mangum, and Pragan, pp. 55–57; Rivlin, "Development of Vocational Education," pp. 162–164.

100. Alice M. Rivlin, *Systematic Thinking for Social Action* (Washington, D.C.: Brookings Institution, 1971), pp. 48–63; idem, "Development of Vocational Education," p. 157; National Planning Association, app. A; Young, Clive, and Miles, pp. 116–117; Taussig, p. 69; "Vocational Education," p. 120.

101. "Career Education," p. 8; National Planning Association, app. A; Stromsdorfer; "Vocational Education."

102. National Planning Association.

103. Somers and Little, pp. 50, 272–274, 277–282; Young, Clive, and Miles pp. 107–111; Taussig.

104. *Careers Education in the 1970's,* Great Britain, Schools Council Working Paper 40 (London: Evans/Methuen Educational, 1972), pp. 32–33.

105. Torsten Husén, "School in a Changing and Industrialized Society," *Educational Leadership,* March 1968, pp. 524–530.

106. "Career Education"; Hoyt et al.; Venn; Somers and Little; Hamburger and Wolfson; Evans, Mangum, and Pragan; "Vocational Education," pp. 83–95; Young, Clive, and Miles; U.S. Department of Health, Education, and Welfare; University of Wisconsin; Mangum; Kaufman and Lewis, *Potential of Vocational Education.*

107. James Nussbaum and William Morsch, "Estimates of Vocational Education Requirements Based upon General Learning Corporation Model" (Paper prepared for Ohio State University Conference on Manpower Forecasting for State Vocational Education, June 1969); Somers and Little, pp. 49–50.

108. National Planning Association, chap. 4, pp. 3–5.

109. Hamburger and Wolfson, p. 42; Somers and Little, p. 47.

110. Hoyt et al.

111. Somers and Little, chaps. 3, 7, 8; Young, Clive, and Miles, pp. 89–94; Banta and Marshall; Evans.

112. Roger Grégoire, *Vocational Education* (Paris: Organization for Economic Cooperation and Development, 1967); Beatrice G. Reubens, "German Apprenticeship: Controversy and Reform," *Manpower,* November 1973.

113. "Career Education"; Hoyt et al., pp. 46, 83; Young, Clive, and Miles, pp. 9–10.

114. "Career Education," pp. 4, 5, 10, 11, 13, 38; Hoyt et al., pp. 2, 94–95.

115. Ginzberg.

116. U. S. Department of Labor, *Manpower Advice for Government* (Washington, D.C.: National Manpower Advisory Committee, 1972), pp. 139–141.

117. Hoyt et al., pp. 35–36, 53; Evans; Venn; Evans, Mangum, and Pragan; University of Wisconsin, p. 57.

118. "Career Education," p. 8.

119. Somers and Little, p. 30.

120. Ibid., p. 268.

121. Myron Roomkin, *High School Dropouts and Vocational Education in Wisconsin* (Madison: University of Wisconsin, Center for Studies in Vocational and Technical Education, 1970), pp. 82–86, 92–94; Young, Clive, and Miles, p. 86.

122. "Career Education," p. 8.

123. Frederick Mosteller and Daniel P. Moynihan, eds., *On Equality of Educational Opportunity* (New York: Random House, Vintage Books, 1972); Jencks.

124. Rivlin, *Systematic Thinking.*

125. National Planning Association, chap. 6, pp. 28–29; app. B, table 15; Stromsdorfer, pp. 73–78.

126. Banta and Marshall; Piker, pp. 269–282.

127. Jesse W. Ullery, "A Comparative Analysis of Selected Student Characteristics and Vocational Cooperation Programs" (Ph.D. diss., University of Illinois at Urbana-Champaign, 1971).

128. "Career Education," pp. 15–17, 48.

129. National Planning Association, app. A, p. 53; Cook and Lanhan.

130. Somers and Little, p. 47; Hamburger and Wolfson, p. 42.

VI Federal Work Strategies

14 Work Experience and Family Life

Frank F. Furstenberg, Jr.

The time-honored assumption that a link exists between the family system and the economic order is hardly a controversial one, and few authorities would question the more specific proposition that family stability in contemporary American society bears a relationship to the occupational prospects of the household head.[1] In times past, the family was generally an economic unit, and its members were integrated by virtue of the fact that they shared a number of work activities. Although the postindustrial family is no longer a work unit, it is still very much an economic entity. For example, the occupational status of the household head determines the social status of his or her family. Moreover, the family is still organized around an economic activity—consumption. The consumption of resources provides a kind of integration of the family and an arena for exchanging economic benefits for psychological rewards.[2]

For a long period, students of the family were content merely to affirm the importance of the association between economic status and family life, but few empirical studies were undertaken that might specify the relationship more precisely. Recently, when researchers finally began to consider this question, a lack of consensus was immediately apparent. Particularly, considerable uncertainty has arisen about which economic actions, if any, might be taken to promote more durable family relations.

Indicative of the state of affairs is the festering debate over the Moynihan report.[3] It has now been nearly ten years since its publication, and the controversy over its conclusions has not subsided. Indeed, the past decade has witnessed far more energy expended in ideological debate than in the fact gathering that might better resolve some of the questions at issue. Surely the time has come to call a cease-fire, to reassess the current state of knowledge about work status and family stability, to identify the issues that have yet to be explored, and to draw what implications we can from the evidence at hand.

Some Methodological Issues
Before setting out, it is worthwhile to recall what William Goode pointed out a decade ago—that one's ideological position inevitably shapes one's definition of family instability.[4] Moreover, Goode reminded us that the harmful effects of family instability are not always self-evident or to be taken for granted. This point has been reiterated in a recent review of the literature on fatherless families which concludes that the absence of a male is not ipso facto a reason for concern.[5] The accumulated evidence suggests that the negative effects of broken homes may be somewhat overrated in socio-logical and psychological literature. Similarly, the deleterious effects of other types of family instability, such as out-of-wedlock parenthood, may be overstated. While recognizing the strong possibility that a wider variety of family forms will become normative in the future, it is nonetheless instruc-tive to examine the sources of family instability in contemporary society. The question I take up in this paper is "What are the prospects of strength-ening the family through improved economic opportunity in our society?" In my discussion I shall consider specifically the effect of certain public policies on the quality of family life.

To answer this question, we must be far more specific about what is meant by both family stability and economic opportunity. As Ray Abrams wrote twenty years ago, it is possible to reach very different conclusions in empirical investigations depending on one's definition of family stability.[6] Abrams's point is no less valid today. There is an uncomfortable lack of clarity in many of the studies that seek to associate family stability with economic factors. Referring to this problem, Reynolds Farley and Albert Hermalin have recently written that ". . . there is no consensus as to how . . . [family stability] is to be measured or how trends over time can be as-sessed." [7] If their point is accepted, then we might expect conflicting and contradictory evidence on the relationship between employment status and family stability.

This methodological problem cannot be solved by edict. Rather than arbitrarily restricting the concept, it seems more prudent to include most of the major indicators of family instability that have been employed in sociological studies. To avoid excessive confusion, it is also useful to make certain distinctions regarding the use of the term. Some writers have used "family instability" to refer to *structural* defects in family composition: the family may be incomplete—childbearing occurs outside marriage. It may be formed precipitately—the timing of marriage is forced by external events such as premarital pregnancy. Or it may be disrupted—either voluntarily through divorce, separation, or desertion, or involuntarily through death or serious illness. Another dimension of family instability, less easily measured, has to do with the *internal role relations* within the family. Many writers characterize the unstable family by referring to strains in the marriage or between parents and children. In this review, I shall include studies that identify both structural and relational sources of instability.

The use of the term is further complicated when one tries to determine the boundary of the family unit. Most researchers have elected not to extend their investigations beyond the nuclear family. This decision to ignore the extended family no doubt reflects an implicit cultural bias on the part of contemporary researchers that the nuclear family is the only viable kinship form in American society.[8] A regrettable consequence of this provincialism has been the tendency to treat multigenerational households as examples of structural weakness rather than as examples of adaptation to meet certain kinds of economic situations.[9]

If there is a lack of clarity in the term "family instability," employment or occupational status presents even greater problems. The vast majority of sociological studies have used greatly simplified measures of the work status of individuals. Either they have merely dichotomized the population into working and nonworking portions, as is typically done in studies of female employment, or they have used some hierarchical categorization of occupational prestige—such as blue-collar versus white-collar. In so doing, these studies have restricted the theoretical analysis of the relationship between work and family life. Since they capture so little of the quality of the work experience, they have relatively little to say about the way that experience impinges on family life (or they are forced to provide improvised and ad hoc explanations, which, though often plausible, are rarely conclusively demonstrated).

Relatively few studies have measured such important features of the work experience as duration of employment, time spent at work, compensation, security, occupational duties, and opportunities for promotion. Presumably all of these factors could have a direct bearing on family relations.[10] Even less studied is the way the job experience is perceived either by the job holder or by other members of the family.[11] Finally, little is known about the families in which more than one member is a job holder. Most studies have examined the effects on family relations of the occupation of the male, disregarding the fact that approximately half of all females are currently employed. While there has been some investigation of the impact that working wives have on family relations,[12] few studies have explored the changes brought about when two or more members are employed.

Contributing to the limited explanatory power of most of the existing studies of employment experience and family stability is the uncertainty over the causal nexus between the two variables. Nearly all the studies that have been conducted to date are cross-sectional—that is, they consider the relationship between employment and family stability only at one time. Typically, they assume that employment conditions are the independent or causal agent that shapes family relations. Daniel Moynihan's insistence that family experience, both past and present, can influence the prospects of stable employment, suggests the possibility of a more complicated interaction between the two factors.[13] There is some evidence, albeit limited, to suggest that family experience, at least early in life, may constrain employment opportunities.[14] Careful consideration of this problem awaits longitudinal studies which would trace individuals' life histories over a period of years, following them through the family life cycle.[15]

Even a cursory examination of the existing literature reveals a preponderance of studies about low-income families, concentrating on poor blacks.[16] While there may be some justification for this special focus, we lack information on employment experience and family life among the middle class. The nearly exclusive focus on lower- and working-class families raises an additional methodological problem. Even if we assume that an individual's employment situation is an important determinant of family disharmony, there are obviously a host of other factors that are sources of instability within the family, such as low levels of education, economic deprivation, poor interpersonal skills, lack of support from extended kin, and pressure from unwanted pregnancies.[17] Since all of these factors are common among the poor, how can we determine whether employment experience, exclusive of these concomitant conditions, exerts an effect on their family life? It would be helpful, of course, to study the impact of employment in a variety of family types, holding constant other factors that might have an impact on family relations, but few studies have introduced this type of control procedure.

In spite of the need for more sophisticated studies, it is useful to take stock of what we now know about the relationship between work experience and family life. While the research may be deficient in the respects I have outlined, it does reveal certain consistent trends. These trends at the very least provide a tentative basis for programmatic recommendations. Further researchers may refine these conclusions, but they are not likely to repudiate them.

Occupational Status and Family Structure

Family Formation

No more than a half dozen studies examine the effect of occupational position on the decision to marry. Several studies of premarital pregnancy refer to the fact that the timing of marriage may be influenced by the economic position of the male when the pregnancy occurs.[18] Extrapolating from this hypothesis, I have suggested in a previous article that the high rate of illegitimacy among lower-income families in general, and poor blacks in particular, may be attributable to the uncertain occupational position of the males.[19] Although compelling demographic evidence has yet to be assembled, several small-scale studies lend support to this interpretation. Case material from studies of black, unwed mothers reveals that expectant mothers often reject the possibility of marriage if their sexual partner is currently unemployed and has limited occupational prospects in the future.[20] In a study that I conducted in Baltimore, young women reported that they would be foolish to marry when their boyfriends were "unsettled" in their jobs.[21] Typically, those who did marry perceived that their husbands would be capable of supporting their families.

The part the occupational situation of the male plays in his willingness to marry when a pregnancy occurs has not been established. It is known that economic status can influence sexual patterns and contraceptive practice among males.[22] It may be hypothesized that men who have a high investment in their careers are more careful in their selection of sexual partners and more scrupulous about using contraception when they engage in premarital sexual relations.[23] Whether or not these men are prepared to marry if a pregnancy occurs may well depend on whether they perceive that their career would be jeopardized by a precipitate marriage.

In one of the few studies on the effect of work on the timing of marriage, Robert Rapoport reasons that men attempt to coordinate their marriages to fit the demands of their occupations: ". . . A higher average age at marriage occurs in occupations that require lengthy specialized training, in occupations that require extraordinary commitment and/or detachment from human involvements, in occupations that defer entry into full status because of inheritance patterns, and in occupations that fail to provide sufficient economic return or stability of employment to support a wife." [24]

In an extensive analysis of the 1960 census data, Hugh Carter and Paul Glick reach the same conclusion.[25] Moreover, they suggest that from the point of view of career earnings, there may be an optimal age to begin family building. Although the data they marshall are extremely sketchy, their findings suggest that lower-class men may be disadvantaged by being constrained to marry either too early or too late. The authors do not explain why men in lower-status occupations are less likely to marry in their early twenties, the age when most middle-class males wed. The discussion points to one obvious determinant, however: these men do not represent an attractive long-range prospect for marriage; to women, their occupational histories appear unstable and their futures uncertain. Thus they marry either quite young when marriage is forced by a premarital pregnancy or much older when women begin to feel that they cannot do appreciably better by deferring marriage any longer. In brief, men whose occupational careers are unpredictable tend to be less predictable in establishing marital relations.

Whatever the reason for these irregular marriage patterns, the effect on family life has been well documented. A large number of studies have shown that early marriages are highly conducive to family instability,[26] and there is some evidence that late marriages also have low prospects for success.[27] Many reasons have been offered to explain the frequent failure of early marriages—such as absence of parental support, immaturity, poor inter-

personal skills, and frequent childbearing. The explanation most relevant
to this discussion is that the male faces limited career opportunities. The
responsibilities of providing for the immediate needs of his family generally
limit his chances of getting further training for occupational advancement.
Unlike the unmarried male, he cannot afford to take chances by returning to
school or searching for a better job. As Burchinal summarizes the situation, ". . . with employment largely limited to unskilled and semi-skilled jobs,
young marriages generally are established and maintained on a meager
economic basis."[28] Thus the situation of the lower-status male who marries
early can be likened to a man caught in a revolving door—he steps in because he has no place to go and he frequently leaves because he is going no
place.

The metaphor of the revolving door points out the artificiality of trying to
establish that career prospects cause marital stability. It is not hard to see
why men with limited hopes of the future might be willing to marry early.
After all, there is little reason for them to wait. But by marrying early they
contribute to their own occupational stagnancy—as their family responsibilities mount their career flexibility diminishes.

Family Permanence

In contrast to the sketchy information on the relation of occupational status
to family formation, there is an abundance of data on its relation to marital
stability. As noted earlier, more attention has been given to the existence of
a link between the two variables than to the reasons why such a link exists.
Some of the earliest information comes from studies of the depression.[29]
Almost all of the data collected in the thirties were based on case histories
and pertained to the effect of unemployment on internal family organization.
The single exception was a study that suggested that high unemployment
decreases both family formation and family dissolution.[30] It is not difficult to
understand why poor economic conditions would reduce marriages rates,
but it is less obvious why they would curtail the incidence of family dissolution. One explanation is that divorce data in times of economic crisis may be
misleading. Those who might otherwise resort to legal means of marital
termination are forced by economic circumstances to resort to unofficial
means such as desertion.

This explanation may also account for the fact that the earliest studies of
marital instability within different occupational groups revealed higher rates
of divorce among professionals and white-collar workers than among the

semiskilled and unskilled. In all likelihood, the cost and difficulty of getting a divorce limited the opportunities of lower-status individuals to use this method of dissolving their marriages. Recently divorce has become more accessible to the poor, although restrictions may still not have completely disappeared. In any event, consistent evidence from a large number of studies has established the fact that divorce is most common in lower-status occupations.[31] And within each class, proneness to divorce varies by occupation.

If we add the number of marriages that break up because of separation and desertion to the number that break up because of divorce, the evidence of a correlation between occupational status and marital disruption is far more powerful. In a study of the 1960 census data, J. Richard Udry reports a strong relationship between the occupational status of males and rates of marital disruption (resulting from divorce, separation, and remarriage). "The relationship between occupational status and marital stability for men," Udry writes, "is direct and unequivocal."[32] Interestingly, he finds that within each occupational group blacks are twice as likely to experience marital failure as whites. A study by Jessie Bernard and one by Hugh Carter and Paul Glick also present evidence of the effect that occupational standing has on marital stability.[33] In general, rates of marital instability are roughly twice as high among service workers and laborers as among professionals, with other occupational groups falling in between. Reiterating Udry's results, these studies report that blacks have much higher rates of marital disruption, even holding occupational status constant.

Jessie Bernard examines the effect on family stability of income, education, and occupation simultaneously. Of the three, income is by far the most powerful determinant of marital instability, although occupation continues to have some effect on marital dissolution even when income is held constant. Bernard's controls are relatively crude, however, and a more precise analysis might reveal that a major reason for the relationship of occupational status to marital instability is income differentials between various job categories.

Income, both in the form of present wages and the prospect of future earnings, may be especially decisive in the erosion of marital relations within the working and lower classes. Goode alludes to this possibility when he cites as one reason for the greater propensity of lower-class marriages to break up the fact that the "costs" of divorce are low for these people—that is, neither partner has a high economic stake in the marriage. The importance of occupational standing, then, in large measure derives from the indication it provides to both husband and wife of their economic future. Perhaps this is one reason why blacks continue to have lower rates of stable marriages even when they possess comparable educational and occupational qualifications. Since blacks are likely to earn less regardless of their qualifications, occupation may serve less well as a prognosticator of future economic position. The importance of occupation as a predictor of future earning power becomes even more apparent later when we consider studies of the impact of occupation on relations within the family.

Occupational Status and Family Relations

Family Disorganization
In studies on the impact of the depression, considerable attention was given to the question of whether loss of employment and downward occupational mobility adversely affected family relations. It should be pointed out that the term "family relations" is a particularly value-laden one, and some of the studies assumed a priori that there was a deterioration in the marriage if the male was forced to share some of his decision-making authority with either his wife or his children. Despite the difficulty of defining such terms as "family integration" and "marital harmony," there is a remarkable degree of uniformity in the findings of these early studies.[34] Typically, the initial reaction to unemployment was disorganization: ". . . when the husband could not find any work, his role suffered in the eyes of other members of the family. Wives sometimes lost their respect or accused their husbands of not trying to find work. Unless the husband could work out some role in the household (difficult to do), he really had no role to play." [35]

Just how seriously the husband's position was undermined depended in part on the type of role he played prior to the time he lost his job. If the husband had had a primarily utilitarian role (that is, if he had earned the respect of his family through the economic support he provided), obviously the impact of unemployment on his position in the family was more severe than if his authority derived from his position as patriarch. In the latter case, he continued to maintain political authority even when his economic position was undercut.

The extent to which we can extrapolate information about the current situation from these early studies of unemployment is questionable. Both the social context and the organization of the family are considerably different today.[36] Several important findings stand out, however, when these early studies are reviewed. First, there is a tremendous variability in the way that families mediate the crisis of unemployment. To a considerable degree, the prior organization of the family either promotes or prevents deterioration. Moreover, it matters greatly whom the family members blame for the loss of employment. If "the system" is blamed, family members rally around the former breadwinner, but if he is deemed responsible, their support is withdrawn. His position within the family is unaffected if unemployment is perceived as temporary. But when joblessness persists, naturally the position of the formerly employed is diminished, particularly when other family members find employment.

These three elements—inflexibility within the family organization, the tendency to blame the jobless breadwinner for his inability to find work, and the perception of low opportunities for future employment—which were characteristic of low stability among depression families, are found in lower-class families today, particularly poor black families. In the ghetto, many marriages begin early, often as the result of premarital pregnancy. Because of low levels of education, the couple often have limited communication skills and are not likely to have common interests and activities.[37] They are placed under considerable economic pressure because of frequent childbearing.[38] When unemployment occurs, the family is ill equipped to handle the strain, for rarely has it had time to accumulate savings, and extended kin can provide only limited assistance.

This high risk family situation is further complicated by the fact that the unemployed husband frequently blames himself and/or is blamed by his wife for his situation. As Lee Rainwater, in a recent study of lower-class family life, has written:

The economic marginality of husbands seemed generally to be converted into a moral issue; the wives maintain not that their husbands cannot but that they will not support them. This may seem an insignificant distinction because the effect is the same: lack of sufficient income to support a family. Within the family, however, it is not a minor issue at all because the moral opprobrium encourages the wife, the children, and the husband himself to locate the nature of the problem in the husband's character rather than in his socioeconomic situation.[39]

Reinforcing the view that the unemployed male is responsible for his

situation is the fact that he is likely to be eligible only for jobs that offer epi-
sodic employment or that pay so little that even full-time employment does
not offer enough compensation to support his family. Elliot Liebow observes
from his study of street-corner men that "a man's chances for working regularly are good only if he is willing to work for less than he can live on, and
sometimes not even then."[40] He is unlikely to be committed to those jobs that
he can get, and as Liebow puts it, "He cannot draw from a job those social
values which other people do not put into it."

The lower-class male's position is further undermined by his wife's ability
to obtain menial employment and her willingness to work at jobs that he, and
the larger society, defines as unacceptable. Thus, at the same time that her
view of him is confirmed, the lower-class male is likely to be put at a competitive disadvantage vis-à-vis his wife. It is little wonder, then, that several
studies have shown that lower-class males, especially blacks, are opposed
to their wives working.[41] Joan Aldous, in a study of working-class wives, discovered that black men are less likely to assume family responsibility if their
wives work. She concluded: ". . . those Negro males who perceive themselves as relative failures, i.e., lower achievers, with little hope of success,
are also more prone to feel that they are failing in their family role performance. . . . intervention attempts to improve the lot of the Negro family should
focus on men and their work. For the Negro man to be an active husband-
father appears to presuppose the Negro man as family breadwinner."[42] Thus,
resentment toward the wife as a secondary wage earner is likely to decrease
only when the lower-class male feels confident of his own earning capacity.

Marital Satisfaction

The erosion of family relations resulting from chronic unemployment or persistent underemployment does not necessarily imply that a low-status job,
if held on a steady basis, will have an adverse effect on family relationships.
But, while the evidence is less than unequivocal, there is reason to believe
that marital satisfaction increases with occupational status. Several recent
studies have reported a disproportionate number of unhappy marriages
among blue-collar and unskilled workers.[43] What is left unanswered by these
studies is whether occupational status has any effect on marital relations
that is independent of effects of income and education. Norman Bradburn
and David Caplovitz do find a tendency for men who are dissatisfied with
their jobs to be dissatisfied in their marriage also. Yet they report that there is
"still considerable independence between adjustment in the marital role and

adjustment in the work role."[44] Karen Renne's findings point to the importance of income, particularly among blacks: "Income is more closely related to marital dissatisfaction than is either education or occupation, probably because it has an independent and very concrete impact on a couple's daily life . . . the domestic problems of black couples can be attributed primarily to economic deprivation."[45] She also discovers that job satisfaction for males is related to marital happiness. Income is a central component of job satisfaction—especially among blacks—and may, again, be the main link between occupational status and marital happiness.[46] As Levinger concludes in a study of the sources of marital dissatisfaction among applicants for divorce, many individuals are "so heavily engaged with coping to satisfy needs at the first and second level (desire for substance and safety) that they are unable . . . to worry about the achievements of mature love and interpersonal respect. . . ."[47] It seems impossible to doubt that economic security is a virtual prerequisite for marital harmony.

In his extensive study of marital relations in working- and middle-class families, John Scanzoni goes further than anyone to date in detailing the process by which low economic status erodes marital cohesion.[48] He is able to demonstrate that men who derive material and symbolic rewards from their work are more likely to gain esteem within the family, as they are able to exchange external rewards for emotional allegiance and deference from other family members. Conversely, Scanzoni has discovered that men who are at the bottom of the status ladder suffer limited bargaining power vis-à-vis their wives and children. Commanding less respect from their families by virtue of their external position, low-status men are forced to draw on traditional sources of power, claiming a historical right to greater authority within the family. Working-class women, in turn, feel resentful and respond by further withdrawing emotional support. Each partner protects his tenuous position by giving as little as possible to the other.[49]

Parent-Child Relations

It is clear that much of what has been said about the corrosive effects of unemployment, underemployment, and menial employment on marital relations applies to parent-child relations also. Elliot Liebow's study of the black men on Tally's Corner bears this out. He discovered that men were propelled away from the home—in part because they could not face the daily reminder of their inability to provide for their children. Consequently, relations were actually better among men who did not live with their offspring: "The man who lives with his wife and children is under legal and social constraints to provide for them. . . . The chances are, however, that he is failing to provide for them, and failure in this primary function contaminates his performance as father in other respects as well."[50]

What Liebow found to be characteristic of the relationship of the lower-class black father to his children may exist in a less dramatic fashion in families of working-class males.[51] A number of studies have pointed out that blue-collar fathers are less inclined than white-collar and professional fathers to become emotionally involved with their children; their parental style tends to be more distant and removed. Whether this pattern of childrearing has conspicuously negative effects has not been established. There is some evidence that children of blue-collar families feel less close to their fathers as they enter adolescence and adulthood than their middle-class counterparts do.[52]

Most of these studies point to the unmistakable conclusion that "the father's occupational achievement has become the cornerstone for his success both as a father and as a man."[53] Again, it is useful to recall the findings of the depression studies on family life: while occupational failure did not guarantee loss of the father's esteem within the family, unless efforts were made to explain, discount, or neutralize the misfortune of the breadwinner, children were likely to resent his economic failure.

Apart from the way occupational prestige influences the character of parent-child relations, a man's work also shapes the values and expectations imparted to his children. Melvin Kohn has conducted the most extensive research on the way that occupational position patterns parental values and childrearing behavior.[54] He finds consistent evidence that certain occupational experiences, particularly those common to unskilled and semiskilled jobs, encourage parents to instill a high degree of behavioral restraint in their children. While these authoritarian patterns need not foster dissent between parents and children, they tend to restrict the children's occupational mobility and reduce their adaptability to changes in their environment. The implication of Kohn's findings is that parents' work experience may have subtle but profound consequences for the social adjustment of their children.

Implications for Policy
Despite the many issues left unsettled, and the occasional points where findings are contradictory, there is a high degree of consistency in the evi-

dence linking occupational experience to family stability. Piecing together conclusions from a variety of studies, there can be little doubt that economic uncertainty brought on by unemployment and marginal employment is a principal reason why family relations deteriorate. Those who hold low-status jobs command less loyalty from spouses primarily because they offer less financial security than other workers. Not only is their current economic contribution unacceptably low, but prospects for betterment in the future are usually nonexistent. Indeed, the lower-class worker cannot even be sure of maintaining the job he currently holds, much less of improving his position over time. In short, in the eyes of his family and himself, he represents a poor investment.

By contrast, white-collar and many working-class occupations afford much greater economic protection. The conscientious worker can usually look forward to a reasonable degree of security, and he generally anticipates a more rewarding, and frequently more interesting position after some years on the job. The fact that these expectations are not always realized is of less importance than the widely held belief that they might come true.

Most jobs are arranged in some kind of progressive sequence, or what might be loosely termed a "career." Particularly in bureaucratic organizations, the worker can expect to "move from less to more desirable positions, and the flow is usually, but not necessarily, related to age."[55] One of the most salient features of lower-class jobs is the absence of a career route, that is, a predictable and prearranged pattern of mobility for the job holder. Indeed, the only predictable feature of the job is that the worker can anticipate low mobility and probably little security. Thus, not only is the lower-class worker relegated to employment that is boring, unappreciated, and poorly paid, but he is also led to expect, unlike most workers, that his situation will not improve. I contend that it is the absence of a work career that has the most unsettling effects on family life.

There is some evidence that when jobs are arranged in an orderly and predictable fashion, the worker's social relations tend to be more stable and more regular. For example, Harold Wilensky has shown that community involvement is greater among people whose occupational career was arranged in an orderly sequence.[56] Similarly, we might expect more enduring relations within the families of such workers. And the worker who is assured of some degree of security and advancement in his job is more likely to have a greater stake in his work. As Marc Fried has written, "Good productive work and self-fulfillment seldom co-exist with fear and lack of hope.''[57] As the breadwinner invests more in his job, he can be expected to invest more in his family, and they, in him.

Work careers and family careers are, then, inextricably bound together. Family members orient their current relations, at least in part, to their expectations of each other's role performance in the future. Concretely, this means that if they cannot foresee the potential of a successful occupational career, there is a reluctance to initiate or maintain a family career. Thus, if patterns of work experience do indeed foreshadow instability in family relations, then it may be necessary to restructure certain types of jobs in order to decrease family instability.

Is it feasible to imagine that menial jobs can be restructured to promote greater investment by the employee in his work? Herbert Gans and others have pointed out that "dirty work," by definition, is work that nobody wants.[58] However, it is unclear whether it is the intrinsic requirements of the work that make them so undesirable or the way the work is organized. As Gans notes, the main reason why these jobs are so despised is that they are low-paying and unstable and lead nowhere. It is entirely possible, therefore, that the difference between "good jobs" and "dirty work" has as much to do with the way that the work is arranged and rewarded as it does with the demands made on the worker. If this is so, many menial jobs might be made far more acceptable if they could be organized into long-term careers. Occupations that are currently regarded as "dirty work" could be upgraded by providing the possibility of advancement and offering other benefits to the employee and his family. All workers who demonstrated reasonable competence and willingness could be guaranteed job security and at least a limited degree of mobility in their "careers."

Let us take a specific case. A young person might become a nursing home attendant without specific skills or a high school diploma. After receiving initial training on the job, he would advance beyond the apprenticeship stage and enter the occupation. Thereafter, the jobholder would be encouraged to take courses to increase his skills and would receive credits toward promotion as he demonstrated higher levels of competence. He would have some latitude in redefining his duties as he acquired further training, experience, and demonstrated special skills. For instance, the experienced attendant would be encouraged to assist in the planning of his work, arrange his own schedule, and aid in the supervision and training of apprentices. During the early part of his career, salary increments would rise steadily; later on, the worker might benefit more from special kinds of compensation such as increased vacation time, educational scholarships for his children, housing allowances, and so on. In short, both the quality of the job and the rewards accorded would induce the worker to remain on the job and invest in his work.

It is not unreasonable, given the evidence presented earlier, to expect that the ready availability of such "careers" might do much to reduce family instability. Couples could marry with the assurance of job security in the present and reasonable economic advancement in the future. More importantly, the position of the lower-class male within the family would not be undermined over time. He and his family could be sure that he would always be in a position to support them.

Some authorities would argue that lower-class males, particularly in their teens, would reject the possibility of such careers even if they were offered them. This would undoubtedly occur in some instances, but there is every reason to believe that the majority would welcome the opportunity to work if decent employment opportunities were available.[59] It is interesting to note how estimates of the number of so-called hard-core unemployed vary considerably depending on the national economic picture. It is difficult to avoid the conclusion that work patterns have less to do with individual values and personalities than with the type of jobs available.

The idea proposed here is not really so far-fetched. After all, many menial jobs, especially those that have become unionized, have already been organized in this fashion. Other jobs that have been considered low-status, such as migrant workers and hospital orderlies, are being restructured along the lines suggested in this paper. The major obstacle to further upgrading is cost. Obviously, it is more expensive to arrange menial labor in the fashion that I have outlined than it is to keep it low-paying and unstable. The indirect costs of menial jobs are rarely considered in such calculations, however. Little effort has been devoted to the difficult task of assigning costs to the consequences of unemployment and underemployment, whether they be the expenses of the criminal justice system, public assistance, mental health clinics, or medical services for the indigent. Considering merely the indirect cost discussed in this paper—the effects of limited employment opportunities on family life—it is clear that the upgrading of "dirty work" jobs might yield a tremendous saving in welfare payments alone by promoting greater family stability within low-income families.

The literature on work experience and family life suggests that manpower policies that attempt to strengthen the family by providing employment to the jobless are not likely to succeed if the jobs offered are low-paying and unstable and offer little chance for advancement. Indeed, relegating people to "dirty work" jobs is more likely to erode family relations than to ameliorate them. It should be the responsibility of the federal government to help create not only jobs but also occupational careers. One of many benefits that might follow from this effort would be a more stable and gratifying family life for many Americans.

Notes

1. Leonard Benson, *Fatherhood* (New York: Random House, 1968).

2. John Scanzoni, *Opportunity and the Family* (New York: Free Press, 1970).

3. Daniel P. Moynihan, "The Moynihan Report: The Negro Family: The Case for National Action," in *The Moynihan Report and the Politics of Controversy,* ed. Lee Rainwater and W. L. Yancey (Cambridge: MIT Press, 1967), pp. 39–124.

4. William J. Goode, "Marital Satisfaction and Instability: A Cross-Cultural Class Analysis of Divorce Rates," *International Social Science Journal* 14 (1962): 507– 526.

5. Elizabeth Herzog and C. E. Sudia, "Boys in Fatherless Families" (Department of Health, Education, and Welfare, Children's Bureau, 1970).

6. Ray H. Abrams, "The Concept of Family Stability," *Annals of the American Academy of Political and Social Science* 272 (November 1950): 1–8.

7. Reynolds Farley and Albert I. Hermalin, "Family Stability: A Comparison of Trends between Blacks and Whites," *American Sociological Review* 36 (February 1971): 1–17.

8. However, a few writers have bucked this trend: R. F. Winch, "Some Observations on Extended Familism in the United States," in *Selected Studies in Marriage and the Family,* ed. R. F. Winch and L. W. Goodman (New York: Holt, Rinehart and Winston, 1968), pp. 127–138; M. B. Sussman, "The Isolated Nuclear Family: Fact or Fiction?" in *Sourcebook in Marriage and the Family,* ed. M. B. Sussman (Boston: Houghton Mifflin, 1968), pp. 89–95; Eugene Litwak, "The Use of Extended Family Groups in Achievement of Social Goals," in *Sourcebook in Marriage and the Family,* ed. M. B. Sussman (Boston: Houghton Mifflin, 1968), pp. 82–89.

9. Charles V. Willie, *The Family Life of Black People* (Columbus: Charles E. Merrill, 1970); Andrew Billingsley and Amy T. Billingsley, *Black Families in White America* (Englewood Cliffs, N.J.: Prentice-Hall, 1969).

358 Frank F. Furstenberg, Jr.

10. Melvin L. Kohn, *Class and Conformity: A Study in Values* (Homewood, Ill.: Dorsey Press, 1969).

11. Scanzoni.

12. F. I. Nye and L. W. Hoffman, *The Employed Mother in America* (Chicago: Rand McNally, 1963); Scanzoni.

13. Moynihan.

14. Beverly Duncan and Otis D. Duncan, "Family Stability and Occupational Success," *Social Problems* 16 (1969), winter: 273–285.

15. Alvin L. Schorr, "The Family Cycle and Income Development," *Social Security Bulletin* 29 (1966), February: 14–25.

16. Robert Staples, "Towards a Sociology of the Black Family: A Theoretical and Methodological Assessment," *Journal of Marriage and the Family* 33 (1971), February: 119–138.

17. Catherine S. Chilman, *Growing Up Poor* (U.S. Department of Health, Education, and Welfare, SRS Publication no. 109, 1966).

18. Lolagene C. Coombs et al., "Premarital Pregnancy and Status before and after Marriage," *American Journal of Sociology* 75 (1970), March: 800–820; Charles E. Bowerman et al., *Unwed Motherhood: Personal and Social Consequences* (Chapel Hill: University of North Carolina, Institute for Research in Social Science, 1963–1966).

19. Frank F. Furstenberg, Jr., "Premarital Pregnancy among Black Teenagers," *Trans-Action,* May 1970, pp. 52–55.

20. Prudence M. Rains, *Becoming an Unwed Mother* (Chicago: Aldine-Atherton, 1971); Lee Rainwater, *Behind Ghetto Walls* (Chicago: Aldine, 1970).

21. Frank F. Furstenberg, Jr., *Unplanned Parenthood* (forthcoming).

22. Lee Rainwater, *Family Design: Marital Sexuality, Family Size and Contraception* (Chicago: Aldine, 1965).

23. William F. Whyte, "A Slum Sex Code," *American Journal of Sociology,* July 1943, pp. 24–31.

24. Robert N. Rapoport, "The Male's Occupation in Relation to His Decision to Marry," *Acta Sociologica* 8 (1964): 68–82.

25. Hugh Carter and Paul C. Glick, *Marriage and Divorce: A Social and Economic Study* (Cambridge: Harvard University Press, 1970).

26. Lawrence L. Bumpass and James A. Sweet, "Differentials in Marital Instability," *American Sociological Review* 37 (1972), December: 754–766; Lee G. Burchinal, "Trends and Prospects for Young Marriages in the United States," *Journal of Marriage and the Family* 27 (1965), May: 243–254; Karen S. Renne, "Correlates

of Dissatisfaction in Marriage," *Journal of Marriage and the Family* 32 (1970), February: 54–67; Robert F. Winch and Scott A. Greer, "The Uncertain Relation between Early Marriage and Marital Stability: A Quest for Relevant Data," *Acta Sociologica* 8 (1964): 83–97.

27. Carter and Glick.

28. Burchinal.

29. Ruth S. Cavan, "Unemployment: Crisis of the Common Man," *Journal of Marriage and the Family* 21 (1959), May: 139–146.

30. Samuel A. Stouffer and Paul F. Lazarsfeld, "Research Memorandum on the Family in the Depression," *Social Science Research Council Bulletin* 29 (1937).

31. J. Richard Udry, "Marital Instability by Race, Sex, Education, and Occupation Using 1960 Census Data," *American Journal of Sociology* 72 (1966), September: 203–209.

32. Ibid.; Goode.

33. Jessie Bernard, "Marital Stability and Patterns of Status Variables," *Journal of Marriage and the Family* 28 (1966), November: 421–439; Carter and Glick.

34. Cavan.

35. Ibid.

36. Ibid.

37. Chilman.

38. Rainwater, *Behind Ghetto Walls.*

39. Ibid., p. 174.

40. Elliot Liebow, *Tally's Corner: A Study of Negro Streetcorner Men* (Boston: Little, Brown, 1967).

41. Rainwater, *Behind Ghetto Walls;* Susan R. Orden and Norman M. Bradburn, "Working Wives and Marriage Happiness," *American Journal of Sociology* 74 (1969), January: 392–407; Joan Aldous, "Wives' Employment Status and Lower-Class Men as Husband-Fathers: Support for Moynihan Thesis," *Journal of Marriage and the Family* 31 (1969), August: 469–476.

42. Ibid.

43. Renne; Scanzoni; Norman M. Bradburn and David Caplovitz, *Reports on Happiness* (Chicago: Aldine, 1965); L. C. Coombs and Zena Zumeta, "Correlates of Marital Dissolution in a Prospective Fertility Study: A Research Note," *Social Problems* 18 (1970), summer: 92–102.

44. Bradburn and Caplovitz, p. 136.

45. Renne.

46. Staples.

47. George Levinger, "Sources of Marital Dissatisfaction among Applicants for Divorce," *American Journal of Orthopsychiatry* 36 (1966), October: 803–807.

48. Scanzoni.

49. Mirra Komarovsky, *Blue-Collar Marriage* (New York: Random House, 1964).

50. Liebow.

51. Donald B. McKinley, *Social Class and Family Life* (New York: Free Press of Glencoe, 1964); Chilman.

52. Ibid.

53. Benson, p. 290.

54. Kohn.

55. Howard S. Becker and Anselm L. Strauss, "Careers, Personality and Adult Socialization," *American Journal of Sociology* 62 (1956), November: 253–263.

56. Harold L. Wilensky, "Orderly Careers and Social Participation: The Impact of Work History on Social Integration in the Middle Mass," *American Sociological Review* 26 (1961), August: 521–539.

57. Mark A. Fried, "Is Work a Career?" *Trans-Action* 3 (1966), September-October: 42–47.

58. Herbert J. Gans, "Income Grants and 'Dirty Work,'" *The Public Interest* 6 (1967), winter: 110–113.

59. Leonard Goodwin, *Do the Poor Want to Work?* (Washington, D.C.: Brookings Institution, 1972).

15 Work, Well-Being, and Family Life

Lee Rainwater

The master goal of domestic public policy is presumably to secure and, if possible, to increase the personal well-being of the nation's citizens. In discussing any particular aspect of public policy, it is useful to specify its relationship to this general goal; otherwise, the ready tendency to substitute the achievement of means for the achievement of ends is reinforced. Let us start, then, with a consideration of the dynamics of personal well-being, first for human beings in general and second for those of us who live in modern, industrial societies.

In all cultures, people seem to judge themselves well-off to the extent that they are able to engage in *validating activities*—those activities that confirm an individual's sense of himself as a full and recognized member of his society and that resonate with his sense of inner needs (whether those be simple physical needs like food gathering or more complex needs like intellectual stimulation). It is through engaging in activities that an individual achieves such a sense of concordance between what others consider him to be (social placement) and what he feels himself to be (personal identity).[1]

Research on which this paper is in part based was supported by Public Health Service grants MH-18635 and MH-15567. Some of the issues dealt with here are treated more extensively in the author's report, "Poverty, Living Standards, and Family Well-Being," prepared for the Subcommittee on Fiscal Policy, Joint Economic Committee of the Congress, June 1972.

Therefore, if we wish to understand the distribution of well-being in a society, we must examine the distribution among its members of possibilities for participating in validating activities. Similarly, if we wish to design public policies to increase the well-being of some or all members of society we need to understand validating activities sufficiently to influence possibilities for participation in them.[2]

Validating Activities
An individual's well-being can be thought of as a product of (1) the access to locales in which validating activities take place and (2) the availability of resources necessary to support engaging in these activities.

Access can be thought of as the proportion of a person's time (in a day, a month, or a year) during which he can participate in a validating activity. The larger this proportion, the better are his possibilities for achieving a sense of well-being. If he feels that there is much "dead time" in his life, much time in which there is "nothing to do," then his chances for achieving well-being are reduced.

The locales of validating activities are quite mundane; depending on his age and other characteristics, the appropriate locales may be school, the workplace, the family, home, a summer vacation in Europe, a ball park, a PTA meeting, and so on. One of the distinguishing marks of modern, industrial society is the incredible range of places in which validating activities are carried on. This range allows people the possibility, in theory at least, of tailoring their validating activities to their own highly personal needs and wishes. Although in general, access itself is not a problem in our society, there is a problem of access in the case of work for many Americans. The American economy does not provide enough jobs for everyone who wants to work at a particular time. As is well known, the unemployment measures tend to underestimate this "no access" rate. Access to jobs for certain groups—teenagers, women who want to work part-time, older people—is sharply restricted.

Access to validating activities in general is problematic only for special categories of persons in society. Thus, suburban teenagers often have "nothing to do" because the suburban world is not organized in such a way that they can get together to engage in activities that confirm their sense of the kind of person they "really" are. Race and ethnic discrimination has the same effect when it prevents access to ongoing activities by which individuals would like to validate themselves.

It is with resources that the most frequent and damaging interference with participation arises. "Resources" means here the broadest possible range of items of personal, social, and physical "capital." Resources may include social contacts, knowledge, political influence, prestige, health, or personal attractiveness. These play a crucial role for some people at some time. Most of the variation in personal well-being in our society can be accounted for by variations in the more familiar resources of income and assets, however. The price of admission to most validating activities has to be paid either by the direct expenditure of money or other assets or by the use of other resources which are themselves contingent upon the availability of economic resources. If one makes a detailed enough description of any activity that is validating in our kind of society, one can attach to it a typical price tag or range of price tags to illustrate the essential tie between economic resources and the ability to engage in it.

For most Americans, the validating activities that consume economic resources have their basis in the nuclear family. Indeed, a very large proportion of nonwork activities are carried out either in the home or in the company of family members away from the home. This is a reflection of the fact that for most Americans, for most of their lives, a very large proportion of the validating activities in which they engage are ones that involve family participation. Many others have the family as an important ultimate reference for the validity of the activity. This is preeminently true of work for many men and women at the working- and lower-middle-class levels. The validating activities that come under the headings of establishing and maintaining a home, pursuing gratifying family activities, and enjoying leisure time and recreational activities consume most of their nonwork time and almost all of their income.[3]

In any historical period, the definition of validating activities for ordinary members of society implicitly carries a definition of the kinds of resources that are necessary in order to succeed at these activities. One needs a home, but the conception of a home in which the validating activities of "average" family relationships take place changes from time to time. The kind of food that the housewife must provide for her family in order to feel validated as at least an ordinary cook also changes. Today's housewife judges herself more in terms of her ability to feed her family meat than the housewife of even twenty years ago. If she had to make do with the shopping basket of twenty years ago she would feel that she was having to skimp drastically and would inevitably feel that she was not able to validate herself as a good cook.[4]

David Riesman and Howard Roseborough have called the conceptions people have of the goods and services necessary to carry out conventional validating activities the consumer's "standard package."[5] There is overwhelming evidence that this standard package changes in an orderly way as per capita personal income increases and that all judgments of how satisfying one's life is are calibrated with reference to a "mainstream package." This means that standards of living are almost completely relative and that the logic often used in government minimum standards budgets is a faulty one. For example, historical analysis of poverty-line budgets and of the public's conceptions of what makes a person poor suggests that poverty is simply not having access to a resource package of at least half that of the average adult.

The relativity of the standard package and therefore of the resources necessary for validating one's identity through participation in validating activities is graphically illustrated by the trend in responses to a question the Gallup poll has asked since 1946: "What is the smallest amount of money a family of four needs to get along in this community?" This question seems to tap the public's feelings about the amount of income that is necessary for a marginal working-class standard of living, for being within striking distance, though not quite a part, of the mainstream.

Most striking in the Gallup findings is the fact that although the absolute purchasing power of the amount thought necessary to get along has increased by 50 percent from 1946 to 1969, there has been no shift in the proportion this amount represents of per capita consumption. With very minor ups and downs, the amounts specified by Gallup's respondents have always been about 55 percent of the per capita consumption of an "average" four-person family. The variations are more marked, but the relationship seems quite stable, for the average worker with three dependents: the "get along" amount is almost always a little more than his take-home pay.

Husbands and fathers traditionally have assessed their validity in the provider role by the extent to which they bring home the resources necessary to approximate the mainstream package. Wives and mothers have felt validated to the extent that they are able to use that income to provide the family with the kind of home it needs to have a mainstream existence. When husbands cannot bring home that level of income, their own and their wives' sense of identity is diminished. The wife often blames her husband for his inability, but inevitably that blame is transformed into self-blame that she is not able to squeeze out of their meager resources a better approximation of mainstream life.

Reciprocity

Most activities in which people engage can be validating only if others also participate in them—that is, people require feedback to tell them that they have done something that validates their identity as a functioning member of the group. But they validate the activity of others only if they feel there is something in it for them. Behind cultural norms, values, and meanings applied to particular activities there lie patterns of reciprocity among members of society. Among persons relatively equal in power, these exchanges are expected to come out more or less evenly. You get what you give. Power differences, however, open the way for exploitative relationships. The inferior is constrained to validate the superior's position whether he wishes to or not, and the superior is free to force onto the inferior a feeling that he is less than a full member of society. When we refer to a situation as oppression, we mean basically that the people caught in that situation are prevented from achieving a full sense of social membership and personality by virtue of the way other people's power is used to deny them access and resources.

Inevitably, standards of reciprocity are applied to every individual by those around him. This means that no one can feel secure about his continued social validity unless he has some reason to believe that he will be able to offer to those who have the power to confirm him as a full member of society something that they value in return. A child can feel secure within the family only if he comes to believe that his behavior can be positively reinforcing for his parents—that he can do things in which they will take pleasure. Similarly, an adult needs to feel that he has something to offer in return for the resources that he needs to participate in validating activities. In our kind of society, "something to offer" is defined at the crudest level as a trade, a skill, or the ability and willingness to work and be productive. In the *traditional* definition of adult roles, men need to feel that they can offer their labor on the market in return for the resources they need, and women need to feel that they can offer their willingness and ability to work as wives and mothers.

Deviance

The need to find validating activities—and to find an audience that, because it gets something from one's action, will confirm one's identity as a valid

member of society—is central to human functioning. When access and resources to the conventional means of achieving identity within society are
denied, people set about busily finding a next-best way of achieving it.
(Sometimes this happens when people are so secure about their position in
the mainstream that they are able to explore the possibility of additional
arenas for validation—as with higher-status youth who have been so much
in the news over the past few years.) This is the process that produces a wide
range of deviance in our society; it results in such things as juvenile delinquency, crime, and drug addiction. The activities that the larger society regards as deviant can generally be understood as a by-product of the search
for validating activities outside the mainstream. The vital connection between
deviance (particularly, destructive forms of deviance that impinge on other
people) and lack of resources emphasizes the fact that reducing the prevalance of such deviance can only come about through changes that provide
the resources necessary for young people as they grow up.

Work

Having a job provides validation and increases an individual's sense of well-
being in several ways. First, it provides the economic resources (such as pay
and credit) that allow one to pursue validating activities in his nonwork life.
It also provides contact with others to whom one can be someone. Even
very menial jobs provide a work group in which an individual can come
to feel that he is known and positively regarded for being the particular person that he is. (Perhaps one of the reasons for the unattractiveness of domestic jobs is that they are highly isolated. Often no one is in the house.
When someone is there, the social distance between worker and employer
is so great as to provide little in the way of personal validation for the worker.)
Perhaps even more important than interpersonal contacts is the sense of
security about future income. The job gives evidence day in and day out that
one has something to offer in return for the resources that he needs.[6] To the
extent that workers must participate in the marginal labor market, they are
not able to acquire this sense fully. Ups and downs in employment are destructive for one's sense of valid identity, not only because he receives less
in the way of economic resources but also because the experience of intermittent employment lowers his sense that in the future he will be able to
earn what he needs.

Finally, at a more intimate level, the experience of work (again, even
menial work) provides a sense of mastery, of personal effectiveness, which

increases one's sense of well-being. Although lower-status workers often complain that their jobs don't give them enough of a sense of personal ful-fillment (in comparison to the fulfillment that they know higher-status jobs can give), with few exceptions jobs do allow an individual to have a sense of structured mastery over external reality that most people cannot have with-out a job. Some unemployed men achieve that sense by developing skills that they practice like hobbies, but most research on unemployment shows that they spend a great deal of time "doing nothing."[7]

The Family

Work in our society can be regarded as a specialized version of the social roles that people carry out in every society. An individual is working when he is engaging in activities that are productive for other people. This broad definition is more useful as a starting place than the traditional economic definition that a person is working when he is paid for what he is doing.

Each of the major family roles (male adult, female adult, child) can be thought of as having a work component. The husband/father is expected to be the provider; that is straightforward enough. But much social policy ig-nores the fact that being a housewife is also a job.[8] There is every reason for counting women with children but without husbands as in the labor force but unemployed. The occupation of these women is that of homemaker, but in order to function in that role they need a partner (if not employer) who fulfills the provider role. Particularly in the working and lower classes this is re-garded as the appropriate and meaningful occupational role for a woman. Jobs in the money labor market are regarded either as temporary or strictly secondary. If we took seriously the homemaker role as a job, we might con-sider a system of unemployment insurance for homemakers (to be paid by their husbands), and we would take as a goal of public policy the creation of opportunities for women to find and keep jobs as homemakers—that is, the facilitation of family stability and of remarriage. Such policies would recog-nize the very great "opportunity cost" a woman incurs when she specializes in making a home for a particular man and their children.

The child's role also involves work elements, but because so much of what children are expected to do is defined as "for their own good," we often don't perceive the child's "production" which he exchanges for the re-sources that significant others provide him with. In fact, children produce values ("services" in economic terms) for parents and siblings. In addition, much of their labor is in the form of investment in themselves as human capital. This is to a considerable extent a validating activity for the parents. (In a more religious age, the child's work in becoming socialized was also regarded as work performed for God.) If in his experiences of the work of socialization the child does not come to feel that he is being productive according to the standards of the significant people around him (parents, peers, teachers), then he readily comes to feel that he is not likely to have something of value to offer on the social labor market when he is grown up.

One observes among women on welfare an effort to create a role as employed out of their situation of being AFDC mothers. That is, women often speak of themselves as working hard to raise their children and of that activity as in some sense meriting compensation. But there is a fictive quality to that stance exactly because they recognize that society does not value their children very much and does not really care whether they are raised well or not. The best the woman can do as she tries to rationalize her situation as a job is to offer the view that by being a good mother she deserves compensation because she is raising her children right and trying to keep them out of trouble. This is a sad kind of claim for the reciprocity of society—that in return for the support she receives from welfare she will try to keep her children from becoming destructive human beings. For women who are on welfare for long periods of time, year in and year out, the absence of a validating work role is very damaging. This is not to say that they would be better off without welfare; clearly they achieve greater validation with that support than if they had to make do on even more meager resources.

Most women on welfare, however, do not receive it for a long period of their careers as homemakers, and if guaranteed income proposals were accepted, presumably there would not be a very large number of men or women for whom the guarantee was the principal source of income for large portions of their adult family careers. For people for whom that was not the case, and for whom there was no legitimate reason in the form of severe disability, the destructiveness of not being able to participate in the validating activities of social and economic exchange that participation in the labor market provides would be cause for concern. One could hardly view as humane a society in which some people are demeaned by being pensioned off in their early adulthood and thereby are made to feel that they have nothing to offer their fellow human beings. A better situation is a society in which whatever "leisure" is required by the economy is relatively evenly distributed among all adults.

Of course, this is an issue that is hardly likely to arise, since the moral imperative to earn what one gets seems to be significantly weakened only among a small segment of the elite—who probably never really believed it anyway. It is much more likely that enthusiasm for a guaranteed annual income, when combined with indifference to the creation of work opportunities, simply represents a hard-headed recognition that it may be cheaper to pay superfluous people to shut up and be quiet than to try to police them.

As a result of increasing affluence and the emphasis on the value of self-realization, there seem to be several family trends that have important consequences for the role played by economic resources in personal well-being. These changes are all reflections of a general value that each person should live only with the people he finds it satisfying to live with. This preference manifests itself demographically in higher rates of household formation. Young people are now more likely to set up households before marriage than they were in the past. Divorce, when one is unhappy, is increasingly institutionalized and accepted. Women with children are less likely to go home to mother when they separate from their husbands and more likely to set up their own households. Living with relatives is less and less attractive as the years go by. This is particularly important with respect to old age. The aged and their children both seem to have a preference for separate accommodations for the older person (in Florida, if possible!). Since a household is generally expected to take care of its own expenses, and interhousehold transfers even among relatives are regarded as delicate, problematic, and to be avoided if at all possible, the income security of each household is more and more crucial for the well-being of the people who live in it—and one can expect this trend to continue. Therefore, there will be an increasingly sharp association between the income and assets that belong to the persons in a particular household and their well-being. The more autonomous each household defines itself as being vis-à-vis those on whom its members might have some claim through kinship, the greater the impact of ups and downs in income. The impact on the up side is greatly valued (you don't have to share with your relatives), but the impact on the down side is magnified because the normative basis for requesting help from relatives is much less solid than it was in the past.

As people grow up and live their lives, they are engaged in a constant implicit assessment of their likelihood of having the access and resources necessary to maintain a sense of valid identity. People's anticipation of their future chances, particularly as children, adolescents, and young adults, seems to affect quite markedly the way they relate to others and the way they make use of the resources available to them. When people feel that their future possibilities for participating in validating activities are low, and particularly when that estimate is constantly confirmed by others in their world (teachers, police, parents), then the process of searching for alternative or deviant validating sources is set in motion. When people decide that they have nothing to lose, they are much less responsive to social control exercised informally by those in their neighborhood and formally by official agencies.

Thus, the lower the level of resources available to the individual in our society is, the higher the risk to his sense of well-being and the higher the risk to the rest of society of his engaging in behavior that is destructive of the well-being of others. This, of course, does not mean that every individual with low resources has a low sense of self-esteem or behaves destructively. Many people in this situation learn to make do; they invent ways of creating a sense of valid identity for themselves. Many are courageous and vigorous in maintaining constructive and respectable behavior vis-à-vis people around them. The fact that many people do so, however, should not be used as an excuse for society's failure to provide the resources that people need if they are not to risk a low level of well-being. A just society is one in which an individual's well-being is not placed in jeopardy by virtue of inadequate resources.

Low resources for participation in validating activities impinges on family patterns in several ways. One kind of impact occurs before marriage. Involvement in the kind of early premarital sexual activity that leads to premarital pregnancies and illegitimate births (or to forced weddings) often seems to arise from the perception by lower-class girls that their prospects do not include a sufficiently more comfortable life. Therefore, they feel they do not have much to lose by beginning a family early and in a not fully respectable way. The validating activities of motherhood or fatherhood are not overshadowed by the losses the individual feels he is likely to incur by not waiting to what he would consider a more appropriate age (the very late teens or early twenties).[9]

Lower-class girls often express a desire to work at a well-paying job for a few years before marriage. But they are seldom confident that this will really be possible, and therefore their ability to strongly resist the blandishments of boyfriends is weakened. (This is not to say, however, that all lower-class girls who become premaritally pregnant choose to have a child. Indeed, the very high rate of abortion for premarital pregnancy where abortion is freely available indicates that the pregnancies are overwhelmingly unwanted.)

Limited access to resources places a couple in a constant risk of tense and conflicting marital relations. Since neither partner can do his job properly with the resources available, the inducements for self- and other-blame are continually present. The tension introduced by chronic low income is exacerbated if the husband also experiences intermittent unemployment. There is always a question in the wife's mind about whether the husband's unemployment is his fault. The husband is often made to feel like a fifth wheel around the house, both because the sharp division of labor in the lower-class family gives him a minimal constructive role there and because the wife feels he really should be out working or looking for work. The longer the work history the man has to his credit, the more forbearance he can generally expect from his family. In many lower-class families, however, bouts of unemployment are frequent and of fairly long duration. This means that the man is constantly vulnerable to others' opinion that something is wrong with him, that perhaps he does not want to work—rather than that he is not able to find a job.

Chronic low income and the consequent patent inability to provide the family with the resources necessary to live an ordinary life encourages a husband to seek validation in other ways. These other ways often involve an extension of the male peer group activities that are so important in adolescence: endless tinkering with cars, gambling, drinking, running around with women, or simply staying away from home a great deal of time. The wife, who feels that her tie to respectability depends on having a conventional family, is constantly anxious lest her husband stray so far that the family falls apart.

Lower-class marriages end in separation and divorce far more often than higher-income marriages.[10] At the end of ten years of marriage, a woman married to a man whose earning capacity is only at the poverty-level range is probably twice as likely to have lost her husband through divorce as a woman whose husband earns the median income or higher. It seems that income is the only socioeconomic factor of great importance here; research suggests that neither educational level nor occupation makes an independent contribution to the greater propensity to separation and divorce.

Finally, low resources also tend to retard second marriages, lengthening the amount of time men and women spend in the divorced status. The United States seems to be moving toward a stabilized but fairly high divorce rate even for couples whose economic resources are well within the mainstream. But this high divorce rate is also accompanied by a very high remarriage rate. Americans don't dislike marriage and its accompanying family life; they simply have a high probability of at least once changing the partner with whom they live this life.

It is with remarriage that the destructive consequences of the present form of welfare assistance are most obvious. Lower-class women who are separated and divorced often feel extremely lonely, and after a while they are inclined to take boyfriends. In the black lower class, these relationships are often institutionalized in such a way that the boyfriend is included within the family in a quasi-father role.[11] A woman on AFDC often gives serious consideration to marrying her boyfriend; often she is pressed toward marriage by him. But even when he is earning more than the woman receives on AFDC, she must think in a very tough-minded way about her family's likely future. She knows that welfare, though pitifully inadequate, is a steady source of income. Her prospective husband's income, she has good reason to fear, is not likely to be as steady. He is always subject to the possibility of unemployment through no fault of his own. Because of the dim view she is likely to have come to take of men, she may also fear that he will prove to be an unstable source of support even if he doesn't lose his job. In this circumstance, the woman has an either/or choice to make. She can marry her boyfriend and take her chances, knowing that it will be difficult, or she can maintain the less-than-satisfactory boyfriend relationship as long as it lasts and count on her secure source of income. A guaranteed income program (in the form of a negative income tax or demogrant) that covers the working poor would do away with the necessity for making these kinds of agonizing decisions.

A Policy for Increasing Family Resources

The connection between resources and family patterns suggests an overall conclusion: if the economy provided stable employment at wage rates above poverty level for all men, and if all women could therefore look forward to marrying men who could serve in the provider role and whom they could serve in the homemaker role, it is likely that fewer girls would become pregnant before marriage, that lower-class couples would marry at a somewhat later age, that relationships in lower-class marriages would be less tense, that fewer lower-class marriages would break up, and that remarriage would take place more quickly for those that did. All these tendencies would be strengthened if women, too, could readily find stable part- and full-time employment. In that case, lower-class girls could realistically look forward to working for a while when they finished school, and lower-class wives could supplement the family income at some points during the family life cycle.

The legitimate expectation of being able to work when one wants to is thus crucial in providing men and women with a sense of full membership in society during all of their life careers. In the prefamily building years, young people need to be able to find validating activities either in school or at work (or both). Even if their wages are somewhat lower than the level necessary to establish and operate a family, they can still be validated through work if it provides meaningful relationships with others and if it assures the possibility of higher wages when the time to become a parent rolls around. Similarly, at the other end of the family life cycle, when the time for retirement comes, people need to have the resources necessary to participate in the validating activities appropriate for people of their age.

One can offer the following as a standard for how just a society is: society owes all its members the resources necessary to be a husband/father or wife/mother in a family that can reproduce itself—that is, a family with two children. Every adult should have access to the resources necessary for forming such a family and pursuing a family life-style at least close to the mainstream level.

A humane social accounting would investigate how much of each person's time is spent in positions that provide access to validating activities (activities in which he can reciprocate the validation provided by others in an appropriate way). Depending on age and family status, these positions could include a job, student status, family roles, relations with the community, and leisure (defined as freely chosen nonwork activities, not enforced idleness). The inventory would assess the extent to which people have the resources necessary to make use of their access.

Every family must have the resources represented by at least one full-time job. For the most part, this means that employment must be available for the able-bodied head of every household. Over the past quarter of a century we have seen a steady increase in the number of housewives who work at least part-time. There is reason to believe that housewives work to purchase the things necessary for the good life and in order to have a sense of personal fulfillment. Part-time work opportunities are important for older children as a way of learning about the world, earning money, and beginning to develop autonomy as a consumer.

The key, however, is the possibility for the central provider to work full-time, and this should be the first goal of public policy. There may well be some real problems in doing this. If policy moves vigorously forward in the area of insuring greater liberty for women who want to work, investments on that front could well take away from resources available for investment to guarantee jobs for principal providers.

In regard to specific policies to achieve these objectives, it is obvious that one needs a combination of guaranteed income and guaranteed work. It is unfortunate that so much of the reformist energies of the past decade have gone into the issue of guaranteed income, and so little into the issue of guaranteed work. One has the impression that guaranteed income appeals both because it is simpler (one thing the federal government knows how to do well is write checks) and, perhaps, also because those who have been most concerned with problems of equality and social justice in recent times have been identified more with education and welfare institutions and thinking than with labor market institutions. If one could start from scratch to design a program of guaranteed work and income, it probably would not take the forms of a combination of welfare and the government-as-employer-of-last-resort programs that are often discussed today.

A program that did not have to address itself to the constraints of our history and current policies might have the following features:

• At the age of fifteen everyone would begin to be paid a modest stipend as compensation for his work in school. He would receive bonuses depending on how well he did in school and perhaps also as pay for work done at school—such as tutoring younger children, monitoring, providing after school day care, etc.

• At the age of eighteen everyone would be entitled to a given amount of support for further education. He could draw on this account at any point in his lifetime (a kind of universal, permanent GI Bill). To the extent that he drew on his account, he would repay it through a small addition to his social security tax. (The account would not be a grant but a loan which might or might not be used, depending on the individual's own judgment of his interests.)

• When an individual left school (at any time after fifteen) he could either find a job on his own or register for work with the employment service. He would be given a job for which there was a scale of compensation based on work experience. Thus, his wage for the first couple of years would be at a relatively low apprentice level but would increase with further years of work or with additional schooling.

• When women had children, they would receive paid furloughs until the children were old enough to enter public school (kindergarten at present, perhaps earlier ages in the future). If they were heads of households, women would be expected to work full-time once they no longer had young children in school. The jobs available would allow a variety of different working hours depending on the child care arrangements available.

• Women with children in school would be guaranteed half-time jobs.

As an accompaniment of such a guaranteed work program, a guaranteed income program in the form of a demogrant would most effectively preserve the incentive to work.[12] The income guarantee could be calculated on a per person (that is, including children), per adult, or per parent basis. There may be good reasons for having a high level of guaranteed income per adult rather than a lower level per person, since per person guarantees tend to bring about significant redistribution toward large families, and it is not really clear that there is a consensus that such a redistribution is equitable. Some balance between these two approaches could be struck by having fairly high guarantees per adult and lower guarantees per child with the guarantees for a large number of children rapidly tapering off to zero.

In any case, it is important to recognize that a guaranteed income is never likely to be high enough to provide families with incomes necessary to participate in mainstream validating activities. For incomes at that level, we must rely on a guaranteed work program. All that a guaranteed income can accomplish is to keep families from living in real social misery.

The results of these programs are illustrated by table 15.1, which shows present income distribution; income distribution if a guaranteed income eliminated poverty; and income distribution if a guaranteed work program eliminated the marginal, near-poor level of living.

This kind of a policy requires, in addition to the particular programs for institutionalizing the guaranteed income and guaranteed job elements, a firm and full commitment by the government to maintain at all times an extremely tight labor market, to create demand for labor at all skill levels (rather than heavier demand for high skill levels than for low ones), and to maintain a near zero rate of people unemployed for more than one or two months. The guaranteed income program would go into effect simultane-

Table 15.1. Effects of Guaranteed Income and Guaranteed Work Programs on Income Distribution

Living Level	Family Income in 1971	Distribution in 1971	Distribution under Guaranteed Income Program	Distribution under Guaranteed Work Program
Poverty	under $5,000	19%		
Marginal	5,000– 7,499	15	28%	
Getting along	$7,500– 9,999	17	23	51%
Comfortable	$10,000– 15,000	27	27	27
Prosperous or rich	over $15,000	22	22	22

ously with a revised income tax system designed to recoup part of the guarantee from employed people with incomes above the guarantee, but the program would primarily be paid for by revised tax rates on families with income and assets greater than twice the median family's income and assets. A tax revision that takes a small amount of additional taxes at and somewhat above the median, and a larger amount from persons well above the median, would be regarded as fair by the great majority of Americans.

In fact, a guaranteed income plus guaranteed jobs program, if properly presented, would command strong public support. A variety of research findings over the past thirty-five years suggests that there has always been an ample reservoir of support for income redistribution if the poor *earned* higher incomes by making greater contributions to society.[13] Thus, the problem in the development of public policy insuring personal well-being through provision of access and resources necessary to participate in validating activities is not one of acceptance by the general public. The difficulty is rather whether the government can meet the challenge to its creativity that such a program will involve.

Notes

1. These issues are dealt with in a cross-cultural context by Melford Spiro, "Social Systems, Personality, and Functional Analysis," in *Studying Personality Cross-*

Culturally, ed. Bert Kaplan (New York: Row Peterson, 1961); Ward Goodenough, *Cooperation and Change* (New York: Russell Sage Foundation, 1963).

2. Lee Rainwater, *Behind Ghetto Walls* (Chicago: Aldine, 1970), chap. 13. This formulation of the relevance of resources defined in a highly general way is well presented in S. M. Miller and Pamela Roby, *The Future of Inequality* (New York: Basic Books, 1970). An initial effort at a cross-national survey of distribution of a variety of resources is contained in S. M. Miller and Martin Rein, "The Possibilities and Limits of Social Policy," prepared for a working meeting of the Research Committee on Poverty, Social Welfare and Social Policy of the International Sociological Association, Bucharest, December 1971.

3. Herbert J. Gans, *The Urban Villagers* (New York: Free Press, 1962); idem, *The Levittowners* (New York: Pantheon, 1967); Mirra Komarovsky, *Blue-Collar Marriage* (New York: Random House, 1964); Sar A. Levitan, ed., *Blue-Collar Workers: A Symposium on Middle America* (New York: McGraw-Hill, 1970); Lee Rainwater, Richard Coleman, and Gerald Handel, *Workingman's Wife* (New York: Oceana, 1959); Arthur B. Shostak, *Blue-Collar Life* (New York: Random House, 1969).

4. A useful exercise for grasping this point is to examine the contents of the budgets developed for city families by the Bureau of Labor Statistics over the past quarter century (U.S. Department of Labor, Bureau of Labor Statistics, *Workers' Budgets in the United States: City Families and Single Persons, 1946 and 1947,* Bureau of Labor Statistics Bulletin 927, 1948; Helen S. Lamale and Margaret S. Stotz, "The Interim City Worker's Family Budget," *Monthly Labor Review,* August 1960; U.S. Department of Labor, Bureau of Labor Statistics, *Three Standards of Living for an Urban Family of Four Persons,* Bureau of Labor Statistics Bulletin 1570–1575, spring 1967).

5. David Riesman and Howard Roseborough, "Careers and Consumer Behavior," in *A Modern Introduction to the Family,* ed. N. Bell and E. F. Vogel (New York: Free Press, 1960). For a discussion of the implications of this point for understanding standards of living see Lee Rainwater, *What Money Buys: Inequality and the Social Meanings of Income* (in press).

6. Peter B. Doeringer and Michael J. Piore, *Internal Labor Markets and Manpower Analysis* (Lexington, Mass.: D. C. Heath, 1971).

7. Studies of unemployment provide some of the best insights into this kind of situation. Those done during the depression are still useful for the insight they give into family employment processes: in particular, E. Wight Bakke, *Citizens Without Work* (New Haven: Yale University Press, 1940); Mirra Komarovsky, *The Unemployed Man and His Family* (New York: Dryden, 1940); Earl L. Koos, *Families in Trouble* (New York: King's Crown Press, 1946). Several papers in A. B. Shostak and W. Gomberg, eds., *Blue-Collar Workers* (Englewood Cliffs, N.J.: Prentice-Hall, 1964), deal with these issues in a more contemporary context: S. M. Miller, "The Outlook of Working Class Youth," H. Kirk Dansereau, "Work and the Teenage Blue Collarite," Michael Schwartz and George Henderson, "The Culture of Unemployment: Some Notes on Negro Children," and William G. Dyer, "Family Reactions to the Father's Job." See also Orville R. Gursslin and Jack L. Roach, "Some Issues in Training the Unemployed," *Social Problems,* summer 1964, pp. 86–98; the classic article by Allison Davis, "The Motivations of the Under-Privileged Worker," in *Industry and Society,* ed. William F. Whyte (New York: McGraw-

Hill, 1946); Marc A. Fried, "The Role of Work in a Mobile Society," in Sam B. Warner, Jr., *Planning for a Nation of Cities* (Cambridge: M.I.T. Press, 1966).

8. Helen Z. Lopata, *Occupation: Housewife* (New York: Oxford University Press, 1972), presents a long overdue, thorough examination of the housewife role in several social classes.

9. The ghetto ethnographies of the 1960s make these points quite forcefully. See Ulf Hannerz, *Soulside* (New York: Columbia University Press, 1969); Elliot Liebow, *Tally's Corner* (Boston: Little, Brown, 1967); Rainwater, *Behind Ghetto Walls;* David A. Schultz, *Coming Up Black* (Englewood Cliffs, N.J.: Prentice-Hall, 1969).

10. See Phillips Cutright, "Income and Family Events: Marital Stability," and Paul C. Glick and Arthur J. Norton, "Frequency, Duration, and Probability of Marriage and Divorce," *Journal of Marriage and the Family,* May 1971, pp. 291–317. Also see U.S. Bureau of the Census, *Current Population Reports,* series P-20, no. 223, "Social and Economic Variations in Marriage, Divorce, and Remarriage: 1967" (Washington, D.C.: U.S. Government Printing Office, 1971); Phillips Cutright and John Scanzoni, "Trends in Marriage and the Family: The Effect of Past and Future Income Supplements," prepared for the Subcommittee on Fiscal Policy, Joint Economic Committee of the Congress, May 1972.

11. The ghetto ethnographies referred to in note 9 are almost unanimous on this point, which is developed most systematically by Schultz. Comparable studies for the white lower class, dealing with quasi-father kinds of relationships, do not exist. Some unpublished studies by Robert S. Weiss suggest that boyfriends are held at a greater distance, filling the kind of role Schultz described as "the supportive companion" rather than a quasi-father role. For both blacks and whites, however, the considerations on the part of the AFDC mother described here would apply.

12. A very useful systematic treatment of these issues is found in James Tobin, "Raising the Incomes of the Poor," in *Agenda for the Nation,* ed. Kermit Gordon (Washington, D.C.: Brookings Institution, 1969).

13. See Rainwater, *What Money Buys;* Michael E. Schiltz, *Public Attitudes towards Social Security, 1935–1965,* Social Security Administration, Report No. 33 (Washington, D.C.: U.S. Department of Health, Education, and Welfare, 1970); Amitai Etzioni and Carol O. Atkinson, *Sociological Implications of Alternative Income Transfer Systems* (New York: Columbia University, Bureau of Social Science Research, September 1969).

16 Work and Welfare

Thomas C. Thomas

Work is one of those important words in the English language that has been
overworked. It has many definitions, and consequently, while everyone
knows what it means, the term is rarely used precisely. In recent years, economists have had an important role in policy analyses involving work, and
their definition of the activity has come to predominate. Technical jargon
aside, economists describe work as any activity that a person is paid to do:
it is made up of those activities whose wage cost is included in the calcula-
tion of the Gross National Product. The limitations of this economic definition
become obvious upon reading any of the psychological, sociological, or
anthropological discussions of work.[1] In this literature one sees that work not
only provides man with his daily bread but also serves to define much about
who he is in society, how he relates to his fellowmen, and how they relate to
him. In short, it defines his status and his self-image.

Nowhere has the overemphasis on the economic and the near exclusion
of the sociopsychological dimensions of work been more harmful than in
welfare policy. From the economic viewpoint, either one works and earns a
wage, or one is on welfare and receives a transfer payment. It may at first
seem that the main problem for the welfare recipient is whether the amount
of the transfer payment is enough to meet his physical needs, but a substantial literature documents that this is far from the only issue—that there is

a whole complex of related psychological and social factors that act to debilitate him. The proposals for a guaranteed annual income are a step toward improving the psychological dimensions of welfare, but they still reflect the economic focus.

Society differentiates sharply between work and welfare, and there is general agreement that all those who can work should work. The analysis leading to this "jobs policy" is usually based only upon economic considerations, and it overlooks so much complexity that the policy it advocates is at best unimaginative and at worst harmful.

In this paper I start from the position that a satisfactory society aims to provide everyone with both the economic and the psychological rewards of work. A welfare policy based upon transfer payments alone degrades and makes pets of welfare recipients, creating long-term problems of alienation and ever increasing economic demands. Rampant idleness is no solution. Psychologically, as well as economically, everyone must work.

Work may be thought of as occurring in those relationships in which an individual contributes something to society and receives economic and/or psychological rewards in return. This expansion of the economic definition is important—consider the role of the housewife. There is no market payment for her services, and her labor is not included in the GNP. But if one housewife decides to work in a child care center and a second housewife is thus freed to come clean the first one's house, both are paid, and cleaning and child care suddenly become part of the GNP.

This example highlights the fact that there are many unpaid roles that would have to be paid for if they weren't filled for nonmonetary reasons. But it is not at all clear that on balance society would be better off (that overall goods, services, and psychological rewards would increase) if, say, the 35 million housewives became part of the labor market and received wages.[2]

There are 45 million students in elementary and secondary schools. Most of them do not have jobs. In fact, those below a certain age are forced not to work by a combination of compulsory school attendance laws and child labor laws. A reasonable conclusion is that society believes that students can contribute more by not working than by working. Students might be said to "work" by studying to improve their skills for later work and not by competing for the existing jobs. (The value of study as work is illustrated more concretely by the fact that some students, primarily in higher education, are company employees and are paid to go to school.)

Finally, there are the 16 million retired persons, many of whom do not desire to work or are not physically able to. Nevertheless, an appreciable number would like a job but have been forced into retirement to make way for younger workers. They are kept out of the labor market to a great extent by the restrictive provisions of the Social Security Act. Since their retirement is in most cases financed in part or fully by taxes on the current income of others,[3] it is reasonable to assume that their nonwork is more valuable to the society than their work.

Solutions to Welfare
The vast majority of welfare recipients are housewives, dependent students, or retired persons, and society penalizes them psychologically as well as economically. The historical evolution of the special treatment of those on public assistance is easy to trace but difficult to justify in terms of equity. Indeed, one can argue for a reduction in their psychological plight (and perhaps some of their economic hardship). If their roles as housewives, students, and retired people were not devalued just because they are on welfare, the social order would be far more egalitarian. Clearly, the distinctions between worker and nonworker, producer and parasite, worthy and unworthy, are as much a question of perception as a description of objective circumstance.

Expansion of the Labor Market
The ostensible solution to welfare is to open up work opportunities until everyone has a suitable job. For nearly forty years, both Keynesian and neo-Keynesian economists have told us that through appropriate fiscal and monetary policies the government can expand or contract business and tune the economy to full employment. While such policies have had some notable successes (in the mid-sixties, for example), it has become clear that achieving full employment depends on favorable conditions, which do not now exist. Factors limiting the ability of fiscal and monetary policy to create jobs in the private sector include the deficit in the balance of payments, the incentive to replace workers with machines as wages rise, persistent inflation despite sluggish demand, and export of employment overseas through foreign subsidiaries.

Our economy is now barely able to absorb the yearly increases in the labor force due to population growth. Rather than creating jobs for those on welfare and better jobs for those who are underemployed, the talk today is of reducing the number of workers by lowering the retirement age and increasing the average number of years of formal schooling. Economic policy is having much too hard a time attempting to reduce the more than 5 million who are classified as unemployed to be expected to provide large quantities of jobs in the private sector for the 10 to 30 million who are underemployed or on welfare.[4]

This leaves the government sector as the place to expand employment. The number of government jobs at all levels—particularly state and local—has been growing rapidly, and this trend is expected to continue. A deliberate expansion of the already large governmental bureaucracies to implement the role of employer of last resort may be unsound, however. One must consider the problem carefully, basing a decision on the answers to a number of fundamental questions about governance: What are the functions of the different levels of government, what are the relative advantages of expansion in the public, private, and nonprofit sectors, and what are the possibilities for creating new institutional forms?

The public sector currently employs about 13.1 million workers, 2.6 million in the federal government (excluding the armed forces) and 10.5 million in state and local government. Ten million new workers would represent a 75 percent increase in total government employment and a 385 percent increase in federal government employment if absorbed by it alone. A new Works Progress Administration or Civilian Conservation Corps would have to be formed so that existing agencies would not be overwhelmed if anywhere near this number of new jobs were contemplated.

Moreover, expansion in the public and private sectors is usually talked about in a very general way—one that tends to assume that jobs and workers are relatively homogeneous. In fact, of course, they are not, and considerably greater understanding of the limitations of a policy of labor market expansion for those on welfare is necessary.

Most policy analyses of poverty and employment have tended to follow the classical economic approach of viewing labor as relatively uniform except for differences in skill levels. The contradictions between this view and observed behavior has led to the development of the *dual labor market* theory, which concludes that even if the demand for workers could be expanded appreciably, the benefits to those who are on welfare or are underemployed would be small.

Michael Piore describes the dual labor market in the following terms:

One sector of [the labor] market . . . termed, the primary market, offers jobs which possess several of the following traits: high wages, good working conditions, employment stability and job security, equity and due process in the administration of work rules, and chances for advancement. The secondary sector has jobs that . . . tend to involve low wages, poor working conditions, considerable variability in employment, harsh and arbitrary discipline, and little opportunity to advance.

The factors which generate the dual market structure and confine the poor to the secondary sector are complex. . . . the most important characteristic distinguishing primary from secondary jobs appears to be the behavioral requirements they impose upon the work force, particularly that of employment stability. Insofar as secondary workers are barred from primary employment by a real qualification [not race, sex, or ethnicity], it is generally their inability to show up for work regularly and on time. Secondary employers are far more tolerant of lateness and absenteeism, and many secondary jobs are of such short duration that these do not matter. Work skills, which receive considerable emphasis in most discussions of poverty and employment, do not appear a major barrier to primary employment (although, because regularity and punctuality are important to successful learning in school and on the job, such behavioral traits tend to be highly correlated with skills).[5]

Piore goes on to describe the factors that generate the secondary labor market, draw the poor to it, and tend over time to lock in even the poor who initially had appropriate traits for the primary labor market.

It would be a mistake to consider the secondary labor market intrinsically bad. It fits the needs of the young, who tend to be excluded from the primary labor market until they are in their twenties, and it matches the preferred life-style of an increasing number of people who do not want to be tied down to a job. It does not, however, meet the needs of those who wish to establish a stable, economically secure, and socially approved family life.

Consequently the following problem emerges: if the expansion is in primary jobs it will not benefit appreciably the underemployed in the secondary labor market or those on welfare (most of whom have secondary labor market characteristics). There is some mobility from the secondary to the primary labor market, and high demand for labor in the primary labor market would tend to increase this mobility. It appears much more likely, however, that the main effect of such demand would be that more middle-class women (with the required behavioral traits) would be drawn into the labor force or that primary jobs would be redesigned to have some secondary characteristics, rather than that people in secondary jobs would move to primary jobs.

Expansion in the secondary labor market would not solve the poverty problem (and would not tend to reduce primary unemployment). Moreover, as several analyses have shown, among them Piore's in the Boston area and Elizabeth Durbin's in New York City,[6] welfare is generally economically competitive and superior to much secondary employment. Many heads of families receiving Aid to Families with Dependent Children (AFDC) literally cannot afford to work.

Proposed changes in welfare rules might alleviate this situation and make secondary employment economically more attractive, but the behavioral traits of secondary employees would not thereby be changed. Poor families need the financial and, more importantly, the psychological rewards associated with primary employment.

Dual labor market economists suggest changes in manpower training and enforcement of equal opportunity laws to help the poor find primary employment. Unfortunately, these proposals appear to be weak, and there is little prospect in this decade for an improvement matched to the size of the problem.

It appears therefore that new institutional structures are required, designed specifically to enable the poor to obtain rewards similar to those derived from primary employment. Otherwise the outlook is bleak. The poor will tend to remain poor, and large groups will become no more than pets. This status implies a profound degradation of the human spirit, and the poor will probably become unruly, requiring the "best available" in surveillance techniques, behavior modification, and chemotherapy to keep them under control. The central city may then become a new reservation.

It appears possible that new institutional structures could be created to avoid this brave new world, but it will not be easy, and it is not likely to be successful unless there is vigorous support from both government and business. In the discussion that follows I am not advancing a panacea, but I believe that some sort of institutional innovation is our only hope.

Institutional Change

Problems of work are greatest for the poor but are by no means limited to them. Job scarcity, job obsolescence, and job irrelevance prevail as a consequence of the current structure of employment. Despite all the talk of leisure, the work week ranges from fifty to sixty hours for the upper middle class, while the poor suffer from enforced idleness. The long-term solution appears to lie in the creation of a large number of work roles supporting learning and planning in the broadest sense. Briefly, the arguments for this are as follows. As it becomes possible for machines to relieve man of burdensome and tedious jobs, there are both economic and humane reasons for supporting such substitution. This leads to the question, "If only a fraction of the available work force is required to supply all necessary goods and services, what are the rest to do and how should society function for them?" Recent economic reasoning has tended to give the answer, "Stimulate demand for more goods and services." For both ecological and psychological reasons, this is an unsatisfactory long-term answer.

There are at least two alternative activities that contribute to human growth and well-being and yet are "nonpolluting." One is *learning*—including enhancement of knowledge and skills, exploration, research, and personal development. The other is *participative planning* (at local, regional, national, and planetary levels and in public, private, and voluntary sectors) of ecologically desirable use of land and of humane application of ever increasing technological powers. Thus, the long-term resolution of questions of how a technologically advanced society employs its citizens appears to require evolution into what might be termed a learning and planning society.

The poor must take part in this transformation and be able eventually to assume new work roles in the future society. As the previous section has indicated, new and different paths to participation will probably be necessary as long as job scarcity and the damaging aspects of division of the labor market into primary and secondary components continue to exist. These alternative paths must be consistent with the evolution of the dominant part of the society and must facilitate crossover to the main path. They must be a viable alternative to primary employment, at least until the problems of job scarcity and unsatisfactory aspects of secondary employment cease to exist.

Thus, in the near future, new institutional forms are needed to provide the poor with the same sorts of economic and psychological rewards that those in the primary labor market receive and to facilitate transition to a future society in which the basic problem of how the society employs *all* of its citizens is more satisfactorily resolved. A multiplicity of institutions will be required, since the poor are not a homogeneous group. American Indians on reservations, poor whites in Appalachia, and blacks and Chicanos in urban ghettos are among the diverse groups who require new forms of work. Although they do have some common handicaps, such as inadequate income and basic services, low status, and little participation in decision making, the removal of these handicaps will have to be keyed to their specific circumstances.

My initial assumption is that the poor have a contribution to make to society at large and to each other and that the task is to find the structure that would encourage this contribution. Using the economic idea of value added, the approach could be stated as follows: each person has some social value added that he can contribute, and for the good of himself and society this contribution should be actualized.

Poor people often make valuable contributions to their family's well-being, even when the institutions of business and government do not appear able to use their abilities. This suggests that, at a group or subeconomy scale, some institution might work that is a cross between an extended family and an industry. There have been attempts in the past to establish similar situations, and from each experience some insight can be obtained. The following two examples show the range of such communities.

If any group is more socially outcast and more resistant to help than the poor it is drug addicts. Nevertheless, through such "communities" as Synanon and Hilltop, large numbers of drug addicts have given up their habits and have begun to lead productive lives in these communities or in the outside world. Each person in the Synanon community is expected to be a contributing member, with some allowance made for his initial physical state. The technical skills required are not great, but the interpersonal skills needed to support relationships in a small community are initially beyond the capability of the addict. But through planned confrontations between members—in which interpersonal problems are dealt with objectively and openly—the former addicts learn to be effective members of a working community (although, of course, Synanon is not a panacea; it does fail with some). All the members are there voluntarily and voluntarily confront their problems. The crucial element of the will to overcome the problem must be present; without it the addict cannot be helped.

Another community, far removed from the world of the drug addict, is that of the Mormons. During the Great Depression, Mormons, like many others, were faced with poverty because the market economy broke down and goods and services could not be distributed. Essentially, their solution was to create their own subeconomy; they issued scrip in lieu of money. Using scrip, Mormon farmers, artisans, and businessmen were once again able to function nearly as effectively as when the money economy was operating properly.

Drug addicts have, in a magnified way, all the problems and liabilities of poor people. The Mormons during the depression had only the lack of necessary goods and services in common with the poor. An amalgam of the solutions in the two examples would appear to have the characteristics of a new institution that could serve the urban poor.

The tasks of the new institution would range from objective ones focused on economic needs to subjective ones focused on social and psychological needs. (This is only to convey the breadth of the task. In fact, the tasks cannot be separated, for they impinge in a highly interactive way upon the poor. Poverty is a systemic situation which yields only marginally to piece-meal solutions.) Some of the more important functions the new institution would perform are as follows:

• Increasing the quantity and effective utilization of goods and services with a minimum of additional governmental cost (and perhaps a long-term reduction in cost)

• Developing personal traits of responsibility for task performance, temporal obligations, team effort, and trustworthiness

• Providing skill training that provides "instant" gratification

• Increasing personal safety and reducing openness to robbery and rape

• Enabling participants to build a life in their community rather than providing escape for the lucky few

• Providing access to the system: teaching participants about the rights they have, how they can work within the system, how they can make the system work for them

• Breaking dependency patterns; increasing the power and control of participants over their own fates

• Creating environments for supportive interpersonal relationships to overcome the depersonalization and loneliness of poverty.

There are more tasks, but this list indicates the kind of aims that a new institution that is an alternate to welfare must have.

The next section outlines the characteristics that a new institution might have. This can only be speculative: the broad outlines appear plausible and the possibilities are exciting, but no detailed feasibility analysis has been carried out. The purpose here is to indicate a direction of high potential, not to provide a specific solution.

Design for a Community Corporation

The design of this exemplary community assumes a membership drawn primarily from urban families receiving AFDC payments. Because most of these families have female heads, however, other categories of poor families and single male adults would need to be included. The community life envisioned would require at least one male adult for every two female adults. The inclusion of different categories of poor families is consistent with the goal of high membership density; most of the people in a confined area, ranging from three or four buildings to a few blocks, would belong to the same community.

The objective is to provide an acceptable economic and psychological standard of living for community members. This would be reached through providing them with cooperative, reinforcing tasks done for their mutual benefit. This does not preclude endeavors outside the community, but, at least in the early days, the internal needs for organization and growth would leave little energy to be directed externally. And we must keep in mind that people who are isolated, dependent, mistrustful, and mutually exploitative and are not task-oriented will not be able to transform their community into a viable, functioning, mutually reinforcing institution without considerable effort and commitment.

The major initial resources of each member of the community would be income and some free time. Some of the members might be working, but most would be on welfare or, in the future, on a guaranteed annual income. Either way, the assumption is that all would have a continuous income that would provide the same basis for rational individual planning that wages in the primary labor market do. The community would not place primary emphasis on getting its members off welfare except to the extent that this would benefit an individual. The central objective would be to make the best use of the money and talents available in the community, not to substitute one source of income for another. (Government, business, and the general public would find it in their interest to support such a community because it would be developing the skills and personal characteristics that the poor will eventually need to participate in a "learning and planning economy.") Under present societal conditions the costs of welfare or a guaranteed

annual income can be considered to be sunk costs. A positive aspect of
the alternative approach offered here is that it would improve the utilization
of these funds so that expenses would not mount further and the intergenerational cycle of poverty would be broken.

The management task for the community would be to use both its small
cash income and its free time to improve the life of its members. Those items
and services that require either heavy capital in their production (such as
appliances and most foodstuffs) or a high level of technical skill (such as
medicine and law) would be purchased from the outside market economy.
Those that require mainly labor (such as cooking, child care, appliance and
house repair, and mending and sewing) would be done with the contributed
time of the community members. Training courses could be short and
provide instant gratification: the new skill could be put to immediate use.
Quality control would result from peer pressure to fulfill the obligations
between community members already agreed upon.

Organizational Structure

To achieve the design criteria specified above, it appears that three different
scales of operation would be needed, the smallest involving clusters of
five to fifteen families who would operate almost as extended families.
Each cluster would provide the basic psychological support structure for its
members and the context within which skills in interpersonal relationships
would be developed. Some services could be provided within the cluster,
such as some meal preparation and child care, but efficient operation both
in buying on the outside market and in scheduling of internal services would
require groups of 100 to 300 families. This group would be the "community
corporation" and would represent the primary governance level; documents
of incorporation or charters would be drawn up for them. This size would
permit the corporation, if concentrated in a small area, to have a large
impact on and control over its environment.

The largest unit, the "development corporation," would primarily perform
administrative, political, public relations, and maintenance functions. It
would be on the same scale as the political unit in which it functioned—
city or borough—and would work with local, state, and federal authorities,
businesses, and civic groups to provide a favorable climate for the community corporations, supplying funds and services whenever possible. It would
furnish the management know-how to get the community corporations
operating effectively. In cooperation with other agencies it would develop

and schedule training sessions so that community members could learn skills that would allow them to provide the services required to improve their life and eventually to take over direction of their own community corporations.

Businesses could offer their managerial capability and capital resources to the development corporation (and even earn a modest return). In cooperation with the development corporation, government could aid the community corporation through funding pilot tests, conducting research on appropriate organizational models, insuring loans or bonding agreements, and assisting the development and community corporations in participating in applicable federal, state, and local programs—urban renewal, job training, or child care, for example. (As weak new institutions, it is mandatory that both development and community corporations avoid competing with established interests. Thus, they might have to steer clear of some programs —to avoid construction or child care lobbies, for example—and could not allow themselves to be seen as threatening to any major business or labor union. Of course, the more internally oriented they are, the less likelihood of conflict. Such an internal orientation is consistent with early organization needs.)

The development corporation, the outside arm and support system for the community corporation, would also act to pool the needs and resources of separate communities when desirable—in establishing a medical clinic, for instance. The community corporation would be directed inward toward its members, interacting with the outside world primarily in its purchase of goods and services on the open market. Of course, each community corporation would be free to take a more active outside role as it matured, but the development corporation would have a continuing and important role to play.

Individual Contributions

One of the first questions a prospective member would ask is "How much of my welfare check and how many hours of my 'free' time will I have to contribute to gain the proposed benefits of the community corporation?" This is an impossible question to answer in the abstract because it critically depends upon the services provided to the families. It also depends upon the size and composition of each family and the size of their welfare payment. Some communities might attempt total sharing of resources and work (consistent with the ideals of the utopian communities of the past or the communes of today). Such a course is not consistent with the mainstream of American experience, however, and it is unlikely that many community corporations would elicit it despite its apparent simplicity.

Nevertheless, the harshness of ghetto life and the need for psychological support suggests that close-knit communities would be called for in most instances. Depending upon the structure of the real estate market, it would probably be desirable for the communities (and certainly the clusters) to purchase contiguous living units for their members. This approach would have the following advantages:

• Probable reduction in the cost of housing
• Incentives and opportunities to improve the property and develop handy-man skills
• Ability to control the immediate environment through collective efforts on litter and garbage collection, vermin and pest control, removal of undesirables (pushers, addicts, winos)
• Provision for mutual protection against crime
• Common facilities, such as day care centers and game rooms.

It might also be advantageous for food to be bought in bulk and for the clusters to share the largest meal of the day. This would provide a focal point for community interaction, maximize the economies of bulk buying, create a position of "dietician" to improve group health, and encourage an adult community life. The two smaller meals of the day, presumably breakfast and lunch, could be handled on a family basis if desired.

Community day care facilities also appear highly desirable. They would meet an obvious need, would build the sense of community, and could make time available for other community tasks, such as sewing and clothing repair, cooking, light appliance and house repair, participation in the management functions of the community (buying food, planning meals, accounting, and scheduling work), and taking courses to train for any of these skills.

If the community were as interactive as this discussion suggests, relatively little would need to be bought by individuals on the outside market. For a family of one adult and three children with a monthly welfare check of $300, perhaps $50 per month would suffice for family funds. Another $50 to $75 per month might be their drawing account for inclusion in community bulk purchases, the rest of the check going to the community for common items such as rent, meals, and capital purchases.[7]

The question of capital purchases deserves special note. The assured income of the community corporation would provide the collateral for loans for group purchases. The largest loans would be for building mortgages if economic and psychological analyses warranted the purchase of housing. (Such mortgages might require government insurance or support.) Smaller items such as sewing machines, tools, repair kits, and some furniture are small capital purchases that could be made out of community funds. Individual ownership of such items would be redundant, given a respect for community goods, and probably would not be financially possible for most families.

Governance and Training

The community corporation would be a highly sophisticated organization, a miniature economy with foreign and domestic trade. It is not to be expected that the poor could head such an enterprise immediately. The development corporation would be expected to provide the outside leadership until the membership was prepared to assume full responsibility. There are many sources for such expertise that would perform the administrative and leadership service for a small fee. Businesses might be interested in the role as part of their social responsibility, and so might the nonprofit sector. Perhaps best of all, existing corporations could some day aid in the establishment of new ones. The main points are that such start-up aid could be made available if time were taken to develop it and that the members of the community corporation would always retain the final word over the hired management concerning the corporation's actions.

The objective is to have the members eventually be fully competent to run their own corporation. They could then train with an assured use of the skills they acquired. They could interact with the larger systems of society in learning how to make society work for the benefit of the corporation, and they could have a feeling of control over their own destiny. The leadership positions in these communities would be responsible management positions. A 100-family community could well have a cash flow of over $100,000 per year and capital stock to manage of over $250,000. If properly supported and trained, members could develop the skills to manage this scale of enterprise, and these are primary labor market skills.

This is not to depreciate the other tasks in the community. For example, six-week programs teaching welfare mothers to sew have had remarkable results not only in terms of the clothing produced but in terms of the effect upon self-image as the women saw what they could accomplish. Training in food preparation, handyman work, and child care could provide the same objective and subjective rewards. While the community corporation is not proposed as a training ground for the primary labor force (it is viewed as an end in itself), it could probably perform such training more effectively than the current manpower training programs, which tend to fit the poor only for the secondary labor force.

One major learning opportunity would be in the resolution of arguments among community members arising in either interpersonal relationships or questions of task performance. A type of governance similar to a New England town hall meeting appears ideal. In addition, complaint sessions, encounter groups, or Synanon-type games would probably be used to bring problems into the open and to help members confront them. The primary requirement for such sessions, whichever model is drawn upon, is that they be seen primarily as a confrontational yet supportive situation for the participants, rather than as a place to undercut or achieve some advantage over each other.

There are innumerable other items that would have to be worked out. Some of them relate to how the development corporation would approach an inner-city neighborhood (and the city power structure) to maximize chances of successfully establishing community corporations. Certain obvious problems of trust would have to be faced (the "man" had better not be the person who tries to convince the minority poor to join), and those handling the corporation's money would need to be bonded. Provisions would also have to be made for those who would have to withdraw from the corporation to receive their share of the accumulated surplus. This list goes on and on.

Clusters, community corporations, and development corporations operating within the rough guidelines that have been sketched here appear to offer a real chance to meet the design objectives that I set forth earlier—and they do not require an increase in welfare costs. They would also reduce the dependency and lack of power of those on welfare. In the past a system like this might have appeared threatening, but the self-interest of the wealthy and the middle class no longer demands a large supply of low-paid, unskilled labor. My hope is that this institution would support family life, aid in breaking the intergenerational cycle of poverty, and create a new and dynamic way to meet the needs of the poor, and perhaps others, in a post-industrial leisure society. A new path for alternative forms of work is badly needed for all of us.

Notes

1. Hannah Arendt, *The Human Condition* (Chicago: University of Chicago Press, 1958); Michael Carter, *Into Work* (Baltimore: Penguin Books, 1966); Thomas F. Green, *Work, Leisure, and the American Schools* (New York: Random House, 1968); Stanley Parker, *The Future of Work and Leisure* (New York: Praeger, 1971); Adriano Tilgher, *Homo Faber: Work through the Ages* (Chicago: Henry Regnery, 1958).

2. If many women are confined to the housewife role through sexual discrimination, the status of this role thereby being lowered both for women who want another role and for those who want to be housewives, then the elimination of the discrimination would benefit society. The "marketization" of all housewife roles is only one way to accomplish this, however, and hardly the best way.

3. Far less than 50 percent of the funds paid out as Old Age Survivors Disability and Health Insurance (OASDHI) benefits comes from funds previously put into the fund through employee contributions.

4. The broad range reflects some uncertainty about the number on public assistance who could work and the number who are underemployed. Some estimates have placed the number underemployed at two to two and a half times the number unemployed in most cities.

5. Michael J. Piore, "Jobs and Training," in *The State and the Poor,* ed. Samuel H. Beer and Richard E. Barringer (Cambridge, Mass.: Winthrop, 1970).

6. Elizabeth F. Durbin, *Welfare Income and Employment: An Economic Analysis of Family Choice* (New York: Praeger, 1969).

7. Nothing in the design of the community corporation is planned to weaken family life. Strengthening family life is a principal objective, though approached indirectly through the removal of the pressure which disrupts the family life of the poor.

Afterword

Edward M. Kennedy

The quality of work in America has been the subject of Upton Sinclair novels, of Chaplin films, and of a libraryful of scholarly tomes. For decades, unions have fought to raise the wages and to improve the working conditions of their members. Yet today there is a growing awareness that new standards are being demanded of work. The content of the job itself is increasingly the subject of collective bargaining by our largest unions and their corporate employers.

At the same time, governments are reacting to the renewed interest and concern for the role and character of work in technologically advanced societies. With slight variations in terminology and emphasis, legislation dealing with job satisfaction is pending in several Western European parliaments.

In Britain, the government already has formed a tripartite board of business, labor, and government to experiment in this area. In France, national reporting on work satisfaction has begun. In Sweden, the Prime Minister has asserted, "The task of the seventies must be to give the worker a better surrounding and more say over his workplace." Throughout the industrialized world, we see a burgeoning movement to take a fresh look at the contemporary worker, at the content of his job, at the condition of his workplace, and at the degree of autonomy and democracy within the workplace.

In the United States, public recognition of this issue perhaps has lagged slightly behind that of other Western industrial nations. Congressional hearings addressed the subject of worker alienation for the first time in August 1972. I served as chairman for those hearings before the Senate Subcommittee on Employment, Manpower, and Poverty which explored what knowledge existed, what still lay uncharted, what remedies already had been discovered, and what the role of the government should be in the process. Those hearings demonstrated that our level of knowledge and understanding of the degree and implications of job discontent was inadequate. To provide a focus for subsequent hearings, to broaden our base of information, and to bring unions, workers, employers, and scholars together to experiment with practical solutions to the problems of job dissatisfaction, I introduced the Worker Alienation Research and Development Act of 1972. I have introduced similar legislation in the Ninety-third Congress which seventeen other senators have cosponsored.

The legislation reflects my belief that government can best act in the private sector as a catalyst, providing a central clearing-house of information, offering models, and providing technical assistance for undertaking pilot projects in collaboration with unions and management. However, government also is itself an employer, the nation's largest, with 2.8 million employees at the federal level alone. For that reason, the legislation mandates an internal review of what the federal government is doing and what it can do in defining the problem of worker dissatisfaction and in seeking immediate methods to resolve it.

Prior to our hearings, a special task force had been named by Elliot Richardson, then Secretary of Health, Education, and Welfare, to reexamine the institution of work in America. That task force, under the auspices of the W. E. Upjohn Institute for Employment Research, submitted its report to the Secretary in December 1972. Underlying that report, titled *Work in America,* whose conclusions and recommendations have generated a wide-ranging discussion, were thirty-nine papers commissioned by the task force on various aspects of work and the workplace. Sixteen of those innovative and intellectually exciting papers are published in this new volume. I am convinced that this collection of papers, the task force's report, and the hearing record of the Senate Subcommittee on Employment, Manpower, and Poverty constitute three basic resources for examining the subject of work in America today. I am sure that discussion of this subject will be enriched by the publication of this volume, which adds new perspectives to our understanding of the institution of work.

If there are few conclusions that can be offered with any confidence one observation surely can be defended. The issue of job discontent—its cost, its character, its implications, and its solutions—will not fade away or be brushed aside. The strong and growing interest that this subject has ignited in the past year lends credence to the view that there is something fundamentally different about the significance and priority being given to the quality of work in America today.

George Gallup, Jr., whose organization took a survey on job satisfaction in the spring of 1973, found a 10 percent decline in worker satisfaction over the past four years. The bulk of that decline seemed to have come in the preceding thirteen months, with over three-quarters of a million men and women leaving the ranks of the satisfied each month. If that trend were to continue, by 1975 over half of the workers in the nation would be dissatisfied with their jobs.

This trend should be watched, for even a lower rate of dissatisfaction would result in a significantly growing body of discontented labor. The critical consequences for our citizens and for our economy of such a development are self-evident. We already have seen a major increase in absenteeism, in worker turnover, in worker grievances, and in disciplinary layoffs. We also know that the quality of the product in major American industries has been challenged in recent years. During 1972, while 11.2 million cars, buses, and trucks were sold, 7.8 million vehicles were ordered recalled for corrections. In some industries, the rate of spoilage has reached the level of one in every four products that come off the production line. And if there is one across-the-board conclusion of pilot efforts to deal with the problems of job dissatisfaction, it is that when the projects succeed, one result is improved quality.

Technology is only one part of the cost equation; the collaboration and cooperation of labor are essential if the fruits of technology are to be realized. In the past, management has spent most of its capital and most of its energies to refine and polish the machine, forgetting all too often that there is a human being struggling to adapt to or keep pace with that machine. The realities of modern competition and the search for ways to improve productivity and to improve product quality are raising corporate awareness of the costs of job discontent.

Some two hundred firms have experimented with improving job satisfaction. There is an eclecticism about these efforts that is more encouraging than any one solution being studied. For the problems of the workplace are as different as the workplaces of America are different. They span the assembly lines and the offices and the telephone switchboards, and they cover blue-collar and white-collar workers, as well as managers.

The wide interest and concern of management is witnessed as well by the rising attendance at conferences and seminars with the words "worker discontent" or "job satisfaction" in their titles. Unfortunately, the vast majority of American corporations still see the problem of worker discontent as the responsibility of the labor relations division. Few have recognized fully that an underlying cause of the discontent has been the failure of industry and business to recognize that the worth and value of the individual must become a part of the complex equation by which corporate goals are set, jobs designed, and success measured.

Labor unions have an equal concern with the rising evidence of discontent, and they have responded in their own ways. For beyond their interest in the ability of American industry to withstand foreign competition, their very nature accords them a special responsibility and a special right to speak for the worker. Over the past generation, unions have achieved substantial improvements in the status of the American worker. In wages, in working conditions, in health and safety standards—vast numbers of American workers have moved beyond their own expectations of a generation ago. These priorities have not disappeared as vital goals for labor unions or for their members. But past successes at the bargaining table have enabled other objectives to claim more attention.

The best evidence of this renewed concern with the quality of work on the part of labor unions is that various aspects of this problem are on the agenda at more than one major national bargaining table. While union leaders may react with some hesitancy to the assertions of behavioral scientists or object to unilateral management decisions to undertake job experimentation, they rarely deny the existence of a problem. They are saying that they have a right to participate both in the definition of the problem and in the complex process of evolving experiments for its solution.

No one can mistake the statement of the worker who testifies: "All we are left with is the dead-end job . . . that offers little challenge to the more educated worker, little chance for advancement and hardly any chance to participate as a worker."

It is the modern cry of Dostoevsky, the cry that "to crush, to annihilate a man utterly, to inflict on him the most terrible punishments so that the most ferocious murderer would shudder at it and dread it beforehand, one need only give work of an absolutely, completely useless and irrational character."

Nor should we be surprised at the rising decibel rating of those cries. We are a better-educated, more demanding population than we ever were before. A generation ago, only 40 percent of the American work force had high school diplomas. Today, nearly 80 percent of workers under thirty-four have a high school degree and a third of those have a year or more of college.

If we find a rejection of static institutions in a rapidly changing era when human values are given more weight and relevance, why should we expect that rejection to stop at the factory door? Demands for change, demands for greater opportunity to express initiative, demands to participate in decisions affecting their jobs—all reflect the character of today's youth. It is a hopeful and encouraging sign, and one with potential for ultimate good, if institutions are willing to respond to those new forces.

This emphasis on the worker as a citizen whose condition of life at the factory or the office inevitably affects his relations with individuals and institutions outside his job is what makes this issue a matter of enormous importance for the nation. The satisfaction of the assembly-line worker may determine not only the quality of the work he performs, the rate at which he changes jobs, and his level of absenteeism. It also may affect his health, his emotional well-being, his family relations, and his community behavior, as *Work in America* so convincingly documented. It is for this reason that I believe that these background papers deserve our close attention. They illuminate new paths toward achieving a more human work environment and in so doing they constitute an important addition to the reexamination of the institution of work in America.

Index

A *t* following a page number indicates a table.